Microsoft®

PowerPoint®

2016

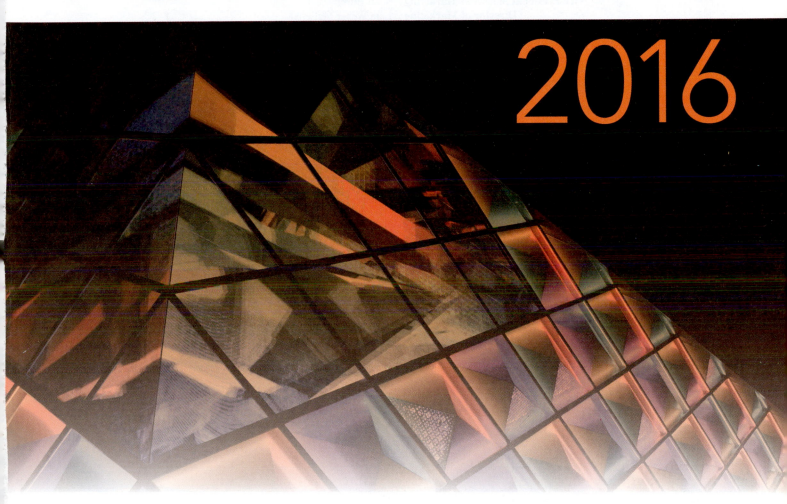

Nita Rutkosky • Audrey Roggenkamp • Ian Rutkosky

PARADIGM
EDUCATION SOLUTIONS

St. Paul

Senior Vice President	Linda Hein
Editor in Chief	Christine Hurney
Director of Production	Timothy W. Larson
Production Editor	Jen Weaverling
Cover and Text Designer	Valerie King
Copy Editors	Communicáto, Ltd.; Page to Portal, LLC
Senior Design and Production Specialist	Jack Ross; PerfecType
Assistant Developmental Editors	Mamie Clark, Katie Werdick
Testers	Janet Blum, Fanshawe College; Traci Post
Instructional Support Writers	Janet Blum, Fanshawe College; Brienna McWade
Indexer	Terry Casey
Vice President Information Technology	Chuck Bratton
Digital Projects Manager	Tom Modl
Vice President Sales and Marketing	Scott Burns
Director of Marketing	Lara Weber McLellan

ISBN 978-0-76386-970-0 (print)
ISBN 978-0-76386-971-7 (digital)

© 2017 by Paradigm Publishing, Inc.
875 Montreal Way
St. Paul, MN 55102
Email: educate@emcp.com
Website: ParadigmCollege.com

Brief Contents

Contents

Benchmark Series: Microsoft® PowerPoint 2016 is designed for students who want to learn how to build eye-catching presentations that communicate key information to audiences in business, academic, and organization settings. No prior knowledge of presentation software is required. After successfully completing a course using this textbook and digital courseware, students will be able to:

- Plan, create, and revise presentations, including executing basic skills such as opening, editing, running, saving, and closing a presentation
- Format slides using design templates, slide and title masters, styles, bullets and numbering, headers and footers, and speaker notes
- Create visual appeal with images, SmartArt, charts, animation effects, and sound and video effects
- Share presentations for collaboration and review with others
- Given a workplace scenario requiring a presentation solution, assess the information requirements and then prepare the materials that achieve the goal efficiently and effectively

Upon completing the text, students can expect to be proficient in using PowerPoint to organize, analyze, and present information.

Well-designed textbook pedagogy is important, but students learn technology skills through practice and problem solving. Technology provides opportunities for interactive learning as well as excellent ways to quickly and accurately assess student performance. To this end, this textbook is supported with SNAP 2016, Paradigm's web-based training and assessment learning management system. Details about SNAP as well as additional student courseware and instructor resources can be found on page xiv.

Achieving Proficiency in PowerPoint 2016

Since its inception several Office versions ago, the *Benchmark Series* has served as a standard of excellence in software instruction. Elements of the *Benchmark Series* function individually and collectively to create an inviting, comprehensive learning environment that produces successful computer users. The following visual tour highlights the structure and features that comprise the highly popular *Benchmark* model.

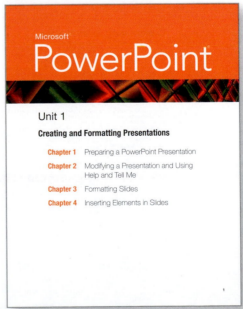

Unit Openers display the unit's four chapter titles. *PowerPoint* contains two units; each unit concludes with a comprehensive unit performance assessment.

Student Textbook and eBook

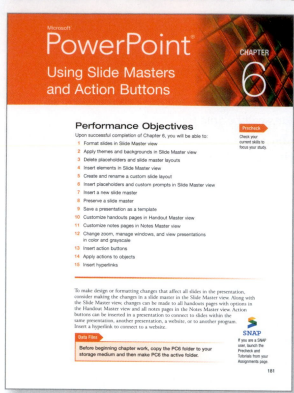

Chapter Openers present the performance objectives and an overview of the skills taught.

Precheck quizzes allow students to check their current skills before starting chapter work.

Data Files are provided for each chapter from the ebook. A prominent note reminds students to copy the appropriate chapter data folder and make it active.

Students with SNAP access are reminded to launch the Precheck quiz and chapter tutorials from their SNAP Assignments page.

Projects Build Skill Mastery within Realistic Context

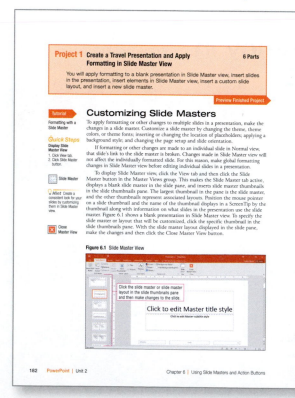

Multipart Projects provide a framework for instruction and practice on software features. A project overview identifies tasks to accomplish and key features to use in completing the work.

Preview Finished Project shows how the file will look after students complete the project.

Tutorials provide interactive, guided training and measured practice.

Quick Steps provide feature summaries for reference and review.

Hint margin notes offer useful tips on how to use features efficiently and effectively.

Typically, a file remains open throughout all parts of the project. Students save their work incrementally. At the end of the project, students save, print, and then close the file.

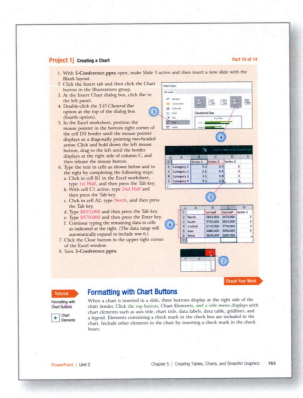

Step-by-Step Instructions guide students to the desired outcome for each project part. Screen captures illustrate what the screen should look like at key points.

Magenta Text identifies material to type.

Check Your Work allows students to confirm they have completed the project activity correctly.

Between project parts, the text presents instruction on the features and skills necessary to accomplish the next section of the project.

Chapter Review Tools Reinforce Learning

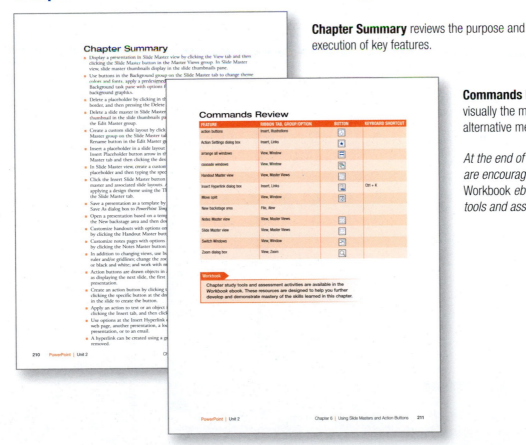

Chapter Summary reviews the purpose and execution of key features.

Commands Review summarizes visually the major features and alternative methods of access.

At the end of each chapter, students are encouraged to go to the Workbook ebook to access study tools and assessment activities.

Workbook eBook Activities Provide a Hierarchy of Learning Assessments

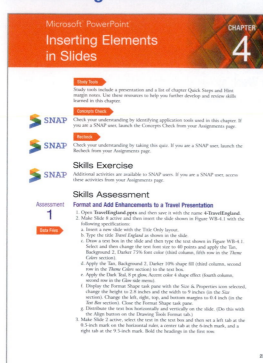

Study Tools are presentations with audio support and a list of chapter Quick Steps and Hint margin notes designed to help students further develop and review skills learned in the chapter.

Concepts Check is an objective completion exercise that allows students to assess their comprehension and recall of application features, terminology, and functions.

Recheck concept quizzes for each chapter enable students to check how their skills have improved after completing chapter work.

Skills Exercises are available to SNAP 2016 users. SNAP will automatically score student work, which is performed live in the application, and provide detailed feedback.

Skills Assessment exercises ask students to develop both standard and customized types of presentations without how-to directions.

Visual Benchmark assessments test problem-solving skills and mastery of application features.

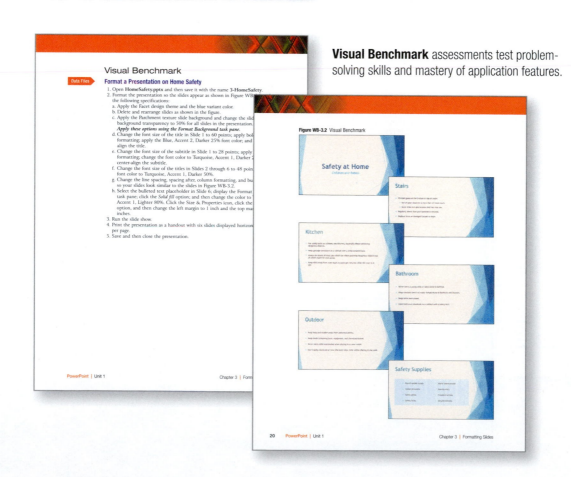

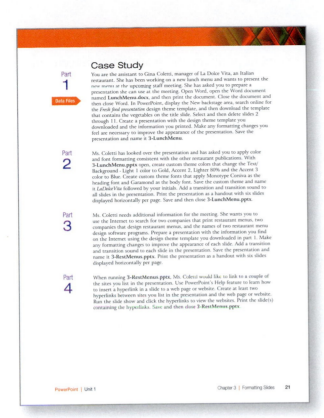

Case Study requires analyzing a workplace scenario and then planning and executing a multipart project.

Students search the web and/or use the program's Help feature to locate additional information required to complete the Case Study.

Unit Performance Assessments Deliver Cross-Disciplinary, Comprehensive Evaluation

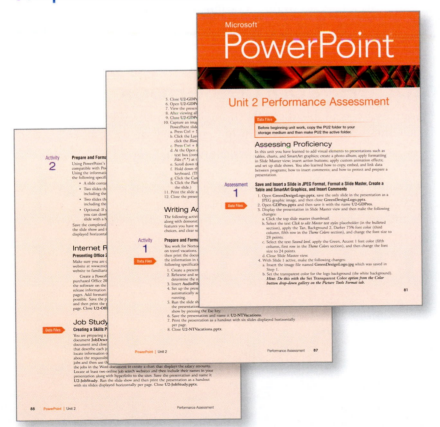

Assessing Proficiency exercises check mastery of features.

Writing Activities involve applying application skills in a communication context.

Internet Research projects reinforce research and information processing skills.

Job Study at the end of Unit 2 presents a capstone assessment requiring critical thinking and problem solving.

SNAP Training and Assessment

SNAP is a web-based training and assessment program and learning management system (LMS) for learning Microsoft Office 2016. SNAP is comprised of rich content, a sophisticated grade book, and robust scheduling and analytics tools. SNAP courseware supports the *Benchmark Series* content and delivers live-in-the-application assessments for students to demonstrate their skills mastery. Interactive tutorials increase skills-focused moments with guided training and measured practice. SNAP provides automatic scoring and detailed feedback on the many activities, exercises, and quizzes to help identify areas where additional support is needed, evaluating student performance both at an individual and course level. The *Benchmark Series* SNAP course content is also available to export into any LMS system that supports LTI tools.

Paradigm Education Solutions provides technical support for SNAP through 24-7 chat at ParadigmCollege.com. In addition, an online User Guide and other SNAP training tools for using SNAP are available.

Student eBook and *Workbook* eBook

The student ebook and *Workbook* ebook available through SNAP or online at Paradigm.bookshelf.emcp.com provide access to the *Benchmark Series* content from any device (desktop, tablet, and smartphone) anywhere, through a live Internet connection. The versatile ebook platform features dynamic navigation tools including a linked table of contents and the ability to jump to specific pages, search for terms, bookmark, highlight, and take notes. The ebooks offer live links to the interactive content and resources that support the print textbook, including the student data files, Precheck and Recheck quizzes, and interactive tutorials. The *Workbook* ebook also provides access to presentations with audio support and to end-of-section Concept Check, Skills Assessment, Visual Benchmark, Case Study, and end-of-unit Performance Assessment activities.

Instructor eResources eBook

All instructor resources are available digitally through a web-based ebook at Paradigm.bookshelf.emcp.com. The instructor materials include these items:

- Planning resources, such as lesson plans, teaching hints, and sample course syllabi
- Presentation resources, such as PowerPoint slide shows with lecture notes
- Assessment resources, including live and annotated PDF model answers for chapter work and workbook activities, rubrics for evaluating student work, and chapter-based exam banks

Office

Getting Started
in Office 2016

Several computer applications are combined to make the Microsoft Office 2016 application suite. The applications are known as *software*, and they contain instructions that tell the computer what to do. Some of the applications in the suite include Word, a word processing applicaton; Excel, a spreadsheet applicaton; Access, a database applicaton; and PowerPoint, a presentation applicaton.

Identifying Computer Hardware

The Microsoft Office suite can run on several types of computer equipment, referred to as *hardware*. You will need access to a laptop or a desktop computer system that includes a PC/tower, monitor, keyboard, printer, drives, and mouse. If you are not sure what equipment you will be operating, check with your instructor. The computer systems shown in Figure G.1 consists of six components. Each component is discussed separately in the material that follows.

Figure G.1 Computer System

PC/tower

monitor

USB drive

printer

keyboard

mouse

1

Figure G.2 PC/Tower

PC/Tower

The PC, also known as the *tower*, is the brain of the computer and is where all processing occurs. A PC/tower consists of components such as the Central Processing Unit (CPU), hard drives, and video cards plugged into a motherboard. The motherboard is mounted inside the case, which includes input and output ports for attaching external peripherals (as shown in Figure G.2). When a user provides input through the use of peripherals, the PC/tower computes that input and outputs the results. Similar hardware is included in a laptop, but the design is more compact to allow for mobility.

Monitor

Hint Monitor size is measured diagonally. For example, the distance from the bottom left corner to the top right corner of the monitor.

A computer monitor looks like a television screen. It displays the visual information that the computer is outputting. The quality of display for monitors varies depending on the type of monitor and the level of resolution. Monitors can also vary in size—generally from 13 inches to 26 inches or larger.

Keyboard

The keyboard is used to input information into the computer. The number and location of the keys on a keyboard can vary. In addition to letters, numbers, and symbols, most computer keyboards contain function keys, arrow keys, and a numeric keypad. Figure G.3 shows an enhanced keyboard.

The 12 keys at the top of the keyboard, labeled with the letter F followed by a number, are called *function keys*. Use these keys to perform functions within each of the Office applications. To the right of the regular keys is a group of special or dedicated keys. These keys are labeled with specific functions that will be performed when you press the key. Below the special keys are arrow keys. Use these keys to move the insertion point in the document screen.

Some keyboards include mode indicator lights. When you select certain modes, a light appears on the keyboard. For example, if you press the Caps Lock key, which disables the lowercase alphabet, a light appears next to Caps Lock. Similarly, pressing the Num Lock key will disable the special functions on the numeric keypad, which is located at the right side of the keyboard.

Figure G.3 Keyboard

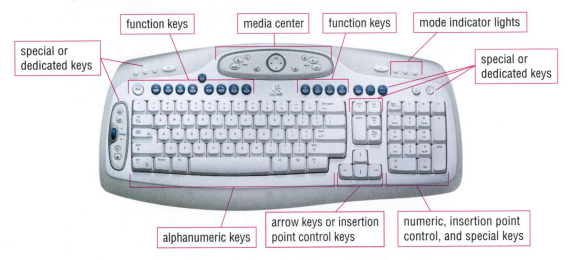

function keys · media center · function keys · mode indicator lights

special or dedicated keys · special or dedicated keys

alphanumeric keys · arrow keys or insertion point control keys · numeric, insertion point control, and special keys

Drives and Ports

A PC includes drives and ports that allow you to input and output data. For example, a hard drive is a disk drive inside of the PC that stores data that may have been inputted or outputted. Other drives may include CD, DVD and BluRay disc drives, although newer computers may not include these drives, because USB flash drives are becoming the preferred technology. Ports are the "plugs" on the PC, and are used to connect devices to the computer, such as the keyboard and mouse, the monitor, speakers, a USB flash drive and so on. Most PCs will have a few USB ports, at least one display port, an audio cable port, and possibly an ethernet port (used to physically connect to the Internet or a network).

Printer

An electronic version of a file is known as a *soft copy*. If you want to create a hard copy of a file, you need to print it. To print documents you will need to access a printer (as shown in Figure G.4), which will probably be either a laser printer or an ink-jet printer. A laser printer uses a laser beam combined with heat and pressure to print documents, while an ink-jet printer prints a document by spraying a fine mist of ink on the page.

Figure G.4 Printer

Mouse

Most functions and commands in the Microsoft Office suite are designed to be performed using a mouse or a similar pointing device. A mouse is an input device that sits on a flat surface next to the computer. You can operate a mouse with your left or right hand. Moving the mouse on the flat surface causes a corresponding pointer to move on the screen, and clicking the left or right mouse buttons allows you to select various objects and commands. Figure G.5 shows an example of a mouse.

Using the Mouse The applications in the Microsoft Office suite can be operated with the keyboard and a mouse. The mouse generally has two buttons on top, which you press to execute specific functions and commands. A mouse may also contain a wheel, which can be used to scroll in a window or as a third button. To use the mouse, rest it on a flat surface or a mouse pad. Put your hand over it with your palm resting on top of the mouse and your index finger resting on the left mouse button. As you move your hand, and thus the mouse, a corresponding pointer moves on the screen.

When using the mouse, you should understand four terms — point, click, double-click, and drag. When operating the mouse, you may need to point to a specific command, button, or icon. To *point* means to position the mouse pointer on the desired item. With the mouse pointer positioned on the item, you may need to click a button on the mouse to select the item. To *click* means to quickly tap a button on the mouse once. To complete two steps at one time, such as choosing and then executing a function, double-click the mouse button. To *double-click* means to tap the left mouse button twice in quick succession. The term *drag* means to click and hold down the left mouse button, move the mouse pointer to a specific location, and then release the button.

> **Hint** This textbook will use the verb *click* to refer to the mouse and the verb press to refer to a key on the keyboard.

Using the Mouse Pointer The mouse pointer will look different depending on where you have positioned it and what function you are performing. The following are some of the ways the mouse pointer can appear when you are working in the Office suite:

- The mouse pointer appears as an I-beam (called the *I-beam pointer*) when you are inserting text in a file. The I-beam pointer can be used to move the insertion point or to select text.
- The mouse pointer appears as an arrow pointing up and to the left (called the *arrow pointer*) when it is moved to the Title bar, Quick Access Toolbar, ribbon, or an option in a dialog box, among other locations.
- The mouse pointer becomes a double-headed arrow (either pointing left and right, pointing up and down, or pointing diagonally) when you perform certain functions such as changing the size of an object.

Figure G.5 Mouse

- In certain situations, such as when you move an object or image, the mouse pointer displays with a four-headed arrow attached. The four-headed arrow means that you can move the object left, right, up, or down.
- When a request is being processed or when an application is being loaded, the mouse pointer may appear as a moving circle. The moving circle means "please wait." When the process is completed, the circle is replaced with a normal mouse pointer.
- When the mouse pointer displays as a hand with a pointing index finger, it indicates that more information is available about an item. The mouse pointer also displays as a hand with a pointing index finger when you hover the mouse over a hyperlink.

Touchpad

If you are working on a laptop computer, you may use a touchpad instead of a mouse. A *touchpad* allows you to move the mouse pointer by moving your finger across a surface at the base of the keyboard. You click and right-click by using your thumb to press the buttons located at the bottom of the touchpad. Some touchpads have special features such as scrolling or clicking something by tapping the surface of the touchpad instead of pressing a button with a thumb.

TouchScreen

Smartphones, tablets, and touch monitors all use TouchScreen technology (as shown in Figure G.6), which allows users to directly interact with the objects on the screen by touching them with fingers, thumbs, or a stylus. Multiple fingers or both thumbs can be used on most modern touchscreens, giving users the ability to zoom, rotate, and manipulate items on the screen. While a lot of activities in this textbook can be completed using a device with a touchscreen, a mouse or touchpad might be required to complete a few activities.

Figure G.6 Touchscreen

Choosing Commands

Once an application is open, you can use several methods in the application to choose commands. A command is an instruction that tells the application to do something. You can choose a command using the mouse or the keyboard. When an application such as Word or PowerPoint is open, the ribbon contains buttons and options for completing tasks, as well as tabs you can click to display additional buttons and options. To choose a button on the Quick Access Toolbar or on the ribbon, position the tip of the mouse arrow pointer on the button and then click the left mouse button.

The Office suite provides accelerator keys you can press to use a command in an application. Press the Alt key on the keyboard to display KeyTips that identify the accelerator key you can press to execute a command. For example, if you press the Alt key in a Word document with the Home tab active, KeyTips display as shown in Figure G.7. Continue pressing accelerator keys until you execute the desired command. For example, to begin checking the spelling in a document, press the Alt key, press the R key on the keyboard to display the Review tab, and then press the letter S on the keyboard.

Choosing Commands from Drop-Down Lists

To choose a command from a drop-down list with the mouse, position the mouse pointer on the option and then click the left mouse button. To make a selection from a drop-down list with the keyboard, type the underlined letter in the option.

Some options at a drop-down list may appear in gray (dimmed), indicating that the option is currently unavailable. If an option at a drop-down list displays preceded by a check mark, it means the option is currently active. If an option at a drop-down list displays followed by an ellipsis (…), clicking that option will display a dialog box.

Choosing Options from a Dialog Box

A dialog box contains options for applying formatting or otherwise modifying a file or data within a file. Some dialog boxes display with tabs along the top that provide additional options. For example, the Font dialog box shown in Figure G.8 contains two tabs—the Font tab and the Advanced tab. The tab that displays in the front is the active tab. To make a tab active using the mouse, position the arrow pointer on the tab and then click the left mouse button. If you are using the keyboard, press Ctrl + Tab or press Alt + the underlined letter on the tab.

To choose an option from a dialog box with the mouse, position the arrow pointer on the option and then click the left mouse button. If you are using the keyboard, press the Tab key to move the insertion point forward from option to option. Press Shift + Tab to move the insertion point backward from option to option. You can also press and hold down the Alt key and then press the

Figure G.7 Word Home Tab KeyTips

Figure G.8 Word Font Dialog Box

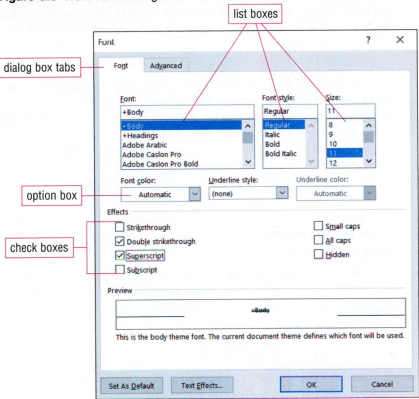

underlined letter of the option. When an option is selected, it displays with a blue background or surrounded by a dashed box called a *marquee*. A dialog box contains one or more of the following elements: list boxes, option boxes, check boxes, text boxes, option buttons, measurement boxes, and command buttons.

List Boxes and Option Boxes The fonts available in the Font dialog box, shown in Figure G.8, are contained in a list box. To make a selection from a list box with the mouse, move the arrow pointer to the option and then click the left mouse button.

Some list boxes may contain a scroll bar. This scroll bar will display at the right side of the list box (a vertical scroll bar) or at the bottom of the list box (a horizontal scroll bar). Use a vertical scroll bar or a horizontal scroll bar to move through the list if the list is longer (or wider) than the box. To move down a list using a vertical scroll bar, position the arrow pointer on the down arrow, and then click and hold down the left mouse button. To scroll up through the list, position the arrow pointer on the up arrow, and then click and hold down the left mouse button. You can also move the arrow pointer above the scroll box and click the left mouse button to scroll up the list or move the arrow pointer below the scroll box and click the left mouse button to move down the list. To navigate in a list with a horizontal scroll bar, click the left arrow to scroll to the left of the list or click the right arrow to scroll to the right of the list.

To use the keyboard to make a selection from a list box, move the insertion point into the box by holding down the Alt key and pressing the underlined letter of the desired option. Press the Up and/or Down Arrow keys on the keyboard to move through the list, and press the Enter key when the desired option is selected.

In some dialog boxes where there is not enough room for a list box, lists of options are contained in a drop-down list box called an *option box*. Option boxes display with a down arrow. For example, in Figure G.8, the font color options are contained in an option box. To display the different color options, click the *Font color* option box arrow. If you are using the keyboard, press Alt + C.

Check Boxes Some dialog boxes contain options preceded by a box. A check mark may or may not appear in the box. The Word Font dialog box shown in Figure G.8 displays a variety of check boxes within the *Effects* section. If a check mark appears in the box, the option is active (turned on). If the check box does not contain a check mark, the option is inactive (turned off). Any number of check boxes can be active. For example, in the Word Font dialog box, you can insert a check mark in several of the boxes in the *Effects* section to activate the options.

To make a check box active or inactive with the mouse, position the tip of the arrow pointer in the check box and then click the left mouse button. If you are using the keyboard, press Alt + the underlined letter of the option.

Text Boxes Some options in a dialog box require you to enter text. For example, the boxes below the *Find what* and *Replace with* options at the Excel Find and Replace dialog box shown in Figure G.9 are text boxes. In a text box, type text or edit existing text. Edit text in a text box in the same manner as normal text. Use the Left and Right Arrow keys on the keyboard to move the insertion point without deleting text and use the Delete key or Backspace key to delete text.

Command Buttons The buttons at the bottom of the Excel Find and Replace dialog box shown in Figure G.9 are called *command buttons*. Use a command button to execute or cancel a command. Some command buttons display with an ellipsis (...), which means another dialog box will open if you click that button. To choose a command button with the mouse, position the arrow pointer on the button and then click the left mouse button. To choose a command button with the keyboard, press the Tab key until the command button is surrounded by a marquee and then press the Enter key.

Option Buttons The Word Insert Table dialog box shown in Figure G.10 contains options in the *AutoFit behavior* section preceded by option buttons. Only one option button can be selected at any time. When an option button is selected, a blue or black circle displays in the button. To select an option button with the mouse, position the tip of the arrow pointer inside the option button or on the option and then click the left mouse button. To make a selection with the keyboard, press and hold down the Alt key, press the underlined letter of the option, and then release the Alt key.

Figure G.9 Excel Find and Replace Dialog Box

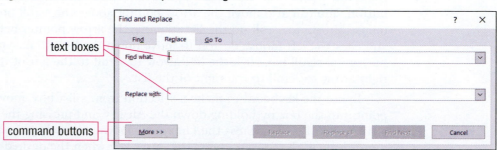

Figure G.10 Word Insert Table Dialog Box

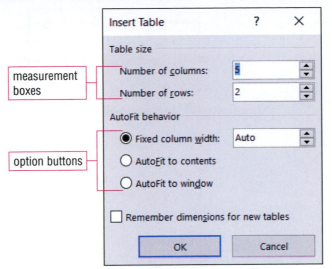

Measurement Boxes Some options in a dialog box contain measurements or amounts you can increase or decrease. These options are generally located in a measurement box. For example, the Word Insert Table dialog box shown in Figure G.10 contains the *Number of columns* and *Number of rows* measurement boxes. To increase a number in a measurement box, position the tip of the arrow pointer on the up arrow at the right of the measurement box and then click the left mouse button. To decrease the number, click the down arrow. If you are using the keyboard, press and hold down the Alt key and then press the underlined letter for the option, press the Up Arrow key to increase the number or the Down Arrow key to decrease the number, and then release the Alt key.

Choosing Commands with Keyboard Shortcuts

Applications in the Office suite offer a variety of keyboard shortcuts you can use to execute specific commands. Keyboard shortcuts generally require two or more keys. For example, the keyboard shortcut to display the Open dialog box in an application is Ctrl + F12. To use this keyboard shortcut, press and hold down the Ctrl key, press the F12 function on the keyboard, and then release the Ctrl key. For a list of keyboard shortcuts, refer to the Help files.

Choosing Commands with Shortcut Menus

The software applications in the Office suite include shortcut menus that contain commands related to different items. To display a shortcut menu, position the mouse pointer over the item for which you want to view more options, and then click the right mouse button or press Shift + F10. The shortcut menu will appear wherever the insertion point is positioned. For example, if the insertion point is positioned in a paragraph of text in a Word document, clicking the right mouse button or pressing Shift + F10 will cause the shortcut menu shown in Figure G.11 to display in the document screen (along with the Mini toolbar).

To select an option from a shortcut menu with the mouse, click the option. If you are using the keyboard, press the Up or Down Arrow key until the option is selected and then press the Enter key. To close a shortcut menu without choosing an option, click outside the shortcut menu or press the Esc key.

Figure G.11 Word Shortcut Menu

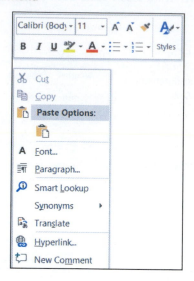

Working with Multiple Programs

As you learn the various applications in the Microsoft Office suite, you will notice many similarities between them. For example, the steps to save, close, and print are virtually the same whether you are working in Word, Excel, or PowerPoint. This consistency between applications greatly enhances your ability to transfer knowledge learned in one application to another within the suite. Another benefit to using Microsoft Office is the ability to have more than one application open at the same time and to integrate content from one program with another. For example, you can open Word and create a document, open Excel and create a spreadsheet, and then copy the Excel spreadsheet into Word.

When you open an application, a button containing an icon representing the application displays on the taskbar. If you open another application, a button containing an icon representing that application displays to the right of the first application button on the taskbar. Figure G.12 shows the taskbar with Word, Excel, Access, and PowerPoint open. To move from one program to another, click the taskbar button representing the desired application.

Customizing Settings

Before beginning computer projects in this textbook, you may need to customize your monitor's settings, change the DPI display setting, and turn on the display of file extensions. Projects in the chapters in this textbook assume that the monitor display is set at 1600 × 900 pixels, the DPI set at 125%, and that the display of file extensions is turned on. If you are unable to make changes to the monitor's resolution or the DPI settings, the projects can still be completed successfully. Some references in the text might not perfectly match what you see on your

Figure G.12 Taskbar with Word, Excel, Access, and PowerPoint Open

screen, so some mental adjustments may need to be made for certain steps. For example, an item in a drop-down gallery might appear in a different column or row than what is indicated in the step instructions.

Before you begin learning the applications in the Microsoft Office 2016 suite, take a moment to check the display settings on the computer you are using. Your monitor's display settings are important because the ribbon in the Microsoft Office suite adjusts to the screen resolution setting of your computer monitor. A computer monitor set at a high resolution will have the ability to show more buttons in the ribbon than will a monitor set to a low resolution. The illustrations in this textbook were created with a screen resolution display set at 1600 × 900 pixels. In Figure G.13, the Word ribbon is shown three ways: at a lower screen resolution (1366 × 768 pixels), at the screen resolution featured throughout this textbook, and at a higher screen resolution (1920 × 1080 pixels). Note the variances in the ribbon in all three examples. If possible, set your display to 1600 × 900 pixels to match the illustrations you will see in this textbook.

Figure G.13 The Home Tab Displayed on a Monitor Set at Different Screen Resolutions

1366 × 768 screen resolution

1600 × 900 screen resolution

1920 × 1080 screen resolution

Project 1 Setting Monitor Display to 1600 × 900

Note: The resolution settings may be locked on lab computers. Also, some laptop screens and small monitors may not be able to display in a 1600 × 900 resolution.

1. At the Windows 10 desktop, right-click in a blank area of the screen.
2. At the shortcut menu, click the *Display settings* option.

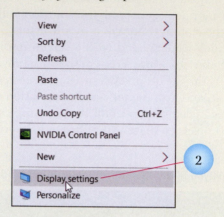

3. At the Settings window with the SYSTEM screen active, scroll down and then click *Advanced display settings*.

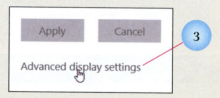

4. Scroll down the Settings window until the *Resolution* option box is visible and take note of the current resolution setting. If the current resolution is already set to 1600 × 900, skip ahead to Step 8.
5. Click in the Resolution option box and then click the 1600 × 900 option at the drop-down list.

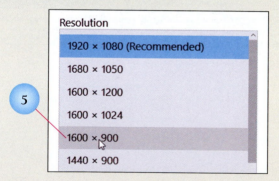

6. Click the Apply button.
7. Click the Keep Changes button.
8. Click the Close button.

Project 2 Changing the DPI Setting

Note: The DPI settings may be locked on lab computers. Also, some laptop screens and small monitors may not allow the DPI settings to be changed.

1. At the Windows 10 desktop, right-click in a blank area of the screen.
2. At the shortcut menu, click the *Display settings* option.
3. At the Settings window, take note of the current DPI percentage next to the text *Change the size of text, apps, and other items*. If the percentage is already set to 125%, skip to Step 5.
4. Click the slider bar below the text *Change the size of text, apps, and other items* and hold down the left mouse button, drag to the right until the DPI percentage is 125%, and then release the mouse button.

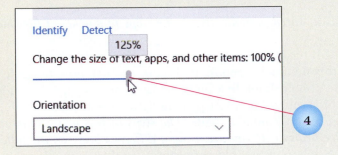

5. Close the computer window.

Project 3 Displaying File Extensions

1. At the Windows 10 desktop, click the File Explorer button on the taskbar.

2. At the File Explorer window, click the View tab.
3. Click the *File name extensions* check box in the Show/hide group to insert a check mark.

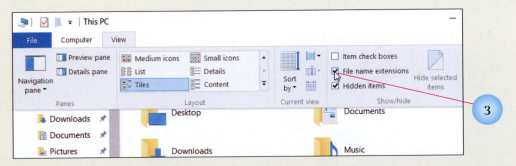

4. Close the computer window.

Completing Computer Projects

Some projects in this textbook require that you open an existing file. Project files are saved on OneDrive in a zip file. Before beginning projects and assessments in this book and the accompanying ebook, copy the necessary folder from the zip file to your storage medium (such as a USB flash drive) using File Explorer. Begin downloading the files for this book by going to the ebook and clicking the Ancillary Links button that displays when the ebook displays this page or any chapter opener page with the Data Files tab on it.

Project 4   Downloading Files to a USB Flash Drive

Note: OneDrive is updated periodically, so the steps to download files may vary from the steps below.

1. Insert your USB flash drive into an available USB port.
2. Navigate to this textbook's ebook. If you are a SNAP user, navigate to the ebook by clicking the textbook ebook link on your Assignments page. If you are not a SNAP user, launch your browser and go to http://paradigm.bookshelf.emcp.com, log in, and then click the textbook ebook thumbnail. *Note: The steps in this activity assume you are using the Microsoft Edge browser. If you are using a different browser, the following steps may vary.*
3. Navigate to the ebook page that corresponds to this textbook page.
4. Click the Ancillary Links button in the menu. The menu that appears may be at the top of the window or along the side of the window, depending on the size of the window.

5. At the Ancillary Links dialog box, click the <u>Data Files: All Files</u> hyperlink.

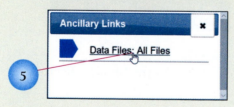

6. Click the Download hyperlink at the top of the window.
7. Click the Open button in the message box when the DataFiles.zip finishes downloading.
8. Right-click the DataFiles folder in the Content pane.
9. Click the *Copy* option in the shortcut menu.

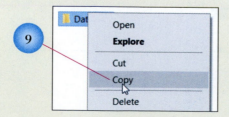

10. Click the USB flash drive that displays in the Navigation pane at the left side of the File Explorer window.
11. Click the Home tab in the File Explorer window.
12. Click the Paste button in the Clipboard group.

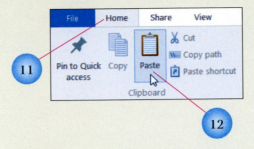

13. Close the File Explorer window by clicking the Close button in the upper right corner of the window.

Project 5 Deleting a File

Note: Check with your instructor before deleting a file.

1. At the Windows 10 desktop, open File Explorer by clicking the File Explorer button on the taskbar.
2. Click the *Downloads* folder in the navigation pane.
3. Right-click *DataFiles.zip*.
4. Click the *Delete* option at the shortcut menu.

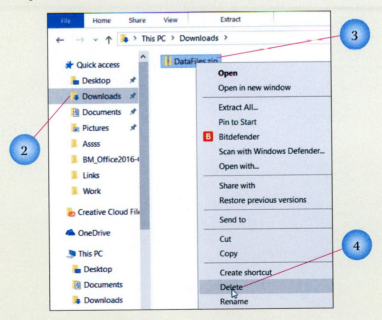

Microsoft®
PowerPoint®

Unit 1

Creating and Formatting Presentations

Microsoft® PowerPoint®

Preparing a PowerPoint Presentation

Performance Objectives

Upon successful completion of Chapter 1, you will be able to:

1. Open a presentation
2. Pin and unpin presentations and folders
3. Run a slide show
4. Plan a presentation
5. Close a presentation
6. Create a presentation using a design theme template
7. Insert slides, insert text in slides, and change slide layouts
8. Change presentation views
9. Save a presentation
10. Navigate and edit slides
11. Preview and print a presentation
12. Apply a design theme and a color variant to a presentation
13. Delete a presentation
14. Prepare a presentation from a blank presentation
15. Prepare a presentation in Outline view
16. Add transitions, transition sounds, and timings to a presentation

Precheck

Check your current skills to help focus your study.

During a presentation, the presenter may use visual aids to strengthen the impact of his or her message as well as help organize the presented information. Visual aids may include transparencies, slides, photographs, or an on-screen slide show. With Microsoft's PowerPoint program, you can easily create visual aids for a presentation and then print copies of the aids as well as run the slide show. PowerPoint is a presentation graphics program that you can use to organize and present information.

SNAP

If you are a SNAP user, launch the Precheck and Tutorials from your Assignments page.

Data Files

Before beginning the projects, copy the PC1 folder to your storage medium and then make PC1 the active folder.

Project 1 **Open a Presentation, Run a Slide Show, and Close a Presentation** **1 Part**

You will open a presentation on using color in publications, run the slide show, and then close the presentation.

Tutorial

Opening a
Presentation
Based on a
Template

Tutorial

Exploring the
PowerPoint
Screen

Creating a Presentation

PowerPoint provides several methods for creating a presentation. Create a presentation using a theme template or starting with a blank presentation. The steps to follow when creating a presentation will vary depending on the chosen method, but will often follow these basic steps:

1. Open PowerPoint.
2. Choose the theme template or start with a blank presentation.
3. Type the text for each slide, adding additional elements, such as images, as needed.
4. If necessary, apply a design theme.
5. Save the presentation.
6. Print the presentation as slides, handouts, notes pages, or an outline.
7. Run the slide show.
8. Close the presentation.
9. Close PowerPoint.

After choosing the specific type of presentation to be created, the PowerPoint window displays in Normal view. The window displayed will vary depending on the type of presentation being created. However, the PowerPoint window contains some consistent elements, as shown in Figure 1.1. Many of these elements are similar to those in other Microsoft Office programs, such as Word and Excel. For example, the PowerPoint window, like the Word and Excel windows, contains a File tab, Quick Access Toolbar, tabs, ribbon, vertical and horizontal scroll bars, and Status bar. The PowerPoint window elements are described in Table 1.1.

PowerPoint, like other Microsoft Office programs, provides enhanced ScreenTips for buttons and options. Hover the mouse pointer over a button or option and, after approximately one second, an enhanced ScreenTip will display the name of the button or option, any shortcut command if one is available, and a description of that button or option.

Figure 1.1 PowerPoint Window

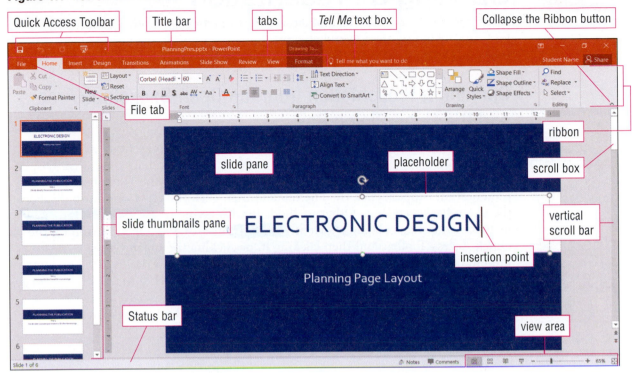

Table 1.1 PowerPoint Window Elements

Feature	Description
Collapse the Ribbon button	when clicked, removes the ribbon from the screen (To redisplay the ribbon, click any tab [except the File tab] and then click the Pin the Ribbon button [previously the Collapse the Ribbon button])
File tab	when clicked, displays the backstage area with options for working with and managing presentations
horizontal scroll bar	used to shift the slide in the slide pane left or right
I-beam pointer	used to move the insertion point or to select text
insertion point	indicates the location of the next character entered at the keyboard
placeholder	location on a slide that holds text or objects
Quick Access Toolbar	contains buttons for commonly used commands
ribbon	area containing the tabs with options and buttons divided into groups
slide pane	displays the slide and slide contents
slide thumbnails pane	area on the left side of the screen that displays slide thumbnails
Status bar	displays the slide number and number of slides, buttons for inserting notes and comments, and the view area
tabs	contain commands and features organized into groups
Tell Me feature	provides information as well as guidance on how to complete a function
Title bar	displays presentation name followed by the program name
vertical scroll bar	displays specific slides
view area	a feature of the Status bar that contains buttons for changing the presentation view or slide display percentage

Opening a Presentation

After a presentation is saved and closed, it can be opened from a variety of locations including the Open dialog box, the *Recent* option list at the Open backstage area, or from the PowerPoint opening screen.

Opening a Presentation from the Open Backstage Area and the Open Dialog Box

The Open dialog box provides one method for opening a presentation. Display the Open dialog box by clicking the *Browse* option at the Open backstage area. Display the Open backstage area, shown in Figure 1.2, by clicking the File tab. If a presentation is open, click the File tab and then click the *Open* option to display the Open backstage area. Other methods for displaying the Open backstage area include using the keyboard shortcut, Ctrl + O, inserting an Open button on the Quick Access Toolbar and then clicking it, or clicking the Open Other Presentations hyperlink in the lower left corner of the PowerPoint 2016 opening screen. Go directly to the Open dialog box without displaying the Open backstage area by pressing Ctrl + F12. At the Open dialog box, navigate to a specific location, open the folder containing the file, and then double-click the file name in the Content pane.

Figure 1.2 Open Backstage Area

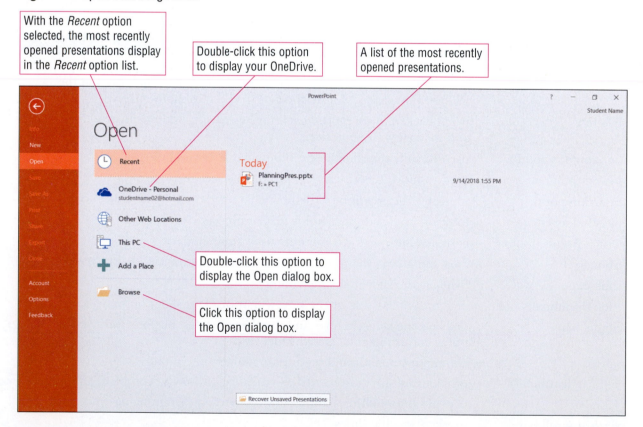

With the *Recent* option selected, the most recently opened presentations display in the *Recent* option list.

Double-click this option to display your OneDrive.

A list of the most recently opened presentations.

Double-click this option to display the Open dialog box.

Click this option to display the Open dialog box.

Opening a Presentation from the *Recent* Option List

At the Open backstage area with *Recent* option selected, the names of the most recently opened presentations display. By default, PowerPoint displays 25 of the most recently opened presentations and groups them into categories such as *Today*, *Yesterday*, and sometimes *Last Week*. The PowerPoint 2016 opening screen also contains a list of the most recently opened presentations. Click a presentation name in the *Recent* option list at the Open backstage area or the Recent list at the opening screen to open the presentation.

Pinning and Unpinning Presentations and Folders

If a presentation is opened on a regular basis, consider pinning it to the *Recent* option list at the Open backstage area. To pin a presentation, hover the mouse pointer over the presentation name in the *Recent* option list and then click the left-pointing push pin at the right of the presentation name. This turns the push pin into a down-pointing push pin and inserts the presentation into a new category named *Pinned*. The *Pinned* category displays at the top of the *Recent* option list, and the next time the Open backstage area displays, the presentation will display in the *Pinned* category of the *Recent* option list.

A presentation can also be pinned to the Recent list at the PowerPoint 2016 opening screen. When a presentation is pinned, it displays at the top of the Recent list as well as the *Recent* option list at the Open backstage area. To "unpin" a document from the Recent list or *Recent* option list, click the pin to change it from a down-pointing push pin to a left-pointing push pin. More than one presentation can be pinned to a list. Another method for pinning and unpinning presentations is to right-click a presentation name in the Recent list or *Recent* option list and then click the *Pin to list* or *Unpin from list* option.

In addition to presentations, folders can be pinned to a list at the Save As backstage area. The third panel in the Save As backstage area displays a list of the most recently opened folders and groups them into categories such as *Today*, *Yesterday*, and *Last Week*. When you pin a folder or folders to the list, a *Pinned* category is created and the folder names display in that category.

Quick Steps

Pin a Presentation to the *Recent* Option List
1. Display PowerPoint 2016 opening screen or Open backstage area.
2. Hover mouse over presentation in list.
3. Click left-pointing push pin.

Running a Slide Show

When a presentation is opened, the presentation displays in Normal view. A presentation can be edited and customized in this view. To run the slide show, click the Start From Beginning button on the Quick Access Toolbar, click the Slide Show button in the view area on the Status bar, or click the Slide Show tab and then click the From Beginning button in the Start Slide Show group. Navigate through the slides in the slide show by clicking the left mouse button.

Closing a Presentation

To remove a presentation from the screen, close the presentation. Close a presentation by clicking the File tab and then clicking the *Close* option or with the keyboard shortcut Ctrl + F4. If any changes are made to the presentation, a message will display asking if the presentation should be saved.

Quick Steps

Close a Presentation
1. Click File tab.
2. Click *Close* option.

1. Open PowerPoint by clicking the PowerPoint 2016 tile at the Windows Start menu. (Depending on your operating system, these steps may vary.)
2. At the PowerPoint opening screen, click the <u>Open Other Presentations</u> hyperlink in the lower left corner of the screen.
3. At the Open backstage area, click the *Browse* option.
4. At the Open dialog box, navigate to the PC1 folder on your storage medium and then double-click **ColorInfo.pptx**.
5. Run the slide show by completing the following steps:
   a. Click the Start From Beginning button on the Quick Access Toolbar.

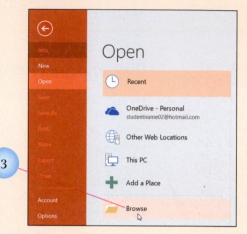

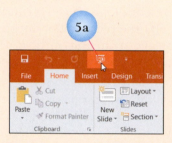

   b. Read the information in the first slide in the presentation and then click the left mouse button.
   c. Continue reading the information in the slides and clicking the left mouse button to advance the slides.
   d. At the black screen with the *End of slide show* message, click the left mouse button. (This returns the presentation to Normal view.)
6. Close the presentation by clicking the File tab and then clicking the *Close* option. (If a message displays asking if you want to save changes, click the No button.)
7. Pin **ColorInfo.pptx** to the *Recent* option list by completing the following steps:
   a. Click the File tab.
   b. At the Open backstage area with the *Recent* option selected, hover your mouse over the **ColorInfo.pptx** presentation name at the top of the *Recent* option list and then click the push pin to the right of the presentation name.

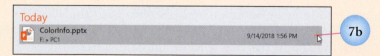

   c. Click the Back button to return to the blank presentation screen. (The Back button is in the upper left corner of the backstage area and displays as a circle with a left-pointing arrow.)
8. Close PowerPoint by clicking the Close button in the upper right corner of the screen.
9. Open PowerPoint by clicking the PowerPoint 2016 tile at the Windows Start menu. (These steps may vary; check with your instructor.)
10. At the PowerPoint 2016 opening screen, notice that **ColorInfo.pptx** is pinned in the *Pinned* section of the Recent list. Open the presentation by clicking **ColorInfo.pptx** at the top of the list.
11. Close **ColorInfo.pptx**.
12. Unpin **ColorInfo.pptx** from the *Recent* option list by completing steps 7a through 7c.

You will use a design theme template to create a presentation, insert text in slides in the presentation, choose a slide layout, insert new slides, change views, navigate through the presentation, edit text in slides, and then print the presentation.

Planning a Presentation

When planning a presentation, first define the purpose of the presentation. Is the intent to inform, educate, sell, motivate, and/or entertain? Also consider the audience who will be listening to and watching the slide show. Determine the content of the presentation and the medium that will be used to convey the message. Will a computer monitor be used to display the presentation or will the presentation be projected onto a screen? Consider these guidelines when preparing the content of a presentation:

- **Determine the main purpose of the presentation.** Do not try to cover too many topics—this may strain the audience's attention or cause confusion. Identifying the main point of the presentation will help to stay focused and convey a clear message to the audience.

- **Show one idea per slide.** Each slide in a presentation should convey only one main idea. Too many thoughts or ideas on a slide may confuse the audience and cause you to stray from the purpose of the slide. Determine the specific message you want to convey and then outline the message to organize your ideas.

- **Determine the display medium.** Is the presentation going to be presented on a computer or will the slides be projected onto a screen? To help determine which type of output to use, consider the availability of equipment, the size of the room where the presentation will be given, and the number of people who will be attending the presentation.

- **Maintain a consistent layout.** Using a consistent layout and color scheme for slides in a presentation will create continuity and cohesiveness. Do not get carried away by using too many colors, pictures, and/or other graphic elements.

- **Keep slides simple.** Keep slides uncluttered so that they are easy for the audience to read. Keep words and other items, such as bullets, to a minimum.

- **Determine the output needed.** Will you be providing audience members with handouts? If so, what format will the handouts take? Will they show the slides either with or without space for taking notes or an outline of the slide content?

Quick Steps

Create a Presentation Using a Design Theme Template

1. Click File tab.
2. Click *New* option.
3. Click design theme template.
4. Click color variant.
5. Click Create button.

Creating a Presentation Using a Design Theme Template

PowerPoint provides built-in design theme templates for creating slides for a presentation. These design theme templates include formatting options such as color, background, fonts, and so on. Choose a design theme template at the New backstage area shown in Figure 1.3. Display the New backstage area by clicking the File tab and then clicking the *New* option. At this backstage area, click the design theme template or search for a template online by typing a category in the

Figure 1.3 New Backstage Area

Click this option to display a blank presentation.

Use this option to search for templates online.

Click one of these design theme templates to open a presentation with the design theme applied.

search text box or clicking one of the categories listed next to *Suggested searches* below the search text box.

Click a design theme template at the New backstage area and a window opens containing a slide with the design theme applied as well as theme color variants. The color variants display at the right side of the window and provide color options for the theme. To change the color of the theme, click the color variant and then click the Create button. This opens a presentation with the design theme and the new theme colors applied.

Inserting Text in a Placeholder

Choose a blank presentation template or design theme template at the New backstage area and a slide displays in the slide pane in Normal view. The slide displays with the default Title Slide layout. This layout contains placeholders for entering the slide title and subtitle. To insert text in a placeholder, click in the placeholder. This moves the insertion point inside the placeholder, removes the placeholder label (the text inside the placeholder), and makes the placeholder active. An active placeholder displays surrounded by a dashed border with sizing handles and a white rotation handle, as shown in Figure 1.4.

With the insertion point positioned in a placeholder, type the text. Edit text in a placeholder in the same manner as editing text in a Word document. Press the Backspace key to delete the character immediately left of the insertion point and press the Delete key to delete the character immediately right of the insertion point. Use the arrow keys on the keyboard to move the insertion point in a specific direction.

Figure 1.4 Slide Placeholders

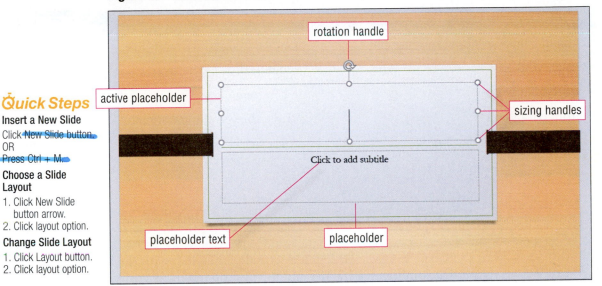

Tutorial

Inserting a New Slide

Tutorial

Choosing a Slide Layout

 New Slide

Tutorial

Changing Slide Layout

Layout

Inserting Slides

Create a new slide in a presentation by clicking the New Slide button in the Slides group on the Home tab or by pressing Ctrl + M. By default, PowerPoint inserts a new slide with the Title and Content layout. However, if a slide with a different layout is selected in the slide thumbnails pane, the layout of the selected slide is applied to the new slide. Choose a different slide layout for a new slide by clicking the New Slide button arrow and then clicking the layout option at the drop-down list.

Changing a Slide Layout

Choose a blank presentation template or design theme template to create a presentation and the slide displays in the Title Slide layout. Change the slide layout with the Layout button in the Slides group on the Home tab. Click the Layout button and a drop-down list of layout options displays. Click a layout at the drop-down list and that layout is applied to the current slide.

Tutorial

Inserting and Deleting Text in Slides

Tutorial

Selecting Text

Inserting, Selecting, and Deleting Text in Slides

Text in a slide may need to be edited, moved, copied, or deleted. Specific text in a slide may need to be replaced with other text. Text is generally inserted in a slide placeholder. Placeholders can be moved, sized, and/or deleted.

To insert or delete text in an individual slide, open the presentation, edit the text as needed, and then save the presentation. To delete more than one character, consider selecting the text first. This will help reduce the number of times the Delete key or Backspace key needs to be pressed. Several methods can be used for selecting text, as described in Table 1.2.

Table 1.2 Selecting Text

To select	Perform this action
text the mouse pointer passes through	Click and drag the mouse.
an entire word	Double-click in the word.
an entire bulleted item	Click the bullet.
an entire paragraph	Triple-click in the paragraph.
all text in a selected placeholder	Click Select button in Editing group on Home tab and then click *Select All*, or press Ctrl + A.

Text in a slide is positioned inside a placeholder. Slide layouts provide placeholders for text and display a label suggesting the type of text to be entered in the slide. For example, the Title and Content slide layout contains a placeholder with the label *Click to add title* and a second placeholder with the label *Click to add text*. Click in the placeholder and the insertion point is positioned inside the placeholder, the default label is removed, and the placeholder is selected.

Saving a Presentation

 Save

After creating or editing a presentation, save it for future use by clicking the Save button on the Quick Access Toolbar, by clicking the File tab and then clicking the *Save* or *Save As* option, or with the keyboard shortcut Ctrl + S. A presentation file name can contain up to 255 characters, including the drive letter and any folder names, and can include spaces. A presentation cannot contain the same name in first uppercase and then lowercase letters. For example, one presentation cannot be named Planning.pptx and another presentation named planning.pptx. Also, some symbols cannot be used in a file name, including /, ?, \, ", >, :, <, ;, *, and |.

Tutorial

Saving to a
Removable Disk

Quick Steps

**Save a Presentation
with a New Name**
1. Click File tab.
2. Click *Save As*.
3. Click *Browse*.
4. Navigate to folder.
5. Type name in *File
   name* text box.
6. Click Save.

Saving a Presentation with a New Name

Save a presentation with a new name using options at the Save As dialog box. Display the Save As dialog box by clicking the File tab and then clicking the *Save As* option. At this backstage area, click the *Browse* option and the Save As dialog box displays. At the Save As dialog box, navigate to a specific folder, type a name for the presentation in the *File name* text box and then press the Enter key or click the Save button. Press the F12 function key to go directly to the Save As dialog box without displaying the Save As backstage area.

Click the OneDrive or *This PC* option at the Save As backstage area and the names of the most recently accessed folders display in the third panel of the backstage area. Open a folder by clicking the folder name.

Tutorial

Saving with the
Same Name

Quick Steps

**Save a Presentation
with the Same Name**
1. Click File tab.
2. Click *Save*.

Saving a Presentation with the Same Name

If changes are made to an existing presentation, save the changes before closing the presentation. Consider saving changes to a presentation on a periodic basis to ensure that no changes are lost if the power is interrupted. Save a presentation with the same name using the Save button on the Quick Access Toolbar or the *Save* option at the backstage area.

1. With PowerPoint open, click the File tab and then click the *New* option.
2. At the New backstage area, click the *Organic* design theme template.
3. At the window, click the Create button.

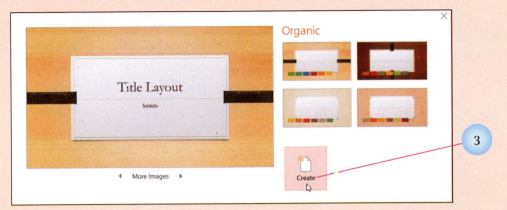

4. Click anywhere in the *Click to add title* placeholder and then type Career Finders.
5. Click anywhere in the *Click to add subtitle* placeholder and then type Resume Writing.

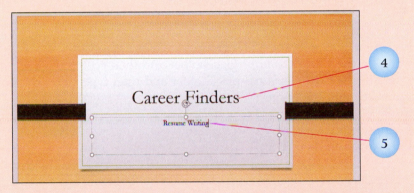

6. Click the New Slide button in the Slides group on the Home tab. (This inserts a slide with the Title and Content slide layout.)

7. Click anywhere in the *Click to add title* placeholder and then type Resume Styles.
8. Click anywhere in the *Click to add text* placeholder and then type Chronological resume.
9. Press the Enter key (this moves the insertion point to the next line and inserts a bullet) and then type Functional resume.
10. Press the Enter key and then type Hybrid resume.

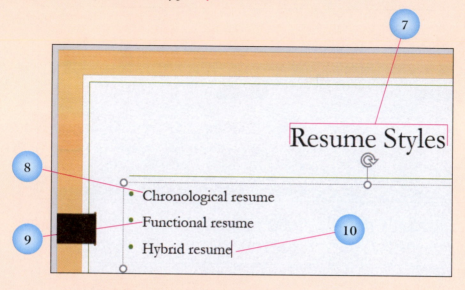

11. Click the New Slide button in the Slides group.
12. Click anywhere in the *Click to add title* placeholder and then type Resume Sections.
13. Click anywhere in the *Click to add text* placeholder and then type Contact information.
14. Press the Enter key and then type Summary or job objective statement.
15. Press the Enter key and then type Work history.
16. Press the Enter key and then type Education details.
17. Press the Enter key and then type References.

18. Click the New Slide button arrow and then click the *Title Only* layout option.

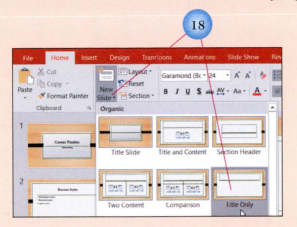

19. Click anywhere in the *Click to add title* placeholder and then type Career Finders.
20. Click the Layout button in the Slides group on the Home tab and then click the *Title Slide* layout option.

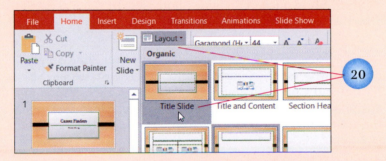

21. Click anywhere in the *Click to add subtitle* placeholder and then type Contact us by calling 1-800-555-2255.
22. Click in the slide pane, but outside the slide. (This deselects the placeholder.)
23. Save the presentation by completing the following steps:
    a. Click the Save button on the Quick Access Toolbar.
    b. At the Save As backstage area, click the *Browse* option.
    c. At the Save As dialog box, navigate to the PC1 folder on your storage medium.
    d. Select the text in the *File name* text box and then type 1-Resumes (*1* for Chapter 1 and *Resumes* because that is the topic of the presentation).
    e. Press the Enter key or click the Save button.

Check Your Work

Normal

 Outline View

Slide Sorter

Notes Page

Reading View

Slide Sorter

Reading View

Normal

Slide Show

Hint In Normal view, you can increase or decrease the size of the slide thumbnails pane.

Changing Views

PowerPoint provides a variety of viewing options. Change the view with buttons in the view area on the Status bar or with options in the Presentation Views group on the View tab. The viewing choices include:

- **Normal view.** This is the default view and displays two panes: The slide pane and the slide thumbnails pane. Enter text in a slide in the slide pane and manage slides in the slide thumbnails pane.

- **Outline view.** In Outline view, the slide thumbnails pane changes to an outline pane where text is typed for slides. *You can easily create an entire presentation by pasting your entire outline from Word into the Outline pane.*

- **Slide Sorter view.** Choosing Slide Sorter view displays all slides in the presentation as thumbnails. In this view, add, move, rearrange, and delete slides.

- **Notes Page view.** Changing to Notes Page view displays an individual slide on a page with any added notes displayed below the slide. *Each page will contain one slide and its speaker notes, which you can edit in this view*

- **Reading view.** Use Reading view to deliver a presentation to people viewing the presentation on their own computers. In this view, a slide show can be played in the PowerPoint window without switching to a full-screen slide show.

- **Slide Show view.** Use Slide Show view to run a slide show. Choose this view and each slide fills the entire screen.

The view area on the Status bar contains four buttons for changing the view: Normal, Slide Sorter, Reading View, and Slide Show. The active button displays with a darker gray background. The Status bar also contains a Notes button and Comments button. Click the Notes button and a notes pane displays at the bottom of the slide in the slide pane. Click the Comments button to display the Comments task pane, in which a comment can be typed.

Previous Slide

Next Slide

Navigating in a Presentation

In Normal view, change slides by clicking the Previous Slide or Next Slide buttons at the bottom of the vertical scroll bar. Or, change to a different slide using the mouse pointer on the vertical scroll bar. To do this, position the mouse pointer on the scroll box on the vertical scroll bar, hold down the left mouse button, drag up or down until a box displays with the desired slide number, and then release the button.

Keyboard keys can also be used to display slides in a presentation. In Normal view, press the Down Arrow or Page Down key to display the next slide or press the Up Arrow or Page Up key to display the previous slide in the presentation. Press the Home key to display the first slide in the presentation and press the End key to display the last slide in the presentation. Navigate in the slide thumbnails pane by clicking the slide thumbnail. Navigate in Slide Sorter view by clicking the slide or using the arrow keys on the keyboard.

1. With **1-Resumes.pptx** open, navigate within the presentation by completing the following steps:
   a. Make sure no placeholders are selected.
   b. Press the Home key to display Slide 1 in the slide pane.
   c. Click the Next Slide button at the bottom of the vertical scroll bar.
   d. Press the End key to display the last slide in the slide pane.
   e. Click the Slide Sorter button in the view area on the Status bar.

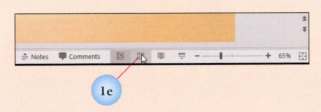

   f. Click Slide 1. (Notice that the active slide displays with an orange border.)
   g. Double-click Slide 3. (This closes Slide Sorter view and displays the presentation in Normal view with Slide 3 active.)
2. Insert text in slides by completing the following steps:
   a. Click in the bulleted text. (This positions the insertion point inside the placeholder.)
   b. Move the insertion point so it is positioned immediately right of *Education details*.
   c. Press the Enter key and then type Professional affiliations.

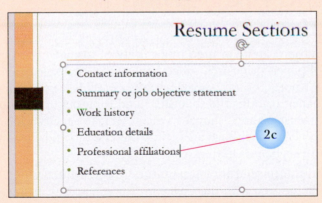

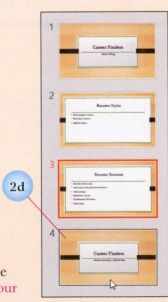

   d. Click Slide 4 in the slide thumbnails pane. (This displays Slide 4 in the slide pane.)
   e. Click in the text containing the telephone number and move the insertion point so it is positioned immediately right of the telephone number. Press the spacebar and then type or visit our website at emcp.net/careerfinders.
3. Type a note in the notes pane by completing the following steps:
   a. Click Slide 2 in the slide thumbnails pane.
   b. Click the Notes button on the Status bar.
   c. Click in the *Click to add notes* placeholder in the notes pane.

d. Type Distribute resume examples to the audience.

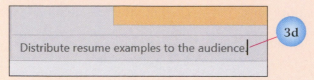

3d

Distribute resume examples to the audience.

e. Display the slide in Notes Page view by clicking the View tab and then clicking the Notes Page button in the Presentation Views group. (Notice the note you typed displays below the slide in this view.)

3e

f. Return to Normal view by clicking the Normal button in the view area on the Status bar.
g. Click the Notes button on the Status bar to close the notes pane.
h. Press the Home key to make Slide 1 the active slide.
4. Save the presentation by clicking the Save button on the Quick Access Toolbar.

Check Your Work

Printing and Previewing a Presentation

A PowerPoint presentation can be printed in a variety of formats. Print each slide on a separate piece of paper; print each slide at the top of the page, leaving the bottom of the page for notes; print a specific number of slides (up to nine slides) on a single piece of paper; or print the slide titles and topics in outline form. Use options in the Print backstage area, shown in Figure 1.5, to specify what is to be printed. To display the Print backstage area, click the File tab and then click the *Print* option or use the keyboard shortcut Ctrl + P.

Click the Print button to send the presentation to the printer and specify the number of copies to be printed with the *Copies* measurement box. Below the Print button are two categories: *Printer* and *Settings*. Use the gallery in the *Printer* category to specify the printer. Click the first gallery in the *Settings* category and options display for specifying what is to be printed, such as all of the presentation or specific slides in the presentation. The *Settings* category also contains a number of galleries that describe how the slides will print.

In the *Settings* category, print a range of slides using the hyphen and print specific slides using a comma. For example, to print Slides 2 through 6, type *2-6* in the *Slides* text box. To print Slides 1, 3, and 7, type *1,3,7*. A hyphen and comma can be combined. For example, to print Slides 1 through 5 and Slide 8, type *1-5,8* in the *Slides* text box.

Figure 1.5 Print Backstage Area

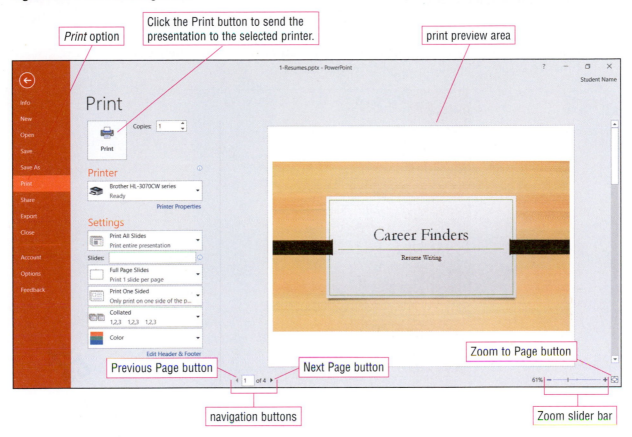

Print option

Click the Print button to send the presentation to the selected printer.

print preview area

Previous Page button

Next Page button

Zoom to Page button

navigation buttons

Zoom slider bar

A preview of how a slide or slides will print displays at the right side of the Print backstage area. If a color printer is selected, the slide or slides at the right side of the Print backstage area display in color, and if a black-and-white printer is selected, the slide or slides will display in grayscale. Use the Next Page button (right-pointing arrow) below and to the left of the page to view the next slide in the presentation; click the Previous Page button (left-pointing arrow) to display the previous slide in the presentation; use the Zoom slider bar to increase or decrease the size of the slide; and click the Zoom to Page button to fit the slide in the viewing area in the Print backstage area.

A presentation can be printed as individual slides, handouts, notes pages, or an outline. If a presentation is printed as handouts or an outline, PowerPoint will automatically print the current date in the upper right corner of the page and the page number in the lower right corner. If the presentation is printed as notes pages, PowerPoint will automatically print the page number in the lower right corner. PowerPoint does not insert the date or page number when individual slides are printed.

1. With **1-Resumes.pptx** open, click the File tab and then click the *Print* option.
2. Click the Next Page button (below and to the left of the slide in the viewing area) two times to display Slide 3 in the print preview area.

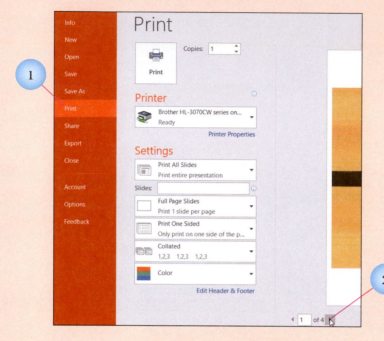

3. Click the Previous Page button two times to display Slide 1.
4. Change the zoom by completing the following steps:
   a. Position the mouse pointer on the Zoom slider bar button (at the bottom right of the Print backstage area), drag the button to the right to increase the size of the slide in the print preview area of the Print backstage area, and then to the left to decrease the size of the slide.
   b. Click the percentage at the left side of the Zoom slider bar. (This displays the Zoom dialog box.)
   c. Click the *50%* option in the Zoom dialog box and then click OK.
   d. Click the Zoom to Page button to the right of the Zoom slider bar. (This changes the size of the slide to fill the print preview area.)

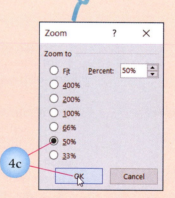

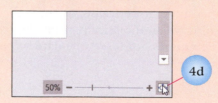

5. Print the presentation as a handout with four slides displayed horizontally on the page by completing the following steps:
   a. At the Print backstage area, click the second gallery (displays with *Full Page Slides*) in the *Settings* category and then click *4 Slides Horizontal* in the *Handouts* section.

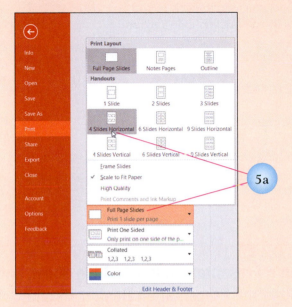

   b. Click the Print button.
6. Print Slide 2 as a notes page by completing the following steps:
   a. Click the File tab and then click the *Print* option.
   b. At the Print backstage area, click in the *Slides* text box in the *Settings* category, and then type 2.
   c. Click the second gallery (displays with *4 Slides Horizontal*) in the *Settings* category and then click *Notes Pages* in the *Print Layout* section.
   d. Click the Print button.

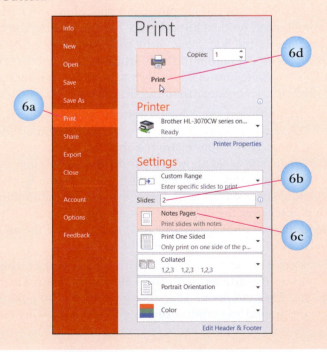

7. Print Slides 1, 2, and 4 by completing the following steps:
   a. Click the File tab and then click the *Print* option.
   b. At the Print backstage area, click in the *Slides* text box in the *Settings* category and then type 1-2,4.
   c. Click the second gallery (displays with *Notes Pages*) in the *Settings* category and then click *4 Slides Horizontal* in the *Handouts* section.
   d. Click the Print button.
8. Close the presentation by clicking the File tab and then clicking the *Close* option.

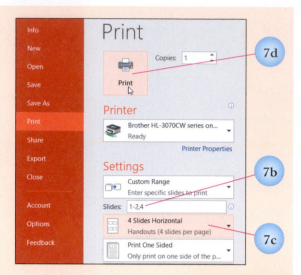

Check Your Work

Project 3 **Open a Presentation, Run a Slide Show, and Change the Presentation Design Theme**   **3 Parts**

You will open a presentation, run the slide show using buttons on the Slide Show toolbar, apply a different design theme and color variant to the presentation, and then delete the presentation.

Preview Finished Project

Tutorial

Running a Slide Show

Tutorial

Changing the Display when Running a Slide Show

Tutorial

Displaying Slide Show Help and Hiding Slides during a Slide Show

Tutorial

Using the Pen Tool during a Slide Show

 From Beginning

 From Current Slide

Using the Slide Show Toolbar

As discussed earlier in this chapter, run a slide show by clicking the Start From Beginning button on the Quick Access Toolbar, clicking the Slide Show button in the view area on the Status bar, or by clicking the Slide Show tab and then clicking the From Beginning button in the Start Slide Show group. This group also contains a From Current Slide button. Use this button to begin running the slide show with the currently active slide rather than the first slide in the presentation.

PowerPoint offers a number of options for navigating through slides in a slide show. Click the left mouse button to advance slides in a slide show, right-click in a slide and then choose options from a shortcut menu, or use buttons on the Slide Show toolbar. The Slide Show toolbar displays in the lower left corner of a slide when running the slide show. Figure 1.6 identifies the buttons on the Slide Show toolbar. To display the Slide Show toolbar, run the slide show and then hover the mouse pointer over the buttons. Click the Next button (displays with a right arrow) on the toolbar to display the next slide and click the Previous button (displays with a left arrow) to display the previous slide.

Click the Pen button (displays with a pen icon) on the Slide Show toolbar and a pop-up list displays with the following options: *Laser Pointer, Pen, Highlighter, Eraser,* and *Erase All Ink on Slide,* along with a row of color options. Click the *Laser Pointer* option and the pointer displays as a red, glowing circle, which can be used

Quick Steps

Run a Slide Show
1. Click Start From Beginning button on Quick Access Toolbar.
2. Click left mouse button to advance slides.
OR
1. Click Slide Show button on Status bar.
2. Click left mouse button to advance slides.
OR
1. Click Slide Show tab.
2. Click From Beginning button.
3. Click left mouse button to advance slides.

Figure 1.6 Slide Show Toolbar

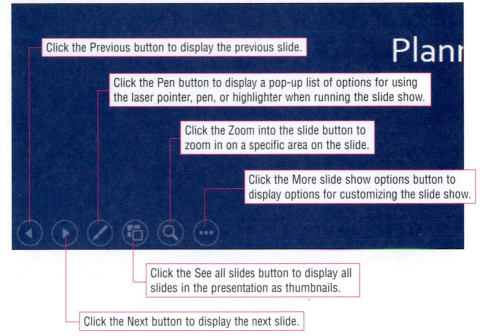

Click the Previous button to display the previous slide.

Click the Pen button to display a pop-up list of options for using the laser pointer, pen, or highlighter when running the slide show.

Click the Zoom into the slide button to zoom in on a specific area on the slide.

Click the More slide show options button to display options for customizing the slide show.

Click the See all slides button to display all slides in the presentation as thumbnails.

Click the Next button to display the next slide.

to point to specific locations on the slide. Use the *Pen* option to draw in the slide, and use the *Highlighter* option to highlight specific items in the slide. Select the *Pen* or *Highlighter* option and then drag the mouse in the slide to draw or highlight items. Erase the drawing or highlighting in a slide by clicking the Pen button on the Slide Show toolbar, clicking the *Eraser* option, and then dragging the mouse to erase the drawing or highlighting. To erase all drawing or highlighting on the slide, click the Pen button and then click the *Erase All Ink on Slide* option.

Quick Steps

Use the Pen or Highlighter During a Slide Show
1. Run slide show.
2. Display slide.
3. Click Pen button on Slide Show toolbar.
4. Click *Pen* or *Highlighter* option.
5. Drag to draw line or highlight text.

💡 **Hint** If you use the pen or highlighter on a slide when running a slide show, choose an ink color that the audience can see easily.

Change the pen or highlighter color by clicking the Pen button and then clicking a color option in the color row. Draw in a slide with the pen or highlighter and PowerPoint will ask if the ink annotations are to be kept or discarded. Reply to this message, and return the laser pointer, pen, or highlighter option back to the mouse pointer by pressing the Esc key on the keyboard.

Click the See all slides button on the Slide Show toolbar and all slides in the slide show display on the screen. Use this feature to display all of the slides in the slide show and/or move to a different slide by clicking the slide.

Zoom in on a portion of a slide by clicking the Zoom into the slide button (contains an image of a magnifying glass) on the Slide Show toolbar. Clicking this button creates a magnification area and dims the remainder of the slide. Drag the magnification area with the mouse to specify what is to be magnified and then click the left mouse button. Return to the normal zoom by pressing the Esc key or right-clicking the slide.

Click the More slide show options button (the last button on the Slide Show ...lbar; depicting three dots) and a pop-up list displays with a variety of options. ...: pop-up list contains options for displaying a custom show or switching to ...senter view; changing the screen display, display settings, and arrow options; ...pausing or ending the show. Click the *Help* option and the Slide Show Help ...og box displays, as shown in Figure 1.7. This dialog box contains various tabs ...describe the keyboard options available when running a slide show.

In addition to the options on the Slide Show toolbar, right-click in a slide and a shortcut menu displays with many of the same options as the options that display when the More slide show options button is clicked.

When running a slide show, the mouse pointer is set, by default, to be hidden automatically after three seconds of inactivity. The mouse pointer will appear again when the mouse is moved. Change this default setting by clicking the More slide show options button on the Slide Show toolbar, clicking *Arrow Options*, and then clicking *Visible* to make the mouse pointer always visible or *Hidden* if the mouse pointer should not display at all when running the slide show. The *Automatic* option is the default setting.

If the mouse pointer displays as the pen or highlighter, return to the regular pointer by pressing the Esc key or clicking the More slide show options button on the Slide Show toolbar, clicking *Arrow Options* at the pop-up list, and then clicking *Visible*.

Figure 1.7 Slide Show Help Dialog Box

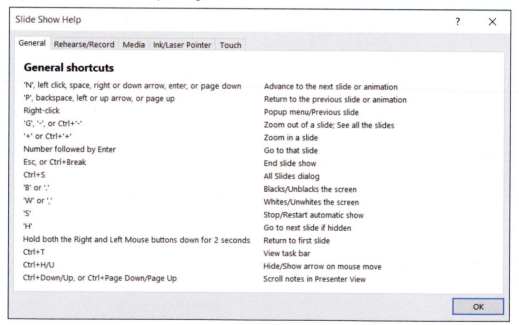

1. Click the File tab and then click the *Open* option.
2. At the Open backstage area, click the *Browse* option.
3. At the Open dialog box, navigate to the PC1 folder on your storage medium and then double-click ***PlanningPres.pptx***.
4. Save the presentation by completing the following steps:
   a. Click the File tab and then click the *Save As* option.
   b. At the Save As backstage area, click the *Browse* option.
   c. At the Save As dialog box, make sure the PC1 folder on your storage medium is active and then type 1-PlanningPres in the *File name* text box.
   d. Press the Enter key or click the Save button.
5. Run the slide show by completing the following steps:
   a. Click the Slide Show button in the view area on the Status bar.
   b. When Slide 1 fills the screen, move the mouse to display the Slide Show toolbar. (This toolbar displays in a dimmed manner in the lower left corner of the slide.)
   c. Click the Next button (contains a right arrow) to display the next slide.
   d. Continue clicking the Next button until a black screen displays.
   e. Click the left mouse button. (This displays the presentation in Normal view.)
6. Run the slide show from the current slide by completing the following steps:
   a. Click Slide 4 in the slide thumbnails pane. (This makes Slide 4 active.)
   b. Click the Slide Show tab.
   c. Click the From Current Slide button in the Start Slide Show group.
7. With Slide 4 active, zoom in on the step text by completing these steps:
   a. Move the mouse to display the Slide Show toolbar.
   b. Click the Zoom into the slide button on the Slide Show toolbar.
   c. Using the mouse, drag the magnification area so it displays the step text and then click the left mouse button.
   d. Press the Esc key to return to the normal zoom.
8. Click the See all slides button on the Slide Show toolbar and then click the Slide 2 thumbnail.
9. With Slide 2 active, use the pen to draw in the slide by completing the following steps:
   a. Move the mouse to display the Slide Show toolbar.
   b. Click the Pen button on the Slide Show toolbar and then click *Pen* at the pop-up list. (This changes the mouse pointer to a small circle.)

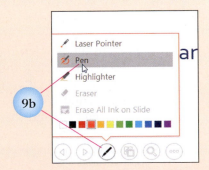

c. Using the mouse, draw a circle around the text *Step 1*.

d. Draw a line below the word *identify*.

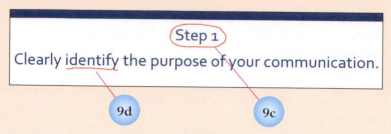

e. Press the Esc key to return the mouse pointer to an arrow.

10. Erase the pen markings by clicking the Pen button on the Slide Show toolbar and then clicking *Erase All Ink on Slide* at the pop-up list.

11. Click the Next button to display Slide 3.

12. Click the Pen button and then click *Highlighter*.

13. Click the Pen button and then click the *Light Green* color (seventh option).

14. Drag through the text *Assess your target audience*.

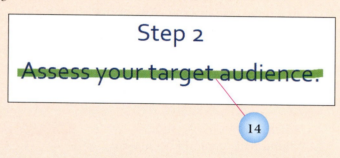

15. Press the Esc key to return the mouse pointer to an arrow.

16. Press the Esc key to end the slide show. Click the Discard button at the message asking if you want to keep or discard the ink annotations.

17. With Slide 3 active, click the Slide Show button on the Status bar to start the slide show.

18. Click the Pen button on the Slide Show toolbar and then click *Laser Pointer* at the pop-up list.

19. Use the laser pointer to point to various locations on the slide.

20. Press the Esc key to return to the mouse pointer to an arrow.

21. Click the Next button on the Slide Show toolbar. (This displays Slide 4.)

22. Turn on the highlighter and then drag through the words *best format* to highlight them.

23. Press the Esc key to return the mouse pointer to an arrow.

24. Continue clicking the left mouse button to move through the presentation.

25. At the black screen, click the left mouse button.

26. At the message asking if you want to keep your ink annotations, click the Keep button.

27. Save the presentation with a new name by completing the following steps:

    a. Click the File tab and then click the *Save As* option.

    b. At the Save As backstage area, click the *Browse* option.

    c. At the Save As dialog box, make sure the PC1 folder on your storage medium is the active folder, type 1-PlanningPres-Ink in the *File name* text box, and then press the Enter key.

28. Print Slide 4 as a handout.

29. Close **1-PlanningPres-Ink.pptx**.

Check Your Work

Applying a Design Theme and Color Variant

PowerPoint provides a variety of built-in design theme templates that can be used when creating slides for a presentation. Choose a design theme template at the New backstage area or with options in the Themes group on the Design tab. Click the Design tab and themes display in the themes gallery in the Themes group. Click one of these themes to apply it to the current presentation. Click the More Themes button at the right side of the themes gallery to display any additional themes. Click the up arrow or down arrow at the right side of the themes gallery to scroll through the list. Hover the mouse pointer over a theme and the active slide in the presentation displays with the theme formatting applied. This is an example of the live preview feature, which displays how theme formatting will affect the presentation.

More Themes

Each design theme contains color variations that display in the Variants group on the Design tab. These are the same theme color variants that display when applying a theme template at the New backstage area. Click a color variant in the Variants group to apply the colors to the slides in the presentation.

Hover the mouse pointer over a theme in the theme gallery and a ScreenTip displays (after approximately a second) containing the theme name. Theme names in PowerPoint are similar to those in Word, Excel, Access, and Outlook and apply similar formatting. With the availability of the themes across these applications, business files such as documents, workbooks, and presentations can be "branded" with a consistent and uniform appearance.

Quick Steps

Apply a Design Theme
1. Click Design tab.
2. Click theme in themes gallery.

Hint Design themes were designed by professional graphic artists who understand the use of color, space, and design.

Project 3b Applying a Design Theme and Color Variant   **Part 2 of 3**

1. Open **1-PlanningPres.pptx**.
2. Make sure Slide 1 is active and that the presentation displays in Normal view.
3. Apply a different design theme to the presentation by completing the following steps:
   a. Click the Design tab.
   b. Hover the mouse pointer over the *Ion* theme in the themes gallery in the Themes group and notice the theme formatting applied to the slide in the slide pane.
   c. Click the *Ion* theme.

4. Run the slide show and notice the formatting applied by the theme.
5. With the presentation displayed in Normal view, apply a different design theme by clicking the *Facet* theme in the themes gallery in the Themes group on the Design tab.

color change

6. Apply a color variant by clicking the fourth option in the Variants group.

Variants

⑥

7. Run the slide show.
8. Print the presentation as a handout by completing the following steps:
   a. Click the File tab and then click the *Print* option.
   b. At the Print backstage area, click the second gallery (displays with *Full Page Slides*) in the *Settings* category and then click *6 Slides Horizontal* in the *Handouts* section.
   c. Click the Print button.
9. Save and then close **1-PlanningPres.pptx**.

Check Your Work ▶

Deleting a Presentation

File management tasks in PowerPoint can be performed at the Open dialog box or Save As dialog box. To delete a PowerPoint presentation, display the Open dialog box, click the presentation to be deleted, click the Organize button on the toolbar, and then click *Delete* at the drop-down list. At the message asking to confirm the deletion, click the Yes button. The presentation file must be closed to be deleted.

If a presentation is deleted from a folder on the computer's hard drive, the confirmation message does not display. This is because the deleted presentation is sent to the Recycle Bin where it can be restored, if needed.

Project 3c Deleting a PowerPoint Presentation   Part 3 of 3

1. Click the File tab and then, if necessary, click the *Open* option.
2. At the Open backstage area, click the *Browse* option.
3. At the Open dialog box, make sure the PC1 folder on your storage medium is the active folder and then click *PlanningPres.pptx* in the Content pane.
4. Click the Organize button on the toolbar and then click *Delete* at the drop-down list.
5. At the message asking if you are sure you want to delete the presentation, click Yes. (If you are deleting the presentation from a folder on your computer's hard drive, the confirmation message will not display because the presentation is sent automatically to the Recycle Bin.)
6. Click the Cancel button to close the Open dialog box.

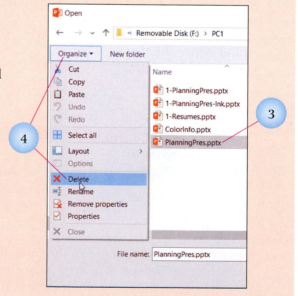

> **Project 4** **Create a Technology Presentation in the**
> **Outline Pane**
> **3 Parts**
>
> You will create a computer technology presentation in the outline pane, add and remove transitions and sounds to the presentation, and set up the presentation to advance slides automatically after a specified amount of time.

Tutorial

Opening a Blank
Presentation

Preparing a Presentation from a Blank Presentation

To create a presentation without a design theme applied, open a blank presentation. Open a blank presentation at the PowerPoint opening screen or at the New backstage area by clicking the *Blank Presentation* template. Another method for opening a blank presentation is to use the keyboard shortcut Ctrl + N.

Tutorial

Entering Text in
the Outline Pane

Quick Steps

**Prepare a
Presentation from a
Blank Presentation**
1. Click File tab.
2. Click *New* option.
3. Click *Blank
   Presentation*.
OR
Press Ctrl + N.

Preparing a Presentation in Outline View

Text can be inserted in a slide by typing the text in the outline pane. Display this pane by clicking the View tab and then clicking the Outline View button in the Presentation Views group. The outline pane replaces the slide thumbnails pane at the left side of the screen. A slide number displays in the pane followed by a small slide icon. When typing text in the outline pane, press the Tab key to move the insertion point to the next tab. This moves the insertion point and also changes the formatting. The formatting will vary depending on the theme applied. Press Shift + Tab to move the insertion point to the previous tab. Moving the insertion point back to the left margin will create a new slide.

Project 4a Preparing a Presentation in Outline View   **Part 1 of 3**

1. At a blank screen, click the File tab and then click the *New* option.
2. At the New backstage area, click the *Blank Presentation* template.
3. At the blank presentation, click the View tab and then click the Outline View button in the Presentation Views group.

4. Click in the outline pane immediately right of the slide icon.
5. Type the first slide title shown in Figure 1.8 (*Computer Technology*) and then press the Enter key. (The text you type displays immediately right of the small orange slide icon in the outline pane.)
6. Type the second slide title shown in Figure 1.8 (*The Motherboard*) and then press the Enter key.
7. Press the Tab key, type the text after the first bullet in Figure 1.8 (*Buses*), and then press the Enter key.
8. Continue typing the text as it displays in Figure 1.8. Press the Tab key to move the insertion point to the next tab or press Shift + Tab to move the insertion point back to a previous tab.

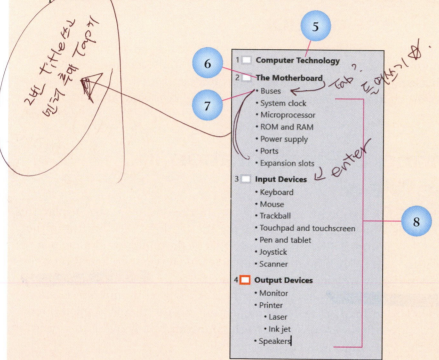

9. After typing all of the information as shown in Figure 1.8, click the Normal button in the Presentation Views group on the View tab.
10. Click the Notes button on the Status bar to close the notes pane.
11. Click Slide 1 in the slide thumbnails pane. (This displays Slide 1 in the slide pane.)
12. Apply a design theme by completing the following steps:
    a. Click the Design tab.
    b. Click the *Ion* theme in the themes gallery in the Themes group.
    c. Click the fourth option in the Variants group (the orange color variant).
13. Save the presentation and name it **1-Computers**.
14. Run the slide show.

Check Your Work

Figure 1.8 Project 4a

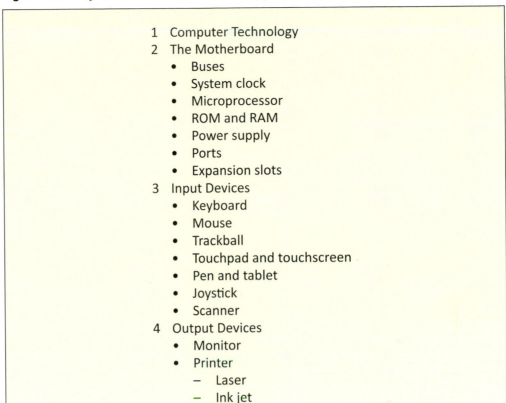

1 Computer Technology
2 The Motherboard
 • Buses
 • System clock
 • Microprocessor
 • ROM and RAM
 • Power supply
 • Ports
 • Expansion slots
3 Input Devices
 • Keyboard
 • Mouse
 • Trackball
 • Touchpad and touchscreen
 • Pen and tablet
 • Joystick
 • Scanner
4 Output Devices
 • Monitor
 • Printer
  – Laser
  – Ink jet
 • Speakers

Adding Transitions and Transition Sounds

Interesting transitions and transition sounds can be applied to a presentation. A transition is how one slide is removed from the screen during a slide show and the next slide is displayed. Transitions such as cut, fade, push, wipe, split, reveal, and random bars can be applied to a presentation. To add transitions and transition sounds, open a presentation, and then click the Transitions tab. This displays transition buttons and options, as shown in Figure 1.9.

 Apply To All

Transitions and transition sounds apply by default to the active slide. To apply transitions and transition sounds to all slides in the presentation, click the Apply To All button in the Timing group. In Slide Sorter view, select all slides by pressing Ctrl + A (or by clicking the Home tab, clicking the Select button, and then clicking *Select All* at the drop-down list) and then apply the transition and/or transition sounds.

Figure 1.9 Transitions Tab

Tutorial

Adding Transitions

Quick Steps

Apply a Transition to All Slides
1. Click Transitions tab.
2. Click transition in transitions gallery in Transition to This Slide group.
3. Click Apply To All button.

Adding Transitions

To add a transition, click an option in the gallery in the Transition to This Slide group on the Transitions tab and the transition displays in the slide in the slide pane. Use the down and up arrows at the right side of the transitions gallery to display additional transitions. Click the More Transitions button at the right side of the transitions gallery and a drop-down list displays with additional options. Use the *Duration* measurement box to specify the duration of slide transitions when running the slide show. Click the *Duration* measurement box up or down arrows to change the duration time. Or, select the current time in the measurement box and then type the specific time.

Use options in the Effect Options button drop-down gallery to change transition effects. The options in the drop-down gallery vary depending on the transition applied. The Effect Options button is located in the Transition to This Slide group on the Transitions tab.

When a transition is applied to slides in a presentation, animation icons display below the slide numbers in the slide thumbnails pane and in Slide Sorter view. Click an animation icon for a particular slide and the slide will display the transition effect.

Tutorial

Adding Sound to Slide Transitions

Adding Sound to Slide Transitions

Quick Steps

Apply Transition Sound to All Slides
1. Click Transitions tab.
2. Click *Sound* option box arrow.
3. Click sound.
4. Click Apply To All button.

To add a sound effect to slide transitions in a presentation, click the *Sound* option box arrow and then click a sound at the drop-down list. Preview a transition and/or transition sound applied to a slide by clicking the Preview button at the left side of the Transitions tab.

Removing Transitions and Transition Sounds

Remove a transition from a slide by clicking the *None* option in the transitions gallery in the Transition to This Slide group. To remove transitions from all slides, click the Apply To All button in the Timing group. To remove a transition sound from a slide, click the *Sound* option box arrow and then click *[No Sound]* at the drop-down gallery. To remove sound from all slides, click the Apply To All button.

Project 4b Adding Transitions and Transition Sounds to a Presentation   **Part 2 of 3**

1. With **1-Computers.pptx** open, click the Transitions tab.
2. Apply transitions and a transition sound to all slides in the presentation by completing the following steps:
   a. Click the More Transitions button at the right side of the transitions gallery in the Transition to This Slide group.

b. Click the *Fall Over* option in the *Exciting* section.
c. Click the Effect Options button in the Transition to This Slide group and then click *Right* at the drop-down list.

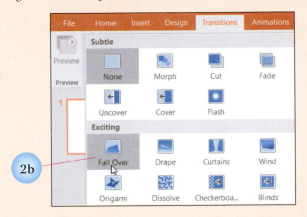
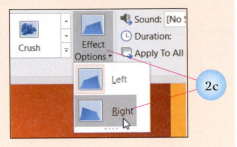

d. Click in the *Duration* measurement box in the Timing group, type 1, and then press the Enter key.

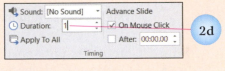

e. Click the *Sound* option box arrow in the Timing group and then click *Chime* at the drop-down list.
f. Click the Apply To All button in the Timing group.

3. Run the slide show. (Notice the transitions and transition sound as you move from slide to slide.)
4. With the presentation in Normal view and the Transitions tab active, remove the transitions and transition sound by completing the following steps:
   a. Click the More Transitions button in the Transition to This Slide group and then click the *None* option in the *Subtle* section.
   b. Click the *Sound* option box arrow and then click *[No Sound]* at the drop-down list.
   c. Click the Apply To All button.
5. Apply transitions and transition sounds to specific slides by completing the following steps:
   a. Make sure the presentation displays in Normal view.
   b. Click Slide 1 in the slide thumbnails pane.
   c. Hold down the Shift key and then click Slide 2. (Slides 1 and 2 will display with orange backgrounds.)
   d. Click the More Transitions button at the right side of the transitions gallery and then click the *Ferris Wheel* option in the *Dynamic Content* section.
   e. Click the *Sound* option box arrow and then click the *Breeze* option.
   f. Click Slide 3 in the slide pane.
   g. Hold down the Shift key and then click Slide 4.
   h. Click the More Transitions button at the right side of the transitions gallery and then click the *Glitter* option in the *Exciting* section.
   i. Click the *Sound* option box arrow and then click the *Wind* option.
6. Run the slide show from the beginning.
7. Remove the transitions and transition sounds from all slides. (Refer to Step 4.)
8. Save **1-Computers.pptx**.

Advancing Slides Automatically

Slides in a slide show can be advanced after a specific number of seconds by selecting options in the Timing group on the Transitions tab. To advance slides automatically, click the *After* check box and then insert the number of seconds in the measurement box. Or, select the current time in the measurement box and then type the time, or click the up or down arrows to increase or decrease the time. Click the *On Mouse Click* check box to remove the check mark. To apply the transition time to all slides in the presentation, click the Apply To All button. In Slide Sorter view, the transition time displays below each affected slide.

Project 4c Advancing Slides Automatically

Part 3 of 3

1. With **1-Computers.pptx** open, make sure the Transitions tab is active.
2. Click the *On Mouse Click* check box to remove the check mark.
3. Click in the *After* check box in the Timing group to insert a check mark.
4. Click the *After* measurement box up arrow until *00:04.00* displays in the box.
5. Click the Apply To All button.
6. Run the slide show from the beginning. (Each slide will advance automatically after four seconds.)
7. At the black screen, click the left mouse button.
8. Print the presentation as an outline by completing the following steps:
   a. Click the File tab and then click the *Print* option.
   b. At the Print backstage area, click the second gallery (displays with *Full Page Slides*) in the *Settings* category and then click *Outline* in the *Print Layout* section.
   c. Click the Print button.
9. Save and then close **1-Computers.pptx**.

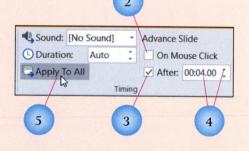

Check Your Work

Chapter Summary

- PowerPoint is a presentation graphics program used for creating slides for an on-screen presentation.

- Open a presentation at the Open dialog box. Display this dialog box by clicking the File tab and then clicking the *Open* option. At the Open backstage area, click the *Browse* option.

- A presentation can be pinned to or unpinned from the Recent list at the PowerPoint opening screen and the *Recent* option list at the Open backstage area.

- Start running a slide show by clicking the Start From Beginning button on the Quick Access Toolbar, clicking the Slide Show button in the view area on the Status bar, or by clicking the View tab and then clicking the From Beginning button.

- Close a presentation by clicking the File tab and then clicking the *Close* option or with the keyboard shortcut Ctrl + F4.

- Before creating a presentation in PowerPoint, plan the presentation by defining the purpose and determining the content and display medium.

- Built-in presentation design theme templates are available at the New backstage area. Display this backstage area by clicking the File tab and then clicking the *New* option.

- To insert text in a slide, click in a placeholder and then type the text.

- Insert a new slide in a presentation with the Title and Content layout by clicking the New Slide button in the Slides group on the Home tab. Insert a new slide with a specific layout by clicking the New Slide button arrow and then clicking the layout at the drop-down list.

- A slide layout provides placeholders for specific data in a slide. Choose a slide layout by clicking the Layout button in the Slides group on the Home tab and then clicking a layout at the drop-down list.

- Save a presentation by clicking the Save button on the Quick Access Toolbar or clicking the File tab and then clicking the *Save As* option. At the Save As backstage area, click the *Browse* option. At the Save As dialog box, navigate to the location where the presentation is to be saved and then type a name for the presentation.

- View a presentation in one of the following six views: Normal view, which is the default view and displays two panes—the slide thumbnails pane and the slide pane; Outline view, which displays the outline pane for typing text in slides; Slide Sorter view, which displays all slides in the presentation in slide thumbnails; Reading view, which delivers a presentation to people viewing it on their computers; Notes Page view, which displays an individual slide with any added notes displayed below the slide; and Slide Show view, which runs the slide show.

- Navigate to various slides in a presentation using the mouse and/or keyboard. Navigate in the presentation using the Previous Slide and Next Slide buttons at the bottom of the vertical scroll bar, the scroll box on the vertical scroll bar, arrow keys on the keyboard, or the Page Up and Page Down keys on the keyboard.

- Click the File tab and the backstage area displays options for working with and managing presentations.

- Use options at the Print backstage area to print presentations with each slide on a separate piece of paper; each slide at the top of the page, leaving room for notes; all or a specific number of slides on a single piece of paper; or slide titles and topics in outline form.

- When running a slide show, the Slide Show toolbar displays in the lower left corner of the slide. This toolbar contains buttons and options for running a slide show. Use the buttons to navigate to slides, make ink notations on slides, display slide thumbnails, zoom in on a specific location in a slide, and display a Help menu.

- Apply a design theme to a presentation by clicking the Design tab and then clicking the theme in the themes gallery in the Themes group. Apply a color variation to a theme by clicking an option in the Variants group on the Design tab.

- Delete a presentation at the Open dialog box by clicking the presentation file name, clicking the Organize button on the toolbar, and then clicking *Delete* at the drop-down list.

- Open a blank presentation by displaying the New backstage area and then clicking the *Blank Presentation* template or with the keyboard shortcut Ctrl + N.

- Type text in a slide in the slide pane or in the outline pane. Display the outline pane by clicking the View tab and then clicking the Outline View button.

- Enhance a presentation by adding transitions (how one slide is removed from the screen and replaced with the next slide) and transition sounds. Add transitions and transition sounds to a presentation with options on the Transitions tab.

- Advance slides automatically in a slide show by removing the check mark from the *On Mouse Click* check box on the Transitions tab, inserting a check mark in the *After* check box, and then specifying the time in the *After* measurement box.

- Click the Apply To All button to apply transitions, transition sounds, and/or time settings to all slides in a presentation.

Commands Review

FEATURE	RIBBON TAB, GROUP/OPTION	BUTTON	KEYBOARD SHORTCUT
close presentation	File, *Close*		Ctrl + F4
design theme	Design, Themes		
New backstage area	File, *New*		
new slide	Home, Slides		Ctrl + M
Normal view	View, Presentation Views		
Notes Page view	View, Presentation Views		
Open backstage area	File, *Open*		Ctrl + O
Outline view	View, Presentation Views		
Print backstage area	File, *Print*		Ctrl + P
run slide show	Slide Show, Start Slide Show OR Quick Access Toolbar		F5
Save As backstage area	File, *Save* OR *Save As*		Ctrl + S
slide layout	Home, Slides		
Slide Sorter view	View, Presentation Views		
transition	Transitions, Transition to This Slide		
transition duration	Transitions, Timing		
transition sound	Transitions, Timing		

Workbook

Chapter study tools and assessment activities are available in the *Workbook* ebook. These resources are designed to help you further develop and demonstrate mastery of the skills learned in this chapter.

PowerPoint®

Modifying a Presentation and Using Help and Tell Me

CHAPTER 2

Performance Objectives

Upon successful completion of Chapter 2, you will be able to:

1 Check spelling
2 Use the Thesaurus
3 Find and replace text in slides
4 Cut, copy, and paste text in slides
5 Rearrange text in the outline pane
6 Size and rearrange placeholders
7 Insert, delete, move, and copy slides
8 Copy slides between presentations
9 Duplicate slides
10 Reuse slides
11 Create and manage sections
12 Customize the Quick Access Toolbar
13 Use the Help and Tell Me features

Precheck

Check your current skills to help focus your study.

When preparing a presentation, you may need to modify the contents by finding and replacing specific text or copying and pasting text in slides. Improve the quality of your presentation by completing a spelling check to ensure that the words in your presentation are spelled correctly and use the Thesaurus to find synonyms and antonyms. Additional modifications you may need to make to a presentation could include sizing and rearranging placeholders and rearranging, inserting, deleting, or copying slides. In this chapter, you will learn how to make these modifications to a presentation as well as how to create sections within a presentation and use the Help and Tell Me features.

SNAP

If you are a SNAP user, launch the Precheck and Tutorials from your Assignments page.

Data Files

Before beginning the projects, copy the PC2 folder to your storage medium and then make PC2 the active folder.

<table>
<tr><td>

Project 1
</td><td>

Check Spelling, Use the Thesaurus, and Manage Text in a Design Presentation
</td><td>

2 Parts
</td></tr>
</table>

You will open a presentation on steps for planning a design publication, complete a spelling check on the text in the presentation, use the Thesaurus to find synonyms, and find and replace specific text in slides.

▸ **Preview Finished Project**

▸ **Tutorial**

Checking Spelling

 Spelling

Quick Steps

Complete a Spelling Check
1. Click Review tab.
2. Click Spelling button.
3. Change or ignore errors.
4. Click OK.

Checking Spelling

When preparing a presentation, perform a spelling check on text in slides using PowerPoint's spelling checker feature. The spelling checker feature compares words in slides in a presentation with words in its dictionary. If a match is found, the word is passed over. If a match is not found, the Spelling task pane displays replacement suggestions. At this task pane, choose to change the word or ignore it and leave it as written. To perform a spelling check, click the Review tab and then click the Spelling button in the Proofing group. Pressing the F7 function key will also start the spelling checker.

When checking the spelling in the presentation in Project 1a, the spelling checker will stop at the misspelled word *Layuot* and display the Spelling task pane as shown in Figure 2.1. The buttons available in the Spelling task pane are described in Table 2.1.

Figure 2.1 Spelling Task Pane

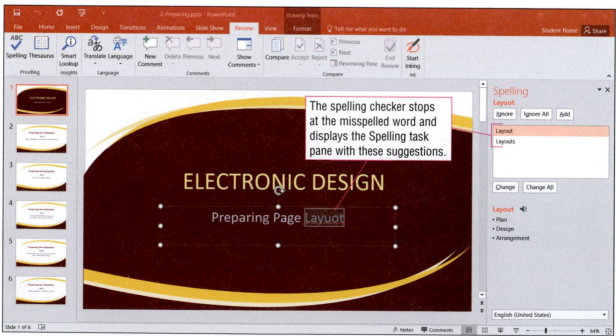

The spelling checker stops at the misspelled word and displays the Spelling task pane with these suggestions.

Table 2.1 Spelling Task Pane Options

Button	Function
Ignore	skips that occurrence of the word
Ignore All	skips that occurrence of the word and all other occurrences of the word in the presentation
Add	adds the selected word to the main spelling check dictionary
Delete	deletes the currently selected word(s)
Change	replaces the selected word with the word selected in the task pane list box
Change All	replaces the selected word and all other occurrences of it in the presentation with the word selected in the task pane list box

Using the Thesaurus

Tutorial

Using the
Thesaurus

 Thesaurus

Quick Steps

Use the Thesaurus
1. Click word.
2. Click Review tab.
3. Click Thesaurus button.
4. Position mouse pointer on replacement word in Thesaurus task pane.
5. Click down-pointing arrow at right of word.
6. Click *Insert*.

Use the Thesaurus to find synonyms, antonyms, and related words for a particular word. Synonyms are words that have the same or nearly the same meaning and antonyms are words with the opposite meanings.

To use the Thesaurus, click in the word, click the Review tab, and then click the Thesaurus button in the Proofing group. This displays the Thesaurus task pane with information about the word where the insertion point is positioned. Hover the mouse over the synonym or antonym, click the down-pointing arrow at the right of the word, and then click *Insert* at the drop-down list. Another method for displaying and inserting a synonym for a word is to right-click the word, point to *Synonyms*, and then click the replacement word at the side menu.

Project 1a   Checking the Spelling in a Presentation   **Part 1 of 2**

1. Open **Preparing.pptx** and then save it with the name **2-Preparing**.
2. With the presentation in Normal view, run a spelling check by completing the following steps:
   a. Click the Review tab.
   b. Click the Spelling button in the Proofing group.
   c. The spelling checker selects the misspelled word *Layuot* and displays the Spelling task pane. The proper spelling (*Layout*) is selected in the Spelling task pane list box, so click the Change button (or the Change All button) to correct the misspelling.

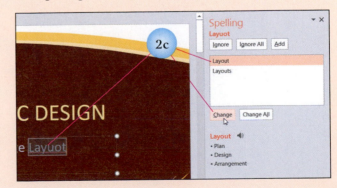

d. The spelling checker selects the misspelled word *Clerly*. The correct spelling is selected in the Spelling task pane list box, so click the Change button (or the Change All button).

e. When the spelling checker selects the misspelled word *massege*, click *message* in the Spelling task pane list box and then click the Change button (or the Change All button).

f. The spelling checker selects the misspelled word *fo*. The correct spelling is selected in the Spelling task pane list box, so click the Change button (or the Change All button).

g. At the message stating that the spelling check is complete, click the OK button.

3. Make Slide 2 active and then use the Thesaurus to find a synonym for *point* by completing the following steps:

a. Click in the word *point*.

b. Click the Review tab, if necessary, and then click the Thesaurus button.

c. At the Thesaurus task pane, scroll down the task pane list box to display *purpose* (below *purpose (n.)*).

d. Hover your mouse pointer over the word *purpose* in the task pane, click the down-pointing arrow, and then click *Insert* at the drop-down list.

e. Close the Thesaurus task pane by clicking the Close button (contains an *X*) in the upper right corner of the task pane.

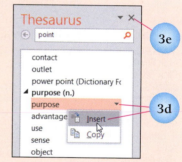

4. Make Slide 6 active and right-click in the word *Gather*.

5. Point to *Synonyms* at the short-cut menu and then click *Collect* at the side menu.

6. Save **2-Preparing.pptx**.

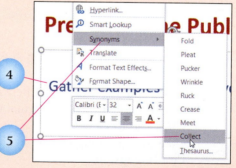

Check Your Work

Managing Text and Placeholders

Text in a placeholder in a slide can be edited, modified, and rearranged. For example, text can be replaced with other text and text can be cut, copied, and pasted to other locations. The placeholder containing text or other objects can be modified by resizing it or moving it to another location.

Finding and Replacing Text in Slides

Use the Find feature to look for specific text in slides in a presentation and use the Find and Replace feature to look for specific text in slides in a presentation and replace it with other text. Begin a search by clicking the Find button in the Editing group on the Home tab. This displays the Find dialog box, as shown in Figure 2.2. In the *Find what* text box, type the text to be found and then click the Find Next button. Continue clicking this button until a message displays indicating that the search is complete. At this message, click OK.

Use options at the Replace dialog box, shown in Figure 2.3, to search for text and replace it with other text. Display this dialog box by clicking the Replace button in the Editing group on the Home tab. Type the text to be found in the *Find what* text box, press the Tab key, and then type the replacement text in the *Replace with* text box. Click the Find Next button to find the next occurrence of the text and then click the Replace button to replace it with the new text, or click the Replace All button to replace all occurrences in the presentation.

Both the Find dialog box and the Replace dialog box contain two additional options. Insert a check mark in the *Match case* check box to specify that the text in the presentation should exactly match the case of the text in the *Find what* text box. For example, search for *Planning* and PowerPoint will stop at *Planning* but not *planning* or *PLANNING*. Insert a check mark in the *Find whole words only* check box to specify that the text to be found is a whole word only and not part of a word. For example, if you search for *plan* and do not check the *Find whole words only* option, PowerPoint will stop at ex*plan*ation, *plan*ned, *plan*ning, and so on.

Figure 2.2 Find Dialog Box

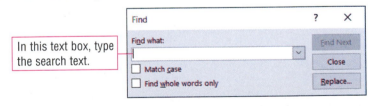

Figure 2.3 Replace Dialog Box

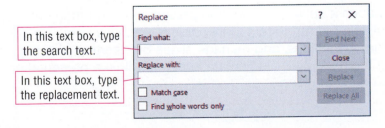

1. With **2-Preparing.pptx** open, make Slide 1 active.
2. Find all occurrences of *Preparing* in the presentation and replace them with *Planning* by completing the following steps:
   a. With Slide 1 active, click the Replace button in the Editing group on the Home tab.
   b. At the Replace dialog box, type Preparing in the *Find what* text box.
   c. Press the Tab key.
   d. Type Planning in the *Replace with* text box.
   e. Click the Replace All button.

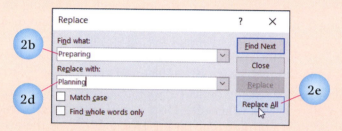

   f. At the message stating that six replacements were made, click the OK button.
   g. Click the Close button to close the Replace dialog box.
3. Find all occurrences of *Publication* and replace them with *Newsletter* by completing steps similar to those in Step 2.
4. Save the presentation.
5. Apply a transition and transition sound of your choosing to all slides in the presentation.
6. Run the slide show.
7. Print Slide 1 by completing the following steps:
   a. Click the File tab and then click the *Print* option.
   b. At the Print backstage area, click in the *Slides* text box in the *Settings* category and then type 1.
   c. Click the Print button.
8. Print the presentation as a handout with six slides displayed horizontally on the page. (Change the second gallery in the *Settings* category to *6 Slides Horizontal* and delete the *1* in the *Slides* text box.)
9. Save and then close **2-Preparing.pptx**.

Check Your Work

Project 2 Cut, Copy, Paste, Rearrange, and Manage Slides in a Network Presentation

5 Parts

You will open a network evaluation presentation and then cut, copy, and paste text in slides; rearrange text in the slide thumbnails pane; size and rearrange placeholders in slides; and manage slides by inserting, deleting, moving, and copying them. You will also create sections within a presentation and copy slides between presentations.

Preview Finished Project

Cut

Copy

Paste

Cutting, Copying, and Pasting Text in Slides

Use buttons in the Clipboard group on the Home tab and/or shortcut menu options to cut, copy, and paste text in slides. For example, to move text in a slide, click in the placeholder containing the text to be moved, select the text, and then click the Cut button in the Clipboard group or use the keyboard shortcut Ctrl + X. Position the insertion point where the text is to be inserted and then click the Paste button in the Clipboard group or use the keyboard shortcut Ctrl + V.

To cut and paste with the shortcut menu, select the text to be moved, right-click in the selected text, and then click *Cut* at the shortcut menu. Position the insertion point where the text is to be inserted, right-click in the placeholder, and then click *Paste* at the shortcut menu. Complete similar steps to copy and paste text, except click the Copy button instead of the Cut button, use the keyboard shortcut Ctrl + C, or click the *Copy* option at the shortcut menu instead of the *Cut* option.

Project 2a Cutting, Copying, and Pasting Text in Slides   **Part 1 of 5**

1. Open **NetworkSystem.pptx** and then save it with the name **2-NetworkSystem**.
2. Insert a new slide by completing the following steps:
   a. Make Slide 4 active.
   b. Click the New Slide button in the Slides group on the Home tab.
   c. Click in the title placeholder and then type TIME.
3. Cut text from Slide 3 and paste it into Slide 5 by completing the following steps:
   a. Make Slide 3 active.
   b. Click in the bulleted text in the slide pane.
   c. Using the mouse, select the bottom three lines of bulleted text. (The bullets will not be selected.)
   d. With the text selected, click the Cut button in the Clipboard group on the Home tab.

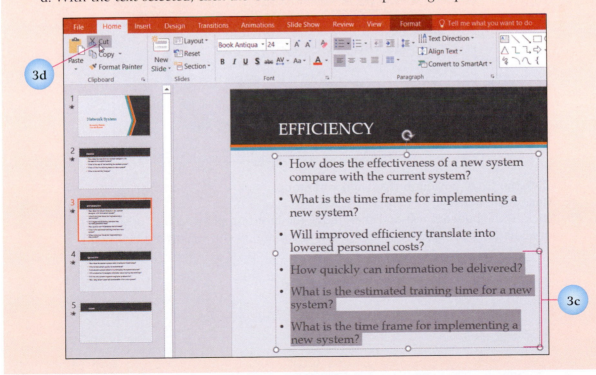

e. Make Slide 5 the active slide (contains the title *TIME*).
f. Click in the text placeholder.
g. Click the Paste button in the Clipboard group.
h. With the insertion point positioned below the third bulleted item following a bullet, press the Backspace key two times. (This removes the bullet and deletes the blank line below that bullet.)

4. Insert a new slide by completing the following steps:
   a. With Slide 5 the active slide, click the New Slide button in the Slides group on the Home tab.
   b. Click in the title placeholder and then type EASE OF USE.

5. Cut text from Slide 4 and paste it into Slide 6 by completing the following steps:
   a. Make Slide 4 active.
   b. Click in the bulleted text.
   c. Select the bottom three bulleted items.
   d. Click the Cut button in the Clipboard group on the Home tab.
   e. Make Slide 6 active (contains the title *EASE OF USE*).
   f. Click in the text placeholder.
   g. Click the Paste button in the Clipboard group.
   h. With the insertion point positioned below the third bulleted item following a bullet, press the Backspace key two times.

6. Copy text from Slide 3 to Slide 5 by completing the following steps:
   a. Make Slide 3 active.
   b. Click in the bulleted text.
   c. Position the mouse pointer over the last bullet until the pointer turns into a four-headed arrow and then click the left mouse button. (This selects the text following the bullet.)

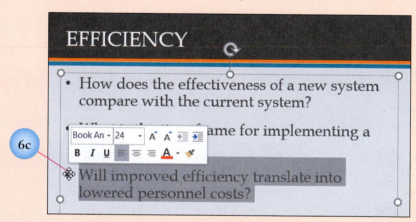

d. Click the Copy button in the Clipboard group.
e. Make Slide 5 active.
f. Click in the bulleted text and then move the insertion point so it is positioned immediately right of the question mark at the end of the second bulleted item.

g. Press the Enter key. (This moves the insertion point down to the next line and inserts another bullet.)

h. Click the Paste button in the Clipboard group.

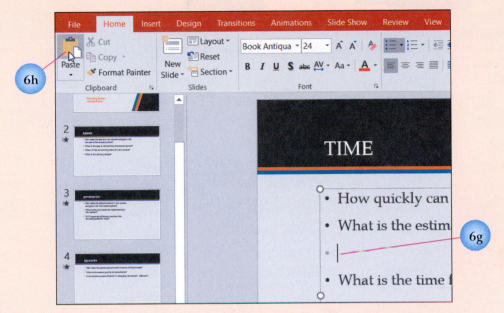

i. If there is a blank line between the third and fourth bullets, press the Backspace key two times to remove it.

7. Save **2-NetworkSystem.pptx**.

Check Your Work

Rearranging Text Using the Outline Pane

Text in slides can be moved and copied in the outline pane. Display the outline pane by clicking the View tab and then clicking the Outline View button in the Presentation Views group or with the keyboard shortcut Ctrl + Shift + Tab. To move text in the outline pane, position the mouse pointer on the slide icon or bullet at the left side of the text until the arrow pointer turns into a four-headed arrow. Click and hold down the left mouse button, drag the arrow pointer (a thin horizontal line displays) to the new location, and then release the mouse button.

Position the arrow pointer on the slide icon and then click the left mouse button and all of the text in the slide is selected. Click a bullet and all text following that bullet is selected.

Dragging selected text with the mouse moves the selected text to a new location in the presentation. Selected text can also be copied. To do this, click the slide icon or the bullet to select the text. Position the arrow pointer in the selected text, press and hold down the Ctrl key, and then click and hold down the left mouse button. Drag the arrow pointer (displays with a light gray box and a plus symbol attached) to the new location, release the mouse button, and then release the Ctrl key.

1. With **2-NetworkSystem.pptx** open, make Slide 1 active.
2. Press Ctrl + Shift + Tab to display the outline pane.
3. Move the first bulleted item in Slide 4 in the outline pane to the end of the list by completing the following steps:
   a. Position the mouse pointer on the first bullet below *QUALITY* until it turns into a four-headed arrow.
   b. Click and hold down the left mouse button, drag the arrow pointer down until a thin horizontal line displays below the last bulleted item, and then release the mouse button.

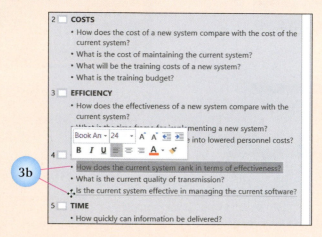

4. Copy and paste text by completing the following steps:
   a. In the outline pane, move the insertion point to the end of the text in Slide 6 and then press the Enter key. (This inserts a new bullet in the slide.)
   b. Scroll up the outline pane until the last bulleted item in Slide 2 is visible in the outline pane as well as the last bullet in Slide 6. (You may need to increase the width of the outline pane to display both bulleted items.)
   c. Position the mouse pointer near the last bulleted item in Slide 2 until it turns into a four-headed arrow and then click the left mouse button. (This selects the text.)
   d. Position the mouse pointer in the selected text, click and hold down the left mouse button, press and hold down the Ctrl key, and then drag down until the arrow pointer and light gray vertical line display on the blank line below the text in Slide 6.
   e. Release the mouse button and then release the Ctrl key.

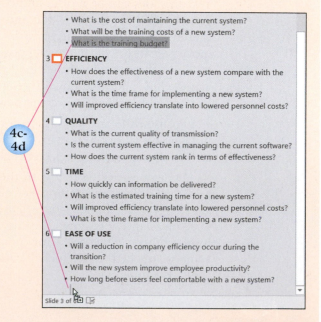

5. Press Ctrl + Shift + Tab to return to the slide thumbnails pane.
6. Click the Notes button on the Status bar to close the notes pane.
7. Save **2-NetworkSystem.pptx**.

Check Your Work

Tutorial

Modifying Placeholders

Modifying Placeholders

Clicking in a placeholder selects the placeholder and displays white sizing handles and a white rotation handle around the placeholder border. Use the sizing handles to increase or decrease the size of the placeholder by positioning the arrow pointer on a sizing handle until the pointer turns into a double-headed arrow and then dragging the placeholder border to the desired size. To move a placeholder, position the arrow pointer on the placeholder border until the arrow pointer displays with a four-headed arrow attached. Click and hold down the left mouse button, drag the placeholder to the new position, and then release the mouse button.

Dragging a selected placeholder with the mouse moves the placeholder. To copy a placeholder, press and hold down the Ctrl key while dragging the placeholder. When the placeholder is in position, release the mouse button, and then release the Ctrl key. If an unwanted change is made to the size and/or location of a placeholder, click the Reset button in the Slides group on the Home tab to return the formatting of the placeholder back to the default.

When dragging a placeholder on a slide, guidelines may display. Use the guidelines to help position placeholders. For example, use the guidelines to help align a title placeholder with a subtitle placeholder.

If a placeholder is no longer necessary, delete the placeholder. To delete a placeholder, click in the placeholder, click the border to change it to a solid line border, and then press the Delete key.

Project 2c Sizing and Rearranging Placeholders

Part 3 of 5

1. With **2-NetworkSystem.pptx** open, make Slide 1 active.
2. Size and move a placeholder by completing the following steps:
   a. Click in the subtitle *Evaluating Current Network System*.
   b. Position the arrow pointer on the sizing handle in the middle of the right border until the pointer turns into a left-and-right-pointing arrow.
   c. Click and hold down the left mouse button, drag to the right until the subtitle text appears on one line, and then release the mouse button.

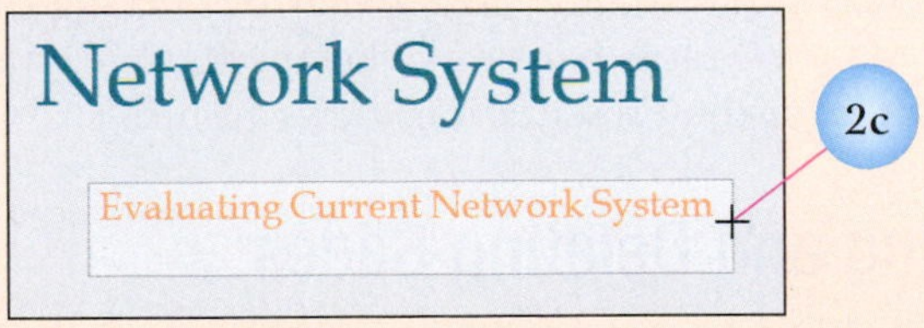

   d. Position the arrow pointer on the border of the placeholder until the pointer turns into a four-headed arrow.
   e. Click and hold down the left mouse button, drag the placeholder up and to the left so the placeholder is positioned as shown at the right, and then release the mouse button. Use the guideline to the left and above the placeholder to align the subtitle placeholder with the title placeholder.

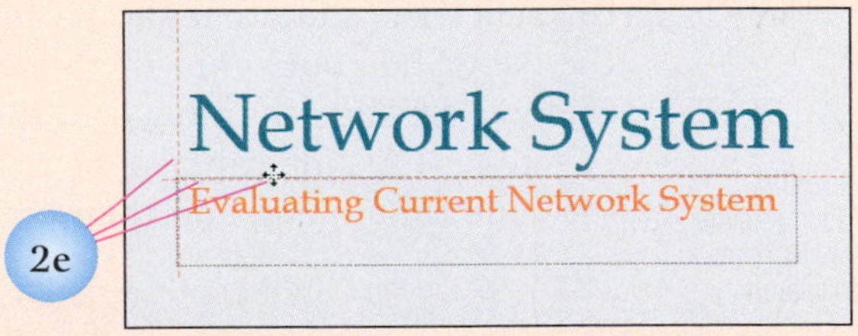

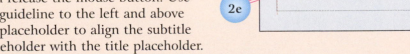

3. Make Slide 4 active.

4. Size and move a placeholder by completing the following steps:
   a. Click in the bulleted text.
   b. Position the arrow pointer on the sizing handle in the middle of the right border until the pointer turns into a left-and-right-pointing arrow.
   c. Click and hold down the left mouse button and then drag to the left until the right border is positioned just to the right of the question mark in the first bulleted item.
   d. Drag the middle sizing handle on the bottom border up until the bottom border of the placeholder is positioned just below the last bulleted item.
   e. Position the arrow pointer on the border of the placeholder until the pointer turns into a four-headed arrow.
   f. Click and hold down the left mouse button and then drag the placeholder to the left until the vertical guideline displays left of the title and then release the mouse button.
5. Save **2-NetworkSystem.pptx**.

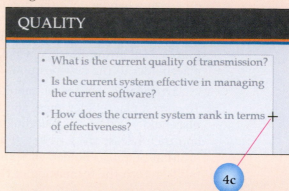

Check Your Work

Managing Slides

Editing a presentation may require reorganizing slides, inserting new slides, or deleting existing slides. Manage slides in the slide thumbnails pane or in Slide Sorter view. Switch to Slide Sorter view by clicking the Slide Sorter button in the view area on the Status bar or by clicking the View tab and then clicking the Slide Sorter button in the Presentation Views group.

Tutorial

Deleting Slides

Quick Steps

Insert a Slide
1. Click Home Tab.
2. Click New Slide Button.

Delete a Slide
1. Click slide in slide thumbnails pane.
2. Press Delete key.

Inserting and Deleting Slides

As explained in Chapter 1, clicking the New Slide button in the Slides group on the Home tab inserts a new slide in the presentation immediately following the currently active slide. A new slide can also be inserted in Slide Sorter view. To do this, click the slide that should immediately precede the new slide and then click the New Slide button in the Slides group. Delete a slide in Normal view by clicking the slide thumbnail in the slide thumbnails pane and then pressing the Delete key. A slide can also be deleted by switching to Slide Sorter view, clicking the slide thumbnail, and then pressing the Delete key.

Rearranging Slides

Rearrange slides in a presentation in Normal view or Slide Sorter view. In Normal view, click a slide in the slide thumbnails pane and then position the mouse pointer on the selected slide. Click and hold down the left mouse button, drag the pointer up or down until the slide thumbnail is in the new location, and then release the mouse button. Complete similar steps to move a slide in Slide Sorter view. Click the desired slide and hold down the left mouse button, drag the slide to the new location, and then release the mouse button.

Copying a Slide

💡 **Hint** Press Ctrl + X to cut the selected slide and then press Ctrl + V to paste the cut slide.

💡 **Hint** Press Ctrl + C to copy the selected slide and then press Ctrl + V to paste the copied slide.

When creating slides in a presentation, some slides may contain similar text, objects, and/or formatting. Rather than creating new slides in these presentations, consider copying an existing slide. To do this, display the presentation in Slide Sorter view, position the mouse on the slide to be copied, press and hold down the Ctrl key, and then click and hold down the left mouse button. Drag the copy of the slide thumbnail to the location where it is to be inserted, release the mouse button, and then release the Ctrl key. Slides can also be copied using the Ctrl key in the slide thumbnails pane in Normal view.

Slides can also be copied in Normal view or Slide Sorter view with buttons in the Clipboard group on the Home tab. To copy a slide, click the slide thumbnail and then click the Copy button in the Clipboard group. Click the slide thumbnail of the slide that will precede the copied slide and then click the Paste button in the Clipboard group.

Project 2d Moving and Copying Slides

1. With **2-NetworkSystem.pptx** open in Normal view, move slides by completing the following steps:
   a. Click Slide 3 (*EFFICIENCY*) in the slide thumbnails pane.
   b. Position the mouse pointer on Slide 3, click and hold down the left mouse button, drag the slide thumbnail up between Slides 1 and 2, and then release the mouse button.
   c. Click Slide 4 (*QUALITY*) in the slide thumbnails pane.
   d. Position the mouse pointer on Slide 4, click and hold down the left mouse button, drag the slide thumbnail down below Slide 6, and then release the mouse button.
2. Move and copy slides in Slide Sorter view by completing the following steps:
   a. Click the Slide Sorter button in the view area on the Status bar.
   b. Click Slide 4 (*TIME*) to make it the active slide. (The slide thumbnail displays with an orange border.)

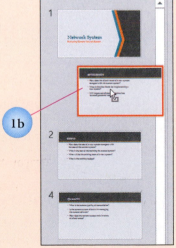

c. Position the mouse pointer on Slide 4, click and hold down the left mouse button, drag the slide thumbnail between Slides 1 and 2, and then release the mouse button.

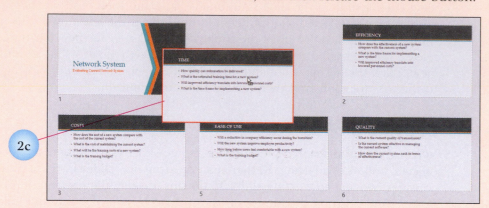

d. Click Slide 1 to make it the active slide.
e. Position the mouse pointer on Slide 1 (*Network System*), click and hold down the left mouse button, and then press and hold down the Ctrl key.
f. Drag the slide thumbnail down and to the right of Slide 6.

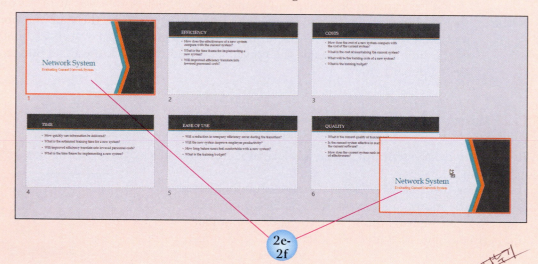

g. Release the mouse button and then release the Ctrl key.
3. Click the Normal button in the view area on the Status bar.
4. Save **2-NetworkSystem.pptx**.

Check Your Work

Copying a Slide between Presentations

Slides can be copied between presentations as well as within them. To copy a slide, click the slide thumbnail of the slide to be copied (either in Slide Sorter view or in the slide thumbnails pane in Normal view) and then click the Copy button in the Clipboard group on the Home tab. Open the presentation into which the slide is to be copied (in either Normal view or Slide Sorter view). Click in the location where the slide is to be positioned and then click the Paste button. The copied slide will take on the design theme of the presentation into which it is copied.

1. With **2-NetworkSystem.pptx** open, open the file named **EvalNetwork.pptx** in the PC2 folder on your storage medium.
2. Copy Slide 2 from **EvalNetwork.pptx** to the **2-NetworkSystem.pptx** file by completing the following steps:
   a. Click Slide 2 in the slide thumbnails pane to make it the active slide.
   b. Click the Copy button in the Clipboard group on the Home tab.
   c. Position the mouse pointer on the PowerPoint button on the taskbar and then click the **2-NetworkSystem.pptx** thumbnail.
   d. Click Slide 4 (*COSTS*) in the slide thumbnails pane.
   e. Click the Paste button in the Clipboard group.
   f. Position the mouse pointer on the PowerPoint button on the taskbar and then click the **EvalNetwork.pptx** thumbnail.
3. Copy Slide 3 from the **EvalNetwork.pptx** to **2-NetworkSystem.pptx** by completing the following steps:
   a. With **EvalNetwork.pptx** active, click Slide 3 in the slide thumbnails pane.
   b. Position the mouse pointer on Slide 3 and then click the right mouse button. (This displays a shortcut menu.)
   c. Click *Copy* at the shortcut menu.
   d. Position the mouse pointer on the PowerPoint button on the taskbar and then click the **2-NetworkSystem.pptx** thumbnail.
   e. Right-click Slide 3 in the slide thumbnails pane.
   f. Click the Use Destination Theme button in the *Paste Options* section.

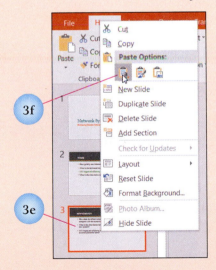

4. Position the mouse pointer on the PowerPoint button on the taskbar and then click the **EvalNetwork.pptx** thumbnail.
5. Close the presentation.
6. With **2-NetworkSystem.pptx** open, delete Slide 9 by completing the following steps:
   a. If necessary, scroll down the slide thumbnails pane until Slide 9 is visible.
   b. Click to select Slide 9.
   c. Press the Delete key.
7. Save the presentation.
8. Print the presentation as a handout with four slides displayed horizontally per page.
9. Close **2-NetworkSystem.pptx**.

Check Your Work

You will open a presentation on Adventure Tours and then insert additional slides by duplicating existing slides in the presentation and reusing slides from another presentation. You will also divide the presentation into sections, rearrange sections, and print a section.

Preview Finished Project

Tutorial

Duplicating Slides

Duplicating Slides 원하는 slide copy

In Project 2, the Copy and Paste buttons in the Clipboard group and options from a shortcut menu were used to copy slides in a presentation. Slides can also be copied in a presentation using the *Duplicate Selected Slides* option from the New Slide button drop-down list or by clicking the Copy button arrow and then clicking *Duplicate* at the drop-down list. In addition to duplicating slides, the *Duplicate* option from the Copy button drop-down list can be used to duplicate a selected object in a slide, such as a placeholder.

Ö*uick Steps*
Duplicate Slides
1. Select slides in slide thumbnails pane.
2. Click New Slide button arrow.
3. Click *Duplicate Selected Slides* at drop-down list.

A single slide or multiple selected slides can be duplicated. To select adjacent (sequential) slides, click the first slide in the slide thumbnails pane, press and hold down the Shift key, and then click the last slide. This will select all slides between that first slide and the last slide. To select nonadjacent (nonsequential) slides, press and hold down the Ctrl key while clicking each slide.

Project 3a Duplicating Selected Slides

Part 1 of 4

1. Open **AdvTours.pptx** and then save it with the name **2-AdvTours**.
2. Make sure the presentation displays in Normal view.
3. Select and then duplicate slides by completing the following steps:
   a. Click Slide 1 in the slide thumbnails pane.
   b. Press and hold down the Ctrl key.
   c. Click Slide 3, Slide 4, and then Slide 5.
   d. Release the Ctrl key.

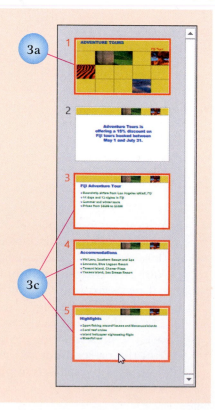

e. Click the New Slide button arrow in the Slides group on the Home tab and then click *Duplicate Selected Slides* at the drop-down list.

4. With Slide 6 active in the slide pane, change *Fiji Tour* to *Costa Rica Tour*.

5. Make Slide 7 active, select *Fiji* in the title and then type Costa Rica. Select and delete the existing bulleted text and then type the following bulleted text:
   • Round-trip airfare from Los Angeles to San Jose, Costa Rica
   • 8 days and 7 nights in Costa Rica
   • Monthly tours
   • Prices from $1099 to $1599

6. Make Slide 8 active, select and delete the existing bulleted text, and then type the following bulleted text:
   • San Jose, Emerald Suites
   • Tortuguero, Plantation Spa and Resort
   • Fortuna, Pacific Resort
   • Jaco, Monteverde Cabanas

7. Make Slide 9 active, select and delete the existing bulleted text, and then type the following bulleted text:
   • San Jose city tour
   • Rainforest tram
   • Canal cruise
   • Forest hike

8. Save **2-AdvTours.pptx**.

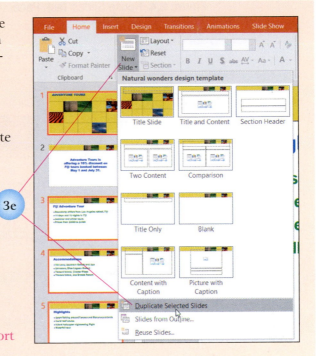

Check Your Work

40:00

Tutorial ►

Reusing Slides

Reusing Slides

Reusing slides is another method for copying slides from one presentation to another. Click the New Slide button arrow and then click the *Reuse Slides* option at the drop-down list to display the Reuse Slides task pane at the right side of the screen, as shown in Figure 2.4. At this task pane, click the Browse button and then click *Browse File* at the drop-down list and the Browse dialog box displays. At this dialog box, navigate to the desired folder and then double-click the presentation. This inserts the presentation slides in the Reuse Slides task pane. Click a slide in the Reuse Slides task pane to insert it into the currently open presentation.

Slides can also be shared and used from a Slide Library on a server running SharePoint Server. Add slides to a Slide Library and then insert slides from a Slide Library into a presentation. Before reusing slides from a Slide Library, the Slide Library must first be created. Refer to the SharePoint help files to learn how to create a Slide Library. To reuse slides from a Slide Library in a presentation, click the Open a Slide Library hyperlink in the Reuse Slides task pane. Or, click the Browse button in the Reuse Slides task pane and then click *Browse Slide Library* at the drop-down list. This displays the Select a Slide Library dialog box. At this dialog box, navigate to the location of the library and then double-click the library.

Quick Steps

Reuse Slides
1. Click New Slide button arrow.
2. Click *Reuse Slides*.
3. Click Browse button.
4. Click *Browse File*.
5. Navigate to folder.
6. Double-click presentation.
7. Click slide in Reuse Slides task pane.

Figure 2.4 Reuse Slides Task Pane

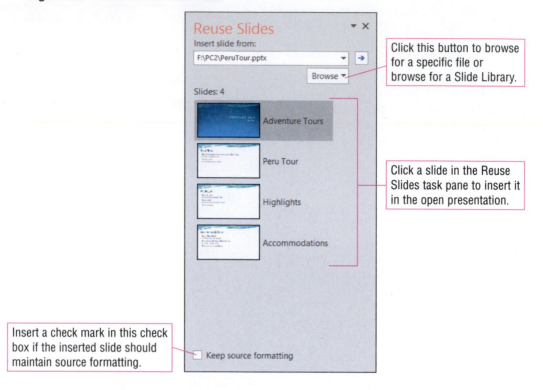

Click this button to browse for a specific file or browse for a Slide Library.

Click a slide in the Reuse Slides task pane to insert it in the open presentation.

Insert a check mark in this check box if the inserted slide should maintain source formatting.

By default, the slides inserted from the Reuse Slides task pane will take on the formatting of the current presentation. To retain the original formatting of the slides when inserted into the current presentation, insert a check mark in the *Keep source formatting* check box at the bottom of the Reuse Slides task pane.

Project 3b Reusing Slides

Part 2 of 4

1. With **2-AdvTours.pptx** open, click the New Slide button arrow in the Slides group on the Home tab and then click *Reuse Slides* at the drop-down list. (This displays the Reuse Slides task pane at the right side of the screen.)
2. Click the Browse button in the Reuse Slides task pane and then click *Browse File* at the drop-down list.
3. At the Browse dialog box, navigate to the PC2 folder on your storage medium and then double-click *PeruTour.pptx*.
4. In the slide thumbnails pane, scroll down the slide thumbnails until Slide 9 displays and then click below Slide 9. (This inserts a thin, horizontal line below the Slide 9 thumbnail in the slide thumbnails pane.)

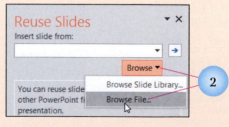

5. Click the first slide thumbnail (*Adventure Tours*) in the Reuse Slides task pane. (This inserts the slide in the open presentation immediately below Slide 9.)

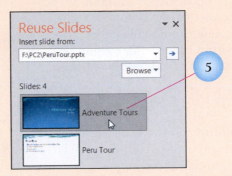

6. Click the second slide thumbnail (*Peru Tour*) in the Reuse Slides task pane.
7. Click the fourth slide thumbnail (*Accommodations*) in the Reuse Slides task pane.
8. Click the third slide thumbnail (*Highlights*) in the Reuse Slides task pane.
9. Close the Reuse Slides task pane by clicking the Close button (contains an *X*) in the upper right corner of the task pane.
10. Save **2-AdvTours.pptx**.

Check Your Work

Tutorial

Creating Sections within a Presentation

Creating Sections within a Presentation 45:00

=) 닫게 있으면 section 나누기

When working on a presentation with others in a group or working in a presentation containing numerous slides, consider dividing related slides in the presentation into sections. Dividing a presentation into sections allows for easy navigating and editing of slides within the presentation.

 Section

Ǫuick Steps

Create Section
1. Select first slide for new section.
2. Click Section button.
3. Click *Add Section*.

Create a section by selecting the first slide in the slide thumbnails pane, clicking the Section button in the Slides group on the Home tab, and then clicking *Add Section* at the drop-down list. A section title bar displays in the slide thumbnails pane. By default, the section title is *Untitled Section*. Rename a section by clicking the Section button in the Slides group on the Home tab and then clicking *Rename Section* at the drop-down list. A section can also be renamed by right-clicking the section title bar in the slide thumbnails pane and then clicking *Rename Section* at the shortcut menu.

Remove, move, collapse, and expand sections with options in the Section button drop-down list or by right-clicking the section title bar and then clicking an option at the shortcut menu. Different formatting can be applied to an individual section by clicking the section title bar to select that section and then applying the formatting.

Creating sections within a presentation provides the option to print only certain sections of the presentation. To print a section of a presentation, click the File tab, click the *Print* option, click the first gallery in the *Settings* category, click the section in the drop-down list, and then click the Print button.

1. With **2-AdvTours.pptx** open, create a section for slides about Fiji by completing the following steps:
   a. Click Slide 1 in the slide thumbnails pane.
   b. Click the Section button in the Slides group on the Home tab and then click *Add Section* at the drop-down list.

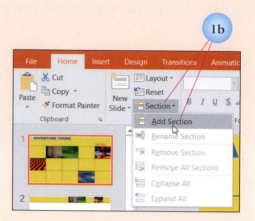

2. Rename the new section by completing the following steps:
   a. Click the Section button and then click *Rename Section* at the drop-down list.
   b. At the Rename Section dialog box, type Fiji Tour and then click the Rename button.

3. Create a section for slides about Costa Rica by completing the following steps:
   a. Click Slide 6 in the slide thumbnails pane.
   b. Click the Section button in the Slides group and then click *Add Section* at the drop-down list.
   c. Right-click in the section title bar (contains the text *Untitled Section*) and then click *Rename Section* at the shortcut menu.
   d. At the Rename Section dialog box, type Costa Rica Tour and then press the Enter key.

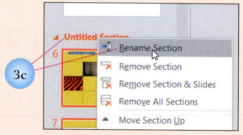

4. Complete steps similar to those in Step 3 to create a section beginning with Slide 10 and rename the section *Peru Tour*.

5. Change the design theme of a section by completing the following steps:
   a. Click the *Fiji Tour* section title bar at the top of the slide thumbnails pane. (This selects all five slides in the *Fiji Tour* section.)
   b. Click the Design tab.
   c. Click the More Themes button in the themes gallery.
   d. Click *Wisp* at the drop-down gallery.

6. Complete steps similar to those in Steps 5a through 5d to apply the Ion design theme to the *Costa Rica Tour* section.

7. Move the Peru Tour section above the *Costa Rica Tour* section by completing the following steps:
   a. Click the Home tab, click the Section button in the Slides group, and then click *Collapse All* at the drop-down list.

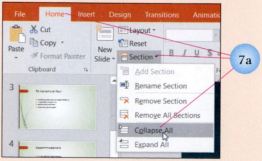

b. Position the mouse pointer on the *Peru Tour* section title bar, click and hold down the left mouse button, drag the title bar up until the title displays above the *Costa Rica* Tour section title bar, and then release the mouse button.

8. Display only slides in the *Costa Rica Tour* section by double-clicking the *Costa Rica Tour* section title bar in the slide thumbnails pane. (Notice that only Slides 10 through 13 display in the slide thumbnails pane and that the slides in the *Fiji Tour* and *Peru Tour* sections are hidden.)

9. Redisplay the *Fiji Tour* section slides by double-clicking the *Fiji Tour* section title bar in the slide thumbnails pane.

10. Display all sections by clicking the Section button in the Slides group and then clicking *Expand All* at the drop-down list.

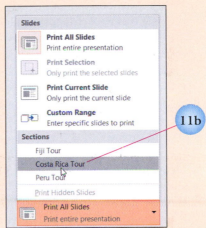

11. Print only the *Costa Rica Tour* section by completing the following steps:
    a. Click the File tab and then click the *Print* option.
    b. At the Print backstage area, click the first gallery in the *Settings* category and then click *Costa Rica Tour* in the *Sections* section (at the bottom of the drop-down list).
    c. Click the second gallery (contains the text *Full Page Slides*) in the *Settings* category and then click *4 Slides Horizontal* in the *Handouts* section.
    d. Click the Print button.

12. Complete steps similar to those in Step 11 to print only the *Peru Tour* section.

13. Save **2-AdvTours.pptx**.

Check Your Work

Tutorial

Customizing the Quick Access Toolbar

Save

Undo

Redo

Start from Beginning

Customize Quick Access Toolbar

Customizing the Quick Access Toolbar

The Quick Access Toolbar contains buttons for some of the most commonly performed tasks. By default, the toolbar contains the Save, Undo, Redo, and Start From Beginning buttons. Buttons can be added to or deleted from the Quick Access Toolbar. To add or delete a button, click the Customize Quick Access Toolbar button at the right side of the toolbar. At the drop-down list, click an option to insert a check mark next to those buttons that should display on the toolbar and click an option to remove the check mark from those that should not.

Click the *More Commands* option at the drop-down list and the PowerPoint Options dialog box displays with *Quick Access Toolbar* selected in the left panel. Use options at this dialog box to add buttons from a list of PowerPoint commands. Click the Reset button at the dialog box to reset the Quick Access Toolbar back to the default.

By default, the Quick Access Toolbar displays above the ribbon tabs. Display the Quick Access Toolbar below the ribbon by clicking the Customize Quick Access Toolbar button at the right side of the toolbar and then clicking the *Show Below the Ribbon* option at the drop-down list.

1. With **2-AdvTours.pptx** open, add a New button to the Quick Access Toolbar by clicking the Customize Quick Access Toolbar button and then clicking *New* at the drop-down list.

2. Add an Open button to the Quick Access Toolbar by clicking the Customize Quick Access Toolbar button and then clicking *Open* at the drop-down list.

3. Add a Print Preview and Print button to the Quick Access Toolbar by clicking the Customize Quick Access Toolbar button and then clicking *Print Preview and Print* at the drop-down list.

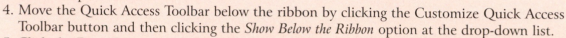

4. Move the Quick Access Toolbar below the ribbon by clicking the Customize Quick Access Toolbar button and then clicking the *Show Below the Ribbon* option at the drop-down list.

5. Click the Print Preview and Print button on the Quick Access Toolbar. (This displays the Print backstage area.)

6. Click the Back button to close the Print backstage area and return to the presentation.

7. Close **2-AdvTours.pptx**.

8. Click the New button to open a new blank presentation.

9. Click the Open button to display the Open backstage area.

10. Press the Esc key to return to the blank presentation and then close the presentation.

11. Move the Quick Access Toolbar back to the original position by clicking the Customize Quick Access Toolbar button and then clicking the *Show Above the Ribbon* option at the drop-down list.

12. Remove the New button by clicking the Customize Quick Access Toolbar button and then clicking *New* at the drop-down list.

13. Remove the Open button by right-clicking the button and then clicking *Remove from Quick Access Toolbar* at the drop-down list.

14. Remove the Print Preview and Print button from the Quick Access Toolbar.

Project 4 **Use the PowerPoint Help and Tell Me Features and Create a Presentation** **2 Parts**

You will use the Help feature to learn more about PowerPoint features. You will also use the Help feature to find information on keyboard shortcuts and then use that information to create a presentation. You will use the Tell Me feature to change the font color for the presentation title.

Preview Finished Project

Tutorial

Using the Help Feature

Using the Help Feature

Microsoft PowerPoint includes a Help feature that contains information about PowerPoint features and commands. This on-screen reference manual is similar to Windows Help and the Help features in Word, Excel, and Access.

Display the PowerPoint Help window, shown in Figure 2.5, by pressing the F1 function key. In this window, click in the search text box, type a topic, feature name, or question, and then press the Enter key. Articles related to the search text display in the PowerPoint Help window. Click an article hyperlink and the article information displays in the window. If the article contains a <u>Show All</u> hyperlink, click this hyperlink to expand the article options to show additional related information. Click the <u>Show All</u> hyperlink and it becomes the <u>Hide All</u> hyperlink.

Getting Help on a Button

Position the mouse pointer on a button and a ScreenTip displays with information about the button. Some button ScreenTips display with a Help icon and the text *Tell me more*. Click this hyperlinked text or press the F1 function key and the PowerPoint Help window opens with information about the button feature.

Getting Help in a Dialog Box or Backstage Area

Some dialog boxes and the backstage area contain a help button. Click this button to display the PowerPoint Help window with specific information about the dialog box or backstage area. After reading and/or printing the information, close a dialog box by clicking the Close button in the upper right corner of the dialog box or close the backstage area by clicking the Back button or pressing the Esc key.

Figure 2.5 PowerPoint Help Window

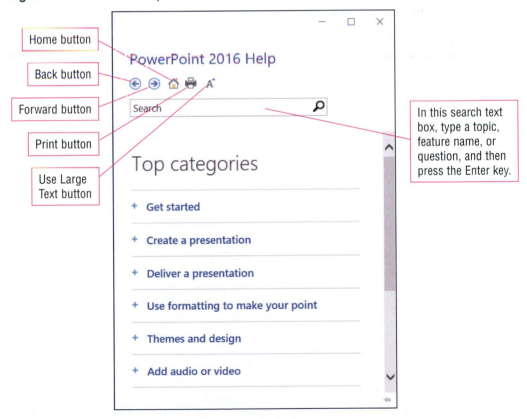

1. At the blank PowerPoint screen, press Ctrl + N to display a blank presentation. (Ctrl + N is the keyboard shortcut to open a blank presentation.)
2. Press the F1 function key.
3. At the PowerPoint Help window, click in the search text box, type basic tasks for creating a presentation, and then press the Enter key.

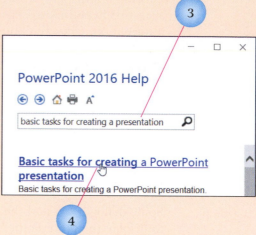

4. When the list of articles displays, click the Basic tasks for creating a PowerPoint presentation hyperlink. (If your PowerPoint Help window does not display this hyperlink, click a similar hyperlink.)
5. Read the information in the article. (If you want a hard copy of the information, you can click the Print button above the search text box in the PowerPoint Help window and then click the Print button at the Print dialog box.)
6. Close the PowerPoint Help window by clicking the Close button in the upper right corner of the window.
7. Hover the mouse over the New Slide button in the Slides group on the Home tab and then click the Tell me more hyperlinked text at the bottom of the ScreenTip.

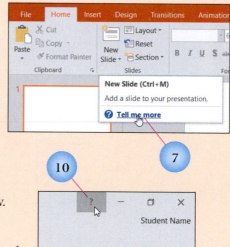

8. At the PowerPoint Help window, read the information on adding, rearranging, and deleting slides and then click the Close button in the upper right corner of the PowerPoint Help window.
9. Click the File tab and then click the *Open* option.
10. At the Open backstage area, click the Microsoft PowerPoint Help button in the upper right corner of the backstage area.
11. Read the information in the PowerPoint Help window.
12. Click in the search text box, type keyboard shortcuts, and then press the Enter key.
13. When the list of articles displays, click the Use keyboard shortcuts to create your presentation hyperlink.
14. Click the Common tasks in PowerPoint hyperlink.
15. Scroll down the *Common tasks in PowerPoint* section to the *Delete and copy text and objects* section. (This section displays a list of keyboard shortcuts for deleting and copying text and objects.)

16. Select the list of keyboard shortcuts for deleting and copying text and objects by positioning the mouse pointer at the left side of the heading *To do this*, Click and hold down the left mouse button, drag down to the lower right corner of the list of keyboard shortcuts, and then release the mouse button.

17. With the information selected, click the Print button above the search text box in the PowerPoint Help window.

18. At the Print dialog box, click the *Selection* option in the *Page Range* section and then click the Print button.

19. Close the PowerPoint Help window.

20. Press the Esc key to return to the blank presentation.

21. At the blank presentation, click in the title placeholder and then type PowerPoint Help.

22. Click in the subtitle placeholder and then type Keyboard Shortcuts.

23. Using the information you printed, create slides with the following information:
    - Slide 2: Type the text Delete Text as the title and then insert the four delete keyboard shortcuts as bulleted text. (For each keyboard shortcut, type the description followed by a colon and then the keyboard shortcut. For example, type Delete one character to the left: Backspace as the first bulleted item in the slide.)
    - Slide 3: Type the text Cut, Copy, Paste Text as the title and then insert the three cut, copy, and paste keyboard shortcuts as bulleted text.
    - Slide 4: Type the text Undo and Redo as the title and then insert the two undo and redo keyboard shortcuts as bulleted text.
    - Slide 5: Type the text Copy and Paste Formatting as the title and then insert the three copy and paste formatting keyboard shortcuts as bulleted text.

24. Apply the Facet design theme with the blue variant to the presentation.

25. Apply a transition and transition sound of your choosing to all slides in the presentation.

26. Save the presentation and name it **2-Shortcuts.pptx**.

Check Your Work

PowerPoint 2016 Help

keyboard shortcuts

Undo the last action.	CTRL+Z
Redo the last action.	CTRL+Y
Copy formatting only.	CTRL+SHIFT+C
Paste formatting only.	CTRL+SHIFT+V
Open **Paste Special** dialog box.	CTRL+ALT+V

Using the Tell Me Feature

Tutorial

Using the Tell Me Feature

PowerPoint 2016 includes a Tell Me feature that provides information as well as guidance on how to complete a function. To use Tell Me, click in the *Tell Me* text box on the ribbon to the right of the View tab and then type the function. Type text in the *Tell Me* text box and a drop-down list displays with options that are refined as the text is typed, which is referred to as "word-wheeling." The drop-down list displays options for completing the function, displaying information on the function from sources on the web, or displaying information on the function in the PowerPoint help window.

The drop-down list also includes a Smart Lookup option. Clicking the Smart Lookup option will open the Smart Lookup task pane at the right side of the screen with information on the function from a variety of sources on the Internet. Smart Lookup can also be accessed with the Smart Lookup button in the Insights group on the Review tab or by selecting text, right-clicking the selected text, and then clicking *Smart Lookup* at the shortcut menu.

1. With **2-Shortcuts.pptx** open, make Slide 1 active.
2. Select the title *PowerPoint Help* by triple-clicking in the title.
3. Use the Tell Me feature to change the font color and increase the font size for the title by completing the following steps:
   a. Click in the *Tell Me* text box.
   b. Type font color.
   c. Click the right arrow at the right side of the *Font Color* option in the drop-down list.
   d. At the side menu of color options, click the *Dark Blue* color option (ninth option in the *Standard Colors* section).
   e. With the title still selected, click in the *Tell Me* text box.
   f. Type font size.
   g. Click the *Increase Font Size* option at the drop-down list.
   h. Click in the slide to deselect the text.

4. Use the Tell Me feature to display the PowerPoint Help window with information on the Quick Access Toolbar by completing the following steps:
   a. Click in the *Tell Me* text box.
   b. Type Quick Access Toolbar.
   c. Click the *Get Help on "Quick Access Toolbar"* option.
   d. At the PowerPoint help window, click the <u>Customize the Quick Access Toolbar</u> hyperlink.
   e. Look at the information in the article on customizing the Quick Access Toolbar and then close the PowerPoint help window by clicking the Close button in the upper right corner of the window.

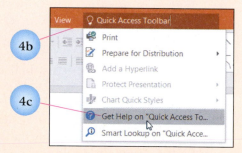

5. Display information in the Smart Lookup task pane on tips for preparing a presentation by completing the following steps:
   a. Click in the *Tell Me* text box.
   b. Type tips for preparing a presentation.
   c. Click the *Smart Lookup on "tips for preparing a presentation"* option (not all of the text is visible). The first time you use the Smart Lookup feature, the Smart Lookup task pane will display with a message indicating that data will be sent to Bing and suggesting that you read the privacy statement for more details. At this message, click the Got it button.
   d. Look at the information in the Smart Lookup task pane on tips for preparing a presentation.
   e. Close the Smart Lookup task pane by clicking the Close button in the upper right corner of the task pane.
6. Print the presentation as a handout with six slides displayed horizontally per page.
7. Save and then close **2-Shortcuts.pptx**.

Check Your Work

Chapter Summary

- Use the spelling checker feature to check the spelling of the text in a presentation. Begin a spelling check by clicking the Review tab and then clicking the Spelling button in the Proofing group.

- Use the Thesaurus to find synonyms and antonyms for words in a presentation. Display synonyms in the Thesaurus task pane or by right-clicking a word and then pointing to *Synonyms* at the shortcut menu.

- Display the Find dialog box by clicking the Find button in the Editing group on the Home tab.

- Display the Replace dialog box by clicking the Replace button in the Editing group on the Home tab.

- Click in a placeholder to select that placeholder and position the insertion point inside the placeholder.

- Cut and paste or copy and paste text in slides using buttons in the Clipboard group or with options from the shortcut menu.

- Use the mouse to move text in the slide thumbnails pane by selecting and then dragging text to a new location. To copy text to a new location, press and hold down the Ctrl key while dragging.

- Use the sizing handles that display around a selected placeholder to increase or decrease the size of the placeholder. Use the mouse to drag a selected placeholder to a new location in the slide.

- Use the New Slide button on the Home tab or Insert tab to insert a slide in a presentation.

- Delete a selected slide by pressing the Delete key.

- Move or delete a selected slide in Normal view in the slide thumbnails pane or in Slide Sorter view.

- Copy a selected slide by pressing and holding down the Ctrl key while dragging the slide to the new location.

- Use the Copy and Paste buttons in the Clipboard group on the Home tab to copy a slide between presentations.

- Select adjacent slides in the slide thumbnails pane or in Slide Sorter view by clicking the first slide, pressing and holding down the Shift key, and then clicking the last slide. Select nonadjacent slides by pressing and holding down the Ctrl key while clicking each slide.

- Duplicate slides in a presentation by selecting the slides in the slide thumbnails pane, clicking the New Slide button arrow, and then clicking the *Duplicate Selected Slides* option or clicking the Copy button arrow and then clicking *Duplicate* at the drop-down list.

- Copy slides from a presentation into the open presentation with options at the Reuse Slides task pane. Display this task pane by clicking the New Slide button arrow and then clicking *Reuse Slides* at the drop-down list.

- Divide a presentation into sections to easily navigate and edit slides in a presentation.

- Customize the Quick Access Toolbar by clicking the Customize Quick Access Toolbar button at the right side of the toolbar and then clicking the button or option at the drop-down list. Buttons can be added to or deleted from the Quick Access Toolbar and the toolbar can be displayed below the ribbon.

- Press the F1 function key to display the PowerPoint Help window.
- Some dialog boxes and the backstage area contain a Help button that, when clicked, will display information specific to the dialog box or backstage area.
- Use the Tell Me feature to provide information and guidance on how to complete a function.

Commands Review

FEATURE	RIBBON TAB, GROUP	BUTTON, OPTION	KEYBOARD SHORTCUT
copy text or slide	Home, Clipboard		Ctrl + C
create section	Home, Slides		
cut text or slide	Home, Clipboard		Ctrl + X
duplicate slide	Home, Slides	, *Duplicate Selected Slides*	
Find dialog box	Home, Editing		Ctrl + F
paste text or slide	Home, Clipboard		Ctrl + V
PowerPoint Help window			F1
Replace dialog box	Home, Editing		Ctrl + H
Reuse Slides task pane	Home, Slides	, *Reuse Slides*	
spelling checker	Review, Proofing		F7
Tell Me feature	*Tell Me* text box		Alt + Q
Thesaurus task pane	Review, Proofing		Shift + F7

Microsoft® PowerPoint®

Formatting Slides

Performance Objectives

Upon successful completion of Chapter 3, you will be able to:

1 Apply font and paragraph formatting to text in slides

2 Apply formatting with the Mini toolbar and Format Painter

3 Replace fonts

4 Customize columns

5 Customize bullets and numbers

6 Customize placeholders

7 Change slide size and page setup

8 Modify design themes

9 Customize slide backgrounds

10 Create custom design themes including custom theme colors and theme fonts

11 Delete custom design themes

Precheck

Check your current skills to help focus your study.

The Font and Paragraph groups on the Home tab contain a number of buttons and options for formatting text in slides. PowerPoint also provides a Mini toolbar and the Format Painter feature to format text. The design theme colors and fonts provided by PowerPoint can be modified and custom design themes can be created. You will learn to use these features in this chapter along with how to change slide size and page setup options.

Data Files

Before beginning chapter work, copy the PC3 folder to your storage medium and then make PC3 the active folder.

SNAP

If you are a SNAP user, launch the Precheck and Tutorials from your Assignments page.

You will open an e-commerce presentation, apply font and paragraph formatting, apply formatting with Format Painter, apply column formatting to text in placeholders, and rotate text in placeholders.

Preview Finished Project

Formatting a Presentation

PowerPoint provides a variety of design themes that can be applied to a presentation. These themes contain formatting options such as font, color, and graphics effect. In some situations, the formatting provided by a theme is appropriate; in other situations, specific formatting can be applied to enhance the presentation.

Tutorial

Applying Font Formatting

Tutorial

Applying Font Formatting at the Font Dialog Box

Applying Font Formatting

The Font group on the Home tab contains a number of buttons and options for applying font formatting to text in a slide. Use these buttons and options to change the font, font size, and font color, as well as apply font effects. Table 3.1 describes the buttons and options in the Font group along with any keyboard shortcuts for applying font formatting.

Changing Fonts   Design themes apply a certain font (or fonts) to text in slides. A different font or font size can be applied to text to change the mood of a presentation, enhance the visual appearance of slides, or increase the readability of the text. Change the font with the *Font* and *Font Size* option boxes in the Font group on the Home tab.

Select text and then click the *Font* option box arrow and a drop-down gallery displays with font options. Hover the mouse pointer over a font option and the selected text in the slide displays with the font applied. Continue hovering the mouse pointer over different font options to see how the selected text displays in the specified font. The *Font* option drop-down gallery is an example of the live preview feature, which displays text with different formatting before actually applying the formatting. The live preview feature is also available at the *Font Size* option drop-down gallery and the Font Color button drop-down gallery.

Hint Consider using a sans serif font for titles and headings and a serif font for body text.

Fonts may be decorative or plain and generally fall into one of two categories: serif fonts or sans serif fonts. A serif is a small line at the end of a character stroke. A serif font is easier to read and is generally used for large blocks of text. A sans serif font does not have serifs (*sans* is French for *without*). Sans serif fonts are generally used for titles and headings.

Hint Use options at the Font dialog box with the Character Spacing tab selected to increase or decrease spacing between characters and to apply kerning to text.

In addition to option boxes and buttons in the Font group on the Home tab, use options at the Font dialog box, shown in Figure 3.1, to apply character formatting to text. Display the Font dialog box by clicking the Font group dialog box launcher or with the keyboard shortcut Ctrl + Shift + F. (The dialog box launcher is the small button containing a diagonal arrow in the lower right corner of the group.) Use options at the Font dialog box to choose a font, font style, and font size and to apply special text effects in slides such as superscript, subscript, and double strikethrough.

Figure 3.1 Font Dialog Box

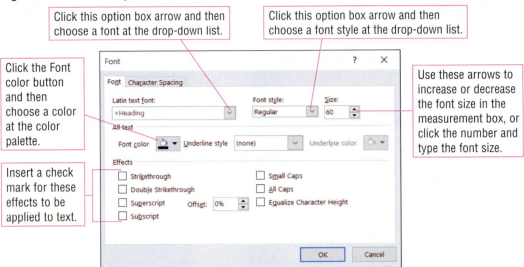

Click this option box arrow and then choose a font at the drop-down list.

Click this option box arrow and then choose a font style at the drop-down list.

Click the Font color button and then choose a color at the color palette.

Use these arrows to increase or decrease the font size in the measurement box, or click the number and type the font size.

Insert a check mark for these effects to be applied to text.

Table 3.1 PowerPoint Home Tab Font Group Option Boxes and Buttons

Button/ Option Box	Name	Function	Keyboard Shortcut
B	Bold	Applies or removes bold formatting to or from selected text.	Ctrl + B
Aa ▾	Change Case	Changes the case of selected text.	Shift + F3
AV ▾	Character Spacing	Adjusts spacing between selected characters.	
A	Clear All Formatting	Clears all character formatting from selected text.	Ctrl + Spacebar
A	Decrease Font Size	Decreases font size of selected text to next smaller size.	Ctrl + Shift + <
Calibri Light (F ▾	*Font*	Changes selected text to a different font.	
A ▾	Font Color	Changes the font color for selected text.	
32 ▾	*Font Size*	Changes selected text to a different font size.	
A	Increase Font Size	Increases font size of selected text to next larger size.	Ctrl + Shift + >
I	Italic	Applies or removes italic formatting to or from selected text.	Ctrl + I
abc	Strikethrough	Inserts or removes a line through the middle of selected text.	
S	Text Shadow	Applies or removes shadow formatting to or from selected text.	
U	Underline	Applies or removes underline formatting to or from selected text.	Ctrl + U

Tutorial

Formatting with
the Mini Toolbar

Formatting with the Mini Toolbar When text is selected, the Mini toolbar displays above the selected text. Click a button or option on the Mini toolbar to apply formatting to selected text. The option to display the Mini toolbar can be turned off. To do this, click the File tab and then click *Options*. At the PowerPoint Options dialog box with the *General* option selected in the left panel, click the *Show Mini Toolbar on selection* check box to remove the check mark.

Project 1a Applying Font Formatting to Text   Part 1 of 6

1. Open **EComm.pptx** and then save it with the name **3-EComm**.
2. Apply the Ion Boardroom design theme with the green variant by completing the following steps:
   a. Click the Design tab.
   b. Click the More Themes button at the right side of the themes gallery.
   c. Click the *Ion Boardroom* theme.
   d. Click the green color variant in the Variants group (second option).
3. Change the font formatting of the Slide 1 subtitle by completing the following steps:
   a. With Slide 1 active, click in the subtitle and then select *ONLINE SERVICES*.
   b. Click the Home tab.
   c. Click the *Font* option box arrow, scroll down the drop-down gallery, and then click *Cambria*.
   d. Click the *Font Size* option box arrow and then click *40* at the drop-down gallery.
   e. Click the Bold button in the Font group.
   f. Click the Text Shadow button.
   g. Click the Font Color button arrow and then click the *Dark Red, Accent 1, Darker 25%* option (fifth column, fifth row) in the *Theme Colors* section.

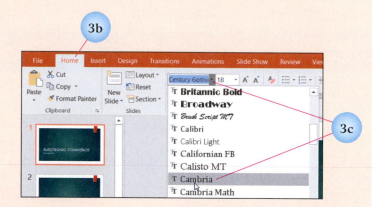

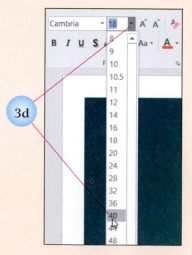

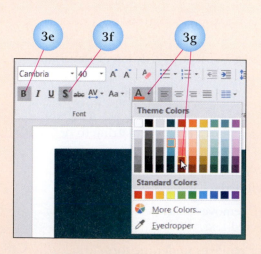

4. Change the size of the title text by completing the following steps:
   a. Click in the title *ELECTRONIC COMMERCE* and then click the placeholder border to change the border line to a solid line.
   b. Click the Decrease Font Size button in the Font group.
5. Change the case of the title text in Slide 2 by completing the following steps:
   a. Make Slide 2 active.
   b. Click in the title *ELECTRONIC COMMERCE* and then click the placeholder border to change the border line to a solid line.
   c. Click the Change Case button in the Font group and then click *Capitalize Each Word* at the drop-down list.

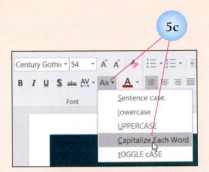

6. Apply and then clear formatting from text by completing the following steps:
   a. Make Slide 3 active.
   b. Click in the bulleted text.
   c. Select the text *m-commerce* (in parentheses).
   d. Click the Underline button in the Font group on the Home tab.
   e. Click the Bold button in the Font group.
   f. After applying underlining and bold formatting, remove the formatting by clicking the Clear All Formatting button in the Font group.
   g. With the text still selected, click the Italic button in the Font group on the Home tab.

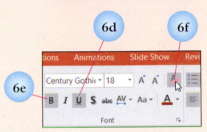

7. Apply italic formatting with the Mini toolbar by completing the following steps:
   a. Select *B2C* in the second bulleted item and then click the Italic button on the Mini toolbar.

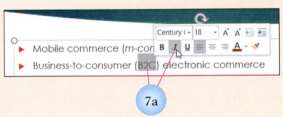

   b. Select *B2B* in the third bulleted item and then click the Italic button on the Mini toolbar.
8. Save **3-EComm.pptx**.

Check Your Work

(handwritten at top) format Painter.
영향을 placeholder click.
⇒ fast way

Tutorial

Formatting with
Format Painter

Format
Painter

Quick Steps

Format with Format Painter
1. Click text containing formatting.
2. Double-click Format Painter button.
3. Select or click text.
4. Click Format Painter button.

💡 **Hint** You can also turn off the Format Painter by pressing the Esc key.

Formatting with Format Painter

If character and/or paragraph formatting is applied to text in a slide and the same formatting should be applied to other text in the presentation, use Format Painter. With Format Painter, the same formatting can be applied in more than one location in a slide or slides. To use Format Painter, apply specific formatting to text, position the insertion point anywhere in the formatted text, and then double-click the Format Painter button in the Clipboard group on the Home tab. Using the mouse, select the additional text to apply the formatting. After applying the formatting in the new locations, click the Format Painter button to deactivate it. To apply formatting in only one other location, click the Format Painter button one time. The first time text is selected and the formatting is applied, the Format Painter button is deactivated.

Project 1b   Applying Formatting with Format Painter

1. With **3-EComm.pptx** open, make sure Slide 3 is active.
2. Apply formatting to the title by completing the following steps:
   a. Click in the title and then click the title placeholder border to change the border line to a solid line.
   b. Click the Font group dialog box launcher on the Home tab.
   c. At the Font dialog box, click the *Latin text font* option box arrow, scroll down the drop-down list, and then click *Candara*.
   d. Click the *Font style* option box arrow and then click *Bold Italic* at the drop-down list.
   e. Select the current measurement in the *Size* measurement box and then type 40.
   f. Click OK to close the dialog box.

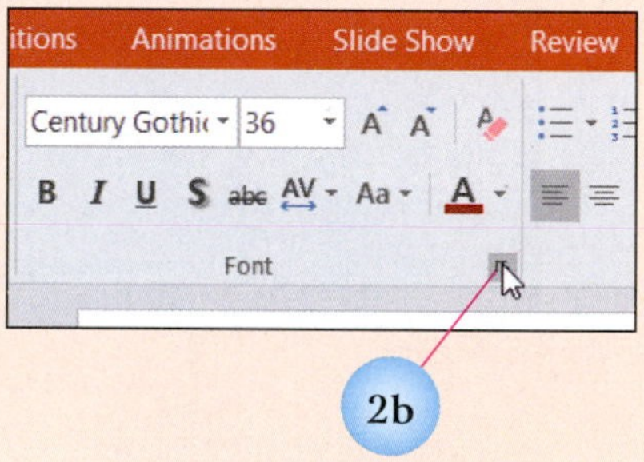

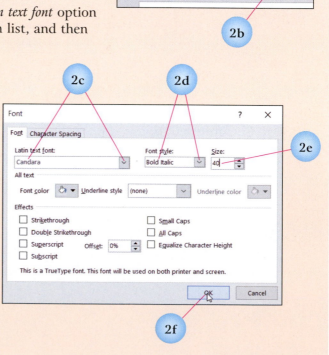

3. Click in the title.
4. Double-click the Format Painter button in the Clipboard group on the Home tab.

5. Make Slide 8 active.
6. Using the mouse, select the title *Advantages of Online Shopping*. (The mouse pointer displays as an I-beam with a paintbrush attached. Instead of selecting the whole title, you can also click each word in the title to apply the formatting. However, clicking individual words will not format the spaces between the words in multiple-word titles.)
7. Make Slide 9 active and then select the title.
8. Make Slide 10 active and then select the title.
9. Click the Format Painter button to deactivate it.
10. If necessary, deselect the text.
11. Save **3-EComm.pptx**.

Check Your Work

Tutorial

Replacing Fonts

 Replace

Quick Steps
Replace Fonts
1. Click Replace button arrow.
2. Click *Replace Fonts*.
3. At Replace Font dialog box, make sure font displays in *Replace* text box.
4. Press Tab.
5. Click *With* option box arrow and click font.
6. Click Replace button.
7. Click Close button.

Replacing Fonts

Search for a specific font in the presentation and replace all occurrences of that font with a different font using options at the Replace Font dialog box. Display the Replace Font dialog box by clicking the Replace button arrow in the Editing group on the Home tab and then clicking the *Replace Fonts* option at the drop-down list. At the Replace Font dialog box, click the *Replace* option box arrow and then click a font to replace at the drop-down list. Click the *With* option box arrow and then click a font with which to replace the existing font at the drop-down list. Click the Replace button to replace all the fonts and then click the Close button to close the Replace Font dialog box.

1. With **3-EComm.pptx** open, make Slide 1 active.
2. Replace the Century Gothic font with Candara in the entire presentation by completing the following steps:
   a. Click the Replace button arrow in the Editing group on the Home tab and then click *Replace Fonts* at the drop-down list.
   b. At the Replace Font dialog box, click the *Replace* option box arrow and then click *Century Gothic* at the drop-down list.
   c. Click the *With* option box arrow, scroll down the drop-down list, and then click *Candara*.
   d. Click the Replace button.
   e. Click the Close button.
3. Scroll through the slides to view the Candara font that has been applied to titles and bulleted text in each slide.
4. Save **3-EComm.pptx**.

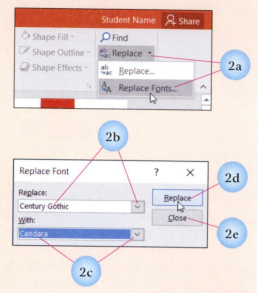

Check Your Work

Formatting Paragraphs *every single bullet is paragraphs*

The Paragraph group on the Home tab contains a number of buttons for applying paragraph formatting to text in a slide, such as applying bullets and numbers, increasing and decreasing list levels, changing the horizontal and vertical alignment of text, changing line spacing, and rotating text in a placeholder. Table 3.2 describes the buttons in the Paragraph group along with any keyboard shortcuts.

Fitting Contents in a Placeholder

 AutoFit Options

If text in a placeholder exceeds the size of the placeholder, use the AutoFit Options button to decrease the spacing between bulleted items or decrease the font size to ensure that all the text fits in the placeholder. The AutoFit Options button displays in the lower left corner of the placeholder when text no longer fits inside the placeholder. Click the AutoFit Options button to display a list of options such as *Autofit Text to Placeholder, Stop Fitting Text to This Placeholder, Split Between Two Slides, Continue on a New Slide, Change to Two Columns,* and *Control AutoCorrect Options.*

টেলাইপা লেখতে হব .

Tutorial

Creating and
Customizing
Columns

Add or
Remove
Columns

💡 **Hint** Format text
into columns to make it
attractive and easy
to read.

Creating and Customizing Columns

Click the Add or Remove Columns button in the Paragraph group to specify one-, two-, or three-column formatting for text. To format text into more than three columns or to control spacing between columns, click the *More Columns* option at the drop-down list. This displays the Columns dialog box, as shown in Figure 3.2. With options at this dialog box, specify the number of columns and the amount of spacing between them.

Figure 3.2 Columns Dialog Box

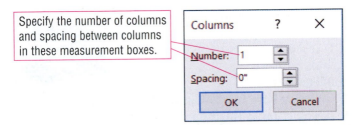

Specify the number of columns and spacing between columns in these measurement boxes.

Table 3.2 Buttons in the Paragraph Group on the Home Tab

Button	Name	Function	Keyboard Shortcut
	Bullets	Adds or removes bullets to or from selected text.	
	Numbering	Adds or removes numbers to or from selected text.	
	Decrease List Level	Moves text to the previous tab (level).	Shift + Tab
	Increase List Level	Moves text to the next tab (level).	Tab
	Line Spacing	Increases or reduces spacing between lines of text.	
	Align Left	Left-aligns text.	Ctrl + L
	Center	Center-aligns text.	Ctrl + E
	Align Right	Right-aligns text.	Ctrl + R
	Justify	Justifies text.	
	Add or Remove Columns	Splits text into two or more columns.	
	Text Direction	Rotates or stacks text.	
	Align Text	Changes the alignment of text within a text box.	
	Convert to SmartArt Graphic	Converts selected text to a SmartArt graphic.	

1. With **3-EComm.pptx** open, change bullets by completing the following steps:
   a. Make Slide 3 active.
   b. Click in the bulleted text.
   c. Select the bulleted text.
   d. Click the Bullets button arrow in the Paragraph group on the Home tab and then click the *Filled Square Bullets* option at the drop-down gallery.
2. Change bullets to letters by completing the following steps:
   a. Make Slide 8 active.
   b. Click in the bulleted text.
   c. Select the bulleted text.
   d. Click the Numbering button arrow in the Paragraph group on the Home tab and then click the *A. B. C.* option at the drop-down gallery.

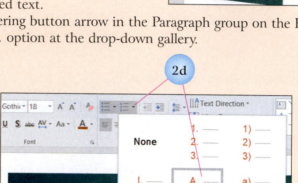

   e. With the lettered text selected, change to numbers by clicking the Numbering button arrow and then clicking the *1. 2. 3.* option at the drop-down gallery.
3. Decrease and increase list levels by completing the following steps:
   a. With Slide 8 active and the numbered text selected, click the Increase List Level button in the Paragraph group.
   b. With the text still selected, click the Font Color button arrow in the Font group on the Home tab and then click *Teal, Accent 5, Darker 50%* at the drop-down gallery (ninth column, last row in the *Theme Colors* section).
   c. Make Slide 10 active.
   d. Click in the bulleted text.

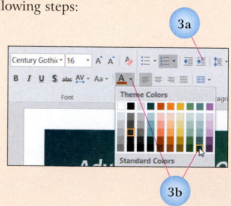

e. Move the insertion point so it is positioned immediately left of the *N* in *Nordstrom*.

f. Click the Decrease List Level button in the Paragraph group.

g. Move the insertion point so it is positioned immediately left of the *M* in *Macy's*.

h. Press Shift + Tab.

i. Move the insertion point so it is positioned immediately left of the first *L.* in *L.L. Bean*.

j. Click the Increase List Level button in the Paragraph group.

k. Move the insertion point so it is positioned immediately left of the *T* in *The Gap*.

l. Press the Tab key.

m. Use the Increase List Level button or Tab key to indent *Bloomingdale's, Expedia, Travelocity,* and *Orbitz* to the next level.

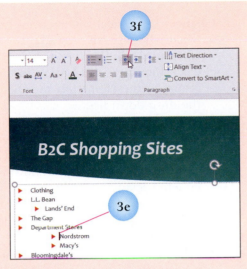

4. Increase the size of the text and make sure the content fits within the Slide 10 placeholder by completing the following steps:

a. With Slide 10 active, select all the bulleted items and then change the font size to 16 points.

b. Click in the bulleted text to deselect the text.

c. Click the AutoFit Options button that displays in the lower left corner of the placeholder and then click *AutoFit Text to Placeholder* at the drop-down list. (This decreases the spacing between the bulleted items to ensure all items fit in the placeholder.)

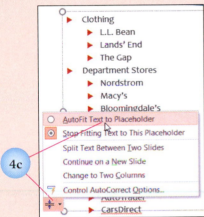

5. Change the line spacing of text by completing the following steps:

a. Make Slide 3 active.

b. Click in the bulleted text and then select the bulleted text.

c. Click the Line Spacing button in the Paragraph group and then click *1.5* at the drop-down list.

d. Make Slide 8 active.

e. Click in the numbered text and then select the numbered text.

f. Click the Line Spacing button and then click *2.0* at the drop-down list.

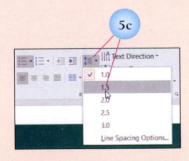

6. Change paragraph alignment by completing the following steps:

a. Make Slide 3 active, click in the title, and then click the Center button in the Paragraph group.

b. Make Slide 8 active, click in the title, and then click the Center button.

c. Make Slide 9 active, click in the title, and then click the Center button.

d. Make Slide 10 active, click in the title, and then click the Center button.

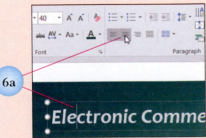

7. Change the vertical alignment of text by completing the following steps:
   a. Make Slide 3 active.
   b. Click in the bulleted text.
   c. Click the Align Text button in the Paragraph group on the Home tab and then click *Middle* at the drop-down list.
8. Split text into two columns by completing the following steps:
   a. Make Slide 9 active.
   b. Click in the bulleted text and then select the bulleted text.
   c. Click the Add or Remove Columns button in the Paragraph group and then click *Two Columns* at the drop-down list.
   d. Select the first sentence in the first bulleted paragraph (*Clear selling terms.*) and then click the Bold button.
   e. Select and then bold the first sentence in each of the remaining bulleted paragraphs in Slide 9.
   f. Drag the bottom border of the bulleted text placeholder up until two bulleted items display in each column.
9. Save **3-EComm.pptx**.

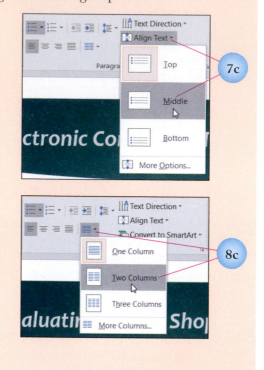

Check Your Work

Tutorial

Customizing Paragraphs

Changing
Paragraph
Spacing

 Line
Spacing

Control paragraph alignment, indenting, and spacing with options at the Paragraph dialog box. Display the dialog box, shown in Figure 3.3, by clicking the Paragraph group dialog box launcher. The dialog box can also be displayed by clicking the Line Spacing button in the Paragraph group and then clicking *Line Spacing Options* at the drop-down list. Use options at this dialog box to specify text alignment, paragraph indentation, spacing before and after paragraphs, and line spacing.

Figure 3.3 Paragraph Dialog Box

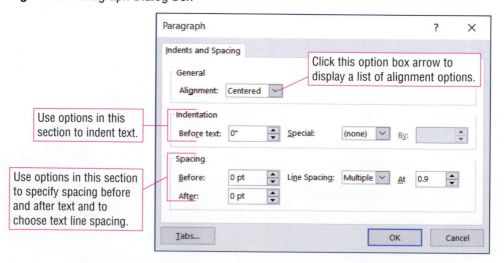

1. With **3-EComm.pptx** open, change line and paragraph spacing by completing the following steps:
   a. Make Slide 3 active.
   b. Click in the bulleted text and then select the text.
   c. Click the Paragraph group dialog box launcher.
   d. In the *Indentation* section at the Paragraph dialog box, click the *Before text* measurement box up arrow three times. (This inserts *0.6"* in the measurement box.)
   e. In the *Spacing* section, click the *After* measurement box up arrow two times. (This inserts *12 pt* in the box.)
   f. Click the *Line Spacing* option box arrow and then click *Multiple* at the drop-down list.
   g. Select the current measurement in the *At* measurement box and then type 1.8.
   h. Click OK.
2. Format text into columns by completing the following steps:

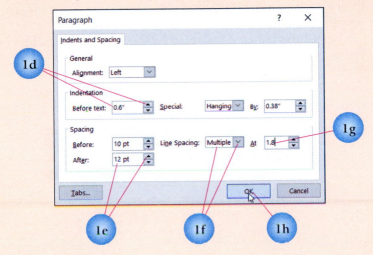

   a. Make Slide 10 active.
   b. Click in the bulleted text and then select the text.
   c. Click the Add or Remove Columns button in the Paragraph group and then click *More Columns* at the drop-down list.
   d. At the Columns dialog box, click the *Number* measurement box up arrow. (This inserts a *2* in the measurement box.)
   e. Click the *Spacing* measurement box up arrow until *0.5"* displays in the measurement box.
   f. Click OK.
   g. With the text still selected, click the Paragraph group dialog box launcher.
   h. In the *Spacing* section at the Paragraph dialog box, click the *After* measurement box up arrow three times. (This inserts *18 pt* in the measurement box.)
   i. Click OK.

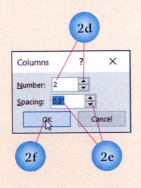

3. With the bulleted text selected, change the font size to 20 points.
4. Save **3-EComm.pptx**.

Check Your Work

Rotating Text

To make specific text stand out or to enhance the appearance of text, consider rotating or stacking text by changing the text direction. For example, text can be rotated so that it displays vertically in the placeholder. Rotate text in a placeholder using the Text Direction button. Click the Text Direction button in the Paragraph group on the Home tab and then click an option at the drop-down gallery.

Project 1f Rotating Text

1. With **3-EComm.pptx** open, make Slide 8 active.
2. Modify the slide so it displays as shown in Figure 3.4 on page 81 by completing the following steps:
   a. Click in the numbered text and then select the text.
   b. Click the Bullets button arrow and then click the *Hollow Square Bullets* option.
   c. With the text selected, change the font size to 20 points.
   d. Decrease the size of the bulleted text placeholder so the placeholder borders display just outside the text.
   e. Drag the placeholder to the middle of the slide until the guideline (a vertical dashed line) displays and then release the mouse button. (Refer to Figure 3.4 for the position of the placeholder.)

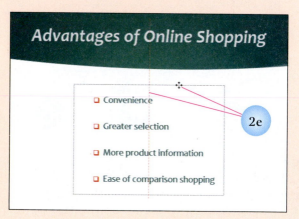

   f. Click in the title *Advantages of Online Shopping*.
   g. Delete the text *of Online Shopping*.
   h. Select *Advantages* and then change the font size to 54 points.
   i. Drag the right border of the placeholder to the left so it is positioned just outside the text.
   j. Click the Text Direction button in the Paragraph group and then click *Rotate all text 270°*.

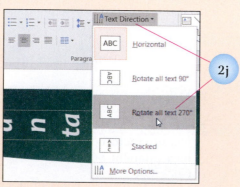

k. Using the sizing handles around the title placeholder, increase the height and decrease the width of the placeholder and then drag the placeholder so the title displays as shown in Figure 3.4. Use the horizontal guideline (a dashed line) to help you vertically center the placeholder on the slide.

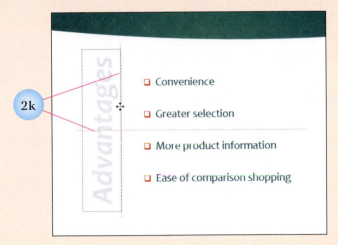

   l. With the title placeholder selected, click the Font Color button arrow in the Font group and then click *Dark Red, Accent 1, Darker 25%* at the drop-down gallery (fifth column, fifth row in the *Theme Colors* section).

3. Apply a transition and transition sound to all slides in the presentation.
4. Print the presentation as a handout with six slides displayed horizontally per page.
5. Save and then close **3-EComm.pptx**.

Check Your Work

Figure 3.4 Project 1f, Slide 8

Tutorial

Customizing
Bullets

Customizing Bullets

Each design theme contains a Title and Content slide layout with bullets. The appearance and formatting of the bullets vary within each design theme. Use the bullet style provided by the design theme or create custom bullets. Customize bullets with options at the Bullets and Numbering dialog box with the Bulleted tab selected, as shown in Figure 3.5. Display this dialog box by clicking in a placeholder containing bulleted text, clicking the Bullets button arrow in the Paragraph group on the Home tab, and then clicking *Bullets and Numbering* at the drop-down gallery.

At the Bullets and Numbering dialog box, choose one of the predesigned bullets from the list box, change the size of the bullets (measured by percentage in relation to the size of the text), change the bullet color, and/or specify an image or symbol to use as a bullet. Click the Picture button at the bottom of the dialog box and the Insert Pictures window displays. Click the Browse button to the right of the *From a file* option, navigate to the desired folder in the Insert Picture dialog box, and then double-click the image. Use the Bing Image Search text box to search for images online. Click the Customize button at the bottom of the Bullets and Numbering dialog box and the Symbol dialog box displays. Choose a symbol bullet option at the Symbol dialog box and then click OK. Image or symbol bullets are particularly effective for adding visual interest to a presentation.

To insert a new, blank bullet point in a bulleted list, press the Enter key. To move the insertion point down to the next line without inserting a new bullet, press Shift + Enter. A new bullet will be inserted the next time the Enter key is pressed.

 Bullets

Quick Steps
Customize Bullets
1. Click in bulleted text.
2. Click Bullets button arrow.
3. Click *Bullets and Numbering*.
4. Make changes.
5. Click OK.

💡 **Hint** Choose a custom bullet that matches the theme or mood of the presentation.

Figure 3.5 Bullets and Numbering Dialog Box with Bulleted Tab Selected

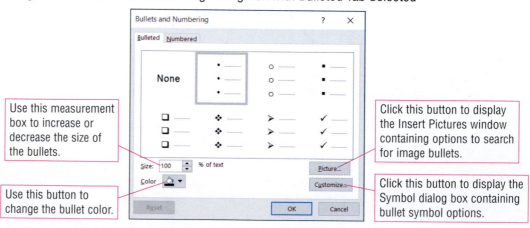

Use this measurement box to increase or decrease the size of the bullets.

Click this button to display the Insert Pictures window containing options to search for image bullets.

Use this button to change the bullet color.

Click this button to display the Symbol dialog box containing bullet symbol options.

1. Open **ColorPres.pptx** and then save it with the name **3-ColorPres**.
2. Increase the list level of text and create custom bullets by completing the following steps:
   a. Make Slide 2 active.
   b. Select the second, third, and fourth bulleted paragraphs.
   c. Click the Increase List Level button in the Paragraph group on the Home tab.
   d. With the three bulleted paragraphs still selected, click the Bullets button arrow and then click *Bullets and Numbering* at the drop-down list.
   e. At the Bullets and Numbering dialog box with the Bulleted tab selected, select the current number (*100*) in the *Size* measurement box and then type 75.
   f. Click the Picture button in the bottom right corner of the dialog box.
   g. At the Insert Pictures window, click the Browse button to the right of the *From a file* option.
   h. At the Insert Picture dialog box, navigate to the PC3 folder on your storage medium and then double-click **Bullet.png**.
3. Insert symbol bullets by completing the following steps:
   a. Make Slide 3 active.
   b. Select all of the bulleted text.
   c. Click the Bullets button arrow and then click *Bullets and Numbering* at the drop-down list.
   d. At the Bullets and Numbering dialog box with the Bulleted tab selected, click the *Size* measurement box down arrow until 90 displays.
   e. Click the Customize button in the bottom right corner of the dialog box.
   f. At the Symbol dialog box, scroll down almost to the bottom of the list box and then click the infinity symbol in the eighth row from the bottom of the list box. (The location may vary.)
   g. Click OK.

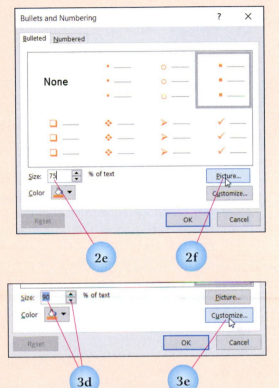

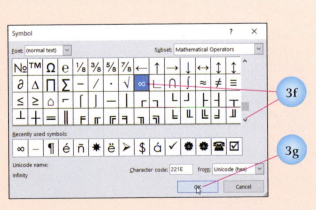

h. At the Bullets and Numbering dialog box, click the Color button and then click *Blue, Accent 5* (ninth column, first row in the *Theme Colors* section).

i. Click OK to close the Bullets and Numbering dialog box. (This applies the blue infinity symbol bullets to the selected text.)

4. Increase the spacing between the bullets and the text by completing these steps:

a. With the bulleted text selected, click the Paragraph group dialog box launcher.

b. At the Paragraph dialog box, select the current measurement in the *By* measurement box (in the *Indentation* section), type 0.5, and then press the Enter key.

5. Save **3-ColorPres.pptx**.

Check Your Work

Tutorial

Customizing Numbers

 Numbering

Quick Steps

Customize Numbers
1. Click in numbered text.
2. Click Numbering button arrow.
3. Click *Bullets and Numbering*.
4. Make changes.
5. Click OK.

Customizing Numbers

Click the Numbering button arrow in the Paragraph group and several numbering options display in a drop-down gallery. Customize numbers with options at the Bullets and Numbering dialog box with the Numbered tab selected, as shown in Figure 3.6. Display this dialog box by clicking in a placeholder containing a numbered list, clicking the Numbering button arrow and then clicking *Bullets and Numbering* at the drop-down gallery. Use options at this dialog box to change the size and color of the numbers as well as the starting number.

To insert a new, blank numbered item in a numbered list, press the Enter key. To move the insertion point down to the next line without inserting the next number, press Shift + Enter. The next number will be inserted the next time the Enter key is pressed.

Figure 3.6 Bullets and Numbering Dialog Box with Numbered Tab Selected

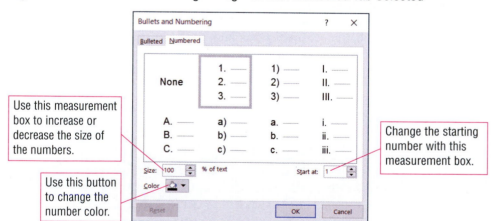

1. With **3-ColorPres.pptx** open, create and insert custom numbers by completing the following steps:
   a. Make Slide 4 active.
   b. Select the bulleted text in the slide.
   c. Click the Numbering button arrow in the Paragraph group on the Home tab and then click the *Bullets and Numbering* option at the drop-down list.
   d. At the Bullets and Numbering dialog box with the Numbered tab selected, click the *1. 2. 3.* option (second column, first row).
   e. Select the measurement in the *Size* measurement box and then type 80.
   f. Click the Color button and then click *Blue, Accent 5* (ninth column, first row in the *Theme Colors* section).
   g. Click OK.

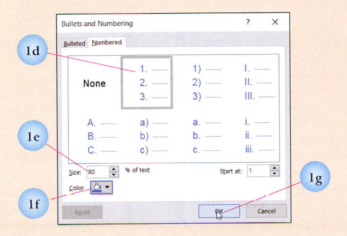

   h. Make Slide 5 active.
   i. Select the bulleted text in the slide.
   j. Click the Numbering button arrow and then click the *Bullets and Numbering* option at the drop-down list.
   k. At the Bullets and Numbering dialog box with the Numbered tab selected, click the *1. 2. 3.* option (second column, first row).
   l. Select the number in the *Size* measurement box and then type 80.
   m. Click the Color button and then click *Blue, Accent 5* (ninth column, first row in the *Theme Colors* section).
   n. Click the *Start at* measurement box up arrow until *6* displays.
   o. Click OK.

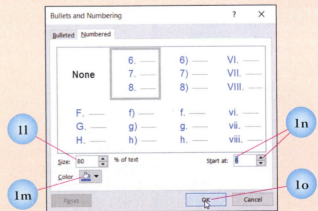

2. Add a transition and transition sound to all slides in the presentation.
3. Run the slide show.
4. Save **3-ColorPres.pptx**.

Check Your Work

Quick
Styles

 Arrange

 Shape
Fill

 Shape
Outline

 Shape
Effects

Hint You can also
use options on the
Drawing Tools Format
tab to customize a
placeholder.

Quick Steps

**Apply Color with the
Eyedropper**
1. Click object.
2. Click Shape Fill
   button arrow.
3. Click *Eyedropper*.
4. Click color.

Customizing Placeholders

Customize a placeholder in a slide with buttons in the Drawing group on the Home tab. Use options in the Drawing group to choose a shape, arrange the placeholder, apply a quick style, change the shape fill and outline colors, and apply a shape effect.

Click the Quick Styles button in the Drawing group and a drop-down gallery of styles displays. Choose a quick style from this gallery or click the *Other Theme Fills* option to display a side menu with additional fills. Arrange, align, and rotate a placeholder with options at the Arrange button drop-down list. Use the Shape Fill button to apply a fill to a placeholder. Click the Shape Fill button arrow and a drop-down gallery displays with options for applying a color, picture, gradient, or texture to the placeholder. Use the Shape Outline button to apply an outline to a placeholder and specify the outline color, weight, and style. Use the Shape Effects button to choose from a variety of effects such as shadow, reflection, glow, and soft edges.

Both the Shape Fill and Shape Outline buttons in the Drawing group contain drop-down galleries with the *Eyedropper* option. Use the eyedropper to capture an exact color from one object and apply it to another object in the slide. To use the eyedropper to apply a fill color, click the object to which the fill color is to be applied, click the Shape Fill button arrow, and then click *Eyedropper* at the drop-down gallery. The mouse pointer displays as an eyedropper. Position the tip of the eyedropper on the desired color and then click the mouse button. The color clicked is applied to the selected object. Move the eyedropper and a live preview box displays above and right of the eyedropper. Use this live preview box to help choose the specific color. To pick a color outside the slide pane, press and hold down the Ctrl key, click and hold down the left mouse button, and then drag outside the slide pane. Position the tip of the eyedropper on the desired color and then release the mouse button and the Ctrl key. The *Eyedropper* option is also available with the Shape Outline and Font Color buttons on the Home tab as well as with buttons on other tabs that apply color.

Customizing Placeholders at the Format Shape Task Pane

With options in the Format Shape task pane, apply shape options to a placeholder or apply text options to the text within a placeholder. The Shape Options tab in the Format Shape task pane displays three icons: Fill & Line, Effects, and Size & Properties, each with different options for formatting a placeholder. After clicking an icon, the icon options may need to be expanded. For example, click the *Fill* option with the Fill & Line icon selected on the Shape Options tab to display options for applying a fill to a placeholder, as shown in Figure 3.7. The Text Options tab in the Format Shape task pane displays three icons: Text Fill & Outline, Text Effects, and Textbox, each with different options for formatting text within a placeholder. Display the Format Shape task pane by clicking the Drawing group task pane launcher on the Home tab.

Align text in a placeholder with options at the Format Shape task pane with the Size & Properties icon selected and options in the *Text Box* section displayed. (If necessary, click the *Text Box* option to expand the list.) Use options in the *Text Box* section to align text in a placeholder as well as change text direction, autofit contents, and change internal margins.

Figure 3.7 Format Shape Task Pane with Shape Options Tab Selected

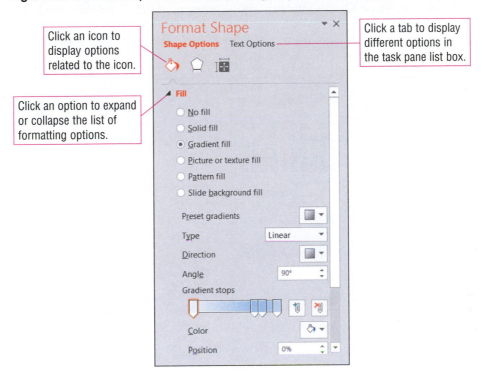

Click an icon to display options related to the icon.

Click an option to expand or collapse the list of formatting options.

Click a tab to display different options in the task pane list box.

Text can be moved within a placeholder with the margin measurements in the Format Shape task pane. Display the margin measurements by clicking the Size & Properties icon and then scrolling down the task pane list box to the *Text Box* section. Use the *Left margin*, *Right margin*, *Top margin*, and *Bottom margin* measurement boxes to specify internal margins for text inside a placeholder.

Project 2c Customizing Placeholders   **Part 3 of 4**

1. With **3-ColorPres.pptx** open, customize the title placeholder in Slide 1 by completing the following steps:
   a. If necessary, make Slide 1 active.
   b. Click in the title to make the title placeholder active.
   c. If necessary, click the Home tab.
   d. Click the Quick Styles button in the Drawing group.
   e. Click the *Subtle Effect - Gold, Accent 4* option at the drop-down gallery (fifth column, fourth row).
   f. Click the Shape Outline button arrow in the Drawing group and then click *Green, Accent 6* (last column, first row in the *Theme Colors* section).

g. Click the Shape Outline button arrow, point to *Weight*, and then click *3 pt* at the side menu.

h. Click the Shape Effects button, point to *Bevel*, and then click *Cool Slant* at the side menu (fourth column, first row in the *Bevel* section).

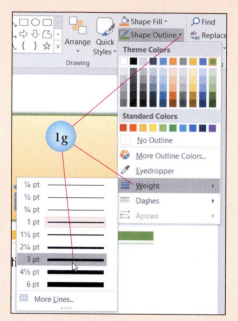 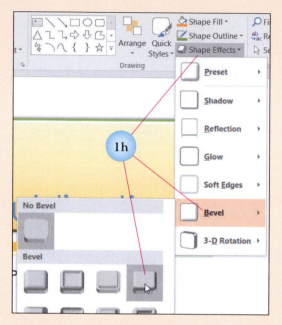

i. Change the fill color by clicking the Quick Styles button in the Drawing group, pointing to *Other Theme Fills* at the bottom of the drop-down gallery, and then clicking *Style 9* at the side menu (first column, third row).

2. Change the alignment of the text within the placeholder by completing the following steps:

a. With the title placeholder active, click the Drawing group task pane launcher.

b. At the Format Shape task pane, make sure the Shape Options tab is selected, and then click the Size & Properties icon.

c. Click the *Text Box* option to display the list of options.

d. Click the *Vertical alignment* option box arrow and then click *Middle* at the drop-down list.

e. Click the *Top margin* measurement box up arrow until *0.3"* displays in the measurement box.

3. Close the Format Shape task pane by clicking the Close button in the upper right corner of the task pane.

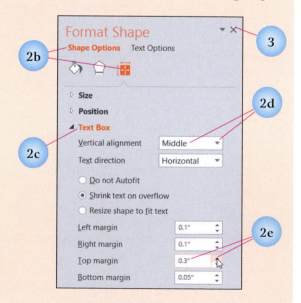

4. Customize the subtitle placeholder by completing the following steps:
   a. Click in the subtitle text to make the subtitle placeholder active.
   b. Click the Shape Fill button arrow in the Drawing group, point to *Texture*, and then click *Blue tissue paper* at the drop-down gallery (first column, fifth row).
   c. Click the Shape Effects button, point to *Bevel*, and then click *Cool Slant* at the side menu (fourth column, first row in the *Bevel* section).

5. You decide the texture fill does not match the theme of the presentation. Change the subtitle placeholder fill by completing the following steps:
   a. With the subtitle placeholder active, click the Drawing group task pane launcher.
   b. At the Format Shape task pane, make sure the Shape Options tab is selected, click the Fill & Line icon, and then click the *Fill* option to display the list of options.
   c. Click *Gradient fill*.
   d. Click the Preset gradients button and then click *Light Gradient, Accent 6* (sixth column, first row).

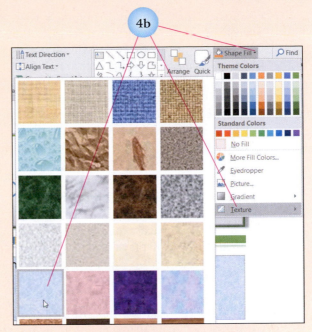

6. At the Format Shape task pane, click the Size & Properties icon, make sure the options in the *Text Box* section are displayed, click the *Vertical alignment* option box arrow, and then click *Middle* at the drop-down list.

7. Make Slide 3 active and then change the spacing after paragraphs by completing the following steps:
   a. Select the bulleted text.
   b. Click the Paragraph group dialog box launcher.
   c. In the *Spacing* section at the Paragraph dialog box, click the *After* measurement box up arrow two times to display *12 pt* in the measurement box.
   d. Click OK to close the dialog box.

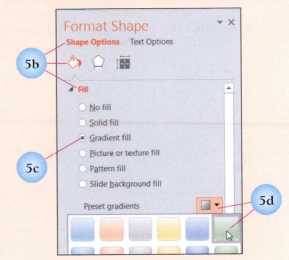

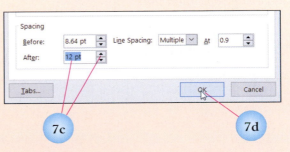

8. Customize and arrange the placeholder by completing the following steps:
   a. With the bulleted text placeholder selected and the Format Shape task pane open, click the Fill & Line icon, make sure the options in the *Fill* section are displayed, and then click *Solid fill*.
   b. Click the Color button and then click *Blue, Accent 5, Lighter 80%* (ninth column, second row in the *Theme Colors* section).

c. Click the Effects icon and then click the *Shadow* option to display the list of options.

d. Click the Presets button and then click *Offset Diagonal Bottom Right* (first column, first row in *Outer* section).

e. Click the Color button and then click *Blue, Accent 5, Darker 50%* (ninth column, bottom row in *Theme Colors* section).

f. Click the *Distance* measurement box up arrow until *15 pt* displays.

g. Click the Size & Properties icon.

h. Click the *Size* option to display the list of options.

i. Click the *Height* measurement box down arrow until *2.8″* displays in the measurement box.

j. Scroll down the task pane and, if necessary, click the *Text Box* option to display the list of options.

k. Change the left and top margin measurements to 0.2 inches.

l. Click the Arrange button in the Drawing group on the Home tab, point to *Align* in the drop-down list, and then click *Distribute Vertically* at the side menu.

9. Make Slide 2 active, click in the bulleted text, and then customize and arrange the placeholder by completing the steps in Step 8. Change the height of the placeholder in Slide 2 to 3 inches.

10. Close the Format Shape task pane.

11. Make Slide 1 active and then use the eyedropper to apply fill color from the subtitle placeholder to the title placeholder by completing the following steps:

a. Click in the title placeholder.

b. Click the Shape Fill button arrow in the Drawing group on the Home tab, and then click the *Eyedropper* option at the drop-down gallery.

c. Position the tip of the eyedropper on the green color above the word *Publications* in the subtitle placeholder and then click the left mouse button.

12. Run the slide show.

13. Print the presentation as a handout with six slides displayed horizontally per page.

14. Save **3-ColorPres.pptx**.

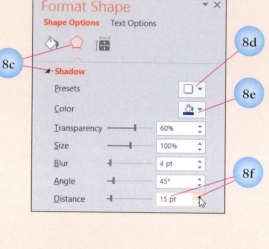

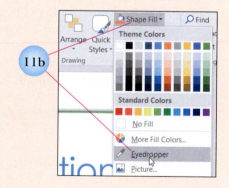

Check Your Work

Slide Size

Changing Slide Size and Page Setup

Control the page setup and the size and orientation of slides using options in the Slide Size dialog box, as shown in Figure 3.8. Display the Slide Size dialog box by clicking the Slide Size button in the Customize group on the Design tab and then clicking *Custom Slide Size* at the drop-down list. With options in the dialog box, change the slide orientation, specify how slides are sized, change the slide size ratio, and change the starting slide number. By default, slides are sized for an on-screen show with a widescreen 16:9 ratio. If a widescreen size (16:9) presentation is changed to a standard size (4:3) presentation, the slide content will need to be maximized or scaled down to fit in the new slide size. Click the *Slides sized for* option box arrow and a drop-down list displays with options for changing the slide size ratio and choosing other paper sizes. The Slide Size dialog box also contains options for changing the orientation of notes, handouts, and outline pages.

Figure 3.8 Slide Size Dialog Box

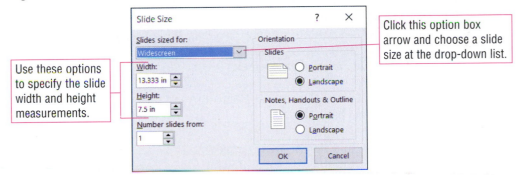

Use these options to specify the slide width and height measurements.

Click this option box arrow and choose a slide size at the drop-down list.

Project 2d **Changing Slide Orientation and Page Setup**   **Part 4 of 4**

1. With **3-ColorPres.pptx** open, change the slide size by completing the following steps:
   a. Click the Design tab.
   b. Click the Slide Size button in the Customize group and then click *Standard (4:3)* at the drop-down list.

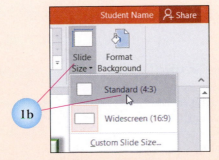

   c. At the Microsoft PowerPoint dialog box, click the Ensure Fit button.
2. Run the slide show to view how the slides appear in the standard size.

3. Change the slide orientation by completing the following steps:
   a. Click the Slide Size button in the Customize group and then click *Custom Slide Size* at the drop-down list.
   b. At the Slide Size dialog box, click the *Portrait* option in the *Slides* section, and then click OK.
   c. Click the Ensure Fit button at the Microsoft PowerPoint dialog box.
4. Run the slide show to view how the slides appear in portrait orientation.
5. After running the slide show, change the page setup by completing the following steps:
   a. Click the Slide Size button and then click *Custom Slide Size* at the drop-down list.
   b. At the Slide Size dialog box, click the *Landscape* option in the *Slides* section.
   c. Click the *Slides sized for* option box arrow and then click *On-screen Show (16:10)*. (Notice that the slide height changed from *10* to *6.25* in the *Height* measurement box.)
   d. Click OK.
   e. Click the Maximize button at the Microsoft PowerPoint dialog box.
6. Run the slide show.
7. Specify slide width and height and change slide numbering by completing the following steps:
   a. Click the Slide Size button and then click *Custom Slide Size* at the drop-down list.
   b. At the Slide Size dialog box, click the *Width* measurement box down arrow until *9 in* displays.
   c. Click the *Height* measurement box down arrow until *6 in* displays.
   d. Click the *Number slides from* measurement box up arrow until *6* displays.
   e. Click OK.
   f. Click the Ensure Fit button at the Microsoft PowerPoint dialog box.
8. Notice that the slide numbering in the slide thumbnails pane begins with Slide 6.
9. Run the slide show.
10. Save and then close **3-ColorPres.pptx**.

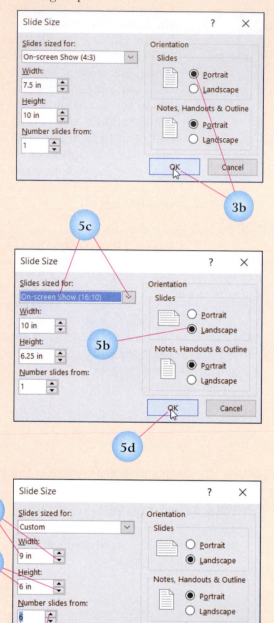

Check Your Work

Project 3 **Modify the Design Theme and Slide Background of a Network Presentation**   **1 Part**

You will open a network presentation, apply a design theme, and then change the theme colors and fonts. You will also apply and customize a background style.

Preview Finished Project

Tutorial

Changing and Modifying Design Themes

💡**Hint** Themes are shared across Office programs such as PowerPoint, Word, Excel, and Access.

Changing and Modifying Design Themes

A design theme is a set of formatting choices that includes a color theme (a set of colors), a font theme (heading and text fonts), and an effects theme (a set of lines and fill effects). Click the More Variants button in the Variants group on the Design tab to display options for changing design theme colors, fonts, and effects.

A theme contains specific color formatting that can be changed with color options. Change color options by clicking the More Variants button in the Variants group, pointing to the *Colors* option, and then clicking a color option in the side menu. Each theme applies specific fonts and these fonts can be changed by pointing to the *Fonts* option at the More Variants button drop-down gallery and then choosing an option at the side menu. Each font group in the side menu contains two choices: The first choice is the font that is applied to slide titles and the second choice is the font that is applied to slide subtitles and text. If a presentation contains graphic elements such as illustrations, images, or text boxes, specify theme effects by pointing to the *Effects* option at the More Variants button drop-down gallery and then choosing an option at the side menu.

Tutorial

Formatting the Slide Background

 Format Background

Formatting the Slide Background

Format the slide background with background styles or with options at the Format Background task pane. Display background styles by clicking the More Variants button in the Variants group on the Design tab and then pointing to the *Background Styles* option. Apply a background style by clicking an option at the side menu.

Click the Format Background button in the Customize group on the Design tab to display the Format Background task pane, as shown in Figure 3.9. Use options in the Format Background task pane to apply fill, effects, or a picture to the slide background. Apply the slide background to all slides in the presentation by clicking the Apply to All button at the bottom of the task pane. If changes are made to the slide background, reset the background to the default by clicking the Reset Background button at the bottom of the Format Background task pane.

Some of the design themes provided by PowerPoint contain a background graphic. The background graphic can be removed from slides by inserting a check mark in the *Hide background graphics* check box in the *Fill* section of the Format Background task pane with the Fill icon selected and then clicking the Apply to All button.

Ⓞ**uick Steps**

Change the Slide Background
1. Click Design tab.
2. Click Format Background button.
3. Make changes at Format Background task pane.

Figure 3.9 Format Background Task Pane

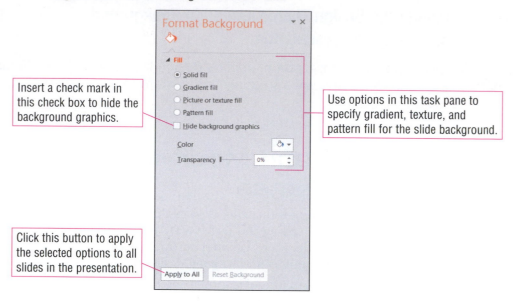

Insert a check mark in this check box to hide the background graphics.

Use options in this task pane to specify gradient, texture, and pattern fill for the slide background.

Click this button to apply the selected options to all slides in the presentation.

Project 3 Changing Theme Colors, Theme Fonts, and Slide Backgrounds

Part 1 of 1

1. Open **NetworkPres.pptx** and then save it with the name **3-NetworkPres.pptx**.
2. Apply a design theme by completing the following steps:
   a. Click the Design tab.
   b. Click the More Themes button at the right side of the themes gallery in the Themes group and then click *Dividend* at the drop-down gallery.
3. Change the theme colors by clicking the More Variants button in the Variants group, pointing to *Colors*, scrolling down the color options in the side menu, and then clicking *Marquee*.

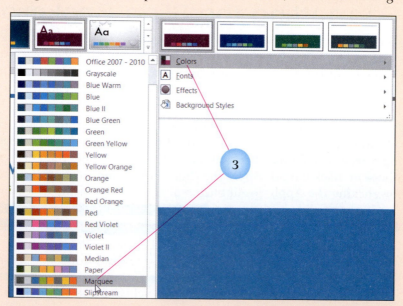

4. Change the theme fonts by clicking the More Variants button, pointing to *Fonts*, scrolling down the side menu, and then clicking *Calibri-Cambria*.

5. Change the background style by clicking the More Variants button, pointing to *Background Styles*, and then clicking *Style 5* at the side menu (first column, second row).

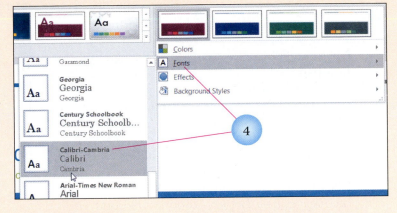

6. With Slide 1 active, run the slide show to view the formatting applied by the design theme, theme colors, theme fonts, and background style.

7. With Slide 1 still active, apply and customize the background style of all slides by completing the following steps:

   a. Click the Format Background button in the Customize group on the Design tab.

   b. At the Format Background task pane with the Fill icon selected and the fill options displayed in the *Fill* section, click the *Picture or texture fill* option.

   c. Click the Texture button (below the Online button) and then click the *Stationery* option (first column, fourth row).

   d. Click the *Transparency* measurement box up arrow until *25%* displays.

   e. Click the Apply to All button at the bottom of the task pane.

   f. Close the Format Background task pane.

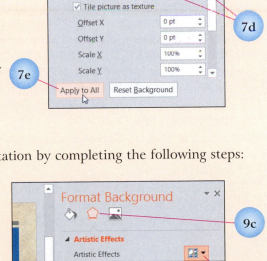

8. Run the slide show to view the background formatting.

9. Apply an artistic effect to all slides in the presentation by completing the following steps:

   a. Make Slide 2 active.

   b. Click the Format Background button in the Customize group on the Design tab.

   c. Click the Effects icon in the Format Background task pane.

   d. Click the Artistic Effects button and then click the *Paint Brush* option (third column, second row).

   e. Click the Apply to All button.

10. Run the slide show to view the artistic effect applied to all slides in the presentation.

11. Change the background to a gradient fill rather than an artistic effect by completing the following steps:
    a. Click the Fill icon in the Format Background task pane.
    b. Click the *Gradient fill* option.
    c. Click the Preset gradients button and then click *Light Gradient - Accent 2* (second column, first row).
    d. Click the *Type* option box arrow and then click *Radial* at the drop-down list.
    e. Click the Direction button and then click the *From Bottom Left Corner* option (second option from the left).
    f. Select the *0%* in the *Position* measurement box, type 25, and then press the Enter key.
    g. Click the Apply to All button.
12. Look at the slides in the slide thumbnails pane to view the gradient fill applied to all slides.
13. Apply a pattern fill to Slide 1 by completing the following steps:
    a. If necessary, make Slide 1 the active slide.
    b. At the Format Background task pane, click the *Pattern fill* option.
    c. Click the *Divot* option in the *Pattern* section (first column, seventh row).
    d. Click the Background button and then click the *Green, Accent 2, Lighter 80%* option (sixth column, second row in the *Theme Colors* section).
14. After viewing the pattern fill in the slide pane, reset the slide background of Slide 1 to the gradient fill background by clicking the Reset Background button at the bottom of the Format Background task pane.
15. Close the Format Background task pane.
16. Run the slide show to view the background formatting.
17. Print the presentation as a handout with six slides displayed horizontally per page.
18. Save and then close **3-NetworkPres.pptx**.

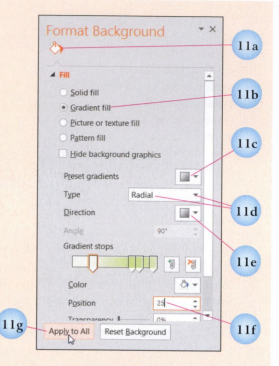

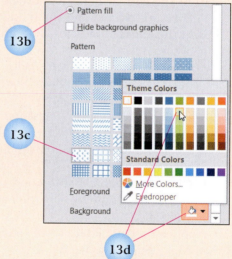

Check Your Work

You will create custom theme colors and custom theme fonts and then save the changes as a custom design theme. You will then apply the custom design theme to a job search presentation and a resume writing presentation.

Preview Finished Project

Creating Custom Design Themes

If the default themes, theme colors, and theme fonts do not provide the necessary formatting for a presentation, create custom theme colors, custom theme fonts, and a custom design theme. A custom design theme will display in the *Custom* section of the Themes drop-down gallery. To create a custom design theme, change the theme colors, theme fonts, and/or theme effects.

Click the More Variants button in the Variants group on the Design tab and the options at the drop-down gallery display a visual representation of the current theme. If the theme colors are changed, the colors are reflected in the small color squares on the *Colors* option. If the theme fonts are changed, the *A* on the *Fonts* option reflects the change.

Tutorial

Creating Custom
Theme Colors

Quick Steps

Create Custom Theme Colors

1. Click Design tab.
2. Click More Variants button.
3. Point to *Colors*.
4. Click *Customize Colors*.
5. Change background, accent, and hyperlink colors.
6. Type name for custom theme colors.
7. Click Save button.

Creating Custom Theme Colors

To create custom theme colors, click the Design tab, click the More Variants button, point to the *Colors* option, and then click *Customize Colors* at the side menu. This displays the Create New Theme Colors dialog box, similar to the one shown in Figure 3.10. Theme colors contain four text and background colors, six accent colors, and two hyperlink colors, as shown in the *Themes colors* section of the dialog box. Change a theme color by clicking the color button at the right side of the color option and then clicking the desired color at the color palette. If changes are made to colors at the Create New Theme Colors dialog box, clicking the Reset button in the lower left corner of the dialog box will change the colors back to the default.

Figure 3.10 Create New Theme Colors Dialog Box

Click this button to reset colors back to the default.

Change a theme color by clicking the color button and then clicking the color at the drop-down palette.

After making color changes, click in the *Name* text box, type a name for the custom theme colors, and then click the Save button. This saves the custom theme colors and applies the color changes to the currently open presentation.

Apply custom theme colors to a presentation by clicking the More Variants button in the Variants group, pointing to the *Colors* option, and then clicking the custom theme colors at the top of the drop-down gallery in the *Custom* section.

Project 4a Creating Custom Theme Colors   Part 1 of 4

Note: If you are running PowerPoint 2016 on a computer connected to a network in a public environment such as a school, you may need to complete all four parts of Project 4 during the same session. Network system software may delete your custom themes when you close PowerPoint. Check with your instructor.

1. At a blank presentation, click the Design tab, click the More Themes button in the Themes group, and then click *Wisp* at the drop-down gallery.
2. Click the third option in the Variants group (light blue color).
3. Create custom theme colors by completing the following steps:
   a. Click the More Variants button in the Variants group, point to the *Colors* option, and then click the *Customize Colors* option at the side menu.
   b. At the Create New Theme Colors dialog box, click the color button at the right side of the *Text/Background - Dark 2* option and then click the *Dark Blue, Accent 3, Darker 25%* option (seventh column, fifth row in the *Theme Colors* section).

   c. Click the color button at the right side of the *Text/Background - Light 2* option and then click the *Purple, Accent 4, Lighter 80%* option (eighth column, second row in the *Theme Colors* section).

   d. Click the color button at the right side of the *Accent 1* option and then click the *Purple, Accent 4, Darker 50%* option (eighth column, last row in the *Theme Colors* section).
4. Save the custom colors by completing the following steps:
   a. Select the text in the *Name* text box.
   b. Type your first and last names.
   c. Click the Save button.
5. Save the presentation and name it **3-CustomTheme**.

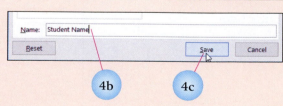

Creating Custom Theme Fonts

To create custom theme fonts, click the Design tab, click the More Variants button in the Variants group, point to the *Fonts* option, and then click *Customize Fonts* at the side menu. This displays the Create New Theme Fonts dialog box, similar to the one shown in Figure 3.11. At this dialog box, choose a heading font and body font. Type the name of the custom theme fonts in the *Name* box and then click the Save button.

Figure 3.11 Create New Theme Fonts Dialog Box

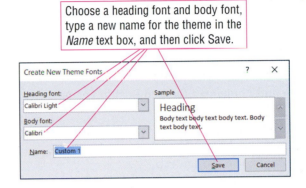

Choose a heading font and body font, type a new name for the theme in the *Name* text box, and then click Save.

Project 4b **Creating Custom Theme Fonts**   **Part 2 of 4**

1. With **3-CustomTheme.pptx** open, create custom theme fonts by completing the following steps:
   a. If necessary, click the Design tab.
   b. Click the More Variants button in the Variants group, point to the *Fonts* option, and then click the *Customize Fonts* option at the side menu.
   c. At the Create New Theme Fonts dialog box, click the *Heading font* option box arrow and then click *Candara*.
   d. Click the *Body font* option box arrow, scroll down the drop-down list, and then click *Constantia*.

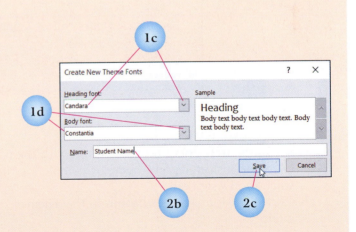

2. Save the custom theme fonts by completing the following steps:
   a. Select the current text in the *Name* text box.
   b. Type your first and last names.
   c. Click the Save button.
3. Save **3-CustomTheme.pptx**.

Saving a Custom Design Theme

When theme colors and fonts have been customized, save these as a custom design theme. To do this, click the More Themes button in the Themes group on the Design tab and then click *Save Current Theme*. This displays the Save Current Theme dialog box with the Document Themes folder active on the computer's hard drive, which contains many of the same options as the Save As dialog box. Type a name for the custom design theme in the *File name* text box and then click the Save button. To apply a custom design theme, click the More Themes button in the Themes group, and then click the theme in the *Custom* section of the drop-down gallery.

Quick Steps

Save a Custom Design Theme
1. Click Design tab.
2. Click More Themes button.
3. Click *Save Current Theme*.
4. Type name for custom theme.
5. Click Save button.

Project 4c Saving and Applying a Custom Design Theme   Part 3 of 4

1. With **3-CustomTheme.pptx** open, save the custom theme colors and fonts as a custom design theme by completing the following steps:
   a. If necessary, click the Design tab.
   b. Click the More Themes button in the Themes group.
   c. Click the *Save Current Theme* option at the bottom of the drop-down gallery.
   d. At the Save Current Theme dialog box with the Document Themes folder active on the computer's hard drive, type **C3** and then type your last name in the *File name* text box.
   e. Click the Save button.

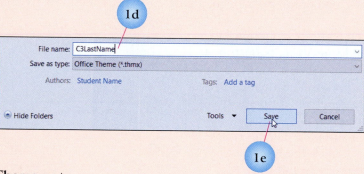

2. Close **3-CustomTheme.pptx**.
3. Open **JobSearch.pptx** and then save it with the name **3-JobSearch**.
4. Apply your custom design theme by completing the following steps:
   a. Click the Design tab.
   b. Click the More Themes button in the Themes group.
   c. Click the custom design theme that begins with *C3* followed by your last name. (The theme will display in the *Custom* section of the drop-down gallery.)

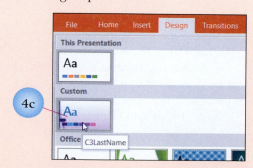

5. Run the slide show to view how the slides display with the custom design theme applied.
6. Print Slide 1 of the presentation.
7. Save and then close **3-JobSearch.pptx**.
8. Open **ResumePres.pptx** and then save it with the name **3-ResumePres**.

Editing Custom Themes

Custom theme colors and custom theme fonts can be edited. To edit the custom theme colors, click the More Variants button in the Variants group on the Design tab and then point to the *Colors* option. At the side menu of custom and built-in themes, right-click the custom theme and then click *Edit* at the shortcut menu. This displays the Edit Theme Colors dialog box, which contains the same options as the Create New Theme Colors dialog box shown in Figure 3.10 on page 97. Make the changes to theme colors and then click the Save button.

To edit custom theme fonts, click the More Variants button in the Variants group on the Design tab, point to the *Fonts* option, right-click the custom theme fonts, and then click *Edit* at the shortcut menu. This displays the Edit Theme Fonts dialog box that contains the same options as the Create New Theme Fonts dialog box shown in Figure 3.11 on page 99. Make the changes and then click the Save button.

Deleting Custom Themes

Delete custom theme colors from the *Colors* option side menu, delete custom theme fonts from the *Fonts* option side menu, and delete custom design themes from the More Themes button drop-down gallery or the Save Current Theme dialog box. To delete custom theme colors, click the More Variants button in the Variants group, point to the *Colors* option, right-click the theme to be deleted, and then click *Delete* at the shortcut menu. At the message asking to confirm the deletion, click the Yes button. Complete similar steps to delete custom theme fonts.

Delete a custom design theme by clicking the More Themes button in the Themes group on the Design tab, right-clicking the custom design theme, and then clicking *Delete* at the shortcut menu. A custom design theme can also be deleted at the Save Current Theme dialog box. To display this dialog box, click the More Themes button in the Themes group on the Design tab and then click *Save Current Theme* at the drop-down gallery. At the Save Current Theme dialog box, click the custom design theme file name, click the Organize button on the toolbar, and then click *Delete* at the drop-down list. At the message asking to confirm the deletion, click the Yes button.

1. Open a new, blank presentation and delete the custom theme colors by completing the following steps:
   a. Click the Design tab.
   b. Click the More Variants button in the Variants group and then point to the *Colors* option.
   c. Right-click the custom theme colors named with your first and last names.
   d. Click *Delete* at the shortcut menu.
   e. At the message asking if you want to delete the theme colors, click Yes.

2. Complete steps similar to those in Step 1 to delete the custom theme fonts you created named with your first and last names.

3. Delete the custom design theme by completing the following steps:
   a. Click the More Themes button in the Themes group.
   b. Right-click the custom design theme that begins with *C3* followed by your last name.
   c. Click *Delete* at the shortcut menu.
   d. At the message asking if you want to delete the theme, click Yes.

4. Close the presentation without saving it.

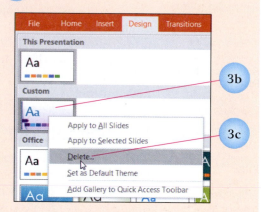

Chapter Summary

- The Font group on the Home tab contains buttons and options for applying character formatting to text in slides.

- Change the default font with the *Font* option box and the *Font Size* option box in the Font group.

- Some options, such as the *Font* and *Font Size* options, contain the live preview feature, which displays how the formatting affects selected text without having to return to the presentation.

- Character formatting can also be applied with options at the Font dialog box. Display this dialog box by clicking the Font group dialog box launcher.

- Select text in a slide and the Mini toolbar displays above the selected text. Apply formatting using the buttons and options on this toolbar.

- Use the Format Painter feature to apply formatting to more than one location in a slide or slides.

- The Paragraph group on the Home tab contains a number of buttons for applying paragraph formatting to text in slides.

- Customize paragraph formatting with options at the Paragraph dialog box with the Indents and Spacing tab selected. Display this dialog box by clicking the Paragraph group dialog box launcher or by clicking the Line Spacing button in the Paragraph group and then clicking *Line Spacing Options* at the drop-down list.

- Use the Add or Remove Columns button in the Paragraph group or options at the Columns dialog box to format selected text into columns. Display the Columns dialog box by clicking the Add or Remove Columns button and then clicking *More Columns* at the drop-down list.

- Use the Text Direction button or options at the Format Shape task pane to rotate or stack text in a slide. Display the Format Shape task pane by clicking the Drawing group task pane launcher on the Home tab.

- The Shape Options tab in the Format Shape task pane displays four icons: Fill & Line, Effects, Size & Properties, and Picture, each with different options for formatting a placeholder.

- Customize bullets with options at the Bullets and Numbering dialog box with the Bulleted tab selected. Display this dialog box by clicking the Bullets button arrow and then clicking *Bullets and Numbering* at the drop-down list.

- Customize numbering with options at the Bullets and Numbering dialog box with the Numbered tab selected. Display this dialog box by clicking the Numbering button arrow and then clicking *Bullets and Numbering* at the drop-down list.

- Click the Quick Styles button in the Drawing group on the Home tab to apply formatting to a placeholder. The Drawing group also contains the Shape Fill, Shape Outline, and Shape Effects buttons for customizing a placeholder, and the Arrange button for arranging slide elements.

- Click the Slide Size button and then click *Custom Slide Size* at the drop-down list to display the Slide Size dialog box. Use options at this dialog box to change the slide size and ratio, the start slide number, and the orientation of slides, notes, handouts, and outline pages.

- Use the Format Background task pane to customize the background of slides. Display the task pane by clicking the Format Background button in the Customize group on the Design tab.

- Create custom theme colors with options at the Create New Theme Colors dialog box. Display this dialog box by clicking the More Variants button in the Variants group on the Design tab, pointing to the *Colors* option, and then clicking *Customize Colors* at the side menu.

- Create custom theme fonts with options at the Create New Theme Fonts dialog box. Display this dialog box by clicking the More Variants button in the Variants group on the Design tab, pointing to the *Fonts* option, and then clicking *Customize Fonts* at the side menu.

- Save a custom design theme at the Save Current Theme dialog box. Display this dialog box by clicking the More Themes button in the Themes group on the Design tab and then clicking *Save Current Theme*.

- Edit custom theme colors with options at the Edit Theme Colors dialog box and edit custom theme fonts with options at the Edit Theme Fonts dialog box.

- Delete custom theme colors by clicking the More Variants button in the Variants group, pointing to the *Colors* option, right-clicking the custom theme, and then clicking the *Delete* option.

- Delete custom theme fonts by clicking the More Variants button in the Variants group, pointing to the *Fonts* option, right-clicking the custom theme, and then clicking the *Delete* option.
- Delete a custom design theme by clicking the More Themes button in the Themes group, right-clicking the custom theme, and then clicking *Delete* at the shortcut menu. A custom design theme also can be deleted at the Save Current Theme dialog box. Display this dialog box by clicking the Themes button and then clicking *Save Current Theme* at the drop-down gallery.

Commands Review

FEATURE	RIBBON TAB, GROUP	BUTTON, OPTION	KEYBOARD SHORTCUT
Bullets and Numbering dialog box with Bulleted tab selected	Home, Paragraph	, *Bullets and Numbering*	
Bullets and Numbering dialog box with Numbered tab selected	Home, Paragraph	, *Bullets and Numbering*	
Columns dialog box	Home, Paragraph	, *More Columns*	
Create New Theme Colors dialog box	Design, Variants	, *Colors, Customize Colors*	
Create New Theme Fonts dialog box	Design, Variants	, *Fonts, Customize Fonts*	
Font dialog box	Home, Font		Ctrl + Shift + F
Format Background task pane	Design, Customize		
Format Painter	Home, Clipboard		
Format Shape task pane	Home, Drawing		
Paragraph dialog box	Home, Paragraph		
Save Current Theme dialog box	Design, Themes	, *Save Current Theme*	
slide size	Design, Customize		

Microsoft

PowerPoint®

Inserting Elements in Slides

Performance Objectives

Upon successful completion of Chapter 4, you will be able to:

1 Insert, format, select, and align a text box

2 Set the default text box format

3 Set tabs in a text box

4 Insert, format, and copy shapes

5 Display rulers, gridlines, and guides

6 Merge, group, and ungroup objects

7 Insert, crop, size, move, and format an image

8 Insert an image as a slide background

9 Insert, size, scale, rotate, and position an online image

10 Copy objects within and between presentations

11 Create and insert a screenshot

12 Create and format WordArt text

13 Insert symbols, headers, footers, the current date, and slide numbers

An audience may overlook a presentation consisting only of text-heavy slides. Adding visual elements, where appropriate, can help by adding interest and impact to the information. In this chapter, you will learn how to create and add visual elements on slides such as text boxes, shapes, images, screenshots, and WordArt text. These elements will make the delivery of your presentation a dynamic experience for your audience.

SNAP

If you are a SNAP user, launch the Precheck and Tutorials from your Assignments page.

Data Files

Before beginning chapter work, copy the PC4 folder to your storage medium and then make PC4 the active folder.

Project 1 | **Create a Company Presentation Containing Text Boxes, Shapes, and Images**   **14 Parts**

You will create a company presentation that includes slides with text boxes, a slide with tabbed text in a text box, slides with shapes and text, and slides with images. You will also insert elements in slides such as slide numbers, headers, footers, the date, and symbols.

Preview Finished Project

Tutorial

Inserting and Formatting Text Boxes

 Text Box

Inserting and Formatting Text Boxes

Many slide layouts contain placeholders for entering text and other elements in a slide. Along with placeholders, a text box can be inserted and formatted in a slide. To insert a text box in a slide, click the Insert tab, click the Text Box button in the Text group, and the mouse pointer displays as a thin, down-pointing arrow. Using the mouse, click and drag in the slide to create the text box. Or, click in a slide to insert a small text box at that location.

Formatting a Text Box

Quick Steps

Draw a Text Box
1. Click Insert tab.
2. Click Text Box button.
3. Click or drag in slide to create box.

Hint Use a text box to place text anywhere in a slide. Text in inserted text boxes does not appear in the Outline view.

When a text box is inserted in a slide, the Home tab displays. Use options in the Drawing group to format the text box by applying a Quick Style or adding a shape fill, outline, or effect. Format a text box in a manner similar to formatting a placeholder. Formatting can also be applied to a text box with options on the Drawing Tools Format tab. Click this tab and the ribbon displays as shown in Figure 4.1. The Shape Styles group contains the same options as the Drawing group on the Home tab. Use other options on the tab to apply WordArt formatting to text and arrange and size the text box.

Move a text box in the same way as a placeholder. Click the text box to select it, position the mouse pointer on the text box border until the pointer displays with a four-headed arrow, and then click and drag the text box to the desired position. Change the size of a selected text box using the sizing handles that display around the box. Use the *Shape Height* and *Shape Width* measurement boxes in the Size group on the Drawing Tools Format tab to adjust the size of the text box to a specific height and width measurement.

PowerPoint provides a task pane with a variety of options for formatting a placeholder. The same task pane is available with options for formatting and customizing a text box. Click the Shape Styles group task pane launcher and the Format Shape task pane displays at the right side of the screen with options for formatting the text box fill, effects, and size; options for formatting an image in the text box; and options for formatting text in a text box. Click the WordArt

Figure 4.1 Drawing Tools Format Tab

Styles group task pane launcher and the Format Shape task pane displays text formatting options. Click the Size group task pane launcher and the Format Shape task pane displays size and position options.

The same formatting applied to a placeholder can also be applied to a text box. For example, use the buttons in the Paragraph group on the Home tab to align text horizontally and vertically in a text box, change text direction, set text in columns, and set internal margins for the text in the text box.

Quick Steps

Select All Text Boxes
1. Click Select button.
2. Click *Select All*.
OR
Press Ctrl + A.

 Select

Selecting Multiple Objects

Multiple text boxes and other objects can be selected in a slide and then the objects can be formatted, aligned, and arranged in the slide. To select all objects in a slide, click the Select button in the Editing group on the Home tab and then click *Select All* at the drop-down list. Or, select all objects in a slide with the keyboard shortcut Ctrl + A. To select specific text boxes or objects in a slide, click the first object, press and hold down the Shift key, and then click each of the other objects.

Aligning Text Boxes

 Align

Use the Align button in the Arrange group on the Drawing Tools Format tab to align the edges of multiple objects in a slide. Click the Align button and a drop-down list of alignment options displays, including options for aligning objects vertically and horizontally and distributing objects in the slide.

Hint To select an object that is behind another object, select the top object and then press the Tab key to cycle through and select the other objects.

Project 1a **Inserting and Formatting Text Boxes**   **Part 1 of 14**

1. Open **AddisonReport.pptx** and then save it with the name **4-AddisonReport**.
2. Insert a new slide with the Blank layout by completing the following steps:
   a. Click the New Slide button arrow in the Slides group on the Home tab.
   b. Click *Blank* at the drop-down list.
3. Insert and format the *Safety* text box shown in Figure 4.2 (on page 110) by completing the following steps:
   a. Click the Insert tab.
   b. Click the Text Box button in the Text group.
   c. Click anywhere in the slide. (This inserts a small text box in the slide.)
   d. Type Safety.
   e. Select the text and then change the font to Copperplate Gothic Bold and the font size to 36 points.

[handwritten note: paragraph box Tabs default tab stops. (1")]

f. Click the Text Direction button in the Paragraph group on the Home tab and then click *Stacked* at the drop-down list.

g. Click the Drawing Tools Format tab.

h. Click the More Shape Styles button in the Shape Styles group and then click the *Moderate Effect - Aqua, Accent 5* option (sixth column, fifth row).

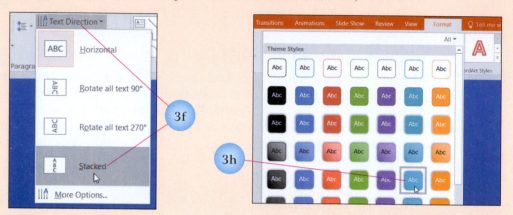

i. Click the Shape Outline button arrow in the Shape Styles group and then click the *Blue* color (eighth option in the *Standard Colors* section).

j. Click the Shape Outline button arrow, point to *Weight*, and then click the *1½ pt* option.

k. Click the Shape Effects button, point to *Bevel*, and then click the *Circle* option (first option in the *Bevel* section).

l. Click the More WordArt Styles button in the WordArt Styles group and then click the *Fill - White, Text 1, Outline - Background 1, Hard Shadow - Background 1* option (first column, third row).

m. Click in the *Shape Height* measurement box, type 4, and then press the Enter key.

n. Drag the text box so it is positioned as shown in Figure 4.2 (on page 110).

4. Insert and size the other text box shown in Figure 4.2 by completing the following steps:

a. Click the Insert tab.

b. Click the Text Box button in the Text group.

c. Drag in the slide to create a text box. (Drag to the approximate width of the text box in Figure 4.2.)

d. Type the text shown in the text box in Figure 4.2 in a single column. Type the text in the first column and then type the text in the second column. (Your text will display as shown at the right in one column, in a smaller font, and with different line spacing than in Figure 4.2.)

e. Select the text and then change the font size to 32 points.

f. Click the Line Spacing button in the Paragraph group and then click *2.0* at the drop-down list. (The text will flow off the slide.)

g. Click the Add or Remove Columns button in the Paragraph group and then click *Two Columns* at the drop-down list. (The text in the slide will not display in two columns until you complete steps 7i and 7j.)
5. Click the Drawing Tools Format tab.
6. Apply a WordArt style by completing the following steps:
   a. Click the More WordArt Styles button in the WordArt Styles group.
   b. Click the *Fill - White, Text 1, Outline - Background 1, Hard Shadow - Background 1* option (first column, third row).
7. Change the height, width, and internal margin measurements of the text box and turn off Autofit in the Format Shape task pane by completing the following steps:
   a. Click the Size group task pane launcher.
   b. At the Format Shape task pane, click the Size & Properties icon if it is not selected.
   c. If necessary, click *Text Box* in the task pane to display the text box options.
   d. Scroll down the task pane list box and click the *Do not Autofit* option.
   e. Select the current measurement in the *Left margin* measurement box and then type 0.8.
   f. Select the current measurement in the *Right margin* measurement box and then type 0.
   g. Select the current measurement in the *Top margin* measurement box, type 0.2, and then press the Enter key.
   h. Scroll up to the top of the task pane list box and, if necessary, click *Size* to display the size options.
   i. Select the current measurement in the *Height* measurement box and then type 4.
   j. Select the current measurement in the *Width* measurement box, type 8, and then press the Enter key.

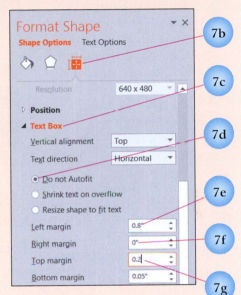

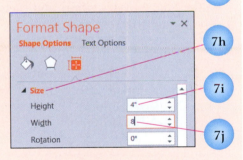

8. Apply fill formatting with options in the Format Shape task pane by completing the following steps:
   a. Click the Fill & Line icon in the task pane.
   b. If necessary, click *Fill* to display the fill options.
   c. Click the *Gradient fill* option to select it. (Notice the options available for customizing the gradient fill.)
   d. Click the *Pattern fill* option to select it. (Notice the options available for applying a pattern fill.)
   e. Click the *Picture or texture fill* option to select it.
   f. Click the File button in the *Insert picture from* section.
   g. At the Insert Picture dialog box, navigate to the PC4 folder on your storage medium and then double-click *Ship.jpg*.

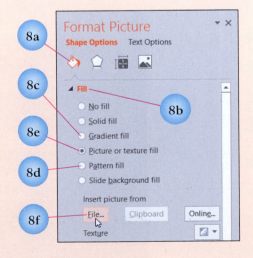

h. Select *0%* in the *Transparency* measurement box, type 10, and then press the Enter key.

i. Close the task pane by clicking the Close button in the upper right corner of the task pane.

9. Click in the slide outside the text box.

10. Arrange the text boxes by completing the following steps:

a. Press Ctrl + A to select both text boxes.

b. Click the Drawing Tools Format tab.

c. Click the Align button in the Arrange group and then click *Align Bottom* at the drop-down list.

d. Drag both boxes to the approximate location in the slide as shown in Figure 4.2.

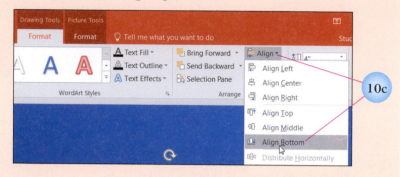

11. Save **4-AddisonReport.pptx**.

12. Print only Slide 2 by completing the following steps:

a. Press Ctrl + P to display the Print backstage area.

b. Click in the *Slides* text box in the *Settings* category and then type 2.

c. Click the Print button.

13. Select the text box containing the image of the ship.

14. Make sure the Drawing Tools Format tab is active, click the More Shape Styles button in the Shape Styles group, and then click the *Moderate Effect - Aqua, Accent 5* option (sixth column, fifth row).

15. Click the Shape Outline button arrow in the Shape Styles group, and then click the *Blue* color (eighth option in the *Standard Colors* section).

16. Click the Shape Outline button arrow, point to *Weight*, and then click the *1½ pt* option.

17. Click the Shape Effects button, point to *Bevel*, and then click the *Circle* option (first option in the *Bevel* section).

18. Save **4-AddisonReport.pptx**.

Check Your Work

Figure 4.2 Project 1a, Slide 2

Setting the Default Text Box Format

The Format Shape task pane can be displayed using the shortcut menu. To do this, position the mouse pointer on the border of the text box until the pointer displays with a four-headed arrow and then click the right mouse button. At the shortcut menu, click the *Size and Position* option to display the Format Shape task pane with the Size & Properties icon active. Click the *Format Shape* option at the shortcut menu and the Format Shape task pane displays with the Fill & Line icon active. Formatting applied to a text box can become the default for other text boxes in the current presentation by clicking the *Set as Default Text Box* option at the shortcut menu.

Project 1b   **Formatting a Text Box and Setting the Default Text Box**   **Part 2 of 14**

1. With **4-AddisonReport.pptx** open, make sure Slide 2 is the active slide and then complete the following steps:
   a. Click the Insert tab, click the Text Box button, and then click in the lower right corner of the slide.
   b. Type Default text box. (In the next step you will change the default text box. You will then use the text box you just inserted to return to the original default text box.)
2. Set as default the text box containing the word *SAFETY* by completing the following steps:
   a. Position the mouse pointer on the border of the text box containing the word *SAFETY* until the pointer displays with a four-headed arrow and then click the right mouse button.
   b. Click the *Set as Default Text Box* option at the shortcut menu.
3. Make Slide 1 active.
4. Insert a text box by clicking the Insert tab, clicking the Text Box button, and then clicking between the company name and the left side of the slide.
5. Type 2018 in the text box.
6. Change the *Autofit* option, wrap text in the text box, and change the size of the text box by completing the following steps:
   a. Position the mouse pointer on the border of the text box until the pointer displays with a four-headed arrow and then click the right mouse button.
   b. Click the *Size and Position* option at the shortcut menu.
   c. At the Format Shape task pane with the Size & Properties icon selected, click *Text Box* to display the options, scroll to the bottom of the task pane list box, and then click in the *Wrap text in shape* check box to insert a check mark.
   d. Click the *Shrink text on overflow* option to select it.
   e. Scroll up to the top of the task pane and then click *Size* if the section is not displayed.

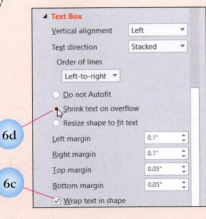

f. Select the current measurement in the *Height* measurement box in the *Size* section and then type 2.4.

g. Select the current measurement in the *Width* measurement box, type 0.8, and then press the Enter key.

7. With the text box selected, change the shape of the text box by completing the following steps:

a. Click the Drawing Tools Format tab.

b. Click the Edit Shape button in the Insert Shapes group, point to *Change Shape*, and then click the *Bevel* option (last option, second row in the *Basic Shapes* section).

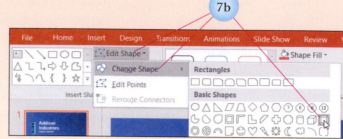

8. Precisely position the text box by completing the following steps:

a. If necessary, scroll down the Format Shape task pane list box to the *Position* section and then click *Position* to display the options.

b. Select the current measurement in the *Horizontal position* measurement box and then type 1.8.

c. Select the current measurement in the *Vertical position* measurement box, type 2, and then press the Enter key.

9. Close the Format Shape task pane.

10. Return to the original text box by completing the following steps:

a. Make Slide 2 active.

b. Click in the text box containing the words *Default text box*.

c. Position the mouse pointer on the border of the text box until the pointer displays with a four-headed arrow and then click the right mouse button.

d. Click the *Set as Default Text Box* option at the shortcut menu.

e. Press the Delete key to delete the text box.

11. Save **4-AddisonReport.pptx**.

Check Your Work

Setting Tabs in a Text Box

💡 **Hint** Setting tabs helps you align text in a slide.

⌐ Left Tab

⊥ Center Tab

⌐ Right Tab

⊥ Decimal Tab

Text inside a text box can be aligned in columns using tabs. A text box, by default, contains left alignment tabs that display as gray marks along the bottom of the horizontal ruler. (If the ruler is not visible, display the horizontal ruler as well as the vertical ruler by clicking the View tab and then clicking the *Ruler* check box in the Show group to insert a check mark.) These default left alignment tabs can be changed to center, right, or decimal. To change to a different tab alignment, click the Alignment button above the vertical ruler and at the left side of the horizontal ruler. Display the desired tab alignment symbol and then click a location on the horizontal ruler. When a tab is set on the horizontal ruler, any default tabs to the left of the new tab are deleted. Move tabs on the horizontal ruler using the mouse to drag the tab to the new position. To delete a tab, use the mouse to drag the tab down and off of the ruler.

Tabs can also be set with option at the Tabs dialog box. To display this dialog box, click the Paragraph group dialog box launcher. At the Paragraph dialog box, click the Tabs button in the lower left corner. At the Tabs dialog box, type a tab position in the *Tab stop position* measurement box, choose a tab alignment with options in the *Alignment* section, and then click the Set button. Clear a specific tab by typing the tab position in the *Tab stop position* measurement box and then clicking the Clear button. Clear all tabs from the horizontal ruler by clicking the Clear All button. When all changes have been made, click OK to close the Tabs dialog box and then click OK to close the Paragraph dialog box.

Project 1c Creating a Text Box and Setting Tabs   Part 3 of 14

1. With **4-AddisonReport.pptx** open, make Slide 1 active and then click the Home tab.
2. Click the New Slide button arrow and then click the *Title Only* layout.
3. Click in the title placeholder and then type Executive Officers.
4. Draw a text box by completing the following steps:
   a. Click the Insert tab.
   b. Click the Text Box button in the Text group.
   c. Draw a text box in the slide that is approximately 10 inches wide and 0.5 inch tall.
5. Change tabs in the text box by completing the following steps:
   a. If necessary, display the horizontal ruler by clicking the View tab and then clicking the *Ruler* check box in the Show group to insert a check mark.
   b. With the insertion point inside the text box, check the Alignment button above the vertical ruler and at the left side of the horizontal ruler and make sure the left tab symbol displays.
   c. Position the tip of the mouse pointer on the horizontal ruler below the 0.5-inch mark and then click the left mouse button.

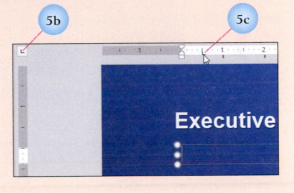

   d. Click the Alignment button to display the Center alignment symbol.
   e. Click immediately below the 5-inch mark on the horizontal ruler.
   f. Click the Alignment button to display the Right alignment symbol.

   g. Click the horizontal ruler immediately below the 9.5-inch mark. (You may need to expand the size of the text box to set the tab at the 9.5-inch mark.)
6. Type the text in the text box as shown in Figure 4.3. Make sure you press the Tab key before typing text in the first column. (This moves the insertion point to the first tab, which is a left alignment tab.) Bold the three column headings—*Name, Title,* and *Number.*
7. When you are finished typing the text in the text box, press Ctrl + A to select all of the text in the text box and then change the font size to 24 points.
8. With the text in the text box still selected, drag the left alignment marker on the horizontal ruler from the 0.5-inch mark to the 0.25-inch mark and then drag the center alignment marker on the horizontal ruler from the 5-inch mark on the ruler to the 5.5-inch mark.

9. Click the Line Spacing button in the Paragraph group on the Home tab and then click the *1.5* option.
10. Position the text box as shown in Figure 4.3.
11. Save **4-AddisonReport.pptx**.

Check Your Work

Figure 4.3 Project 1c, Slide 2

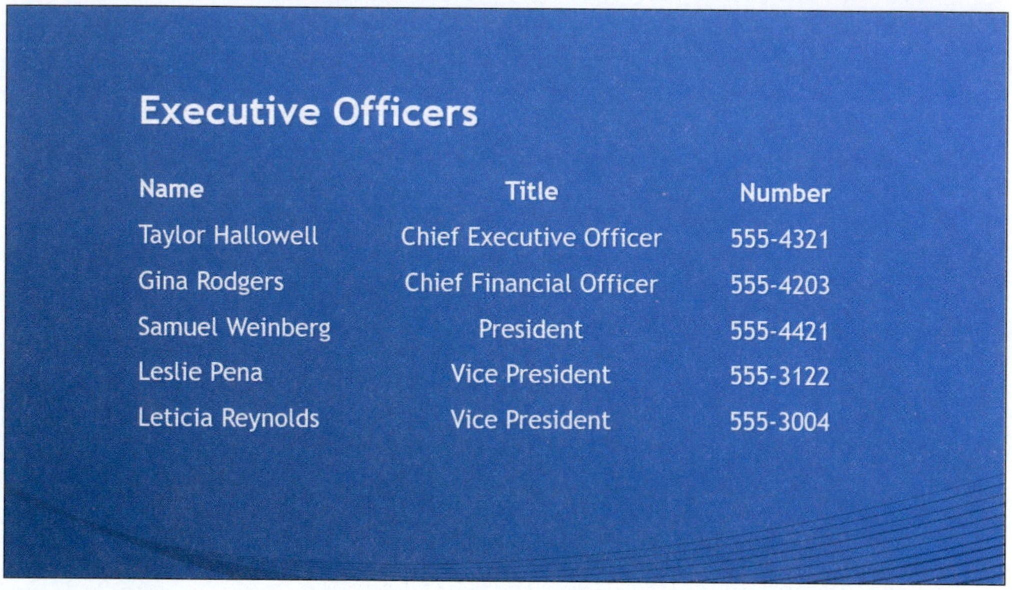

Executive Officers
Name
Title
Number
Taylor Hallowell
Chief Executive Officer
555-4321
Gina Rodgers
Chief Financial Officer
555-4203
Samuel Weinberg
President
555-4421
Leslie Pena
Vice President
555-3122
Leticia Reynolds
Vice President
555-3004

Tutorial

Inserting, Sizing, and Positioning Shapes

Tutorial

Formatting Shapes

Shapes

Quick Steps

Insert a Shape
1. Click Insert tab.
2. Click Shapes button.
3. Choose shape at drop-down list.
4. Click or drag in slide to create shape.

Quick Steps

Copy a Shape
1. Select shape.
2. Click Copy button.
3. Position insertion point at new location.
4. Click Paste button.

Inserting, Formatting, and Copying Shapes

Draw shapes in a slide with shapes in the Drawing group or with the Shapes button in the Illustrations group on the Insert tab. Use the Shapes button drop-down list to draw shapes including lines, basic shapes, block arrows, flow chart symbols, callouts, stars, and banners. Click a shape and the mouse pointer displays as crosshairs (plus sign). Click in the slide to insert the shape, or position the crosshairs in the slide and then click and drag to create the shape.

Apply formatting to a shape in a manner similar to formatting a text box. Format a shape with buttons in the Drawing group on the Home tab, with buttons on the Drawing Tools Format tab, using options in the Format Shape task pane, or with options at the shortcut menu. When drawing an enclosed object, maintain the proportions of the shape by holding down the Shift key while dragging with the mouse to create the shape. The formatting applied to a shape can be saved as the default formatting. To do this, right-click the border of the shape and then click *Set as Default Shape*.

To copy a shape, select the shape and then click the Copy button in the Clipboard group on the Home tab. Position the insertion point and then click the Paste button. A selected shape can also be copied by pressing and holding down the Ctrl key while dragging the shape to the new location.

Tutorial

Displaying Rulers,
Gridlines, and
Guides; Copying
and Rotating
Shapes

Displaying Rulers, Gridlines, and Guides

PowerPoint provides a number of features for positioning objects such as placeholders, text boxes, and shapes. Display horizontal and vertical rulers, gridlines, and/or drawing guides and use Smart Guides as shown in Figure 4.4. Turn the horizontal and vertical rulers on and off with the *Ruler* check box in the Show group on the View tab as you did in Project 1c. The Show group also contains a *Gridlines* check box. Insert a check mark in this check box and gridlines display in the active slide. Gridlines are intersecting lines that create a grid on the slide and are useful for aligning objects. Turn the gridlines on and off with the keyboard shortcut, Shift + F9.

Turn on drawing guides to help position objects on a slide. Drawing guides are a horizontal dashed line and a vertical dashed line that display on the slide in the slide pane as shown in Figure 4.4. To turn on the drawing guides, display the Grid and Guides dialog box shown in Figure 4.5. Display this dialog box by clicking the Show group dialog box launcher on the View tab. At the dialog box, insert a check mark in the *Display drawing guides on screen* check box. By default, the horizontal and vertical drawing guides intersect in the middle of the slide. Move these guides by dragging the guide with the mouse. Drag a guide and a measurement displays next to the mouse pointer. Drawing guides and gridlines display on the slide but do not print.

Figure 4.4 Rulers, Gridlines, Drawing Guides, and Smart Guides

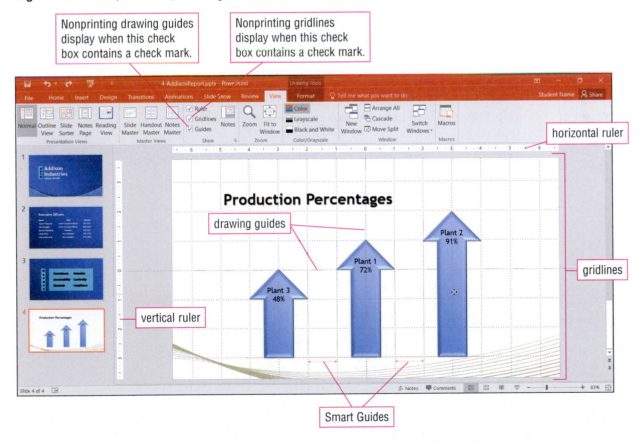

(handwritten annotation: view → show group launcher)

Figure 4.5 Grid and Guides Dialog Box

When this check box contains a check mark, objects will snap into alignment with the gridlines.

Insert a check mark in this check box to display gridlines.

Insert a check mark in this check box to display drawing guides.

Grid and Guides

Snap to
☑ Snap objects to grid

Grid settings
Spacing: 1/12" ⌄   0.08" ⌃⌄
☐ Display grid on screen

Guide settings
☐ Display drawing guides on screen
☑ Display smart guides when shapes are aligned

Set as Default   OK   Cancel

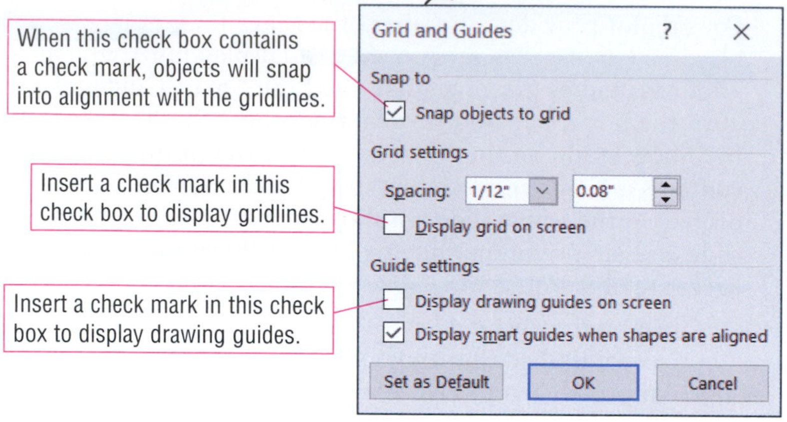

PowerPoint includes Smart Guides, which appear when objects that are close together are moved on a slide. Use these guides to help align and evenly space the objects on the slide. Turn on gridlines by inserting a check mark in the *Gridlines* check box on the View tab or by inserting a check mark in the *Display grid on screen* check box at the Grid and Guides dialog box. The horizontal and vertical spacing between the gridlines is 0.08 inch by default. This measurement can be changed with the *Spacing* option at the Grid and Guides dialog box.

As an object is moved on the slide, it is pulled into alignment with the nearest intersection of gridlines. This is because the *Snap objects to grid* check box at the Grid and Guides dialog box contains a check mark by default. To position an object precisely, turn off this option by removing the check mark from the *Snap objects to grid* check box or by holding down the Alt key while dragging an object. Smart Guides display when shapes are aligned. To turn off the display of Smart Guides, click the *Display smart guides when shapes are aligned* check box in the Grid and Guides dialog box to remove the check mark.

Project 1d Drawing and Formatting Shapes

Part 4 of 14

1. With **4-AddisonReport.pptx** open, make Slide 3 active and then insert a new slide by clicking the New Slide button arrow in the Slides group on the Home tab and then clicking the *White Background* layout at the drop-down list.
2. Turn on the display of gridlines by clicking the View tab and then clicking *Gridlines* to insert a check mark in the check box.
3. Click in the title placeholder and then type Production Percentages.
4. Turn on the drawing guides and turn off the snap-to-grid feature by completing the following steps:
   a. Make sure the View tab is active and then click the Show group dialog box launcher.

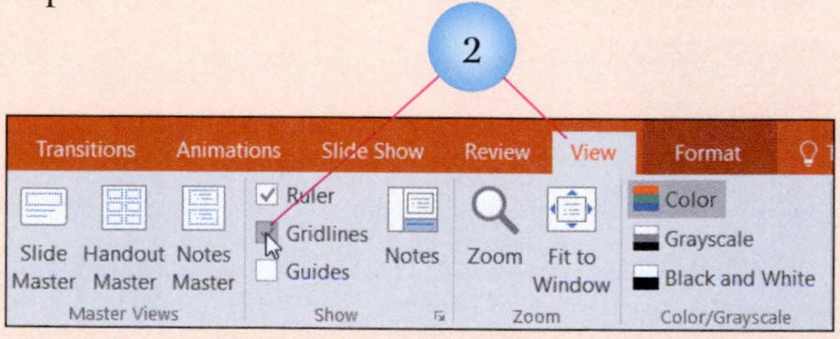

b. At the Grid and Guides dialog box, click the *Snap objects to grid* check box to remove the check mark.

c. Make sure the *Display grid on screen* check box contains a check mark.

d. Click the *Display drawing guides on screen* check box to insert a check mark.

e. Click OK.

5. Insert the left-most arrow in the slide, as shown in Figure 4.6 (on page 119), by completing the following steps:

a. Click outside the title placeholder to deselect it.

b. Click the Insert tab.

c. Click the Shapes button in the Illustrations group and then click the *Up Arrow* shape (third column, first row in the *Block Arrows* section).

d. Position the crosshairs at the intersection of the horizontal drawing guide and the third vertical gridline from the left.

e. Click and hold down the left mouse button, drag down and to the right until the crosshairs are positioned on the intersection of the fifth vertical line from the left and the first horizontal line from the bottom, and then release the mouse button. (Your arrow should be the approximate size shown in Figure 4.6.)

f. With the arrow selected and the Drawing Tools Format tab active, click the Shape Fill button arrow in the Shape Styles group, and then click *Aqua, Accent 5* at the drop-down gallery (ninth column, first row in the *Theme Colors* section).

g. Click the Shape Outline button arrow and then click *Dark Blue* at the drop-down gallery (ninth option in the *Standard Colors* section).

h. Apply a shape style to the arrow by clicking the More Shape Styles button in the Shapes Styles group and then clicking the *Subtle Effect - Blue, Accent 1* option (second column, fourth row).

i. Click the Shape Effects button in the Shape Styles group, point to *Bevel*, and then click the *Soft Round* option (second column, second row in the *Bevel* section).

6. Insert text in the arrow by completing the following steps:

a. With the arrow selected, type Plant 3, press the Enter key, and then type 48%.

b. Click the Home tab, click the Align Text button in the Paragraph group, and then click the *Top* option at the drop-down list.

7. Copy the arrow by completing the following steps:

a. Position the mouse pointer on the border of the selected arrow until the mouse pointer displays with a four-headed arrow.

b. Press and hold down the Ctrl key, click and hold down the left mouse button, drag the arrow to the intersection of the horizontal and vertical drawing guides, and then release the Ctrl key and the mouse button.

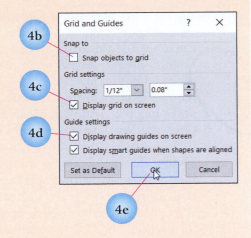

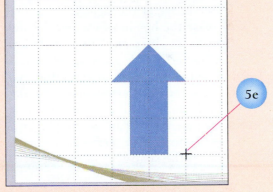

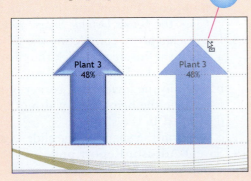

8. Move the vertical drawing guide and then copy the right arrow by completing the following steps:

a. Click outside the arrow to deselect the arrow.

b. Position the mouse pointer on the vertical drawing guide, click and hold down the left mouse button, drag right until the mouse pointer displays with *3.00* and a right-pointing arrow in a box, and then release the mouse button.

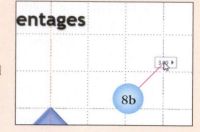

c. Click the right arrow, press and hold down the Ctrl key, click and hold down the left mouse button, drag the arrow to the right so the tip of the arrow is positioned at the intersection of the horizontal and vertical drawing guides, and then release the Ctrl key and the mouse button. Watch for the Smart Guides to display indicating that the arrows are aligned and evenly spaced (see image at the right).

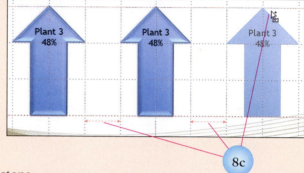

9. Increase the height of the middle and right arrows by completing the following steps:

a. Click the middle arrow to select it.

b. Use the mouse to drag the top middle sizing handle up to the next horizontal gridline.

c. Click the right arrow and then drag the top middle sizing handle up to the second horizontal gridline (see Figure 4.6).

d. Change the text in the middle arrow to *Plant 1 72%* and change the text in the right arrow to *Plant 2 91%* (see Figure 4.6).

10. Turn on the snap-to-grid feature and turn off the gridlines and drawing guides by completing the following steps:

a. Click the View tab.

b. Click the Show group dialog box launcher.

c. At the Grid and Guides dialog box, click the *Snap objects to grid* check box to insert a check mark.

d. Click the *Display grid on screen* option to remove the check mark.

e. Click the *Display drawing guides on screen* check box to remove the check mark.

f. Click OK.

11. Change the slide layout by clicking the Home tab, clicking the Layout button in the Slides group, and then clicking the *Title Only* layout.

12. Set the formatting of the arrow shape as the default by completing the following steps:

a. Click the left arrow shape.

b. Position the mouse pointer on the arrow shape border until the pointer displays with a four-headed arrow and then click the right mouse button.

c. Click the *Set as Default Shape* option at the shortcut menu.

13. Draw a shape by completing the following steps:

a. Click the Insert tab, click the Shapes button, and then click the *Bevel* option (first column, third row in the *Basic Shapes* section).

b. Click in the lower right corner of the slide.

c. Change the height and width of the shape to 0.6 inch.

d. Type AI in the shape.

e. Position the shape in the slide as shown in Figure 4.6.

14. Save **4-AddisonReport.pptx**.

Check Your Work

Figure 4.6 Project 1d, Slide 4

Merging Shapes

Merge
Shapes

Use the Merge Shapes button on the Drawing Tools Format tab to merge shapes to create custom shapes that are not available with the default shapes. To merge shapes, draw the shapes in the slide, select the shapes, and then click the Merge Shapes button in the Insert Shapes group on the Drawing Tools Format tab. At the drop-down list, choose one of the following options: *Union*, *Combine*, *Fragment*, *Intersect*, and *Subtract*. Each option merges the shapes in a different manner.

Project 1e Merging Shapes   **Part 5 of 14**

1. With **4-AddisonReport.pptx** open, make Slide 4 active and then insert a slide from another presentation by completing the following steps:
   a. Click the Home tab.
   b. Click the New Slide button arrow and then click *Reuse Slides* at the drop-down list.
   c. At the Reuse Slides task pane, click the Browse button and then click *Browse File* at the drop-down list.
   d. At the Browse dialog box, navigate to the PC4 folder on your storage medium and then double-click *IEC.pptx*.
   e. Click the second slide thumbnail in the Reuse Slides task pane.
   f. Close the Reuse Slides task pane by clicking the Close button in the upper right corner of the task pane.

2. The slide you inserted contains a circle shape and four rectangle shapes. Merge the shapes to create an image for the International Energy Consortium by completing the following steps:
   a. Click the slide in the slide pane and then press Ctrl + A to select all of the shapes in the slide.
   b. Click the Drawing Tools Format tab.
   c. Click the Merge Shapes button in the Insert Shapes group.
   d. Hover your mouse over each option in the drop-down list to view how the option merges the shapes in the slide, and then click the *Subtract* option. (This merges the shapes into one shape.)

3. Apply formatting to the shape and type text in the shape by completing the following steps:
   a. Click the Shape Fill button arrow in the Shape Styles group and then click the *White, Text 1* option (second column, first row in the *Theme Colors* section).
   b. Click the Text Fill button arrow in the WordArt Styles group and then click the *Black, Background 1* option (first column, first row in the *Theme Colors* section).
   c. Type the following in the shape pressing the Enter key to end each line as shown:

International Energy
Consortium
Global Summit
March 7 to 9, 2018
Paris, France

   d. Select the text you just typed and then change the font size to 20 points.
4. Save **4-AddisonReport.pptx**.

Check Your Work

Grouping and Ungrouping Objects

Tutorial

Grouping and Ungrouping Objects

Quick Steps

Group Objects
1. Select objects.
2. Click Drawing Tools Format tab.
3. Click Group button.
4. Click *Group*.

 Group

Hint Group objects so you can move, size, flip, or rotate objects at the same time.

To apply the same formatting or make the same adjustments to the size or rotation of objects, group the objects. When objects are grouped, any formatting applied such as a shape fill, effect, or shape style, is applied to each object within the group. To group objects, select the objects to be included in the group by clicking each object while holding down the Shift key or, using the mouse, click and drag a border around all the objects. With the objects selected, click the Drawing Tools Format tab, click the Group button in the Arrange group, and then click *Group* at the drop-down list.

An individual object within a group can be formatted. To do this, click any object in the group and the group border displays around the objects. Click the individual object and then apply the desired formatting. To ungroup objects, click the group to select it, click the Drawing Tools Format tab, click the Group button in the Arrange group, and then click *Ungroup* at the drop-down list.

1. With **4-AddisonReport.pptx** open, make Slide 3 active.
2. Group the objects and apply formatting by completing the following steps:
   a. Using the mouse, click and drag a border around the two text boxes in the slide to select them.
   b. Click the Drawing Tools Format tab.
   c. Click the Group button in the Arrange group and then click *Group* at the drop-down list.

   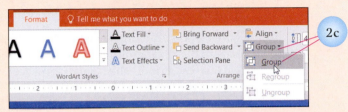

   d. Click the More Shape Styles button in the Shape Styles group and then click the *Subtle Effect - Blue, Accent 1* option (second column, fourth row).
   e. Click the Shape Outline button arrow and then click the *Dark Blue* color (ninth color in the *Standard Colors* section).
   f. Click the Shape Outline button arrow, point to *Weight*, and then click *4½ pt*.
3. With the text boxes selected, ungroup the text boxes by clicking the Group button in the Arrange group and then clicking *Ungroup* at the drop-down list.
4. Click the text box containing the columns of text, click the More WordArt Styles button in the WordArt Styles group, and then click the *Fill - White, Text 1, Outline - Background 1, Hard Shadow - Background 1* option (first column, third row).
5. Make Slide 1 active, click the text box containing the text *2018*, click the Quick Styles button in the Drawing group on the Home tab, and then click the *Subtle Effect - Blue, Accent 1* option (second column, fourth row).
6. Save **4-AddisonReport.pptx**.

Check Your Work

Inserting an Image

Tutorial

Inserting, Sizing, and Moving an Image

 Pictures

Insert an image such as a picture or clip art in a slide using the buttons in the Images group on the Insert tab. To insert an image in a presentation, click the Insert tab and then click the Pictures button in the Images group. At the Insert Picture dialog box, navigate to the folder containing the image and then double-click the image. Use buttons on the Picture Tools Format tab to format and customize the image.

Customizing and Formatting an Image

Tutorial

Formatting an Image

Ǫuick Steps

Insert an Image
1. Click Insert tab.
2. Click Pictures button.
3. Navigate to folder.
4. Double-click image.

When an image that has been inserted in a slide is selected, the Picture Tools Format tab becomes active, as shown in Figure 4.7. Use buttons on this tab to apply formatting to the image. Use options in the Adjust group on the Picture Tools Format tab to crop or remove unwanted portions of the image, correct the brightness and contrast, change the image color, apply artistic effects, compress the size of the image file, change to a different image, and reset the image back to its original formatting.

Use buttons in the Picture Styles group to apply a predesigned style to the image, change the image border, or apply other effects to the image. The Arrange group contains options for positioning the image, specifying how text will wrap around it, aligning the image with other elements in the document, and rotating the image. Use options in the Size group to crop the image and change the image size.

Figure 4.7 Picture Tools Format Tab

Sizing, Cropping, and Moving an Image

Change the size of an image with the *Shape Height* and *Shape Width* measurement boxes in the Size group on the Picture Tools Format tab or with the sizing handles that display around the selected image. To change the size with a sizing handle, position the mouse pointer on a sizing handle until the pointer turns into a double-headed arrow and then click and hold down the left mouse button. Drag the sizing handle in or out to decrease or increase the size of the image and then release the mouse button. Use the middle sizing handles at the left or right side of the image to make the image wider or thinner. Use the middle sizing handles at the top or bottom of the image to make the image taller or shorter. Use the sizing handles at the corners of the image to change both the width and height at the same time.

 Crop

Hint Insert a picture from your camera by downloading the picture to your computer and then copying or inserting the picture into PowerPoint.

The Size group on the Picture Tools Format tab contains a Crop button. Use this button to remove portions of an image. Click the Crop button and the mouse pointer displays with the crop tool attached, which is a black square with overlapping lines, and the image displays with cropping handles around the border. Drag a cropping handle to remove a portion of the image.

Move a selected image by dragging it to the new location. Move the image by positioning the mouse pointer on the image border until the arrow pointer turns into a four-headed arrow. Click and hold down the left mouse button, drag the image to the new position, and then release the mouse button. The arrow keys on the keyboard can be used to move the image in the desired direction. To move the image in small increments (called *nudging*), press and hold down the Ctrl key while pressing an arrow key.

Use the rotation handle to rotate an image by positioning the mouse pointer on the white, round rotation handle until the pointer displays as a circular arrow. Click and hold down the left mouse button, drag in the desired direction, and then release the mouse button.

Arranging Images

 Bring Forward

 Send Backward

Use the Bring Forward and Send Backward buttons in the Arrange group on the Drawing Tools Format tab or the Picture Tools Format tab to layer one object on top of another. Click the Bring Forward button and the selected object is moved forward one layer. For example, if three objects are layered on top of each other, select the object at the bottom of the layers and then click the Bring Forward button to move the object in front of the second object (but not the first object). To move an object to the top layer, select the object, click the Bring Forward button arrow, and then click the *Bring to Front* option at the drop-down list. To move the selected object back one layer, click the Send Backward button. To move the selected object behind all other objects, click the Send Backward button arrow and then click the *Send to Back* option at the drop-down list.

1. With **4-AddisonReport.pptx** open, make Slide 4 active and click the Insert tab.
2. Insert a new slide by clicking the New Slide button arrow in the Slides group and then clicking *Blank* at the drop-down list.
3. Insert a text box by completing the following steps:
   a. Click the Text Box button in the Text group on the Insert tab.
   b. Click in the middle of the slide.
   c. Change the font to Arial Black and the font size to 36 points.
   d. Click the Center button in the Paragraph group.
   e. Type Alternative, press the Enter key, and then type Energy Resources.
   f. With the text box selected, click the Drawing Tools Format tab.
   g. Click the Align button in the Arrange group and then click *Distribute Horizontally* at the drop-down list.
   h. Click the Align button and then click *Distribute Vertically* at the drop-down list.

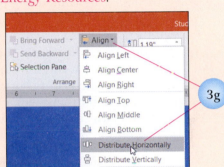

4. Insert an image by completing the following steps:
   a. Click the Insert tab.
   b. Click the Pictures button in the Images group.
   c. At the Insert Picture dialog box, navigate to the PC4 folder on your storage medium and then double-click **Mountain.jpg**.
5. You decide to insert an image of the ocean rather than a mountain. Change the image by completing the following steps:
   a. With the image of the mountain selected, click the Change Picture button in the Adjust group.
   b. At the Insert Pictures window, click the Browse button at the right of the *From a file* option.
   c. At the Insert Picture dialog box, make sure the PC4 folder on your storage medium is selected and then double-click **Ocean.jpg**.

6. Crop the image by completing the following steps:
   a. With the image selected, click the Crop button in the Size group on the Picture Tools Format tab.
   b. Position the mouse pointer (displays with the crop tool attached) on the cropping handle in the middle of the right side of the image.
   c. Click and hold down the left mouse button and then drag to the left approximately 0.25 inch. (Use the guideline on the horizontal ruler to crop the image 0.25 inch.)
   d. Click the Crop button to turn off cropping.

e. Click the Crop button arrow, point to the *Crop to Shape* option at the drop-down list, and then click the *Oval* shape (first option) in the *Basic Shapes* section of the side menu.

7. Click in the *Shape Height* measurement box in the Size group, type 5, and then press the Enter key.

8. Click the Send Backward button in the Arrange group. (This moves the image behind the text in the text box.)

9. Align the image by completing the following steps:

   a. Click the Align button in the Arrange group on the Picture Tools Format tab and then click the *Distribute Horizontally* option.

   b. Click the Align button and then click the *Distribute Vertically* option.

10. Format the image by completing the following steps:

   a. Click the Artistic Effects button in the Adjust group and then click the *Cutout* option (first column, bottom row).

   b. Click the Corrections button in the Adjust group and then click the *Soften: 25%* option (second option in the *Sharpen/Soften* section).

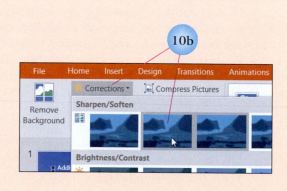

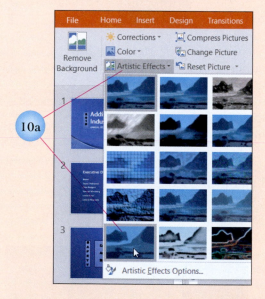

c. Click the Picture Border button arrow in the Picture Styles group and then click the *Dark Blue* color (ninth option in the *Standard Colors* section).

11. After viewing the effects applied to the image, reset the image to the original formatting by clicking the Reset Picture button arrow in the Adjust group and then clicking *Reset Picture* at the drop-down list.

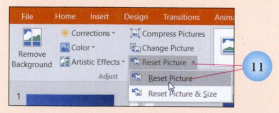

12. Format the image by completing the following steps:
   a. Click the Corrections button in the Adjust group and then click the *Brightness: -20% Contrast: +40%* option (second column, last row in the *Brightness/Contrast* section).
   b. Click the Corrections button and then click the *Sharpen: 25%* option (fourth option in the *Sharpen/Soften* section).
   c. Click the More Picture Styles button in the Picture Styles group and then click the *Soft Edge Oval* option at the drop-down gallery (sixth column, third row).

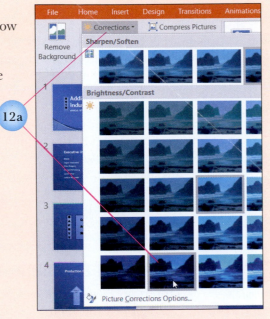

   d. Click the Compress Pictures button in the Adjust group. At the Compress Pictures dialog box, click OK.
13. Make Slide 6 active and then insert a new slide by clicking the Home tab, clicking the New Slide button arrow in the Slides group, and then clicking *Title Only* at the drop-down list.
14. Click in the title placeholder and then type Shipping Contracts.
15. Insert an image by completing the following steps:
   a. Click the Insert tab and then click the Pictures button in the Images group.
   b. At the Insert Picture dialog box, make sure the PC4 folder on your storage medium is active and then double-click **Ship.jpg**.
16. With the image selected, remove some of the background by completing the following steps:
   a. Click the Remove Background button in the Adjust group on the Picture Tools Format tab.
   b. Using the left middle sizing handle, drag the border to the left to include the back of the ship (see image at the right).
   c. Click the Mark Areas to Remove button in the Refine group on the Background Removal tab.
   d. Click anywhere in the water below the ship. (This removes the water from the image. If all of the water is not removed, you will need to click again in the remaining water.)
   e. Using the right middle sizing handle, drag the border to the left so the border is near the front of the ship.
   f. If part of the structure above the front of the ship has been removed, include it in the image. To begin, click the Mark Areas to Keep button in the Refine group. (The mouse pointer displays as a pencil.)

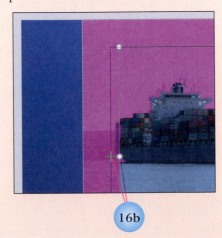

g. Using the mouse, position the pencil at the top of the structure (as shown at the right), drag down to the top of the containers on the ship, and then release the mouse button.

h. Click the Keep Changes button in the Close group on the Background Removal tab.

17. Click the Corrections button in the Adjust group on the Picture Tools Format tab and then click the *Brightness: +40% Contrast: +40%* option at the drop-down gallery (last column, last row in the *Brightness/Contrast* section).

18. Click the Corrections button in the Adjust group and then click the *Sharpen: 50%* option at the drop-down gallery (last option in the *Sharpen/Soften* section).

19. Drag the image down to the middle of the slide.

20. Click outside the image to deselect it.

21. Save **4-AddisonReport.pptx**.

Check Your Work

Tutorial

Inserting an Image as a Slide Background

Inserting an Image as a Slide Background

Insert an image, such as a picture or clip art, as a slide background by clicking the Design tab and then clicking the Format Background button in the Customize group. This displays the Format Background task pane with the Fill icon selected. Click the *Picture or texture fill* option in the *Fill* section of the task pane and then click the File button. At the Insert Picture dialog box, navigate to the desired folder and then double-click the image. To display the image background on all slides, click the Apply to All button at the Format Background task pane.

Use options in the Format Background task pane to apply formatting to the background image. When an image is inserted in a slide, the Format Background task pane (with the Fill icon selected) includes options for hiding background graphics, applying a texture, changing the image transparency, and offsetting the image on the slide either at the left, right, top, or bottom. Click the Effects icon and then click the Artistic Effects button and a drop-down palette of artistic options displays. Click the Picture icon and options display in the task pane for correcting the sharpness, softness, brightness, and contrast of the image and for changing the color saturation and tone of the image.

Quick Steps

Insert an Image as a Slide Background
1. Click Design tab.
2. Click Format Background button.
3. Click *Picture or texture fill* option.
4. Click File button.
5. Navigate to folder.
6. Double-click image.
7. Click Close button.

Project 1h Inserting an Image as a Slide Background

Part 8 of 14

1. With **4-AddisonReport.pptx** open, make sure both Slide 7 and the Home tab are active.

2. Click the New Slide button arrow in the Slides group and then click the *Title Only* layout at the drop-down list.

3. Insert an image background on Slide 8 by completing the following steps:
   a. Click the Design tab.
   b. Click the Format Background button in the Customize group.

c. At the Format Background task pane, click the *Picture or texture fill* option in the *Fill* section to select it.

d. Click the File button in the task pane below the text *Insert picture from*.

e. At the Insert Picture dialog box, navigate to the PC4 folder on your storage medium and then double-click **EiffelTower.jpg**.

4. Apply formatting to the image background by completing these steps:

a. Click the *Hide background graphics* check box to insert a check mark.

b. Select the current percentage in the *Transparency* measurement box, type 5, and then press the Enter key.

c. Select the current number in the *Offset top* measurement box, type -50, and then press the Enter key. (Decreasing the negative number displays more of the top of the Eiffel Tower.)

d. Click the Effects icon in the task pane and then, if necessary, click *Articist Effects* to display the formatting options.

e. Click the Artistic Effects button and then click the *Glow Diffused* option (fourth column, second row).

f. Click the Picture icon and, if necessary, expand the *Picture Corrections* section.

g. Select the current number in the *Contrast* measurement box, type 25, and then press the Enter key.

h. If necessary, expand the *Picture Color* section.

i. Select the current number in the *Saturation* measurement box, type 80, and then press the Enter key.

5. Remove the artistic effect by clicking the Effects icon, clicking the Artistic Effects button, and then clicking the *None* option (first option).

6. Close the Format Background task pane.

7. Click in the title placeholder, type European, press the Enter key, and then type Division 2020. Drag the placeholder so it is positioned attractively on the slide in the upper left corner.

8. Save **4-AddisonReport.pptx**.

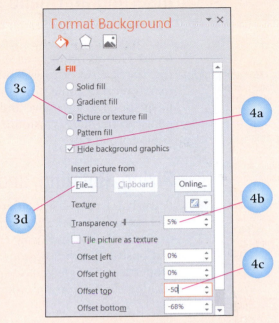

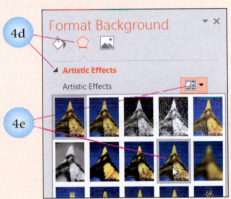

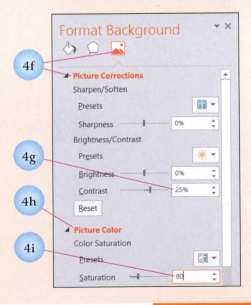

Check Your Work

Inserting an Online Image

Use the Bing Image Search feature to search for images online. To use this feature, click the Insert tab and then click the Online Pictures button. This displays the Insert Pictures window as shown in Figure 4.8. Click in the search text box, type the search term or topic, and then press the Enter key. Images that match the search term or topic display in the window. To insert an image, double-click the image or click the image and then click the Insert button. This downloads the image to the slide. Customize the image with options and buttons on the Picture Tools Format tab.

Sizing, Rotating, and Positioning Objects

PowerPoint provides a variety of methods for sizing and positioning an object such as a shape, text box, or image on a slide. In addition to using sizing handles to size an image and using the mouse to drag an image, an object can be sized and positioned with options at the Format Picture task pane with the Size & Properties icon selected. Display this task pane by selecting an object and then clicking the Size group task pane launcher on the Picture Tools Format tab.

Figure 4.8 Insert Pictures Window

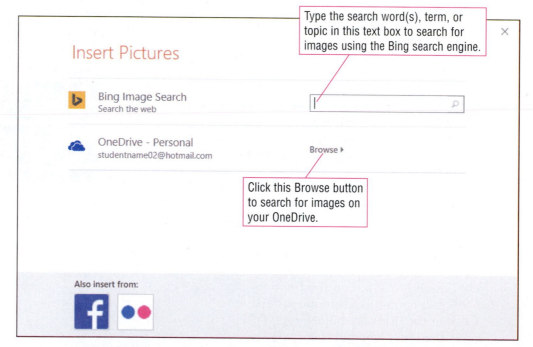

1. With **4-AddisonReport.pptx** open, make Slide 4 active.
2. Click the New Slide button arrow in the Slides group on the Home tab and then click the *Two Content* layout at the drop-down list.
3. Click in the title placeholder and then type Technology.
4. Click in the content placeholder at the right side of the slide.
5. Click the Bullets button in the Paragraph group to turn off bullets.
6. Change the font size to 24 points and turn on bold formatting.
7. Type Equipment and then press the Enter key two times.
8. Type Software and then press the Enter key two times.
9. Type Personnel.
10. Insert an image by completing the following steps:
    a. Click the Online Pictures button in the middle of the placeholder at the left side of the slide.
    b. At the Insert Pictures window, type computer in the search text box and then press the Enter key.
    c. Double-click the image in the window as shown below. If this image is not available online, click the Pictures button on the Insert tab. At the Insert Picture dialog box, navigate to the PC4 folder and then double-click *Computer.png*.

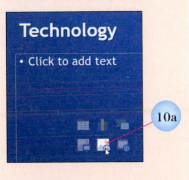

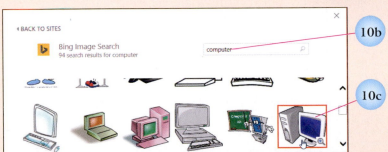

11. Scale, rotate, and position the computer image by completing the following steps:
    a. With the image selected, click the Rotate button in the Arrange group on the Picture Tools Format tab and then click *Flip Horizontal* at the drop-down list.
    b. Click the Size group task pane launcher.

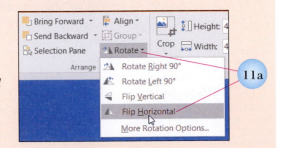

c. At the Format Picture task pane with the Size & Properties icon selected, if necessary, click *Size* to expand the options.

d. Select *0°* in the *Rotation* measurement box and then type -10.

e. Select the current percentage in the *Scale Height* measurement box and then type 50.

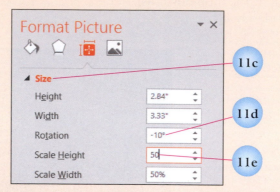

f. If necessary, click *Position* to expand the options.

g. Select the current measurement in the *Horizontal position* measurement box and then type 2.9.

h. Select the current measurement in the *Vertical position* measurement box, type 2.2, and then press the Enter key.

i. Close the Format Picture task pane.

12. Save **4-AddisonReport.pptx**.

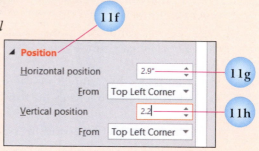

Check Your Work

Copying Objects within and between Presentations

💡**Hint** An object pasted to a different slide is positioned in the same location as the copied object.

Objects can be copied within a presentation and also between presentations. To copy an object, select the object and then click the Copy button in the Clipboard group on the Home tab. Make the slide in which the object is to be pasted active or open another presentation and then click the Paste button in the Clipboard group. Another method for copying an object is to right-click the object and then click *Copy* at the shortcut menu. To paste the object, make the slide in which the object is to be pasted active, click the right mouse button, and then click *Paste* at the shortcut menu.

Project 1j Copying an Object within and between Presentations   **Part 10 of 14**

1. With **4-AddisonReport.pptx** open, make Slide 1 active.
2. Open **Addison.pptx**.
3. Click the image in Slide 1, click the Copy button in the Clipboard group, and then close **Addison.pptx**.
4. With **4-AddisonReport.pptx** open, click the Paste button. (This inserts the image in Slide 1.)
5. With the image selected, make Slide 2 active and then click the Paste button.

6. Decrease the size and position of the image by completing the following steps:
   a. Click the Picture Tools Format tab.
   b. Click in the *Shape Height* measurement box, type 0.8, and then press the Enter key.

   c. Drag the image so that it is positioned in the upper right corner of the slide.
7. Copy the image to other slides by completing the following steps:
   a. With the image selected in Slide 2, click the Home tab and then click the Copy button in the Clipboard group.
   b. Make Slide 3 active and then click the Paste button in the Clipboard group.
   c. Paste the image in Slide 5 and Slide 7.
8. Save **4-AddisonReport.pptx**.

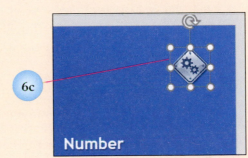

Check Your Work

Tutorial

Creating Screenshot Images

Inserting and Formatting Screenshot and Screen Clipping Images

 Screenshot

Quick Steps

Insert a Screenshot Image
1. Open presentation.
2. Open another file.
3. Display information.
4. Make presentation active.
5. Click Insert tab.
6. Click Screenshot button.
7. Click window at drop-down list.
OR
6. Click Screenshot button.
7. Click *Screen Clipping*.
8. Drag to specify capture area.

The Images group on the Insert tab contains a Screenshot button for capturing the contents or a portion of a screen as an image. This is useful for capturing information from a web page or from a file in another program. To capture the entire screen, display a web page, or open a file, make PowerPoint active, and then open a presentation. Click the Insert tab, click the Screenshot button, and then click the specific screen thumbnail at the drop-down list. The currently active presentation does not display as a thumbnail at the drop-down list. Instead, any other open file or program displays. If no other file or program is open, the Windows desktop displays. Click a thumbnail at the drop-down list and a screenshot of the screen is inserted as an image in the active slide in the open presentation, the image is selected, and the Picture Tools Format tab is active. Use options and buttons on this tab to customize the screenshot image.

In addition to making a screenshot of an entire screen, make a screenshot of a specific portion of the screen by clicking the *Screen Clipping* option at the Screenshot button drop-down list. Click this option and the open web page, file, or Windows desktop displays in a dimmed manner and the mouse pointer displays as crosshairs. Using the mouse, draw a border around a specific area of the screen. The identified area is inserted in the active slide in the presentation as an image, the image is selected, and the Picture Tools Format tab is active.

1. With **4-AddisonReport.pptx** open, make sure that no other programs are open.
2. Make Slide 9 active and then insert a new slide by clicking the New Slide button arrow in the Slides group on the Home tab and then clicking the *Title Only* layout.
3. Click in the title placeholder and then type Draft Invitation.
4. Open Word and then open the document named **AddIndInvite.docx** from the PC4 folder on your storage medium.
5. Make sure the entire invitation displays in the Word window. If necessary, decrease the size of the invitation using the Zoom Out button on the Status bar.
6. Click the PowerPoint button on the taskbar.
7. Insert a screenshot of the draft invitation in the Word document by completing the following steps:
   a. Click the Insert tab.
   b. Click the Screenshot button in the Images group and then click *Screen Clipping* at the drop-down list.
   c. When the invitation displays in a dimmed manner, position the mouse crosshairs in the upper left corner of the invitation, click and hold down the left mouse button, drag down to the lower right corner of the invitation, and then release the mouse button.

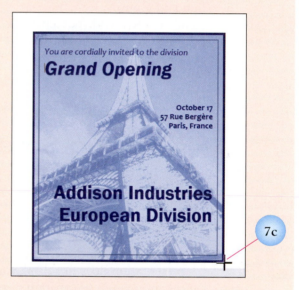

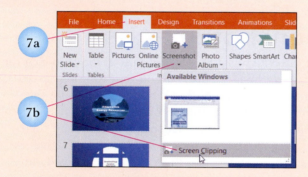

8. With the screenshot image inserted in the slide in the presentation, make the following changes:
   a. Click in the *Shape Width* measurement box in the Size group on the Picture Tools Format tab, type 4.5, and then press the Enter key.
   b. Click the Corrections button in the Adjust group and then click the *Sharpen: 25%* option (fourth option in the *Sharpen/Soften* section).
   c. Using the mouse, drag the screenshot image so it is centered on the slide.

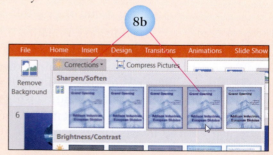

9. Click outside the screenshot image to deselect it.
10. Save **4-AddisonReport.pptx**.
11. Click the Word button, close **AddIndInvite.docx**, and then close Word.

Check Your Work

Creating and Formatting WordArt Text

Use the WordArt feature to insert preformatted, decorative text in a slide and to modify text to conform to a variety of shapes. Consider using WordArt to create a company logo, letterhead, flyer title, or heading. Insert WordArt in a slide by clicking the Insert tab and then clicking the WordArt button in the Text group. This displays the WordArt drop-down list as shown in Figure 4.10. Click a WordArt style at the drop-down list and a text box is inserted in the slide containing the text *Your Text Here*. Type the WordArt text and then use the options and buttons on the Drawing Tools Format tab to customize the WordArt text.

Apply predesigned formatting to WordArt text with a WordArt style. Customize the text with the Text Fill, Text Outline, and Text Effects buttons in the WordArt Styles group. Use the Text Fill button to change the fill color; the Text Outline button to change the text outline color, width, and style; and the Text Effects button to apply a variety of text effects and shapes.

Click the Text Effects button and then point to *Transform* and a side menu displays with shaping and warping options as shown in Figure 4.11. Use these options to conform the WordArt text to a specific shape.

Figure 4.10 WordArt Drop-down List

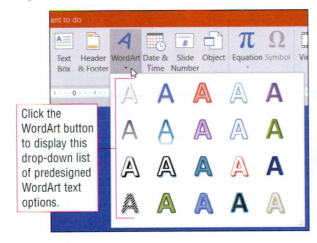

Click the WordArt button to display this drop-down list of predesigned WordArt text options.

Figure 4.11 Text Effects *Transform* Side Menu

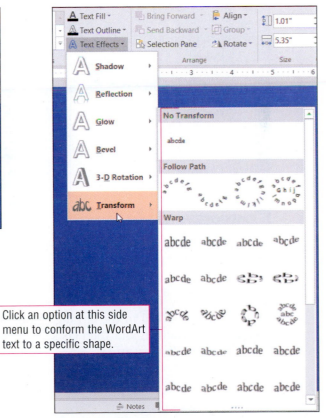

Click an option at this side menu to conform the WordArt text to a specific shape.

1. With **4-AddisonReport.pptx** open, make sure Slide 10 and the Home tab are active.
2. Click the New Slide button arrow in the Slides group and then click the *Blank* layout.
3. Click the Insert tab.
4. Click the WordArt button in the Text group and then click the *Fill - White, Text 1, Outline - Background 1, Hard Shadow - Accent 1* option (second column, third row).

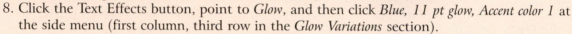
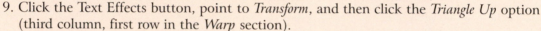

5. Type Addison Industries, press the Enter key, and then type 2018.
6. Click the WordArt text border to change the border from a dashed line to a solid line. (This selects the text box.)
7. Click the Text Outline button arrow in the WordArt Styles group and then click the *Dark Blue* color (ninth option in the *Standard Colors* section).
8. Click the Text Effects button, point to *Glow*, and then click *Blue, 11 pt glow, Accent color 1* at the side menu (first column, third row in the *Glow Variations* section).
9. Click the Text Effects button, point to *Transform*, and then click the *Triangle Up* option (third column, first row in the *Warp* section).

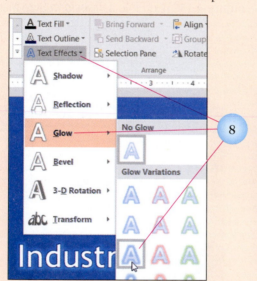
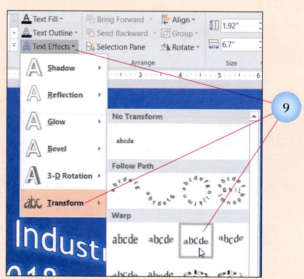

10. Click in the *Shape Height* measurement box, type 5, and then press the Enter key.
11. Click in the *Shape Width* measurement box, type 10, and then press the Enter key.
12. Click the Align button in the Arrange group and then click *Distribute Horizontally*.
13. Click the Align button and then click *Distribute Vertically*.
14. Save **4-AddisonReport.pptx**.

Check Your Work

Inserting Symbols

Inserting Symbols

 Symbol

Insert symbols in a slide using options at the Symbol dialog box. Display this dialog box by clicking the Symbol button in the Symbols group on the Insert tab. At the Symbol dialog box, choose a symbol font with the *Font* option in the dialog box, click a symbol in the list box, click the Insert button, and then click the Close button. The symbol is inserted in the slide at the location of the insertion point.

Project 1m Inserting Symbols in a Presentation   **Part 13 of 14**

1. With **4-AddisonReport.pptx** open, insert a symbol by completing the following steps:
   a. Make Slide 2 active.
   b. Click in the text box containing the names, titles, and telephone numbers.
   c. Delete the *n* in *Pena* (the last name of the fourth person).
   d. Click the Insert tab and then click the Symbol button in the Symbols group.
   e. At the Symbol dialog box, click the *Font* option box arrow, scroll down the drop-down list to the *Trebuchet MS* option, and then click that option.
   f. Scroll down the symbol list box and then click the ñ symbol (in approximately the twelfth row).
   g. Click the Insert button and then click the Close button.
2. Save **4-AddisonReport.pptx**.

Check Your Work

Inserting Headers and Footers

Inserting Headers and Footers

 Header & Footer

 Date & Time

Slide Number

If a presentation is printed as a handout or an outline, PowerPoint automatically prints the current date in the upper right corner of the page and the page number in the lower right corner. Print the presentation as notes pages and PowerPoint automatically prints the page number on individual slides. The date and page numbers are considered header and footer elements. These existing header and footer elements can be modified or additional elements can be inserted using options in the Header and Footer dialog box. Display the Header and Footer dialog box shown in Figure 4.12 by clicking the Header & Footer button in the Text group on the Insert tab, clicking the Date & Time button in the Text group, or clicking the Slide Number button in the Text group. Another method for displaying the Header and Footer dialog box is to display the Print backstage area and then click the Edit Header & Footer hyperlink below the galleries in the *Settings* category.

The Header and Footer dialog box has two tabs, the Slide tab and the Notes and Handouts tab, and the options in the dialog box are similar with either tab selected. Use options in the dialog box to insert the date and time, a header, a footer, and page numbers. Insert the date and time in a presentation and then choose the *Update automatically* option to update the date and time when the presentation is opened. Choose the date and time formatting by clicking the *Update automatically* option box arrow and then clicking the desired formatting at the drop-down list. Choose the *Fixed* option and then type the desired date and/or time in the *Fixed* text box. Type header text in the *Header* text box and type footer text in the *Footer* text box.

To print the slide number on slides, insert a check mark in the *Slide number* check box in the Header and Footer dialog box with the Slide tab selected. To include page numbers on handouts, notes pages, or outline pages, insert a check mark in the *Page number* check box in the Header and Footer dialog box with the Notes and Handouts tab selected. Apply changes to all slides or all handouts, notes pages, and outline pages, by clicking the Apply to All button in the lower right corner of the dialog box.

Figure 4.12 Header and Footer Dialog Box with the Notes and Handouts Tab Selected

Insert a check mark in this check box to insert the date and/or time.

To update the time when a presentation is opened, click *Update automatically* and then choose the formatting at the option box drop-down list.

Text typed in the *Header* text box or *Footer* text box will print when the presentation is printed as notes pages, handouts, or an outline.

Project 1n Inserting Headers and Footers

1. With **4-AddisonReport.pptx** open, insert slide numbers on each slide in the presentation by completing the following steps:
   a. Make Slide 1 active.
   b. Click the Insert tab.
   c. Click the Slide Number button in the Text group.
   d. At the Header and Footer dialog box with the Slide tab selected, click the *Slide number* check box to insert a check mark.
   e. Click the Apply to All button.
   f. Scroll through the slides to view the slide number in the lower right corner of each slide, except for the first slide.

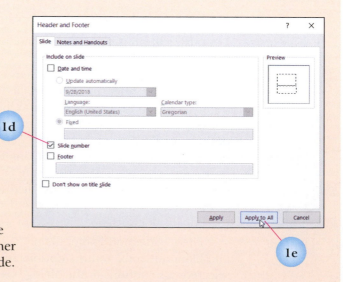

2. Insert your name as a footer on each slide (except the first slide) in the presentation by completing the following steps:
   a. Click the Header & Footer button in the Text group.
   b. Click the *Footer* check box to insert a check mark, click in the *Footer* text box, and then type your first and last names.
   c. Make sure a check mark displays in the *Slide number* check box.
   d. Click the Apply to All button.
   e. Run the slide show to confirm that your name displays at the bottom left side of each slide (except the first slide).

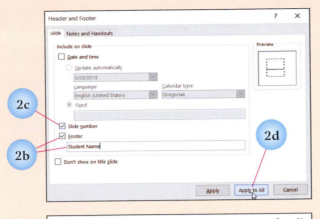

3. You decide that you also want your name to print as a footer on handouts pages. To do this, complete the following steps:
   a. Click the Header & Footer button in the Text group.
   b. At the Header and Footer dialog box, click the Notes and Handouts tab.
   c. Click the *Footer* check box to insert a check mark, click in the *Footer* text box, and then type your first and last names.
   d. Click the Apply to All button.

4. Insert the current date as a header that prints on handouts pages by completing the following steps:
   a. Click the Date & Time button in the Text group.
   b. At the Header and Footer dialog box, click the Notes and Handouts tab.
   c. Click the *Date and time* check box to insert a check mark.
   d. Click the Apply to All button.

5. Insert the presentation name as a header that prints on handouts pages by completing the following steps:
   a. Click the File tab and then click the *Print* option.
   b. At the Print backstage area, click the Edit Header & Footer hyperlink below the galleries in the *Settings* category.

c. At the Header and Footer dialog box, click the Notes and Handouts tab.
d. Click the *Header* check box to insert a check mark, click in the *Header* text box, and then type 4-AddisonReport.pptx.
e. Click the Apply to All button.
f. Click the second gallery in the *Settings* category and then click *6 Slides Horizontal* at the drop-down list. (If a number apears in the *Slides* text box, delete the number.)
g. Display the next handout page by clicking the Next Page button at the bottom of the Print backstage area.
h. Click the Previous page button to display the first handout page.

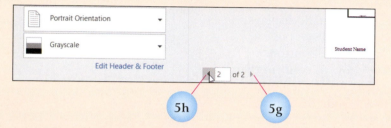

i. Click the Print button to print the presentation as a handout with six slides displayed horizontally per page.
6. Save and then close **4-AddisonReport.pptx**.

Check Your Work

Chapter Summary

- Insert a text box in a slide using the Text Box button in the Text group on the Insert tab. Format a text box with options in the Drawing group on the Home tab, with options on the Drawing Tools Format tab, with options at the shortcut menu, or with options at the Format Shape task pane.

- Select all objects in a slide by clicking the Select button in the Editing group on the Home tab and then clicking *Select All* or by using the keyboard shortcut, Ctrl + A.

- Align selected objects using options from the Align button in the Arrange group on the Drawing Tools Format tab.

- Set tabs in a text box by clicking the Alignment button at the left side of the horizontal ruler until the desired tab alignment symbol displays and then clicking a location on the ruler. Set left, center, right, and/or decimal tabs.

- Insert a shape in a slide by clicking a shape in the Drawing group on the Home tab and then clicking or clicking and dragging in the slide. Or, click the Shapes button in the Illustrations group on the Insert tab, click a shape at the drop-down list and then click or click and drag in the slide.

- Use options in the Shapes button drop-down list to draw a line, basic shapes, block arrows, flow chart symbols, callouts, stars, and banners.

- Copy a shape by selecting the shape, clicking the Copy button in the Clipboard group, positioning the insertion point in the new position, and then clicking the Paste button in the Clipboard group. A shape can also be copied by holding down the Ctrl key and then dragging the shape to the new location.

- Turn the horizontal and vertical rulers on and off with the *Ruler* check box in the Show group on the View tab and turn gridlines on and off with the *Gridlines* check box. Turn gridlines as well as drawing guides and the snap-to-grid feature on and off with options at the Grid and Guides dialog box.

- Group objects together to apply the same formatting to all the objects in that group. To group objects, select the objects, click the Group button in the Arrange group on the Drawing Tools Format tab, and then click *Group* at the drop-down list.

- Size images with the *Shape Height* and *Shape Width* measurement boxes on the Picture Tools Format tab or with the sizing handles that display around a selected image.

- Use the Crop button in the Size group on the Picture Tools Format tab to remove portions of an image.

- Move an image by dragging it to a new location. Move an image in small increments, called *nudging*, by holding down the Ctrl key while pressing an arrow key on the keyboard.

- Specify the order in which objects are to be layered with the Bring Forward and Send Backward buttons in the Adjust group on the Drawing Tools Format tab or the Picture Tools Format tab.

- Insert an image in a slide with the Pictures button in the Images group on the Insert tab.

- Insert an image as a slide background using options at the Format Background task pane. Display this task pane by clicking the Format Background button in the Customize group on the Design tab.

- Insert an online image using the Insert Pictures window. Display this window by clicking the Online Pictures button in the Images group on the Insert tab or clicking the Online Pictures button in a layout content placeholder.

- Size objects with options at the Format Shape or Format Picture task pane with the Size & Properties icon selected.

- Use the Screenshot button in the Images group on the Insert tab to capture the contents of a screen or a portion of a screen.

- Use the WordArt feature to distort or modify text to conform to a variety of shapes. Insert WordArt with the WordArt button in the Text group on the Insert tab. Format WordArt using options and buttons on the Drawing Tools Format tab.

- Insert symbols in a slide with options at the Symbol dialog box. Display this dialog box by clicking the Symbol button in the Symbols group on the Insert tab.

- Click the Header & Footer button, the Date & Time button, or the Slide Number button in the Text group on the Insert tab to display the Header and Footer dialog box. Another method for displaying this dialog box is to click the Edit Header & Footer hyperlink at the Print backstage area.

Commands Review

FEATURE	RIBBON TAB, GROUP	BUTTON, OPTION	KEYBOARD SHORTCUT
date and time	Insert, Text		
Format Background task pane	Design, Customize		
Format Picture task pane	Picture Tools Format, Picture Styles OR Size		
Grid and Guides dialog box	View, Show		
gridlines	View, Show	*Gridlines*	Shift + F9
guides	View, Show	*Guides*	
header and footer	Insert, Text		
Insert Picture dialog box	Insert, Images		
Insert Pictures window	Insert, Images		
rulers	View, Show	*Ruler*	
screenshot	Insert, Images		
shape	Insert, Illustrations OR Home, Drawing		
slide number	Insert, Text		
Symbol dialog box	Insert, Symbols		
text box	Insert, Text		
WordArt	Insert, Text		

Workbook

Chapter study tools and assessment activities are available in the *Workbook* ebook. These resources are designed to help you further develop and demonstrate mastery of the skills learned in this chapter.

Unit assessment activities are also available in the *Workbook*. These activities are designed to help you demonstrate mastery of the skills learned in this unit.

Microsoft® PowerPoint®

Unit 2

Customizing and Enhancing Presentations

Performance Objectives

Upon successful completion of Chapter 5, you will be able to:

1 Create a table
2 Modify the design and layout of a table
3 Insert an image in a table
4 Insert an Excel spreadsheet
5 Draw a table
6 Create SmartArt graphics
7 Modify the design and layout of SmartArt
8 Convert text and WordArt to a SmartArt graphic
9 Convert a SmartArt graphic to text and shapes
10 Create and format charts
11 Modify the design and layout of charts
12 Select and format chart elements
13 Create, edit, and format a photo album

Precheck

Check your current skills to focus your study.

PowerPoint allows you to present information using different formats. Use the Tables feature to present numbers and lists in a slide in columns and rows in a manner similar to a spreadsheet. Use the SmartArt feature to present data in a more visual way by creating a SmartArt graphic. While a table does an adequate job of representing data, create a chart from data to provide a more visual representation. Use the Photo Album feature to attractively display personal or business photographs and then format the appearance of the images in the presentation.

Data Files

Before beginning chapter work, copy the PC5 folder to your storage medium and then make PC5 the active folder.

SNAP

If you are a SNAP user, launch the Precheck and Tutorials from your Assignments page.

Project 1 Create a Company Sales Conference Presentation   14 Parts

You will create a sales conference presentation for Nature's Way that includes a table, a column chart, a pie chart, and four SmartArt graphics.

Preview Finished Project

Creating a Table

Use the Tables feature to create boxes of information called *cells*. A cell is the intersection between a row and a column. A cell can contain text, characters, numbers, data, graphics, or formulas. To arrange the content of a slide in columns and rows, insert a new slide with a slide layout that includes a content placeholder. Click the Insert Table button in the content placeholder and the Insert Table dialog box displays. At the Insert Table dialog box, type the number of columns, press the Tab key, type the number of rows, and then press the Enter key or click OK. A table can also be inserted using the Table button in the Tables group on the Insert tab. Click the Table button, position the mouse pointer in the grid until the correct number for columns and rows displays above the grid, and then click the left mouse button.

When a table is inserted in a slide, the insertion point is in the cell in the upper left corner of the table. Cells in a table contain a cell designation. Columns in a table are lettered from left to right, beginning with *A*. Rows in a table are numbered from top to bottom beginning with *1*. The cell in the upper left corner of the table is cell A1. The cell to the right of A1 is B1, the cell to the right of B1 is C1, and so on.

Quick Steps

Insert a Table
1. Click Insert Table button in content placeholder.
2. Type number of columns.
3. Press Tab.
4. Type number of rows.
5. Click OK.
OR
1. Click Insert tab.
2. Click Table button.
3. Position mouse pointer in grid until correct number for columns and rows displays above grid and then click left mouse button.

Entering Text in Cells

With the insertion point positioned in a cell, type or edit text. Move the insertion point to other cells by clicking in the cell, or press the Tab key to move the insertion point to the next cell or press Shift + Tab to move the insertion point to the previous cell.

If the text typed does not fit on one line, it wraps to the next line within the same cell. Press the Enter key in a cell and the insertion point is moved to the next line within the same cell. The cell vertically lengthens to accommodate the text, and all cells in that row also lengthen. Pressing the Tab key in a table causes the insertion point to move to the next cell. To move the insertion point to a tab position within a cell, press Ctrl + Tab. If the insertion point is in the last cell of a table pressing the Tab key will add another row to the bottom of the table.

Hint Add a row to the bottom of a table by positioning the insertion point in the last cell and then pressing the Tab key.

Selecting Cells

Formatting can be applied to an entire table or to specific cells, rows, or columns in a table. To identify cells for formatting, select the specific cells using the mouse or the keyboard. Press the Tab key to select the next cell or press Shift + Tab to select the previous cell. Refer to Table 5.1 for additional methods for selecting in a table.

Table 5.1 Selecting in a Table

To select this	Do this
A cell	Position the mouse pointer at the left side of the cell until the pointer turns into a small, black, diagonally pointing arrow and then click the left mouse button.
A column	Position the mouse pointer outside the table at the top of the column until the pointer turns into a small, black, down-pointing arrow and then click the left mouse button. Drag to select multiple columns.
A row	Position the mouse pointer outside the table at the left edge of the row until the pointer turns into a small, black, right-pointing arrow and then click the left mouse button. Drag to select multiple rows.
All cells in a table	With the insertion point positioned in the table, drag to select all cells or press Ctrl + A.
Text within a cell	Position the mouse pointer at the beginning of the text, click and hold down the left mouse button, drag the mouse across the text, and then release the mouse button. (When a cell is selected, the cell background color changes to gray. When text within a cell is selected, only those lines containing text are highlighted in gray.)

Project 1a   Creating a Table   Part 1 of 14

1. Open **Conference.pptx** and then save it with the name **5-Conference**.
2. Make Slide 3 active.
3. Insert a table in the slide and enter text into the cells by completing the following steps:
   a. Click the Insert Table button in the middle of the slide in the content placeholder.
   b. At the Insert Table dialog box, select the current number in the *Number of columns* measurement box and then type 2.
   c. Press the Tab key.
   d. Type 5 in the *Number of rows* measurement box.
   e. Click OK or press the Enter key.
   f. Type the text as displayed in the table below. Press the Tab key to move the insertion point to the next cell or press Shift + Tab to move the insertion point to the previous cell. Do not press the Tab key after typing the last cell entry.

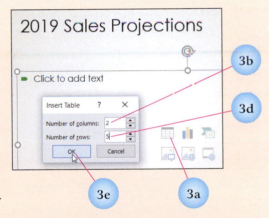

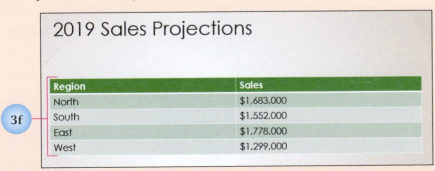

Region	Sales
North	$1,683,000
South	$1,552,000
East	$1,778,000
West	$1,299,000

4. Apply formatting to text in specific cells by completing the following steps:
   a. With the insertion point positioned in the table, press Ctrl + A to select all of the text in the table.
   b. Click the Home tab and then change the font size to 32 points.
   c. Set the text below the headings in a smaller point size by positioning the mouse pointer at the left edge of the second row (to the left of the cell containing *North*) until the pointer turns into a small, black, right-pointing arrow. Click and hold down the left mouse button, drag down so the remaining rows are selected, and then release the mouse button. Change the font size to 28 points.
   d. Click outside the table to deselect it.
5. Save **5-Conference.pptx**.

Check Your Work

Changing the Table Design

Tutorial

Changing the Table Design

 Shading

 Borders

 Effects

 Draw Table

 Eraser

When a table is inserted in a slide, the Table Tools Design tab is active. This tab contains a number of options for enhancing the appearance of the table, as shown in Figure 5.1. With options in the Table Styles group, select a predesigned style that applies color and border lines to a table. Maintain further control over the predesigned style formatting applied to columns and rows with options in the Table Style Options group. For example, to format the first column differently than the other columns in a table, insert a check mark in the *First Column* check box. Apply additional design formatting to cells in a table with the Shading, Borders, and Effects buttons in the Table Styles group and the options in the WordArt Styles group. Draw a table or draw additional rows and/or columns in a table by clicking the Draw Table button in the Draw Borders group. Click this button and the mouse pointer turns into a pencil. Drag in the table to create the columns and rows. Click the Eraser button and the mouse pointer turns into an eraser. Drag through the column and/or row lines to erase the lines.

Figure 5.1 Table Tools Design Tab

1. With **5-Conference.pptx** open, make sure Slide 3 is active, click in a cell in the table, and then click the Table Tools Design tab.

2. Click the *First Column* check box in the Table Style Options group to insert a check mark. (This applies bold formatting to the text in the first column and applies darker shading to the cells.)

3. Click the More Table Styles button in the Table Styles group and then click the *Themed Style 1 - Accent 1* option (second column, first row in the *Best Match for Document* section).

4. Select the first row of the table and then apply the following formatting options:

   a. Click the Quick Styles button in the WordArt Styles group and then click the *Fill - White, Outline - Accent 2, Hard Shadow - Accent 2* option (fourth column, third row).

   b. Click the Text Fill button arrow in the WordArt Styles group and then click the *Lime, Accent 3, Lighter 80%* option (seventh column, second row in the *Theme Colors* section).

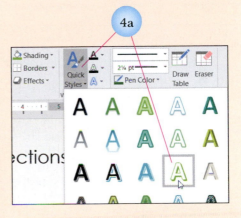

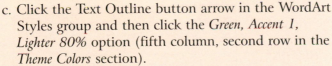

   c. Click the Text Outline button arrow in the WordArt Styles group and then click the *Green, Accent 1, Lighter 80%* option (fifth column, second row in the *Theme Colors* section).

5. Click the *Pen Weight* option box arrow in the Draw Borders group and then click the *2¼ pt* option. (This activates the Draw Table button.)

6. Click the Pen Color button in the Draw Borders group and then click the *Green, Accent 1, Darker 25%* option (fifth column, fifth row in the *Theme Colors* section).

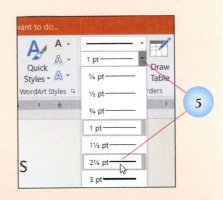

7. Draw along the border that separates the two columns from the top of the first row to the bottom of the last row.

8. Draw along the border that separates the first row from the second row.

9. Click the Draw Table button to deactivate the tool.

10. Save **5-Conference.pptx**.

Check Your Work

Tutorial

Changing the
Table Layout

Hint If you make
a mistake while
formatting a table,
immediately click the
Undo button on the
Quick Access Toolbar.

Changing the Table Layout

To further customize a table, consider changing the table layout by inserting or deleting columns or rows and specifying cell alignments. Change the table layout with options on the Table Tools Layout tab, shown in Figure 5.2. Use options and buttons on the tab to select specific cells, delete and insert rows and columns, merge and split cells, specify cell and table height and width, specify text alignment in cells, and arrange elements in a slide.

Figure 5.2 Table Tools Layout Tab

Project 1c Modifying the Table Layout

1. With **5-Conference.pptx** open, make sure Slide 3 is active.
2. Click in any cell in the table and then click the Table Tools Layout tab.
3. Click in the cell containing the word *East*.
4. Click the Insert Above button in the Rows & Columns group.
5. Type Central in the new cell at the left, press the Tab key, and then type $1,024,000 in the new cell at the right.
6. Click in the cell containing the word *Region*.
7. Click the Insert Left button in the Rows & Columns group.
8. Click the Merge Cells button in the Merge group.
9. Type Sales Projections in the new cell.
10. Click the Text Direction button in the Alignment group and then click *Rotate all text 270°* at the drop-down list.
11. Click the Center button in the Alignment group and then click the Center Vertically button in the Alignment group.
12. Click in the *Width* measurement box in the Cell Size group, type 1.2, and then press the Enter key.

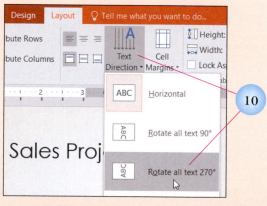

13. Click the Table Tools Design tab.
14. With the insertion point positioned in the cell containing the text *Sales Projections*, click the Borders button arrow in the Table Styles group and then click *Bottom Border* at the drop-down list.

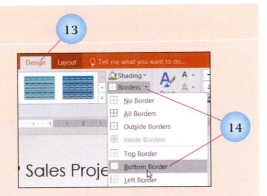

15. Click in the cell containing the text *Sales* and then click the Table Tools Layout tab.
16. Click in the *Height* measurement box in the Cell Size group and then type 0.7.
17. Click in the *Width* measurement box in the Cell Size group, type 2.5, and then press the Enter key.
18. Click in the cell containing the text *Region*.
19. Click in the *Width* measurement box in the Cell Size group, type 4, and then press the Enter key.
20. Click in the *Height* measurement box in the Table Size group, type 4.2, and then press the Enter key.

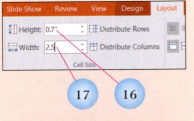

21. Click the Select button in the Table group and then click *Select Table* at the drop-down list.
22. Click the Center button and then click the Center Vertically button in the Alignment group.
23. After looking at the text in cells, you decide that you want the text in the second column left-aligned. To do this, complete the following steps:
    a. Click in the cell containing the text *Region*.
    b. Click the Select button in the Table group and then click *Select Column* at the drop-down list.
    c. Click the Align Left button in the Alignment group.
    d. Click in any cell in the table.

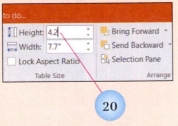

24. Align the table by completing the following steps:
    a. Click the Align button in the Arrange group on the Table Tools Layout tab and then click *Distribute Horizontally* at the drop-down list.

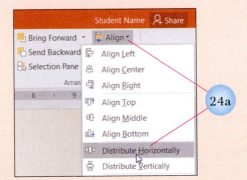

   b. Click the Align button and then click *Distribute Vertically* at the drop-down list.
   c. Looking at the table, you decide that it should be moved down in the slide. To do this, position the mouse pointer on the table border until the pointer displays with a four-headed arrow attached. Click and hold down the left mouse button, drag down approximately 0.5 inch, and then release the mouse button.

25. Insert an image in the table by completing the following steps:
    a. Click the Insert tab.
    b. Click the Pictures button in the Images group.
    c. At the Insert Picture dialog box, navigate to the PC5 folder on your storage medium and then double-click **Sales.png**.
    d. With the image selected, click the Color button on the Pictures Tools Format tab and then click the *Green Accent color 1 Dark* option (second column, second row in the *Recolor* section).
    e. Click in the *Shape Height* measurement box in the Size group, type 2.5, and then press the Enter key.
    f. Drag the image so it is positioned in the table as shown in Figure 5.3.
    g. Click outside the image to deselect it.
26. Save **5-Conference.pptx**.

Check Your Work

Figure 5.3 Project 1c, Slide 3

Inserting an Excel Spreadsheet

In addition to a table, an Excel worksheet can be inserted in a slide, which provides some Excel functions in PowerPoint. To insert an Excel worksheet, click the Insert tab, click the Table button in the Tables group, and then click the *Excel Spreadsheet* option. This inserts a small worksheet in the slide with two columns and two rows visible and the ribbon displays with Excel tabs. Increase the number of visible cells by dragging the sizing handles that display around the selected worksheet. Click outside the worksheet and the cells display as an object that can be formatted with options on the Drawing Tools Format tab. To format the worksheet with Excel options, double-click the worksheet and the Excel tabs display.

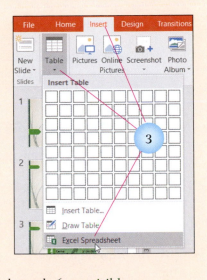

1. With **5-Conference.pptx** open, make sure Slide 3 is active and then insert a new slide with the Title Only layout.
2. Click in the title placeholder and then type Projected Increase.
3. Insert an Excel worksheet by clicking the Insert tab, clicking the Table button in the Tables group, and then clicking *Excel Spreadsheet*.
4. Increase the size of the worksheet by completing the following steps:
   a. Position the mouse pointer on the sizing handle (small black square) in the lower right corner of the worksheet until the pointer displays as a black, diagonal, two-headed arrow.
   b. Click and hold down the left mouse button; drag down and to the right and then release the mouse button. Continue dragging the small black square and releasing the mouse button until columns A, B, and C and rows 1 through 6 are visible.
5. Copy a Word table into the Excel worksheet by completing the following steps:
   a. Open Word and then open **NWSalesInc.docx** from the PC5 folder on your storage medium.
   b. Hover your mouse pointer over the table and then click the table move handle (small square containing a four-headed arrow) in the upper left corner of the table. (This selects all cells in the table.)
   c. Click the Copy button in the Clipboard group on the Home tab.
   d. Click the PowerPoint button on the taskbar.
   e. With Slide 4 and the first cell in the worksheet active, click the Paste button in the Clipboard group on the Home tab.
6. Size and position the worksheet object by completing the following steps:
   a. Click outside the worksheet to remove the Excel ribbon tabs.
   b. With the worksheet object selected, click the Drawing Tools Format tab.
   c. Click in the *Shape Width* measurement box, type 7, and then press the Enter key.
   d. Using the mouse, drag the worksheet object so it is centered on the slide.
7. Format the worksheet and insert a formula by completing the following steps:
   a. Double-click in the worksheet. (This displays the Excel ribbon tabs.)
   b. Click in cell C2, type the formula =b2*1.02, and then press the Enter key.

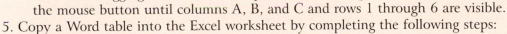

8. Copy the formula in C2 to cells C3 through C6 by completing the following steps:
   a. Position the mouse pointer (white plus symbol) in cell C2, click and hold down the left mouse button, drag down to cell C6, and then release the mouse button.
   b. Click the Fill button in the Editing group on the Home tab and then click *Down* at the drop-down list.
   c. With cells C2 through C6 selected, click the Decrease Decimal button in the Number group two times.
9. Click outside the worksheet to remove the Excel ribbon tabs.

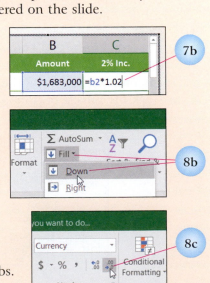

10. Make the following changes to the table:
    a. Click the Drawing Tools Format tab.
    b. Click the Align button and then click *Distribute Horizontally* at the drop-down list.
    c. Click the Align button and then click *Distribute Vertically* at the drop-down list.
11. Click the Word button on the taskbar, close the document, and then close Word.
12. Save **5-Conference.pptx**.

Check Your Work

Drawing a Table

A table can be drawn in a slide using the *Draw Table* option at the Table button drop-down list. Click the Table button and then click the *Draw Table* option and the mouse pointer displays as a pen. Drag in the slide to create the table. Use buttons on the Table Tools Design tab and Table Tools Format tab to format the table.

Project 1e Drawing a Table

1. With **5-Conference.pptx** open, make sure Slide 4 is active.
2. Draw a table and then split the table into two columns and two rows by completing the following steps:
    a. Click the Insert tab, click the Table button in the Tables group, and then click the *Draw Table* option at the drop-down list.
    b. Position the mouse pointer (displays as a pen) below the worksheet and then drag to create a table that is approximately 7 inches wide and 1 inch tall.
    c. Click the Table Tools Layout tab and then click the Split Cells button in the Merge group.
    d. At the Split Cells dialog box, press the Tab key, type 2, and then click OK. (This splits the table into two columns and two rows.)
    e. Select the current measurement in the *Height* measurement box in the Table Size group and then type 1.
    f. Select the current measurement in the *Width* measurement box in the Table Size group, type 7, and then press the Enter key.
3. With the table selected, make the following formatting changes:
    a. Click the Table Tools Design tab.
    b. Click the More Table Styles button in the Table Styles group and then click the *Themed Style 2 - Accent 1* option (second column, second row in the *Best Match for Document* section).
    c. Click the Effects button in the Table Styles group, point to *Cell Bevel*, and then click the *Relaxed Inset* option (second column, first row in the *Bevel* section).

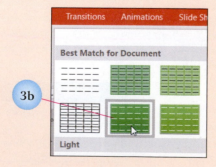

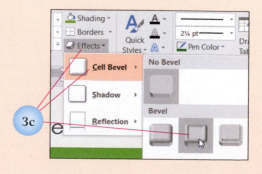

d. Click the Home tab, click the Bold button, and then click the Center button.

e. Click the Align Text button and then click *Middle* at the drop-down list.

f. Make sure the table is positioned evenly between the bottom of the top table and the bottom of the slide.

g. Click the Arrange button in the Drawing group, point to *Align*, and then click *Distribute Horizontally* at the side menu.

4. Type Maximum in the first cell in the table, press the Tab key, and then type $1,813,560.

5. Press the Tab key and then type Minimum.

6. Press the Tab key and then type $1,044,480.

7. Click outside the table to deselect it.

8. Save **5-Conference.pptx**.

Check Your Work

Tutorial

Inserting, Sizing, and Moving SmartArt

 SmartArt

Quick Steps

Insert a SmartArt Graphic

1. Click Insert a SmartArt Graphic button in content placeholder.
2. Double-click graphic.
OR
1. Click Insert tab.
2. Click SmartArt button.
3. Double-click graphic.

Creating SmartArt

Use the SmartArt feature to insert graphics such as diagrams and organizational charts in a slide. SmartArt offers a variety of predesigned graphics that are available at the Choose a SmartArt Graphic dialog box, shown in Figure 5.4. Display the Choose a SmartArt Graphic dialog box by clicking the Insert a SmartArt Graphic button in a content placeholder or by clicking the Insert tab and then clicking the SmartArt button in the Illustrations group. At the dialog box, *All* is selected in the left panel and all available predesigned graphics display in the middle panel.

Predesigned graphics display in the middle panel of the Choose a SmartArt Graphic dialog box. Use the scroll bar at the right side of the middle panel to scroll down the list of graphic choices.

Figure 5.4 Choose a SmartArt Graphic Dialog Box

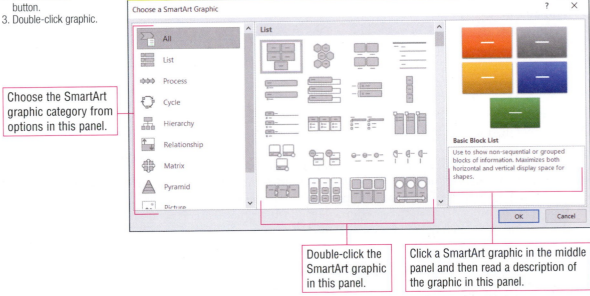

Choose the SmartArt graphic category from options in this panel.

Double-click the SmartArt graphic in this panel.

Click a SmartArt graphic in the middle panel and then read a description of the graphic in this panel.

Hint Use SmartArt to communicate your message and ideas in a visual manner.

Hint Limit the number of shapes and the amount of text in a slide to key points.

Click a graphic in the middle panel and the name of the graphic displays in the right panel along with a description of the graphic type. SmartArt includes graphics for presenting a list of data; showing data processes, cycles, and relationships; and presenting data in a matrix or pyramid. Double-click a graphic in the middle panel of the dialog box and the graphic is inserted in the slide.

When a graphic is inserted in the slide, a text pane may display at the left side of the graphic. Type text in the text pane or directly in the graphic. Apply design formatting to a graphic with options on the SmartArt Tools Design tab, shown in Figure 5.5. This tab is active when the graphic is selected in the slide. Use options and buttons on this tab to change the graphic layout, apply a style to the graphic, and reset the graphic back to the original formatting.

Figure 5.5 SmartArt Tools Design Tab

Project 1f Inserting and Modifying a SmartArt Graphic

Part 6 of 14

1. With **5-Conference.pptx** open, make sure Slide 4 is active and then insert a new slide with the Title and Content layout.
2. Click in the title placeholder and then type Division Reorganization.
3. Click the Insert a SmartArt Graphic button in the middle of the slide in the content placeholder.
4. At the Choose a SmartArt Graphic dialog box, click *Hierarchy* in the left panel of the dialog box.
5. Double-click the *Horizontal Hierarchy* option (as shown at the right).
6. If a *Type your text here* pane displays at the left side of the organizational chart, close the pane by clicking the Text Pane button in the Create Graphic group.

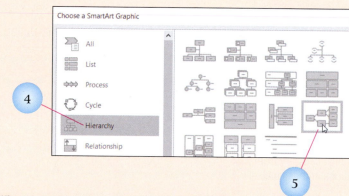

7. Delete one of the boxes in the organizational chart by clicking the border of the top box at the right side of the slide (the top box of the three stacked boxes) and then pressing the Delete key. (Make sure that the selection border that surrounds the box is a solid line and not a dashed line. If a dashed line displays, click the box border again. This should change it to a solid line.)

8. Click the *[Text]* placeholder in the first box at the left, type Andrew Singh, press Shift + Enter, and then type Director. Click in each of the remaining box placeholders and type the text as shown below. (Press Shift + Enter after each name.)

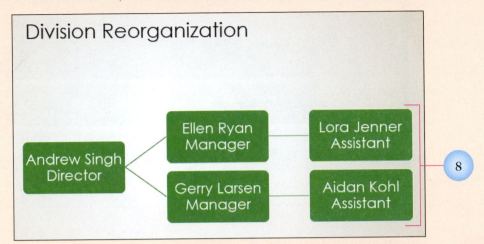

9. Click inside the SmartArt border, but outside of any shape, and then click the SmartArt Tools Design tab.
10. Click the More SmartArt Styles button in the SmartArt Styles group and then click the *Polished* option (first column, first row in the *3-D* section).

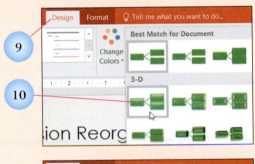

11. Click the Change Colors button in the SmartArt Styles group and then click the *Colorful Range - Accent Colors 3 to 4* option (third option in the *Colorful* section).
12. Change the layout of the organizational chart by clicking the More Layouts button in the Layouts group and then clicking *Table Hierarchy*. Your slide should now look like the slide shown in Figure 5.6.

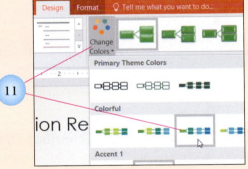

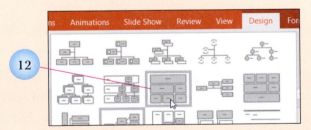

13. Save **5-Conference.pptx**.

Check Your Work

Figure 5.6 Project 1f, Slide 5

Division Reorganization

Andrew Singh
Director

Ellen Ryan
Manager

Gerry Larsen
Manager

Lora Jenner
Assistant

Aidan Kohl
Assistant

Tutorial

Formatting
SmartArt

💡 *Hint* Nudge
selected shape(s) with
the up, down, left, or
right arrow keys on the
keyboard.

Formatting SmartArt

Apply formatting to a SmartArt graphic with options on the SmartArt Tools Format tab, shown in Figure 5.7. Use options and buttons on this tab to change the size and shape of objects in the graphic; apply shape styles and WordArt styles; change the shape fill, outline, and effects; and arrange and size the graphic. Move the graphic by positioning the arrow pointer on the graphic border until the pointer turns into a four-headed arrow, clicking and holding down the left mouse button, dragging the graphic to the new location, and then releasing the mouse button.

Figure 5.7 SmartArt Tools Format Tab

Project 1g Inserting and Formatting a SmartArt Graphic

Part 7 of 14

1. With **5-Conference.pptx** open, make Slide 1 active and then insert a new slide with the Blank layout.
2. Click the Insert tab and then click the SmartArt button in the Illustrations group.
3. At the Choose a SmartArt Graphic dialog box, click *Relationship* in the left panel.
4. Double-click the *Basic Venn* option shown at the right. (You will need to scroll down the list to display this graphic.)
5. Click in the top shape and type Health.

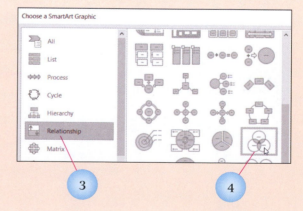

---

6. Click in the shape at the left and type Happiness.
7. Click in the shape at the right and type Harmony.
8. Click inside the SmartArt border but outside of any shape.
9. Click the Change Colors button in the SmartArt Styles group and then click the *Colorful Range - Accent Colors 3 to 4* option (third option in the *Colorful* section).
10. Click the More SmartArt Styles button in the SmartArt Styles group and then click the *Cartoon* option (third column, first row in the *3-D* section).

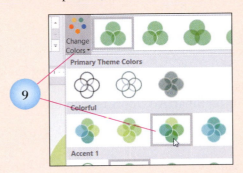

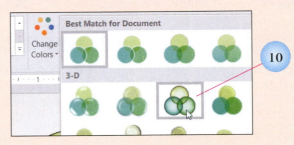

11. Click the SmartArt Tools Format tab.
12. Click the More WordArt Styles button in the WordArt Styles group and then click the *Pattern Fill - Green, Accent 1, 50%, Hard Shadow - Accent 1* option (third column, bottom row).

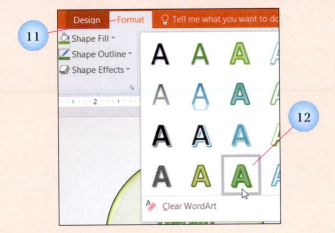

13. Click the Text Outline button arrow in the WordArt Styles group and then click the *Green, Accent 1, Darker 50%* option (fifth column, bottom row in the *Theme Colors* section).
14. Click in the *Shape Height* measurement box in the Size group and then type 6.
15. Click in the *Shape Width* measurement box in the Size group, type 9, and then press the Enter key.
16. Save **5-Conference.pptx**.

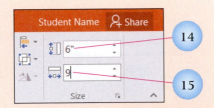

Check Your Work

Tutorial

Converting Text
and WordArt to a
SmartArt Graphic

Convert to
SmartArt
Graphic

Converting Text and WordArt to a SmartArt Graphic

To improve the visual display of text or WordArt and to create a professionally designed image, consider converting text or WordArt to a SmartArt graphic. To do this, select the placeholder containing the text or WordArt and then click the Convert to SmartArt Graphic button in the Paragraph group on the Home tab. Click the SmartArt graphic at the drop-down gallery or click the *More SmartArt Graphics* option and then choose a SmartArt graphic at the Choose a SmartArt Graphic dialog box.

Tutorial

Inserting Text in
the Text Pane

Text Pane

Inserting Text in the Text Pane

Enter text in a SmartArt shape by clicking in the shape and then typing the text or by typing text in the Text pane. Display the Text pane by clicking the Text Pane button in the Create Graphic group on the SmartArt Tools Design tab.

Project 1h Creating a SmartArt Graphic with Text and WordArt   **Part 8 of 14**

1. With **5-Conference.pptx** open, make Slide 7 active. (This slide contains WordArt text.)
2. Click anywhere in the WordArt text.
3. If necessary, click the Home tab.
4. Click the Convert to SmartArt Graphic button in the Paragraph group.
5. Click the *More SmartArt Graphics* option.
6. At the Choose a SmartArt Graphic dialog box, click *Cycle* in the left panel and then double-click *Diverging Radial* in the middle panel.

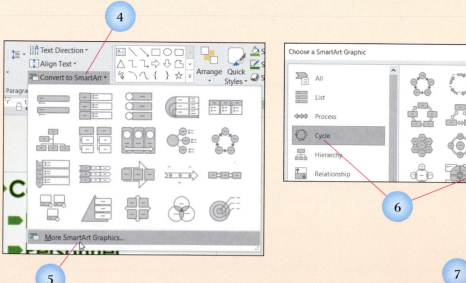

7. Click the Add Shape button in the Create Graphic group on the SmartArt Tools Design tab and then type Supplies in the new shape.
8. Change the order of the text in the shapes at the left and right sides of the graphic by clicking the Right to Left button in the Create Graphic group.

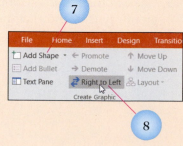

9. Click the Change Colors button in the SmartArt Styles group and then click the *Colorful - Accent Colors* option (first option in the *Colorful* section).

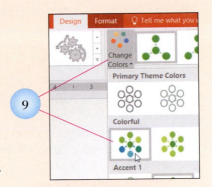

10. Click the More SmartArt Styles button in the SmartArt Styles group and then click the *Inset* option (second column, first row in the *3-D* section).
11. Click the SmartArt Tools Format tab.
12. Click the middle circle (contains the text *Central Division*).
13. Click the Larger button in the Shapes group three times.

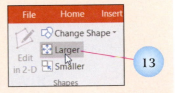

14. Click inside the SmartArt border but outside of any shape.
15. Click in the *Shape Height* measurement box in the Size group and then type 6.6.
16. Click in the *Shape Width* measurement box, type 8.2, and then press the Enter key.
17. With the SmartArt graphic selected, click the Align button in the Arrange group and then click *Distribute Horizontally*.
18. Click the Align button in the Arrange group and then click *Distribute Vertically*.
19. Click the Home tab.
20. Click the Bold button in the Font group.
21. Make Slide 9 active.
22. Click anywhere in the bulleted text and, if necessary, click the Home tab.
23. Click the Convert to SmartArt Graphic button in the Paragraph group and then click the *Vertical Block List* option (second column, first row).
24. Click the shape containing the text *Sales over $2 million* and then click the Demote button in the Create Graphic group on the SmartArt Tools Design tab.

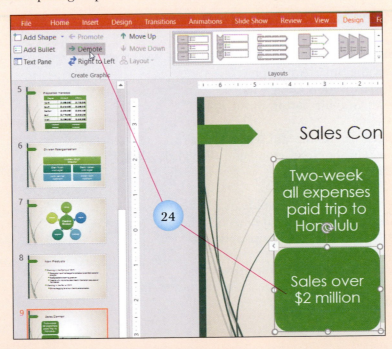

25. Click anywhere in the text *One-week all expenses paid trip to Las Vegas* and then click the Promote button in the Create Graphic group.

26. Click the Text Pane button in the Create Graphic group to display the *Type your text here* text pane.
27. Click immediately right of the *s* in *Vegas* in the text pane and then press the Enter key.
28. Press the Tab key and then type Sales over $1 million.
29. Close the text pane by clicking the Close button in the upper right corner of the pane.
30. Click the More SmartArt Styles button in the SmartArt Styles group and then click the *Inset* option (second column, first row in the *3-D* section).
31. Save **5-Conference.pptx**.
32. Print Slides 7 and 9.

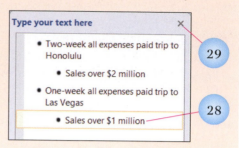

Check Your Work

Tutorial

Converting SmartArt to Text and to Shapes

 Reset Graphic

 Convert

Converting SmartArt Graphic to Text and to Shapes

To remove all formatting from a SmartArt graphic, click the Reset Graphic button in the Reset group on the SmartArt Tools Design tab. Use the Convert button to convert a SmartArt graphic to text or shapes. Click the Convert button and then click the *Convert to Text* option to convert the SmartArt graphic to bulleted text or click the *Convert to Shapes* option to convert a SmartArt graphic to shapes. Once the SmartArt graphic has been converted to shapes, those shapes can be moved, sized, or deleted independently from the other shapes.

Project 1i Converting SmartArt to Text and to Shapes   Part 9 of 14

1. With **5-Conference.pptx** open, make sure Slide 9 is active.
2. Click to select the SmartArt graphic.
3. Click the SmartArt Tools Design tab.
4. Click the Reset Graphic button in the Reset group.
5. With the SmartArt graphic still selected, click the Convert button in the Reset group and then click *Convert to Text*.
6. Make Slide 7 active.
7. Click to select the SmartArt graphic.
8. Click the SmartArt Tools Design tab, click the Convert button in the Reset group, and then click *Convert to Shapes*.
9. Select and then delete each of the arrows that points from the middle circle to each of the outer circles.
10. Save **5-Conference.pptx**.

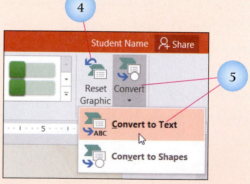

Check Your Work

Creating a Chart

A variety of charts can be created in a slide including bar and column charts, pie charts, area charts, and much more. To create a chart, click the Insert Chart button in a content placeholder or click the Insert tab and then click the Chart button in the Illustrations group. This displays the Insert Chart dialog box, as shown in Figure 5.8. At this dialog box, choose the chart type in the list at the left side, click the chart style, and then click OK. Table 5.2 describes the fifteen basic chart types that can be created.

Click OK at the Insert Chart dialog box and a sample chart is inserted in the slide and an Excel window opens with a worksheet containing sample data, as shown in Figure 5.9. Type the data in the Excel worksheet cells over the existing data. As data is typed, the chart in the slide reflects the new data. To type data in the Excel worksheet, click in the cell, type the data, and then press the Tab key to make the next cell active, press Shift + Tab to make the previous cell active, or press the Enter key to make the cell below active.

The sample worksheet contains a data range of four columns and five rows and the cells in the data range display with a light fill color. Excel uses the data in the range to create the chart in the slide. The data is not limited to four columns and five rows. Simply type data in cells outside the data range and Excel will expand the data range and incorporate the new data in the chart. This is because the table AutoExpansion feature is on by default. If data is typed in a cell outside the data range, an AutoCorrect Options button displays in the lower right corner of the cell. This button can be used to turn off AutoExpansion. If data is not entered in the four columns and five rows, decrease the size of the data range. To do this, position the mouse pointer on the small, square, blue icon in the lower right corner of cell E5 until the pointer displays as a diagonally pointing two-headed arrow and then drag up to decrease the number of rows in the range and/or drag left to decrease the number of columns.

Once all data is entered in the worksheet, click the Close button in the upper right corner of the Excel window. This closes the Excel window and displays the chart in the slide.

Quick Steps

Insert a Chart
1. Click Insert Chart button in content placeholder.
2. Click chart style and type.
3. Enter data in Excel worksheet.
4. Close Excel.
OR
1. Click Insert tab.
2. Click Chart button.
3. Click chart type and style.
4. Enter data in Excel worksheet.
5. Close Excel.

Figure 5.8 Insert Chart Dialog Box

Choose a chart style in this section.

Choose a chart type from this list.

Preview the chart in this section.

Table 5.2 Types of Charts

Type	Description
Area	Emphasizes the magnitude of change, rather than time and rate of change. It also shows the relationship of parts to a whole by displaying the sum of the plotted values.
Bar	Shows individual figures at a specific time, or shows variations between components but not in relationship to the whole.
Box & Whisker	Displays median, quartiles, and extremes of a data set on a number line to show distribution of data. Lines extending vertically are called whiskers and indicate variability outside the upper and lower quartiles.
Column	Compares separate (noncontinuous) items as they vary over time.
Combo	Combines two or more chart types to make data easier to understand.
Histogram	Condenses a data series into a visual representation by grouping data points into logical ranges called *bins*.
Line	Shows trends and changes over time at even intervals. It emphasizes the rate of change over time rather than the magnitude of change.
Pie	Shows proportions and relationships of parts to the whole.
Radar	Emphasizes differences and amounts of change over time, and variations and trends. Each category has its own value axis radiating from the center point. Lines connect all values in the same series.
Stock	Shows four values for a stock—open, high, low, and close.
Sunburst	Displays hierarchical data with each level represented by one ring with the innermost ring as the top of the hierarchy.
Surface	Shows trends in values across two dimensions in a continuous curve.
Treemap	Provides a hierarchical view of data and compares proportions within the hierarchy.
X Y (Scatter)	Either shows the relationships among numeric values in several data series or plots the interception points between *x* and *y* values. It shows uneven intervals of data and is commonly used in scientific data.
Waterfall	Determines how an initial value is affected by a series of positive and negative values.

Figure 5.9 Sample Chart

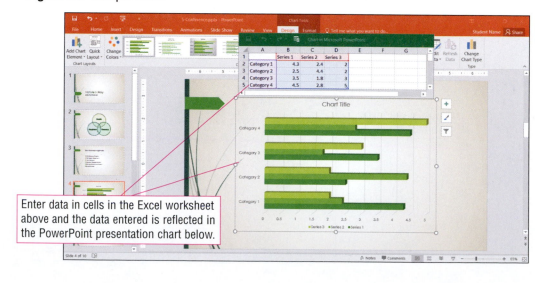

Enter data in cells in the Excel worksheet above and the data entered is reflected in the PowerPoint presentation chart below.

1. With **5-Conference.pptx** open, make Slide 3 active and then insert a new slide with the Blank layout.
2. Click the Insert tab and then click the Chart button in the Illustrations group.
3. At the Insert Chart dialog box, click *Bar* in the left panel.
4. Double-click the *3-D Clustered Bar* option at the top of the dialog box (fourth option).
5. In the Excel worksheet, position the mouse pointer in the bottom right corner of the cell D5 border until the mouse pointer displays as a diagonally pointing two-headed arrow. Click and hold down the left mouse button, drag to the left until the border displays at the right side of column C, and then release the mouse button.
6. Type the text in cells as shown below and to the right by completing the following steps:
   a. Click in cell B1 in the Excel worksheet, type 1st Half, and then press the Tab key.
   b. With cell C1 active, type 2nd Half and then press the Tab key.
   c. Click in cell A2, type North, and then press the Tab key.
   d. Type $853,000 and then press the Tab key.
   e. Type $970,000 and then press the Enter key.
   f. Continue typing the remaining data in cells as indicated at the right. (The data range will automatically expand to include row 6.)
7. Click the Close button in the upper right corner of the Excel window.
8. Save **5-Conference.pptx**.

Check Your Work

Tutorial

Formatting with Chart Buttons

Chart Elements

Formatting with Chart Buttons

When a chart is inserted in a slide, three buttons display at the right side of the chart border. Click the top button, Chart Elements, and a side menu displays with chart elements such as axis title, chart title, data labels, data table, gridlines, and a legend. Elements containing a check mark in the check box are included in the chart. Include other elements in the chart by inserting a check mark in the check boxes.

Apply a chart style to a chart by clicking the Chart Styles button that displays at the right side of the chart. At the side menu that displays, scroll down the gallery and then click an option. In addition to applying a chart style, use the Chart Styles button side menu to change the chart colors. Click the Chart Styles button and then click the Color tab to the right of the Style tab. Click a color option at the color palette that displays.

Chart Styles

Chart Filters

Use the Chart Filters button to isolate specific data in a chart. Click the button and then, at the side menu that displays, specify the series or categories to include in the chart. To do this, remove check marks from those elements that should not appear in the chart. After removing the check marks, click the Apply button at the bottom of the side menu. Click the Names tab at the Chart Filters button side menu and options display for turning the display of column and row names on or off.

Project 1k Formatting a Chart with Chart Buttons

Part 11 of 14

1. With **5-Conference.pptx** open, make sure Slide 4 is the active slide and that the chart in the slide is selected. (Make sure the entire chart is selected and not just an element in the chart.)
2. Insert and remove chart elements by completing the following steps:

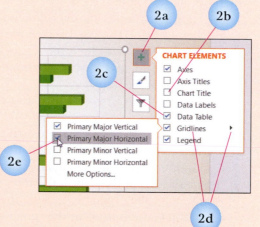

   a. Click the Chart Elements button that displays outside the upper right side of the chart.
   b. At the side menu, click the *Chart Title* check box to remove the check mark.
   c. Click the *Data Table* check box to insert a check mark.
   d. Hover your mouse pointer over *Gridlines* in the Chart Elements button side menu and then click the right-pointing arrow that displays.
   e. At the other side menu, click the *Primary Major Horizontal* check box to insert a check mark.
   f. Click the *Legend* check box to remove the check mark.
   g. Hover your mouse pointer over *Axis Titles* in the Chart Elements button side menu and then click the right-pointing arrow that displays.
   h. At the other side menu, click the *Primary Vertical* check box to insert a check mark.
   i. With *Axis Title* selected in the rotated box at the left side of the chart, type Region.
3. Apply a different chart style by completing the following steps:

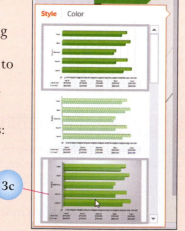

   a. Click the chart border to redisplay the chart buttons.
   b. Click the Chart Styles button that displays to the right of the chart below the Chart Elements button.
   c. At the side menu gallery, click the *Style 3* option (third option in the gallery).

d. Click the Color tab at the top of the side menu and then click the *Color 2* option (second row in the *Colorful* section).

e. Click the Chart Styles button to remove the side menu.

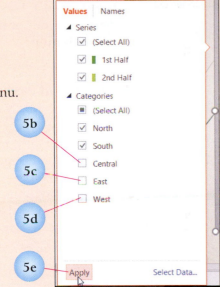

4. Remove the horizontal axis title by completing these steps:

a. Click the Chart Elements button.

b. Hover your mouse pointer over *Axes* in the Chart Elements button side menu and then click the right-pointing arrow that displays.

c. At the other side menu that displays, click the *Primary Horizontal* check box to remove the check mark.

d. Click the Chart Elements button to remove the side menu.

5. Display only the North and South sales by completing the following steps:

a. Click the Chart Filters button that displays below the Chart Styles button.

b. Click the *Central* check box in the *Categories* section to remove the check mark.

c. Click the *East* check box in the *Categories* section to remove the check mark.

d. Click the *West* check box in the *Categories* section to remove the check mark.

e. Click the Apply button at the bottom of the side menu.

f. Click the Chart Filters button to remove the side menu.

g. After viewing only the *North* and *South* sales, redisplay the other regions by clicking the Chart Filters button, clicking the *Central*, *East*, and *West* check boxes to insert check marks, and then clicking the Apply button.

h. Click the Chart Filters button to remove the side menu.

6. Save **5-Conference.pptx**.

Check Your Work

Tutorial

Changing Chart Design

Changing Chart Design

In addition to the buttons that display outside the chart border, a chart can be customized with options on the Chart Tools Design tab, shown in Figure 5.10. Use options on this tab to add a chart element, change the chart layout and colors, apply a chart style, select data and switch rows and columns, and change the chart type.

After creating a chart, the chart type can be changed by clicking the Change Chart Type button in the Type group on the Chart Tools Design tab. This displays the Change Chart Type dialog box. This dialog box contains the same options as the Insert Chart dialog box shown in Figure 5.8. At the Change Chart Type dialog box, click the chart type in the left panel and click the chart style in the right panel.

Use options in the Data group on the Chart Tools Design tab to change the grouping of the data in the chart, select specific data, edit data, and refresh the data. When a chart is created, the cells in the Excel worksheet are linked to the chart in the slide. Click the Select Data button in the Data group and Excel opens

Quick Steps

Change the Chart Type and Style

1. Make the chart active.
2. Click Chart Tools Design tab.
3. Click Change Chart Type button.
4. Click chart type.
5. Click chart style.
6. Click OK.

Change Chart Type

Figure 5.10 Chart Tools Design Tab

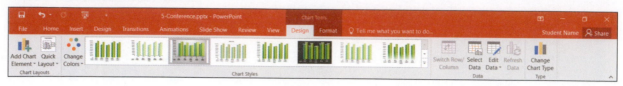

Select Data

Switch Row/ Column

Edit Data

Change Colors

Quick Layout

and the Select Data Source dialog box displays. At the Select Data Source dialog box, click the Switch Row/Column button to change the grouping of the selected data. Filter data at the dialog box by removing the check mark from those items that should not appear in the chart. To edit data in the chart, click the Edit Data button and the Excel worksheet opens. Make edits to cells in the Excel worksheet and then click the Close button.

Apply predesigned chart styles with options in the Chart Styles group and use the Change Colors button to change the color of the selected element or chart. Click the Quick Layout button in the Chart Layouts group to display a drop-down gallery of layout options and add an element to the chart with the Add Chart Element button.

Project 1l Changing the Chart Design

Part 12 of 14

1. With **5-Conference.pptx** open, make sure Slide 4 is active and the chart is selected. Click the Chart Tools Design tab to make it active.
2. Looking at the chart, you decide that the bar chart was not the best choice for the data and decide to change to a column chart. Do this by completing the following steps:
   a. Click the Change Chart Type button in the Type group on the Chart Tools Design tab.
   b. At the Change Chart Type dialog box, click the *Column* option in the left panel.
   c. Click the *3-D Clustered Column* option (fourth option at the top of the dialog box).

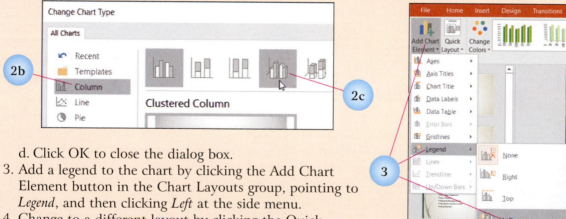

   d. Click OK to close the dialog box.
3. Add a legend to the chart by clicking the Add Chart Element button in the Chart Layouts group, pointing to *Legend*, and then clicking *Left* at the side menu.
4. Change to a different layout by clicking the Quick Layout button in the Chart Layouts group and then clicking the *Layout 10* option (the last option).

166 **PowerPoint** | Unit 2   Chapter 5 | Creating Tables, Charts, and SmartArt Graphics

5. Click the Add Chart Element button in the Chart Layouts group, point to *Chart Title* at the drop-down list, and then click *Above Chart* at the side menu.

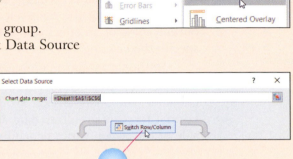

6. Type 2018 Regional Sales as the chart title.
7. Click the chart border to deselect the chart title.
8. Click the *Style 1* option in the chart styles gallery in the Chart Styles group (first option).
9. Select data and switch rows and columns by completing the following steps:
   a. Click the Select Data button in the Data group. (This opens Excel and displays the Select Data Source dialog box.)
   b. Click the Switch Row/Column button in the Select Data Source dialog box.
   c. Click OK. (This switches the grouping of the data from *Region* to *Half Yearly Sales*.)

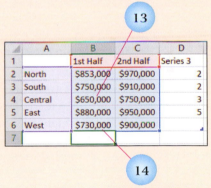

10. After viewing the chart, switch the rows and columns back to the original groupings by dragging the Excel window so the Switch Row/Column button is visible in the Data group on the Chart Tools Design tab, clicking in the chart, and then clicking the Switch Row/Column button.
11. Close the Excel window by clicking the Close button in the upper right corner of the Excel window.
12. Click the Edit Data button in the Data group.
13. Click in cell B4 (the cell containing the amount *$720,000*), type 650000, and then press the Enter key. (When you press the Enter key, a dollar symbol is automatically inserted in front of the number and a thousand separator comma is inserted.)
14. Click in cell B6 (the cell containing the amount *$830,000*), type 730000, and then press the Enter key.
15. Click the Close button in the upper right corner of the Excel window.
16. Save 5-Conference.pptx.

	A	B	C	D
1		1st Half	2nd Half	Series 3
2	North	$853,000	$970,000	2
3	South	$750,000	$910,000	2
4	Central	$650,000	$750,000	3
5	East	$880,000	$950,000	5
6	West	$730,000	$900,000	
7				

Check Your Work

Tutorial

Changing Chart Format

Hint Right-click text in a chart element to display the Mini toolbar.

Format Selection

Formatting a Chart and Chart Elements

Apply formatting to a chart or chart elements using options in the Drawing group on the Home tab. Apply a predesigned style to a chart or chart element with the Quick Styles button. Use other buttons in the group to add fill and outline color and apply effects.

In addition to the buttons in the Drawing group on the Home tab, a chart and chart elements can be formatted using options on the Chart Tools Format tab, as shown in Figure 5.11. To format or modify a specific element in a chart, select the element. Do this by clicking the element or by clicking the *Chart Elements* option box arrow in the Current Selection group and then clicking the element at the drop-down list. With the element selected, apply the formatting. Click the Format Selection button in the Current Selection group and a task pane displays with options for formatting the selected element. Insert shapes with options in the Insert Shapes group. Click a shape, or click the More Shapes button and then click a shape at the drop-down list, and then drag in the chart to create the shape. Click the Change Shape button to change the shape to a different shape.

The Shape Styles group on the Chart Tools Format tab contains predesigned styles that can be applied to elements in the chart. Click the More Shape Styles button at the right side of the shape styles gallery and a drop-down gallery displays shape styles. Use the buttons that display at the right side of the Shape Styles group to apply fill, an outline, and an effect to a selected element. The WordArt Styles group contains predesigned styles for applying formatting to text in a chart. Use the buttons at the right side of the WordArt Styles group to apply fill color, an outline color, or an effect to text in a chart. Use options in the Arrange group to specify the layering, alignment, rotation, and size of a chart or chart element.

Additional formatting options are available at various task panes. Display a task pane by the clicking Format Selection button or by clicking a group task pane launcher. The Shape Styles, WordArt Styles, and Size groups on the Chart Tools Format tab contain a task pane launcher. The task pane that opens at the right side of the screen varies depending on the chart or chart element selected.

Figure 5.11 Chart Tools Format Tab

Project 1m Formatting a Chart and Chart Elements

1. With **5-Conference.pptx** open, make sure Slide 4 is active and the chart is selected.
2. Reposition and format the legend by completing the following steps:
   a. Click the Chart Elements button that displays at the right side of the chart.
   b. Hover your mouse pointer over *Legend*, click the right-pointing arrow at the right side of *Legend* in the side menu, and then click the *Right* option at the other side menu.

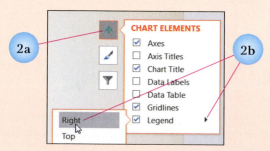

   c. Click the Chart Elements button again to remove the side menu.
   d. Click the legend to select it.
   e. If necessary, click the Home tab.

f. Click the Quick Styles button in the Drawing group and then click the *Subtle Effect - Lime, Accent 3* option (fourth column, fourth row).

g. Click the Shape Outline button arrow in the Drawing group and then click the *Green, Accent 1, Darker 50%* option (fifth column, bottom row in the *Theme Colors* section).

h. Increase the size of the legend by dragging down the bottom middle sizing handle about 0.25 inch.

3. Format the title by completing the following steps:
   a. Click the Chart Tools Format tab.
   b. Click the *Chart Elements* option box arrow in the Current Selection group and then click *Chart Title* at the drop-down list.
   c. Click the More Shape Styles button at the right side of the gallery in the Shape Styles group and then click the *Intense Effect - Green, Accent 1* option (second column, bottom row).
   d. Click the Shape Effects button, point to *Bevel*, and then click the *Cross* option (third column, first row in the *Bevel* section).

4. Customize the chart wall and floor by completing the following steps:
   a. Click the *Chart Elements* option box arrow in the Current Selection group and then click *Back Wall* at the drop-down list.
   b. Click the Format Selection button in the Current Selection group. (This displays the Format Wall task pane with the Fill & Line icon selected.)

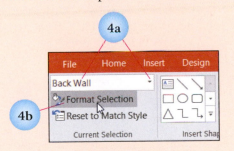

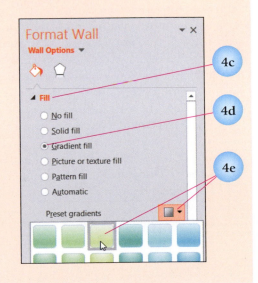

c. If necessary, click *Fill* to display the options.
d. Click the *Gradient fill* option.
e. Click the Preset gradients button and then click the *Light Gradient - Accent 3* option (third column, first row).
f. Click the *Chart Elements* option box arrow and then click *Floor*. (This displays the Format Floor task pane.)
g. Click the *Solid fill* option.

5. Customize the 1st Half data series by completing the following steps:
   a. Click the *Chart Elements* option box arrow in the Current Selection group and then click *Series "1st Half"* at the drop-down list.
   b. Click the Effects icon in the Format Data Series task pane.
   c. Click *3-D Format* to display the options.
   d. Click the Material button in the task pane.
   e. At the gallery that displays, click the *Dark Edge* option (first option in the *Special Effect* section).
   f. Click the Bottom bevel button and then click the *Hard Edge* option (third column, third row in the *Bevel* section).
6. Complete steps similar to those in Step 5a through Step 5f to format the *Series "2nd Half"* chart element.
7. Customize the chart by completing the following steps:
   a. Click the *Chart Elements* option box arrow in the Current Selection group and then click *Chart Area* at the drop-down list.
   b. Click the Fill & Line icon and make sure fill options display in the Format Chart Area task pane. (If necessary, click *Fill* to expand the options.)
   c. Click the *Picture or texture fill* option.
   d. Click the Texture button (located below the Online button)
   e. Click the *Parchment* option (last column, third row).
   f. Scroll down the task pane to the *Border* section and, if necessary, click *Border* to expand the options.
   g. Click the *Solid line* option in the *Border* section.
   h. Click the Size & Properties icon.
   i. If necessary, click *Size* to display the options.
   j. Select the current measurement in the *Height* measurement box and then type 6.
   k. Select the current measurement in the *Width* measurement box, type 9, and then press the Enter key.
   l. Click *Position* to display the options.
   m. Select the current measurement in the *Horizontal position* measurement box and then type 2.5.
   n. Select the current measurement in the *Vertical position* measurement box, type 0.8, and then press the Enter key.
   o. Close the task pane by clicking the Close button in the upper right corner of the task pane.
8. Save **5-Conference.pptx**.

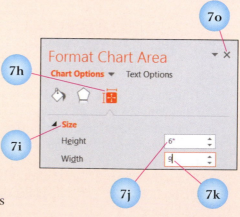

Check Your Work

Another method for formatting a chart or chart elements is to use options at the shortcut menu. Some of the options on the shortcut menu vary depending on the chart or chart element selected. Some common options include deleting the element, editing data, rotating the element, and adding data labels. To display the shortcut menu, right-click the element or the chart. In addition to the shortcut menu, the Mini toolbar also displays. The Mini toolbar contains options for applying fill color and outline color.

Project 1n   Creating and Formatting a Pie Chart

1. With **5-Conference.pptx** open, make Slide 6 active and then insert a new slide with the Blank layout.
2. Click the Insert tab and then click the Chart button in the Illustrations group.
3. At the Insert Chart dialog box, click *Pie* in the left panel.
4. Double-click the *3-D Pie* option at the top of the dialog box (second option).
5. Type the text in cells in the Excel worksheet as shown at the right.
6. When all data is entered, click the Close button in the upper right corner of the Excel window.
7. Click the Chart Styles button that displays at the right side of the pie chart, click the *Style 3* chart style, and then click the Chart Styles button again to remove the side menu.

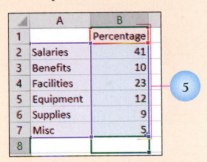

8. Move the data labels to the outside of the pie by completing the following steps:
   a. Click the Chart Elements button that displays at the right side of the chart.
   b. Hover your mouse pointer over the *Data Labels* option in the side menu and then click the right-pointing arrow that displays.
   c. Click the *Outside End* option.
   d. Click the Chart Elements button to remove the side menu.

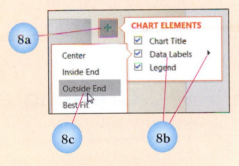

9. Apply formatting to the legend by completing the following steps:
   a. Hover your mouse just above the word *Salaries* in the legend until the mouse pointer displays with a four-headed arrow attached and then click the right mouse button.
   b. Click the Fill button on the Mini toolbar and then click *Tan, Background 2* (third column, first row in the *Theme Colors* section).
   c. Click the Outline button on the Mini toolbar and then click the *Green, Accent 1, Darker 50%* option (fifth column, bottom row in the *Theme Colors* section).
   d. Increase the size of the legend by dragging the bottom middle sizing handle down about 0.25 inch.

10. Edit the title by completing the following steps:
   a. Right-click the title *Percentage* and then click *Edit Text* in the shortcut menu.
   b. With the insertion point positioned in the title, press the End key to move the insertion point to the right of *Percentage*, press the spacebar, and then type of 100k Division Budget.

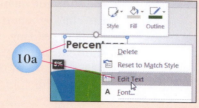

11. Click outside the title but inside the chart to select the chart.
12. Click the Chart Tools Format tab.
13. Change the chart height to 6.5 inches and the chart width to 9 inches.
14. Click the Align button in the Arrange group and then click *Distribute Horizontally*.
15. Click the Align button in the Arrange group and then click *Distribute Vertically*.
16. Apply a transition and transition sound of your choosing to all slides in the presentation.
17. Save **5-Conference.pptx**.
18. Run the slide show.
19. Print the presentation as a handout with six slides displayed horizontally per page.
20. Close **5-Conference.pptx**.

Check Your Work

Project 2 Create and Format a Travel Photo Album   3 Parts

You will use the photo album feature to create a presentation containing travel photographs. You will also apply formatting and insert elements in the presentation.

Preview Finished Project

Tutorial

Creating a Photo Album

Creating a Photo Album

 Photo Album

Quick Steps
Create a Photo Album
1. Click Insert tab.
2. Click Photo Album button arrow.
3. Click *New Photo Album.*
4. Click File/Disk button.
5. Double-click picture.
6. Repeat Steps 4 and 5 for all pictures.
7. Make changes at Photo Album dialog box.
8. Click Create button.

Use PowerPoint's photo album feature to create a presentation containing personal or business pictures. Customize and format the appearance of pictures by applying interesting layouts, frame shapes, and themes and insert elements such as captions and text boxes. To create a photo album, click the Insert tab, click the Photo Album button arrow in the Images group, and then click *New Photo Album* at the drop-down list. This displays the Photo Album dialog box, as shown in Figure 5.12.

To insert pictures in the photo album, click the File/Disk button to display the Insert New Pictures dialog box. At this dialog box, navigate to the desired folder and then double-click the picture to be inserted in the album. This inserts the picture name in the *Pictures in album* list box in the dialog box and also displays the picture in the *Preview* section. As pictures are inserted in the photo album, the picture names display in the *Pictures in album* list box in the order in which they will appear in the presentation. When all pictures have been inserted into the photo album, click the Create button. This creates the photo album as a presentation and displays the first slide. The photo album feature creates the first slide with the title *Photo Album* and the user's name.

Figure 5.12 Photo Album Dialog Box

Choose a picture and then preview it in this *Preview* box.

Insert a picture by clicking the File/Disk button and then double-clicking the picture at the Insert New Pictures dialog box.

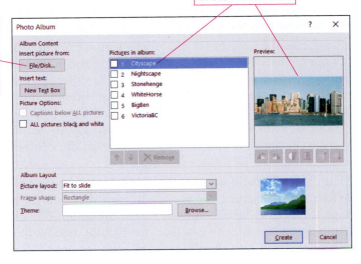

Project 2a Creating a Travel Photo Album

Part 1 of 3

1. At a blank screen, click the Insert tab, click the Photo Album button arrow in the Images group and then click *New Photo Album* at the drop-down list.
2. At the Photo Album dialog box, click the File/Disk button.
3. At the Insert New Pictures dialog box, navigate to the PC5 folder on your storage medium and then double-click **Cityscape.jpg**.
4. At the Photo Album dialog box, click the File/Disk button, and then double-click **Nightscape.jpg** at the Insert New Pictures dialog box.
5. Insert the following additional pictures: **Stonehenge.jpg**, **WhiteHorse.jpg**, **BigBen.jpg**, and **VictoriaBC.jpg**.
6. Click the Create button. (This opens a presentation with each image in a separate slide. The first slide contains the default text *Photo Album* followed by your name (or the user name for the computer).
7. Save the presentation and name it **5-Album.pptx**.
8. Run the slide show.

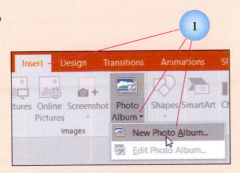

Check Your Work

Editing and Formatting a Photo Album

To make changes to a photo album presentation, open the presentation, click the Insert tab, click the Photo Album button arrow in the Images group, and then click *Edit Photo Album* at the drop-down list. This displays the Edit Photo Album dialog box, which contains the same options as the Photo Album dialog box.

Rearrange the slide order in a photo album presentation by clicking a slide in the *Pictures in album* list box and then clicking the button containing the up-pointing arrow to move the slide up in the order or clicking the button containing the down-pointing arrow to move the slide down in the order. Remove a slide by clicking the slide in the list box and then clicking the Remove button. Use buttons below the *Preview* box in the Edit Photo Album dialog box to rotate the picture in the slide and increase or decrease the contrast or brightness of the picture.

The *Picture layout* option in the *Album Layout* section has a default setting of *Fit to slide*. At this setting the picture in each slide will fill most of the slide. Change this setting by clicking the *Picture layout* option box arrow. With options at the drop-down list, specify whether one picture, two pictures, or four pictures should be inserted into the slide and whether or not titles should be included with the pictures.

Change the *Picture layout* option to something other than the default of *Fit to slide* and the *Frame shape* option becomes available. Click the *Frame shape* option box arrow and a drop-down list displays with options for applying a rounded, simple, or double frame around the picture, or a soft or shadow effect frame.

Apply a theme to the photo album presentation by clicking the Browse button at the right side of the *Theme* option box and then double-clicking the theme in the Choose Theme dialog box. This dialog box contains the predesigned themes provided by PowerPoint.

Captions can be included with the pictures by changing the *Picture layout* to one, two, or four slides and then clicking the *Captions below ALL pictures* check box in the *Picture Options* section. When the *Captions below ALL pictures* check box contains a check mark, PowerPoint will insert a caption containing the name of the picture below each picture. The caption can be edited in the slide in the presentation. All pictures in the photo album can be displayed in black and white by inserting a check mark in the *ALL pictures black and white* check box in the *Picture Options* section of the dialog box.

Click the New Text Box button in the Edit Photo Album dialog box and a new slide containing a text box is inserted in the presentation. The information in the text box can be edited in the presentation. Once all changes have been made to the photo album, click the Update button at the bottom right side of the dialog box.

1. With **5-Album.pptx** open, make sure the Insert tab is active, click the Photo Album button arrow in the Images group, and then click *Edit Photo Album* at the drop-down list.
2. At the Edit Photo Album dialog box, make the following changes:
    a. Click the *ALL pictures black and white* check box to insert a check mark.
    b. Click in the *VictoriaBC* check box in the *Pictures in album* list box to insert a check mark and then click the up-pointing arrow button below the list box three times. (This moves *VictoriaBC* so it is positioned between *Nightscape* and *Stonehenge*).

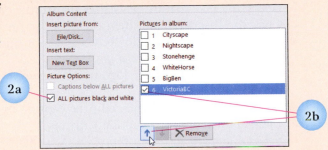

    c. Click the Rotate button below the *Preview* box (the first button from the left below the picture). Click the Rotate button three times to return the image to the original orientation.
    d. Click the *VictoriaBC* check box in the *Pictures in album* list box to remove the check mark.
    e. Click the *Cityscape* check box in the *Pictures in album* list box to insert a check mark and then click the Increase Contrast button below the *Preview* box two times (the third button from the left below the picture preview).

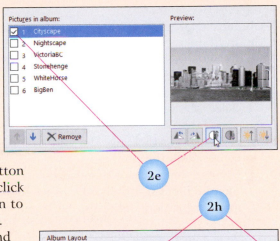

    f. Click the *Cityscape* check box to remove the check mark.
    g. Click the *Stonehenge* check box in the *Pictures in album* list box to insert a check mark, click the Increase Contrast button below the *Preview* box two times and then click the Increase Brightness button (fifth button to the right of the Remove button) two times.
    h. Click the *Picture layout* option box arrow and then click *1 picture* at the drop-down list.
    i. Click the *Frame shape* option box arrow and then click *Center Shadow Rectangle* at the drop-down list.
    j. Click the Browse button at the right side of the *Theme* option box. At the Choose Theme dialog box, double-click **Facet.thmx**.
    k. Click the *Captions below ALL pictures* check box to insert a check mark.
    l. Click the *Stonehenge* check box in the *Pictures in album* list box to remove the check mark and then click the *BigBen* check box in the *Pictures in album* list box to insert a check mark.
    m. Click the New Text Box button at the left side of the list box. (This inserts a new slide containing a text box at the end of the presentation.)
    n. Click the Update button in the lower right corner of the dialog box.

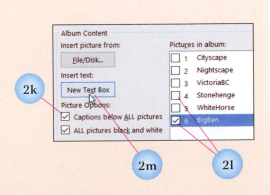

3. At the presentation, make the following formatting changes:
    a. Click the Design tab.
    b. Click the blue variant in the Variants group (second variant).
4. With Slide 1 active, make the following changes:
    a. Select the text *Photo Album* and then type Travel Album.
    b. Select any text that displays after the word *by* and then type your first and last names.
    c. Click the Insert tab and then click the Pictures button.
    d. At the Insert Picture dialog box, navigate to the PC5 folder on your storage medium and then double-click ***FCTLogo.jpg***.
    e. Change the height of the logo to 2.0 inches and then position the logo attractively in the slide.
5. Make Slide 2 active and then edit the caption by completing the following steps:
    a. Click anywhere in the caption *Cityscape*.
    b. Select *Cityscape* and then type New York City Skyline.

6. Complete steps similar to those in Step 5 to change the following captions:
    a. In Slide 3, change *Nightscape* to *New York City at Night*.
    b. In Slide 4, change *VictoriaBC* to *Victoria, British Columbia*.
    c. In Slide 5, change *Stonehenge* to *Stonehenge, Wiltshire County*.
    d. In Slide 6, change *WhiteHorse* to *White Horse, Wiltshire County*.
    e. In Slide 7, change *BigBen* to *Big Ben, London*.
7. Make Slide 8 active and then make the following changes:
    a. Select the text *Text Box* and then type Call First Choice Travel at 213-555-4500 to book your next travel tour.
    b. Select the text, change the font size to 48 points, apply the standard blue font color, and center align the text.
    c. Change the width of the placeholder to 9 inches. (Do this with the *Shape Width* measurement box on the Drawing Tools Format tab.)
8. Apply a transition and transition sound of your choosing to all slides.
9. Run the slide show.
10. Save **5-Album.pptx**.

Check Your Work

Formatting Pictures

If slides are formatted in the presentation instead of using the Edit Photo Album dialog box, some of those changes may be lost if changes are made at the Edit Photo Album dialog box and the Update button is clicked. Consider making initial editing and formatting changes at the Edit Photo Album dialog box and then make any final editing and formatting changes in the presentation slides.

Since a picture in a slide in a photo album is an object, it can be formatted with options on the Drawing Tools Format tab and the Picture Tools Format tab. With options on the Drawing Tools Format tab, insert shapes, apply a shape style to the picture and caption (if one is displayed), apply a WordArt style to caption text, and arrange and size the picture. Use options on the Picture Tools Format tab to adjust the color of the picture, apply a picture style, and arrange and size the picture.

1. With **5-Album.pptx** open, make Slide 2 active.
2. Change the pictures back to color by completing the following steps:
   a. Click the Insert tab.
   b. Click the Photo Album button arrow in the Images group and then click *Edit Photo Album* at the drop-down list.
   c. Click the *ALL pictures black and white* check box to remove the check mark.
   d. Click the Update button.
3. Format the picture in Slide 2 by completing the following steps:
   a. Click the picture to select it.
   b. Click the Drawing Tools Format tab.
   c. Click the More Shape Styles button in the Shape Styles group and then click the *Subtle Effect - Turquoise, Accent 1* option (second column, fourth row).
4. Apply the same style to the pictures in Slides 3 through 7 by making each slide active, clicking the picture, and then pressing the F4 function key. (Pressing F4 repeats the style formatting.)
5. Make Slide 2 active and then apply a WordArt style to the caption text by completing the following steps:
   a. With Slide 2 active, click the picture to select it.
   b. Click the Drawing Tools Format tab.
   c. Click the More WordArt Styles button in the WordArt Styles group and then click the *Fill - Blue, Accent 2, Outline - Accent 2* option (third column, first row).

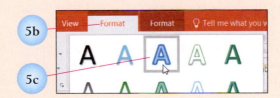

6. Apply the same WordArt style to the caption text in Slides 3 through 7 by making each slide active, clicking the picture, and then pressing the F4 function key.
7. Make Slide 8 active and then change the width of the placeholder to 9 inches.
8. Run the slide show.
9. Print the presentation as a handout with four slides displayed horizontally per page.
10. Save and then close **5-Album.pptx**.

Check Your Work

Chapter Summary

- Use the Table button in the Tables group on the Insert tab to create a table, insert an Excel worksheet, and draw a table in a slide.

- Change the table design with options and buttons on the Table Tools Design tab. Change the table layout with options and buttons on the Table Tools Layout tab.

- Use the SmartArt feature to insert predesigned graphics, such as diagrams and organizational charts, in a slide.

- Use options and buttons on the SmartArt Tools Design tab to change the graphic layout, apply a style to the graphic, and reset the graphic back to the original formatting.

- Use options and buttons on the SmartArt Tools Format tab to change the size and shape of objects in the graphic; apply shape styles; change the shape fill, outline, and effects; and arrange and size the graphic.

- Insert text directly into a SmartArt graphic shape or at the Text pane. Display this pane by clicking the Text Pane button in the Create Graphic group on the SmartArt Tools Design tab.

- Text or WordArt can be converted to a SmartArt graphic and a SmartArt graphic can be converted to text or shapes.

- A chart is a visual presentation of data. A variety of charts can be created as described in Table 5.2.

- To create a chart, display the Insert Chart dialog box by clicking the Insert Chart button in a content placeholder or clicking the Chart button in the Illustrations group on the Insert tab.

- Enter chart data in an Excel worksheet. When entering data, press the Tab key to make the next cell active, press Shift + Tab to make the previous cell active, and press the Enter key to make the cell below active.

- Modify a chart design with options and buttons on the Chart Tools Design tab.

- Cells in the Excel worksheet used to create a chart are linked to the chart in the slide. To edit chart data, click the Edit Data button on the Chart Tools Design tab and then make changes to the text in the Excel worksheet.

- Customize the format of a chart and chart elements with options and buttons on the Chart Tools Format tab. A style can be applied to a shape in a chart, a WordArt style can be applied to text in a chart, and a chart can be sized and arranged in the slide.

- Use the Photo Album feature in the Images group on the Insert tab to create a presentation containing pictures and then edit and format the pictures.

- At the Photo Album dialog box (or the Edit Photo Album dialog box), insert pictures and then use options to customize the photo album.

- Use options on the Drawing Tools Format tab and the Picture Tools Format tab to format pictures in a photo album presentation.

Commands Review

FEATURE	RIBBON TAB, GROUP	BUTTON, OPTION
Choose a SmartArt Graphic dialog box	Insert, Illustrations	
convert bulleted text to SmartArt	Home, Paragraph	
convert SmartArt to text or shapes	SmartArt Tools Design, Reset	
create photo album	Insert, Images	, *New Photo Album*
edit photo album	Insert, Images	, *Edit Photo Album*
Insert Chart dialog box	Insert, Illustrations	
Insert Table dialog box	Insert, Tables	, *Insert Table*
Text pane	SmartArt Tools Design, Create Graphic	

Workbook

Chapter study tools and assessment activities are available in the *Workbook* ebook. These resources are designed to help you further develop and demonstrate mastery of the skills learned in this chapter.

Microsoft®
PowerPoint®

Using Slide Masters and Action Buttons

Performance Objectives

Upon successful completion of Chapter 6, you will be able to:

1. Format slides in Slide Master view
2. Apply themes and backgrounds in Slide Master view
3. Delete placeholders and slide master layouts
4. Insert elements in Slide Master view
5. Create and rename a custom slide layout
6. Insert placeholders and custom prompts in Slide Master view
7. Insert a new slide master
8. Preserve a slide master
9. Save a presentation as a template
10. Customize handouts pages in Handout Master view
11. Customize notes pages in Notes Master view
12. Change zoom, manage windows, and view presentations in color and grayscale
13. Insert action buttons
14. Apply actions to objects
15. Insert hyperlinks

Precheck

Check your current skills to focus your study.

To make design or formatting changes that affect all slides in the presentation, consider making the changes in a slide master in the Slide Master view. Along with the Slide Master view, changes can be made to all handouts pages with options in the Handout Master view and all notes pages in the Notes Master view. Action buttons can be inserted in a presentation to connect to slides within the same presentation, another presentation, a website, or to another program. Insert a hyperlink to connect to a website.

SNAP

If you are a SNAP user, launch the Precheck and Tutorials from your Assignments page.

Data Files

Before beginning chapter work, copy the PC6 folder to your storage medium and then make PC6 the active folder.

Tutorial

Formatting with a
Slide Master

Quick Steps

**Display Slide
Master View**
1. Click View tab.
2. Click Slide Master
   button.

Slide Master

Hint Create a
consistent look for your
slides by customizing
them in Slide Master
view.

Close
Master View

Customizing Slide Masters

To apply formatting or other changes to multiple slides in a presentation, make the changes in a slide master. Customize a slide master by changing the theme, theme colors, or theme fonts; inserting or changing the location of placeholders; applying a background style; and changing the page setup and slide orientation.

If formatting or other changes are made to an individual slide in Normal view, that slide's link to the slide master is broken. Changes made in Slide Master view will not affect the individually formatted slide. For this reason, make global formatting changes in Slide Master view before editing individual slides in a presentation.

To display Slide Master view, click the View tab and then click the Slide Master button in the Master Views group. This makes the Slide Master tab active, displays a blank slide master in the slide pane, and inserts slide master thumbnails in the slide thumbnails pane. The largest thumbnail in the pane is the slide master, and the other thumbnails represent associated layouts. Position the mouse pointer on a slide thumbnail and the name of the thumbnail displays in a ScreenTip by the thumbnail along with information on what slides in the presentation use the slide master. Figure 6.1 shows a blank presentation in Slide Master view. To specify the slide master or layout that will be customized, click the specific thumbnail in the slide thumbnails pane. With the slide master layout displayed in the slide pane, make the changes and then click the Close Master View button.

Figure 6.1 Slide Master View

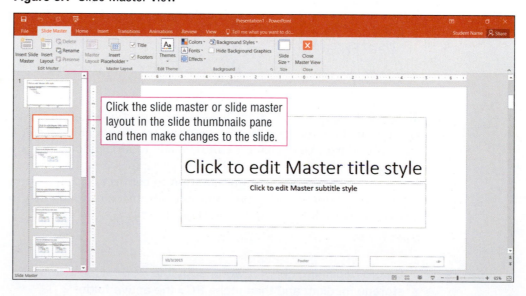

Applying Themes to Slide Masters

Themes

Colors

Fonts

Effects

Apply themes, theme colors, theme fonts, and theme effects to a slide master using buttons in the Edit Theme group and the Background group on the Slide Master tab. Click the Themes button and a drop-down gallery displays with available predesigned themes as well as any custom themes. Click a theme and the theme formatting is applied to the slide master. Use the Colors button in the Background group to change theme colors, use the Fonts button to change theme fonts, and apply a theme effect using the Effects button.

Project 1a **Formatting a Slide Master**   **Part 1 of 6**

1. Open a blank presentation.
2. Click the View tab and then click the Slide Master button in the Master Views group.
3. Scroll up the slide thumbnails pane and then click the top (and largest) slide master thumbnail in the slide thumbnails pane (*Office Theme Slide Master*). This displays the slide master layout in the slide pane.
4. Click the Themes button in the Edit Theme group on the Slide Master tab.
5. Click the *Retrospect* option.
6. Click the Colors button in the Background group and then click the *Blue* option at the drop-down gallery.
7. Click the Fonts button in the Background group, scroll down the drop-down gallery, and then click the *Arial Black-Arial* option.
8. Change the font color for the title style by completing the following steps:
   a. Click the *Click to edit Master title style* placeholder border in the slide master in the slide pane.
   b. Click the Home tab.
   c. Click the Font Color button arrow in the Font group and then click the *Black, Text 1* option (second column, first row in the *Theme Colors* section).
9. Change the font size and color and apply custom bullets by completing the following steps:
   a. Select the text *Edit Master text styles*.
   b. With the Home tab selected, click the *Font Size* option box arrow and then click *24* at the drop-down gallery.
   c. Click the Font Color button arrow and then click the *Light Blue, Background 2, Darker 50%* option (third column, fourth row in the *Theme Colors* section).

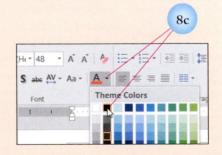

d. Click the Bullets button arrow in the Paragraph group and then click *Bullets and Numbering* at the drop-down gallery.

e. At the Bullets and Numbering dialog box, click the *Hollow Square Bullets* option.

f. Click the Color button and then click the *Light Blue, Background 2, Darker 50%* option (third column, fourth row in the *Theme Colors* section).

g. Select *100* in the *Size* measurement box and then type 80.

h. Click OK to close the dialog box.

i. Click the Paragraph group dialog box launcher.

j. At the Paragraph dialog box, select the measurement in the *By* measurement box and then type 0.4.

k. Click OK to close the dialog box.

10. Click the Slide Master tab.

11. Click the Close Master View button.

12. Save the presentation and name it **6-TravelMaster.pptx**.

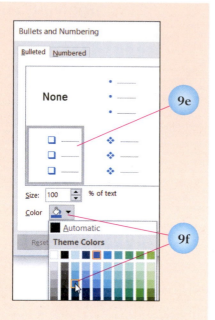

Applying and Formatting Backgrounds

In addition to the theme colors, fonts, and effects buttons, the Background group on the Slide Master tab contains the Background Styles button and the *Hide Background Graphics* check box. To change the background graphic for all slides, display the presentation in Slide Master view and then click the specific slide master layout in the slide thumbnails pane. Click the Background Styles button and then click a background at the drop-down gallery. Or, click the *Format Background* option at the drop-down gallery and then make changes at the Format Background task pane. To remove the background graphic from all slides, click the *Hide Background Graphics* check box to insert a check mark.

Deleting Placeholders

Hint You can also delete a slide master layout by right-clicking the layout in the slide thumbnails pane and then clicking *Delete Layout* at the shortcut menu.

In Slide Master view, if a placeholder is removed from a slide layout it is then removed from all slides based on that layout. To remove a placeholder from a layout, display the presentation in Slide Master view, click the specific slide layout thumbnail, click the placeholder border (make sure the border displays as a solid line), and then press the Delete key. The title placeholder can also be removed from a slide layout by clicking the *Title* check box in the Master Layout group to remove the check mark. Remove footer placeholders by clicking the *Footer* check box to remove the check mark.

Quick Steps

Delete a Slide Master Layout
1. Display presentation in Slide Master view.
2. Click slide layout thumbnail.
3. Click Delete button.

 Delete

Deleting Slide Master Layouts

In Slide Master view, a slide master displays for each available layout. If a particular layout will not be used in the presentation, the slide layout can be deleted. To do this, display the presentation in Slide Master view, click the specific slide layout thumbnail in the slide thumbnails pane, and then click the Delete button in the Edit Master group.

1. With **6-TravelMaster.pptx** open, click the View tab and then click the Slide Master button in the Master Views group.
2. Apply a picture to the background of the title slide layout (the picture will appear only on slides with this layout applied) by completing the following steps:
   a. Make sure the second slide layout thumbnail (*Title Slide Layout*) is selected in the slide thumbnails pane.
   b. Click the *Click to edit Master title style* placeholder border, click the Home tab, change the font size to 48 points, apply the Black, Text 1 font color (second column, first row in the *Theme Colors* section), and click the Center button in the Paragraph group.
   c. Click the Slide Master tab and then make sure the *Hide Background Graphics* check box in the Background group contains a check mark.
   d. Click the Background Styles button in the Background group and then click *Format Background* at the drop-down list.

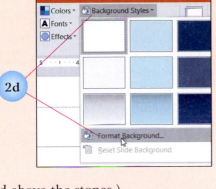

   e. At the Format Background task pane, click the *Picture or texture fill* option.
   f. Click the File button.
   g. At the Insert Picture dialog box, navigate to the PC6 folder on your storage medium and then double-click **Stonehenge.jpg**.
   h. Close the Format Background task pane.
   i. Drag the master title placeholder so it is positioned above the stones and centered horizontally. (Make sure the bottom border of the placeholder is positioned above the stones.)

   j. Delete the master subtitle placeholder by clicking the placeholder border (make sure the border displays as a solid line) and then pressing the Delete key.
   k. Click the thin horizontal line that displays below the stones and then press the Delete key.
3. Delete slide layouts that you will not be using in the presentation by completing the following steps:
   a. Click the fourth slide layout thumbnail (*Section Header Layout*) in the slide thumbnails pane.
   b. Scroll down the pane until the last slide layout thumbnail is visible.
   c. Press and hold down the Shift key, click the last slide layout thumbnail, and then release the Shift key.
   d. Click the Delete button in the Edit Master group. (The slide thumbnails pane should now contain only one slide master and two associated layouts.)
4. Click the Close Master View button.
5. Delete the slide that currently displays in the slide pane. (This displays a gray background with the text *Click to add first slide*. The presentation does not contain any slides, just formatting.)
6. Save **6-TravelMaster.pptx**.

Inserting Slides in a Customized Presentation

If slides in a presentation have been customized in Slide Master view, the presentation formatting can be used in other presentations. To do this, either save the formatted presentation as a template or save the presentation in the normal manner, open the presentation, save it with a new name, and then type text in slides. Slides can also be inserted into the current presentation using the Reuse Slides task pane. (You learned about this task pane in Chapter 2.) To use this task pane, click the Home tab, click the New Slide button arrow, and then click *Reuse Slides* at the drop-down list. This displays the Reuse Slides task pane at the right side of the screen. Click the Browse button and then click the *Browse File* option at the drop-down list. At the Browse dialog box, navigate to the desired folder and then double-click the presentation. Insert slides into the current presentation by clicking specific slides in the task pane.

Project 1c Inserting Slides in a Presentation · **Part 3 of 6**

1. With **6-TravelMaster.pptx** open, save it with the name **6-England**.
2. With the Home tab active, click the New Slide button arrow, and then click the *Title Slide* option.
3. Click in the title placeholder and then type Wiltshire, England.
4. Insert slides into the current presentation from an existing presentation by completing the following steps:

   a. Click the New Slide button arrow and then click the *Reuse Slides* option.
   b. Click the Browse button in the Reuse Slides task pane and then click *Browse File* at the drop-down list.
   c. At the Browse dialog box, navigate to the PC6 folder on your storage medium and then double-click *TravelEngland.pptx*.
   d. Click the *Wiltshire* slide in the Reuse Slides task pane. (This inserts the slide in the presentation and applies the custom formatting to the slide.)
   e. Click the *Ancient Stone Circles* slide in the Reuse Slides task pane.
   f. Click the *Ancient Wiltshire* slide in the Reuse Slides task pane.
   g. Click the *White Horses* slide in the Reuse Slides task pane.
   h. Click the Close button in the upper right corner of the Reuse Slides task pane.

5. With Slide 5 active, format the bulleted text into two columns by completing the following steps:
   a. Click anywhere in the bulleted text.
   b. Press Ctrl + A to select all of the bulleted text.
   c. Click the Line Spacing button in the Paragraph group and then click the *2.0* option.
   d. Click the Add or Remove Columns button in the Paragraph group and then click the *Two Columns* option.
6. With Slide 5 active, insert a new slide by completing the following steps:
   a. Click the New Slide button arrow and then click the *Title Slide* option.
   b. Click in the title placeholder and then type Call Lucy at 213-555-4500.
7. Save **6-England.pptx**.

Check Your Work

Inserting Elements in a Slide Master

A header, footer, or the date and time can be inserted in a presentation that will print on every slide in the presentation. These elements can also be inserted in a slide master. To insert a header or footer in a slide master, display the presentation in Slide Master view, click the Insert tab, and then click the Header & Footer button in the Text group. At the Header and Footer dialog box with the Slide tab selected, make the changes, click the Notes and Handouts tab, make the changes, and then click the Apply to All button. A picture, clip art image, shape, SmartArt graphic, or chart can also be inserted in Slide Master view. These elements are inserted in Slide Master view in the same manner as inserting them in Normal view.

Project 1d Inserting Elements in Slide Master View   **Part 4 of 6**

1. With **6-England.pptx** open, display the presentation in Slide Master view by clicking the View tab and then clicking the Slide Master button in the Master Views group.
2. Insert a header, a footer, and the date and time by completing the following steps:
   a. Click the slide master thumbnail (the top slide thumbnail in the slide thumbnails pane).
   b. Click the Insert tab.
   c. Click the Header & Footer button in the Text group.
   d. At the Header and Footer dialog box with the Slide tab selected, click the *Date and time* check box to insert a check mark.
   e. Make sure the *Update automatically* option is selected. (With this option selected, the date and/or time will automatically update each time you open the presentation.)
   f. Click the *Slide number* check box to insert a check mark.
   g. Click the *Footer* check box to insert a check mark, click in the *Footer* text box, and then type your first and last names.
   h. Click the Notes and Handouts tab.
   i. Click the *Date and time* check box to insert a check mark.
   j. Make sure the *Update automatically* option is selected.
   k. Click the *Header* check box to insert a check mark, click in the *Header* text box, and then type the name of your school.
   l. Click the *Footer* check box to insert a check mark, click in the *Footer* text box, and then type your first and last names.
   m. Click the Apply to All button.

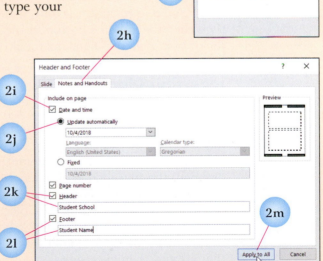

3. Insert the First Choice Travel logo in the upper right corner of the slide master by completing the following steps:

   a. Click the Pictures button in the Images group.

   b. At the Insert Picture dialog box, navigate to the PC6 folder on your storage medium and then double-click *FCTLogo.jpg*.

   c. Click in the *Shape Height* measurement box in the Size group on the Picture Tools Format tab, type 0.6, and then press the Enter key.

   d. Drag the logo to position it in the upper right corner of the slide as shown at the right.

   e. Click outside the logo to deselect it.

4. If necessary, click the Slide Master tab.

5. Click the Close Master View button.

6. Run the slide show to view the logo and other elements in the slides.

7. Save **6-England.pptx**.

3d

Check Your Work

Creating and Renaming a Custom Slide Layout

 Insert Layout

A custom slide layout can be created in Slide Master view and then further customized by inserting or deleting elements and applying formatting to placeholders and text. To create a new slide layout, click the Insert Layout button in the Edit Master group on the Slide Master tab. This inserts in the slide pane a new slide containing a master title placeholder and footer placeholders. Customize the layout by inserting or deleting placeholders and applying formatting to placeholders.

PowerPoint automatically assigns the name *Custom Layout* to a custom slide layout. If another custom slide layout is created, PowerPoint will name it *1_Custom Layout*, and so on. Consider renaming a custom layout with a name that describes that layout. To rename a layout, make sure the specific slide layout is active and

 Rename

then click the Rename button in the Edit Master group. At the Rename Layout dialog box, type the name for the layout and then click the Rename button.

Inserting Placeholders

A placeholder can be inserted in a predesigned or custom slide layout. Insert a placeholder by clicking the Insert Placeholder button arrow in the Master Layout group and then clicking the specific placeholder option at the drop-down list. If the slide master layout is selected, the Insert Placeholder button is dimmed. If a placeholder is deleted from the slide master, it can be reinserted with options at the Master Layout dialog box. Display this dialog box by clicking

Insert Placeholder

 Master Layout

the Master Layout button. Any placeholder that has been removed from the slide master displays in the dialog box as an active option with an empty check box. Reinsert the placeholder by clicking the check box to insert a check mark in the box and then clicking OK to close the dialog box.

Creating Custom Prompts

Some placeholders in a custom layout may contain generic text such as *Click to add Master title style* or *Click to edit Master text styles*. In Slide Master view, this generic text can be replaced with custom text. For example, custom text may describe what should be inserted in the placeholder. Insert a custom prompt by clicking the Insert Placeholder button in the Master Layout group on the Slide Master tab and then clicking the type of placeholder to be inserted in the slide. After clicking the placeholder type, the mouse pointer will display as crosshairs. Click and drag in the slide to create the placeholder and then customize the text in the placeholder.

Project 1e Inserting a Layout and Placeholder   Part 5 of 6

1. With **6-England.pptx** open, click the View tab and then click the Slide Master button in the Master Views group.
2. Click the bottom slide layout thumbnail in the slide thumbnails pane.
3. Click the Insert Layout button in the Edit Master group. (This inserts in the slide pane a new slide with a master title placeholder, the logo, and the footer information.)
4. Remove the footer by clicking the *Footers* check box in the Master Layout group to remove the check mark.
5. Format and move the placeholder by completing the following steps:
   a. Click the *Click to edit Master title style* placeholder border.
   b. Click the Home tab, change the font size to 28 points, apply the Light Blue, Background 2, Darker 50% font color (third column, fourth row in the *Theme Colors* section), and then click the Center button in the Paragraph group.
   c. Move the placeholder so it is positioned along the bottom of the slide, just above the bottom blue border line (as shown below).

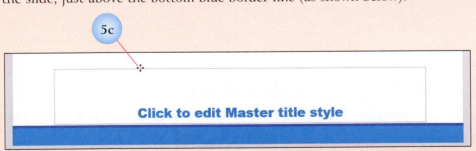

6. Click the Slide Master tab.
7. Insert a picture placeholder by completing the following steps:
   a. Click the Insert Placeholder button arrow.
   b. Click *Picture* at the drop-down list.
   c. Click in the slide to insert a placeholder.
   d. With the Drawing Tools Format tab active, click in the *Shape Height* measurement box and then type 3.5.

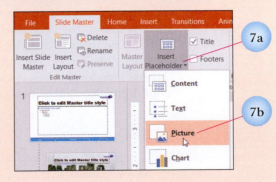

e. Click in the *Shape Width* measurement box, type 12, and then press the Enter key.

f. Drag the placeholder so it is positioned about 0.5 inch below the thin black line in the slide and centered horizontally. (The picture placeholder will overlap the title placeholder.)

g. Click anywhere in the word *Picture* in the placeholder. (This removes the word *Picture* and positions the insertion point in the placeholder.)

h. Type Insert company logo and then click outside of the placeholder.

8. Rename the custom slide layout by completing the following steps:

a. Click the Rename button in the Edit Master group on the Slide Master tab.

b. At the Rename Layout dialog box, select the text that displays in the *Layout name* text box and then type Logo.

c. Click the Rename button.

9. Click the Close Master View button.

10. Insert a slide using the new slide layout by completing the following steps:

a. Make Slide 6 active.

b. Click the New Slide button arrow.

c. Click *Logo* at the drop-down list.

d. Click the Pictures button in the slide.

e. At the Insert Picture dialog box, navigate to the PC6 folder on your storage medium and then double-click *FCTLogo.jpg*.

f. Click in the title placeholder and then type Monthly special: 20% discount on Wiltshire tour.

11. Save **6-England.pptx**.

Check Your Work

Inserting a New Slide Master

Insert Slide Master

A PowerPoint presentation can contain more than one slide master (and associated layouts). To insert a new slide master, display the presentation in Slide Master view and then click the Insert Slide Master button in the Edit Master group. This inserts a new slide master and all associated layouts below the existing slide master and layouts in the slide thumbnails pane. A slide master and all associated layouts can also be inserted with a design theme applied. To do this, click below the existing slide master and associated layouts, click the Themes button in the Edit Theme group, and then click the theme at the drop-down gallery. A slide master containing the chosen design theme is inserted below the existing thumbnails.

Preserving Slide Masters

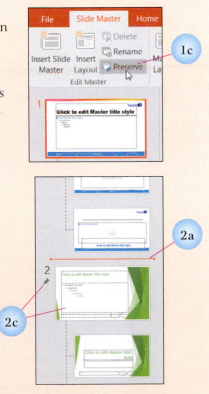

Preserve

If all of the slide layouts that follow a slide master are deleted, PowerPoint will automatically delete the slide master. A slide master can be protected from being deleted by preserving the master. To do this, click the slide master thumbnail and then click the Preserve button in the Edit Master group. If a slide master is inserted using the Insert Slide Master button, the Preserve button is automatically active. When a slide master is preserved, a preservation icon displays below the slide number in the slide thumbnails pane.

Ōuick Steps

Preserve a Slide Master
1. Display presentation in Slide Master view.
2. Click slide master thumbnail.
3. Click Preserve button.

Changing Page Setup

Click the Slide Size button in the Size group on the Slide Master tab and a drop-down list displays with options for choosing standard or widescreen size. In addition to these two options, the drop-down list also includes the *Custom Slide Size* option. Click this option and the Slide Size dialog box displays. This is the same dialog box covered in Chapter 3. The dialog box contains options for changing slide width, height, and numbering, as well as applying slide orientation to slides, notes, handouts, and outline pages.

Project 1f Applying a Second Slide Master   **Part 6 of 6**

1. With **6-England.pptx** open, preserve the Retrospect slide master by completing the following steps:
   a. Click the View tab and then click the Slide Master button in the Master Views group.
   b. Click the first slide master (*Retrospect Slide Master*) in the slide thumbnails pane.
   c. Click the Preserve button in the Edit Master group. (This inserts a preservation icon below the slide number in the slide thumbnails pane).

2. Insert a second slide master by completing the following steps:
   a. Click below the bottom slide layout in the slide thumbnails pane. (You want the second slide master and associated layouts to display below the original slide master and not take the place of the original.)
   b. Click the Themes button in the Edit Theme group and then click *Facet* at the drop-down gallery.
   c. Notice that the slide master and associated layouts display in the slide thumbnails pane below the original slide master and associated layouts and that the preservation icon displays below the second slide master.
   d. Click the new slide master (*Facet Slide Master*) in the slide thumbnails pane.
   e. Click the Colors button in the Background group and then click the *Blue* option.
   f. Click the Fonts button and then click the *Arial Black-Arial* option.

3. Click the first layout below the new slide master (*Title Slide Layout*) and then select and delete the master subtitle placeholder.
4. Click the third layout below the new slide master (*Section Header Layout*), scroll down to the bottom of the slide thumbnails pane, press and hold down the Shift key, click the bottom thumbnail, release the Shift key, and then click the Delete button in the Edit Master group. (This deletes all but two of the layouts associated with the new slide master.)
5. Click the Close Master View button.
6. Insert a new slide by completing the following steps:
   a. Make Slide 7 active.
   b. Click the New Slide button arrow and then click *Title Slide* in the *Facet* section.

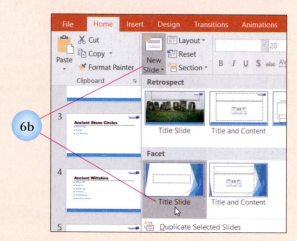

   c. Click in the title placeholder and then type New York City Tour.
7. Insert a new slide by completing the following steps:
   a. With Slide 8 active, click the New Slide button. (This inserts a slide with the Facet Title and Content layout.)
   b. Click in the title placeholder and then type Manhattan Tour.
   c. Click in the text placeholder and then type the following bulleted text:
      Times Square
      Madison Square Garden
      Greenwich Village
      Soho
      Little Italy
      Battery Park
8. Insert slides using the Reuse Slides task pane by completing the following steps:
   a. Click the New Slide button arrow and then click *Reuse Slides* at the drop-down list.
   b. Click the Browse button in the Reuse Slides task pane and then click *Browse File* at the drop-down list.
   c. At the Browse dialog box, navigate to the PC6 folder on your storage medium and then double-click *FCTNewYork.pptx*.
   d. Click the *Dinner Cruise* slide in the Reuse Slides task pane. (This inserts the slide in the presentation and applies the custom formatting to that slide.)
   e. Click the *City Pass* slide in the Reuse Slides task pane.
   f. Click the *Museum Passes* slide in the Reuse Slides task pane.
   g. Click the Close button in the upper right corner of the Reuse Slides task pane to close the task pane.

9. Assume that the presentation is going to be inserted into a larger presentation and that the starting slide will be Slide 12 (instead of Slide 1). Change the beginning slide number by completing the following steps:

a. Click the View tab and then click the Slide Master button.

b. Click the top slide master in the slide thumbnails pane.

c. Click the Slide Size button in the Size group and then click *Custom Slide Size* at the drop-down list.

d. At the Slide Size dialog box, select the current number in the *Number slides from* measurement box and then type 12.

e. Click OK to close the dialog box.

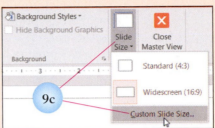

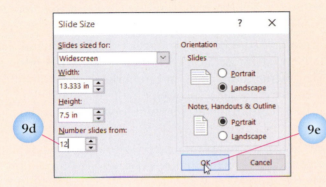

f. Click the second slide master in the slide thumbnails pane (*Facet Slide Master* thumbnail).

g. Click the Insert tab and then click the Slide Number button in the Text group.

h. At the Header and Footer dialog box with the Slide tab selected, click the *Slide number* check box to insert a check mark and then click the Apply to All button.

i. Click the Slide Master tab.

j. Click the Close Master View button.

10. Make Slide 12 active (the first slide in the presentation) and then run the slide show.

11. Print the presentation as a handout with six slides displayed horizontally per page.

12. Save and then close **6-England.pptx**.

Check Your Work

Project 2 Save a Template and Create a Travel Presentation with the Template

4 Parts

You will save a travel presentation as a template and then use that template to create and format a travel presentation. You will insert elements in the presentation in Handout Master view and Notes Master view, change the presentation zoom, and view the presentation in grayscale and black and white.

Preview Finished Project

Saving a Presentation as a Template

If custom formatting will be used for future presentations, consider saving the presentation as a template. The advantage to saving a presentation as a template is that the template cannot accidentally be overwritten. Save a custom template in the Custom Office Templates folder in the Documents folder on the hard drive. Check to determine the default custom template folder location by displaying the PowerPoint Options dialog box with *Save* selected in the left panel. The *Default personal templates location* option should display the Custom Office Templates folder in the Documents folder as the default location. If this is not the default location, check with your instructor.

To save a presentation as a template, display the Save As dialog box, click the *Save as type* option button, and then click *PowerPoint Template (*.potx)* at the drop-down list. Type a name for the template in the *File name* text box and then click the Save button.

To create a presentation based on a template, click the File tab and then click the *New* option. At the New backstage area, click the *PERSONAL* option that displays above the design theme thumbnails and thumbnails for templates saved in the Custom Office Templates folder display. Open a template by double-clicking the template thumbnail. PowerPoint opens a presentation based on the template, not the original template file.

By default, PowerPoint saves a template in the Custom Office Templates folder in the Documents folder on the computer's hard drive. In addition to this folder, a template can be saved to a specific folder and then a presentation based on the template can be opened using File Explorer, which is a file management application included with Microsoft Windows. To use File Explorer, click the File Explorer icon on the taskbar and, at the window that displays, navigate to the folder containing the template and then double-click the template.

If a template is no longer needed, delete the template at the Custom Office Templates folder. Open this folder by displaying the Open dialog box, displaying the Documents folder, and then double-clicking the Custom Office Templates folder. Click the template file to be deleted, click the Organize button, and then click *Delete* at the drop-down list.

Project 2a Saving a Presentation as a Template   Part 1 of 4

Note: If you are using PowerPoint 2016 in a school setting on a network system, you may need to complete Project 2a and 2b on the same day Or, you may need to save a template to your PC6 folder and then use File Explorer to open a presentation based on the template. Check with your instructor for any specific instructions.

1. Open **6-TravelMaster.pptx**.
2. Press F12 to display the Save As dialog box.
3. At the Save As dialog box, type **XXXTravelTemplate** in the *File name* text box. (Type your initials in place of the *XXX*.)
4. Click the *Save as type* option box and then click *PowerPoint Template (*.potx)* at the drop-down list.
5. Click the Save button.

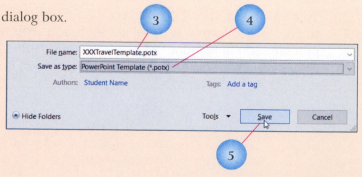

6. Close **XXXTravelTemplate.potx**.
7. Open the template and save it as a presentation by completing the following steps:
   a. Click the File tab and then click the *New* option.
   b. At the New backstage area, click the *PERSONAL* option.
   c. Double-click the ***XXXTravelTemplate*** thumbnail.

8. Save the presentation with the name **6-ParisTour**.

Check Your Work

Tutorial

Customizing the
Handout Master

 Handout
Master

Customizing the Handout Master

When a presentation is printed as handouts or an outline, PowerPoint will automatically print the current date in the upper right corner of the page and the page number in the lower right corner. Customize handouts with options in the Handout Master view. Display a presentation in Handout Master view by clicking the View tab and then clicking the Handout Master button in the Master Views group. Use options on the Handout Master tab to move, size, and format header and footer placeholders; change page orientation; add or remove placeholders; and specify the number of slides to be printed on each page.

With buttons in the Page Setup group, change the handout orientation, display the Slide Size dialog box with options for changing the size and orientation of the handouts page, and specify the number of slides to be printed on the handouts page. By default, a handouts page will contain a header, footer, date, and page number placeholder. Remove any of these placeholders by removing the check mark before the placeholder check boxes in the Placeholders group.

The Edit Theme group contains buttons for changing the theme color, font, and effects. Click the Themes button and the options in the drop-down gallery are dimmed, indicating that the themes are not available for the handouts pages. If a background style is applied to the handout master, theme colors can be changed by clicking the Colors button and then clicking a color theme at the drop-down gallery. Apply theme fonts by clicking the Fonts button and then clicking a font theme at the drop-down gallery.

 Background
Styles

Apply a background style to the handouts page by clicking the Background Styles button in the Background group and then clicking one of the predesigned styles. Or, click the *Format Background* option at the Background Styles button drop-down list and then make changes at the Format Background task pane. Remove any background graphics by clicking the *Hide Background Graphics* check box to insert a check mark.

1. With **6-ParisTour.pptx** open and displayed in Normal view, click the New Slide button arrow in the Slides group on the Home tab and then click *Reuse Slides* at the drop-down list.
2. In the Reuse Slides task pane, click the Browse button and then click the *Browse File* option at the drop-down list.
3. Navigate to the PC6 folder on your storage medium and then double-click *ParisTour.pptx*.
4. Insert the second, third, fourth, and fifth slides from the Reuse Slides task pane into the current presentation.
5. Close the Reuse Slides task pane.
6. Edit the Title Slide Layout in Slide Master view by completing the following steps:
   a. Click the View tab and then click the Slide Master button.
   b. Click the second thumbnail in the slide thumbnails pane (*Title Slide Layout*).
   c. Click the Background Styles button in the Background group and then click *Format Background* at the drop-down list.
   d. At the Format Background task pane, click the File button (below the text *Insert picture from*).
   e. At the Insert Picture dialog box, navigate to the PC6 folder on your storage medium and then double-click *EiffelTower.jpg*.
   f. Close the Format Background task pane.
   g. If necessary, click the *Hide Background Graphics* check box in the Background group to insert a check mark.
   h. Select the text *Click to edit Master title style*, click the Home tab, click the Font Color button arrow, and then click the *Turquoise, Accent 2, Lighter 60%* option (sixth column, third row in the *Theme Colors* section).
   i. Click the Slide Master tab.
   j. Click the Close Master View button.
   k. Make Slide 1 active and then type Paris Tour in the title placeholder.
   l. Size and move the text placeholder so *Paris Tour* displays in a blue area of the slide (not over the tower).

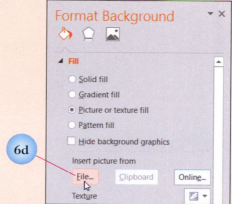

7. Make Slide 5 active and then create a new slide with the Title Slide layout. Type Call Greg at 213-555-4500 in the title placeholder. (Leave the placeholder in the default location.)
8. Save **6-ParisTour.pptx**.
9. Click the View tab and then click the Handout Master button in the Master Views group.

10. Click the Handout Orientation button in the Page Setup group and then click *Landscape* at the drop-down list.

11. Click in the Header placeholder on the page and then type your first and last names.
12. Click in the Footer placeholder and then type *Paris Tour*.
13. Click the Background Styles button and then click *Style 9* at the drop-down list (first column, third row).
14. Click the Colors button in the Background group and then click the *Blue* option.
15. Click the Fonts button in the Background group, scroll down the drop-down gallery, and then click the *Arial Black-Arial* option.
16. Edit the header text by completing the following steps:
    a. Click in the Header placeholder.
    b. Move the insertion point so it is positioned immediately to the right of the last character in your last name.
    c. Type a comma, press the spacebar, and then type your course number and title.
    d. Click in the handouts page outside of any placeholder.
17. Click the Close Master View button.
18. Save **6-ParisTour.pptx**

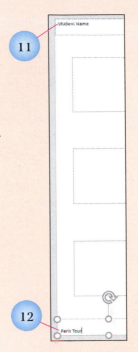

Check Your Work

Tutorial

Customizing the Notes Master

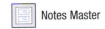 Notes Master

Customizing the Notes Master

If notes are inserted in a presentation, the presentation can be printed as notes pages with the notes printed below the slides. To insert or format text or other elements as notes on all slides in a presentation, consider making the changes in the Notes Master view. Display this view by clicking the View tab and then clicking the Notes Master button in the Master Views group. This displays a notes page along with the Notes Master tab. Many of the buttons and options on this tab are the same as those on the Handout Master tab.

Project 2c **Customizing the Notes Master**   **Part 3 of 4**

1. With **6-ParisTour.pptx** open, click the View tab and then click the Notes Master button in the Master Views group.
2. Click the *Body* check box in the Placeholders group to remove the check mark.
3. Click the Fonts button in the Background group, scroll down the drop-down gallery, and then click the *Arial Black-Arial* option.
4. Click the Insert tab.
5. Click the Text Box button in the Text group.
6. Click in the notes page below the slide.
7. Type Visit www.first-choice.emcp.net for a listing of all upcoming tours.

8. Size and position the text box below the slide as shown below and to the right.
9. Click the Insert tab and then click the Pictures button in the Images group.
10. At the Insert Picture dialog box, navigate to the PC6 folder on your storage medium and then double-click *FCTLogo.jpg*.
11. Change the height of the logo to 0.5 inch. (This changes the width to approximately 1.75 inches.)
12. Drag the logo so it is positioned below the text as shown below.

13. Click the Notes Master tab and then click the Close Master View button.
14. Print Slides 2 and 4 as notes pages by completing the following steps:
    a. Display the Print backstage area.
    b. Click the second gallery in the *Settings* category and then click *Notes Pages* in the *Print Layout* section.
    c. Click in the *Slides* text box located below the first gallery in the *Settings* category and then type 2,4.
    d. Click the Print button.
15. Save **6-ParisTour.pptx**.

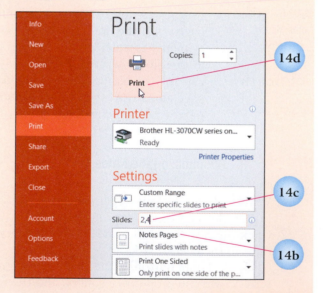

Check Your Work

Using View Tab Options

The View tab contains buttons for displaying a presentation in various views such as Normal, Slide Sorter, Slide Master, Handout Master, and Notes Master. In addition to viewing buttons, the View tab also includes options for showing or hiding the ruler and gridlines; displaying the Notes pane below the slide pane; zooming in or out in the slide; viewing the slide in color, grayscale, or black and white; and working with windows.

Tutorial

Changing the
Display of a Slide
in the Slide Pane

Zoom

Changing the Zoom

Change the display size of the slide in the slide pane or the slides in the slide thumbnails pane with the Zoom button on the View tab or with the Zoom slider bar at the right side of the Status bar. Click the Zoom button on the View tab and the Zoom dialog box displays. Use options in this dialog box to increase or decrease the display size of slides in the slide pane or slide thumbnails pane.

To change the zoom with the Zoom slider bar, use the mouse to drag the slider bar button to the left to decrease the display size or to the right to increase the display size. Click the Zoom Out button (the minus symbol at the left side of the Zoom slider bar) to decrease the display percentage or click the Zoom In button (the plus symbol at the right side of the Zoom slider bar) to increase the display percentage. Click the Zoom level button, which displays as a percentage number at the right side of the slider bar, and the Zoom dialog box displays.

Managing Windows

Use buttons in the Window group on the View tab to work with presentation windows. Work in two locations in the same presentation by opening the presentation and then opening a new window with the same presentation. This is helpful for viewing and editing slides in two different locations in the presentation. Open a new window by clicking the New Window button in the Window group.

 New Window

 Arrange All

 Cascade

If more than one presentation is open, the presentations can be arranged so a portion of each presentation displays. Click the Arrange All button in the Window group and each open presentation displays as a tile on the screen. Click the Cascade button in the Window group and the open presentations are displayed in a layered manner with the title bar of each presentation visible. Slides can be copied from one presentation to another when the presentations are arranged on the screen by dragging a slide from the slide thumbnails pane in one presentation to the slide thumbnails pane in the other presentation.

  Switch Windows

With more than one presentation open, switch between presentations by clicking the Switch Windows button in the Window group. Click this button and a drop-down list with the names of the open presentations displays with a check mark in front of the active presentation. Make another presentation active by clicking the presentation name at the drop-down list.

  Move Split

Maximize

Minimize

Restore
Down

Increase or decrease the viewing area of each section of the presentation window with the Move Split button. Click this button and the mouse pointer displays as a four-headed arrow. Use the arrow keys on the keyboard to increase or decrease the viewing area of the slide pane and slide thumbnails pane. Click the left mouse button to deactivate the feature. Use the Maximize and Minimize buttons in the upper right corner of the active presentation to change the size of the window. If all open presentations are arranged in the window, click the Maximize button in the active presentation to fill the presentation screen. In addition, the Maximize button changes to the Restore Down button. To return the active presentation back to its size before it was maximized, click the Restore Down button. Click the Minimize button in the active presentation to reduce the presentation to a button that displays on the taskbar.

Viewing in Color and Grayscale

Color

Grayscale

Black and White

By default, the slides in a presentation display in color. This can be changed to grayscale or black and white with buttons in the Color/Grayscale group on the View tab. Click the Grayscale button and the slides in the presentation display in grayscale and the Grayscale tab becomes active. This tab contains a variety of options for changing the grayscale display, such as light grayscale, inverse grayscale, and gray or black with grayscale fill. Return to the color view by clicking the Back to Color View button on the Grayscale tab. Click the Black and White button in the Color/Grayscale group and the slides in the presentation display in black and white and the Black And White tab becomes active. This tab contains many of the same options as the Grayscale tab.

Project 2d Viewing a Presentation

Part 4 of 4

1. With **6-ParisTour.pptx** open, make Slide 1 active and then click the slide in the slide pane.
2. Click the View tab.
3. Increase and decrease the zoom by completing the following steps:
   a. Click the Zoom button in the Zoom group.
   b. At the Zoom dialog box, click the *33%* option and then click OK.
   c. Click the Zoom button, click the *100%* option in the Zoom dialog box, and then click OK.
   d. Click the Slide 2 thumbnail in the slide thumbnails pane.
   e. Click the Zoom button, click the *66%* option in the Zoom dialog box, and then click OK. (Because the slide was active in the slide thumbnails pane, the percentage display changed for the thumbnails in the pane.)
   f. Position the mouse pointer on the Zoom slider bar button (at the right side of the Status bar), drag the button to the right to increase the size of the slide in the slide pane, and then drag the slider bar to the left to decrease the size of the slide.
   g. Click the Zoom level button (the percentage number at the right side of the Zoom slider bar). This displays the Zoom dialog box.
   h. Click the *100%* option in the Zoom dialog box and then click OK.
   i. Click the Fit to Window button in the Zoom group on the View tab.
4. View the slides in grayscale by completing the following steps:
   a. Click the Grayscale button in the Color/Grayscale group on the View tab.
   b. Click the slide in the slide pane.
   c. Click the buttons on the Grayscale tab to display the slides in varying grayscale options.
   d. Click the Back To Color View button.
5. View the slides in black and white by completing the following steps:
   a. Click the View tab and then click the Black and White button in the Color/Grayscale group.
   b. Click some of the buttons on the Black And White tab to display the slides with varying black and white options applied.
   c. Click the Back To Color View button.

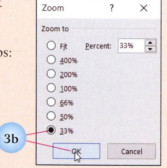

6. Open another presentation and then arrange the presentations by completing the following steps:
   a. Open **ParisTravelInfo.pptx** from the PC6 folder.
   b. Click the View tab and then click the Cascade button in the Window group. (This arranges the two presentations with the presentations overlapping with the title bar for each presentation visible.)
   c. Click the Switch Windows button in the Window group and then click the *6-ParisTour.pptx* option at the drop-down list.
   d. Click the Arrange All button in the Window group to arrange the two presentations in two side-by-side windows.

7. Copy a slide from one presentation to another by completing the following steps:
   a. Click Slide 2 (*Accommodations*) in the slide thumbnails pane of **ParisTravelInfo.pptx** and hold down the left mouse button.
   b. Drag the slide so it is positioned below the Slide 5 thumbnail in the slide thumbnails pane in **6-ParisTour.pptx** (an orange line will display) and then release the mouse button.

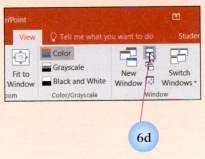

8. Click the Close button in the upper right corner of the **ParisTravelInfo.pptx** file.
9. Click the Maximize button in the upper right corner of the presentation window. (The Maximize button displays immediately to the left of the Close button.)
10. Use the Move Split button by completing these steps:
    a. Click the Move Split button in the Window group. (The mouse displays as a four-headed arrow.)
    b. Press the Right Arrow key on the keyboard several times and notice the slide thumbnails pane increasing in size.
    c. Press the Left Arrow key several times.
    d. Press the Up Arrow key several times and notice that the slide in the slide pane decreases in size and the notes pane displays.
    e. Press the Down Arrow key until the slide in the slide pane returns to the original size and the notes pane has closed.
11. With the View tab active, click the Grayscale button in the Color/Grayscale group and then click the Light Grayscale button in the Change Selected Object group.
12. Print the presentation by completing the following steps:
    a. Display the Print backstage area.
    b. If any text displays in the *Slides* text box, select and then delete the text.
    c. If you are using a color printer, click the *Color* gallery that displays at the bottom of the *Settings* category and then click *Grayscale*. (Skip this step if you are using a black and white printer.)
    d. Click the second gallery in the *Settings* category and then click *4 Slides Horizontal* in the *Handouts* section.
    e. Click the Print button.
13. Click the Back To Color View button on the Grayscale tab.
14. Make Slide 1 active and then run the slide show.
15. Save and then close **6-ParisTour.pptx**.

Check Your Work

You will open a job search presentation and then insert action buttons that display the next slide, the first slide, a website, and another presentation. You will also create a hyperlink from text, a graphic image, and a chart in a slide to a website, a Word document, and another presentation.

Preview Finished Project

Tutorial

Inserting Action
Buttons

Inserting Action Buttons

Action buttons are drawn objects on a slide that have a routine attached to them which is activated when the viewer or the presenter clicks the button. For example, an action button can be inserted in a slide that displays the next slide in the presentation, a file in another program, or a specific web page. Creating an action button is a two-step process. The button is drawn in the slide using an Action Button shape in the Shapes button drop-down list and then the action that will take place is defined with options in the Action Settings dialog box. Customize an action button in the same manner as customizing a drawn object. When the viewer or presenter moves the mouse over an action button during a presentation, the pointer changes to a hand with the index finger pointing upward to indicate clicking will result in an action.

To display the available action buttons, click the Insert tab and then click the Shapes button in the Illustrations group. Action buttons display at the bottom of the drop-down list. Hover the mouse pointer over a button and the name and the action it performs will display in a ScreenTip above the button. The action attached to an action button occurs when the button is clicked during the running of the slide show.

Quick Steps

Insert an Action Button

1. Make slide active.
2. Click Insert tab.
3. Click Shapes button.
4. Click action button.
5. Click or drag in slide to create button.
6. Make changes at Action Settings dialog box.
7. Click OK.

Hint Apply formatting to an action button with options on the Drawing Tools Format tab.

Project 3a Inserting Action Buttons

Part 1 of 5

1. Open **JobSearch.pptx** and then save it with the name **6-JobSearch**.
2. Make the following changes to the presentation:
   a. Apply the Dividend design theme.
   b. Click the Insert tab and then click the Header & Footer button in the Text group.
   c. At the Header and Footer dialog box with the Slide tab selected, click the *Date and time* check box and make sure *Update automatically* is selected.
   d. Click the *Slide number* check box to insert a check mark.
   e. Click the Notes and Handouts tab.
   f. Click the *Date and time* check box and make sure *Update automatically* is selected.
   g. Click the *Header* check box to insert a check mark, click in the *Header* text box, and then type the name of your school.
   h. Click the *Footer* check box to insert a check mark, click in the *Footer* text box, and then type your first and last names.
   i. Click the Apply to All button.

3. Insert an action button in Slide 1 that will display the next slide by completing the following steps:

a. Make sure Slide 1 is active.

b. Click the Insert tab and then click the Shapes button in the Illustrations group.

c. Scroll down the drop-down list and then click the *Action Button: Forward or Next* button (second button in the *Action Buttons* group).

d. Move the crosshairs to the lower right corner of the slide and then drag to create a button that is approximately 0.5 inch in height and width (see below).

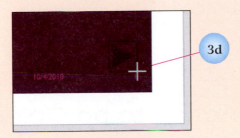

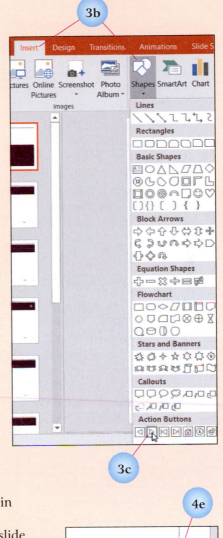

e. At the Action Settings dialog box, click OK. (The default setting is *Hyperlink to Next Slide*.)

4. Insert an action button in Slide Master view that will display the next slide by completing the following steps:

a. Display the presentation in Slide Master view.

b. Click the top slide master thumbnail (*Dividend Slide Master*).

c. Click the Insert tab and then click the Shapes button in the Illustrations group.

d. Scroll down the drop-down list and then click the *Action Button: Forward or Next* button (second button in the *Action Buttons* group).

e. Move the crosshairs to the lower right corner of the slide master and then drag to create a button as shown at the right.

f. At the Action Settings dialog box, click OK. (The default setting is *Hyperlink to Next Slide*.)

g. Click the Slide Master tab and then click the Close Master View button.

5. Make Slide 1 active and then run the slide show, clicking the action button to advance slides. When you click the action button on the last slide (Slide 9) nothing happens because it is the last slide. Press the Esc key to end the slide show.

6. Change the action button on Slide 9 by completing the following steps:

a. Make Slide 9 active.

b. Click the Insert tab and then click the Shapes button in the Illustrations group.

c. Scroll down the drop-down list and then click the *Action Button: Home* button (fifth button in the *Action Buttons* group).

d. Drag to create a button on top of the previous action button. (Make sure it completely covers the previous action button.)

e. At the Action Settings dialog box with the *Hyperlink to: First Slide* option selected, click OK.

f. Deselect the button.

7. Display Slide 1 in the slide pane and then run the slide show. Navigate through the slide show by clicking the action button. When you click the action button on the last slide, the first slide displays. End the slide show by pressing the Esc key.

8. Save **6-JobSearch.pptx**.

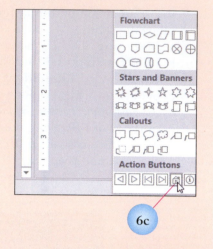

6c

Check Your Work ▶

Tutorial ▶

Applying an Action to an Object

 Action

Applying an Action to an Object

The Links group on the Insert tab contains an Action button for specifying an action for a selected object. To use this button, select the object in the slide, click the Insert tab, and then click the Action button. This displays the Action Settings dialog box, which is the same dialog box that displays when an action button is drawn in a slide.

The action button or a selected object can be linked to another PowerPoint presentation, another file, or a website. To link to another PowerPoint presentation, click the *Hyperlink to* option at the Action Settings dialog box, click the *Hyperlink to* option box arrow, and then click *Other PowerPoint Presentation* at the drop-down list. At the Hyperlink to Other PowerPoint Presentation dialog box, navigate to the specific folder, and then double-click the PowerPoint presentation. To link to another file, click the *Hyperlink to* option at the Action Settings dialog box, click the *Hyperlink to* option box arrow, and then click *Other File* at the drop-down list. At the Hyperlink to Other File dialog box, navigate to the specific folder and then double-click the file name. To link to a website, click the *Hyperlink to* option at the Action Settings dialog box, click the *Hyperlink to* option box arrow, and then click *URL* at the drop-down list. At the Hyperlink to URL dialog box, type the web address in the *URL* text box, and then click OK. Other locations that can be linked to using the *Hyperlink to* drop-down list include *Next Slide*, *Previous Slide*, *First Slide*, *Last Slide*, *Last Slide Viewed*, *End Show*, *Custom Show*, *Slide*, and *Other File*.

Project 3b Linking to Another Presentation and a Website

Part 2 of 5

1. With **6-JobSearch.pptx** open, add an action button that will link to another presentation by completing the following steps:

a. Make Slide 4 active.

b. Click the Insert tab and then click the Shapes button in the Illustrations group.

c. Scroll down the drop-down list and then click *Action Button: Help* (eleventh button in the *Action Buttons* section).

d. Draw the action button to the left of the existing button in the lower right corner of the slide.

e. At the Action Settings dialog box, click the *Hyperlink to* option.

f. Click the *Hyperlink to* option box arrow and then click *Other PowerPoint Presentation* at the drop-down list.

g. At the Hyperlink to Other PowerPoint Presentation dialog box, navigate to the PC6 folder on your storage medium and then double-click **Contacts.pptx**.

h. At the Hyperlink to Slide dialog box, click OK.

i. Click OK to close the Action Settings dialog box.

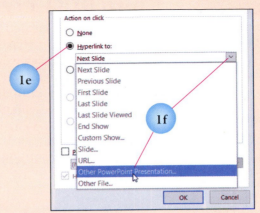

2. Apply an action to the image in Slide 5 that links to a website by completing the following steps:

a. Make Slide 5 active and then click the image to select it.

b. Click the Insert tab and then click the Action button in the Links group.

c. At the Action Settings dialog box, click the *Hyperlink to* option.

d. Click the *Hyperlink to* option box arrow, and then click *URL* at the drop-down list.

e. At the Hyperlink to URL dialog box, type www.usajobs.gov in the *URL* text box and then click OK.

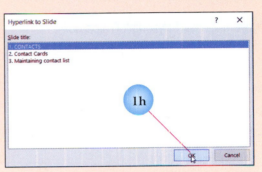

f. Click OK to close the Action Settings dialog box.

g. Click outside the image to deselect it.

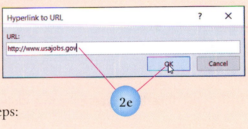

3. Run the slide show by completing the following steps:

a. Make sure you are connected to the Internet.

b. Make Slide 1 active.

c. Click the Slide Show button in the view area on the Status bar.

d. Navigate through the slide show to Slide 4.

e. Click the action button in Slide 4 containing the question mark. (This displays Slide 1 of **Contacts.pptx**.)

f. Navigate through the three slides in **Contacts.pptx**. Continue clicking the mouse button until you return to Slide 4 of **6-JobSearch.pptx**.

g. Display Slide 5 and then click the image. (If you are connected to the Internet, the job site of the United States Federal Government displays.)

h. Search for information on a specific job title that interests you and then click a few hyperlinks at the website.

i. When you have finished viewing the website, close your web browser.

j. Continue viewing the remainder of the slide show by clicking the action button in the lower right corner of each slide.

k. When Slide 1 displays, press the Esc key to end the slide show.

4. Save **6-JobSearch.pptx**.

Check Your Work

Inserting Hyperlinks

Inserting
Hyperlinks

 Hyperlink

Quick Steps

Insert a Hyperlink
1. Click Insert tab.
2. Click Hyperlink button.
3. Make changes at Insert Hyperlink dialog box.
4. Click OK.

Hyperlinks can be created with options at the Action Settings dialog box or with options at the Insert Hyperlink dialog box shown in Figure 6.2. To display this dialog box, select a key word, phrase, or object in a slide, click the Insert tab, and then click the Hyperlink button in the Links group, or press Ctrl + K, which is the keyboard shortcut to display the Insert Hyperlink dialog box. Link to a website, another presentation, a place in the current presentation, a new presentation, or to an email address. To insert a hyperlink to a website or an existing presentation, click the Existing File or Web Page button in the *Link to* group at the Insert Hyperlink dialog box.

Figure 6.2 Insert Hyperlink Dialog Box

Type the text that will display in the hyperlink.

Click this button to edit the hyperlink ScreenTip.

Click a button in this group to indicate the hyperlink location.

Select a file name or type a web address to specify a hyperlink location.

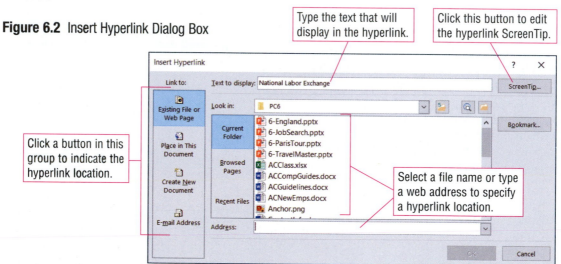

Project 3c Inserting Hyperlinks to a Website

Part 3 of 5

1. With **6-JobSearch.pptx** open, insert a new slide by completing the following steps:
   a. Make Slide 5 active.
   b. Click the Home tab.
   c. Click the New Slide button arrow and then click the Title and Content layout option.
   d. Type Internet Job Resources as the slide title.
   e. Click the text placeholder, type National Labor Exchange, press the Enter key, and then type Monster.
2. Add a hyperlink to the National Labor Exchange site by completing the following steps:
   a. Select the text *National Labor Exchange* in Slide 6.
   b. Click the Insert tab and then click the Hyperlink button in the Links group.
   c. At the Insert Hyperlink dialog box, type www.us.jobs in the *Address* text box. (PowerPoint automatically inserts *http://* at the beginning of the address.)
   d. Click OK to close the Insert Hyperlink dialog box.

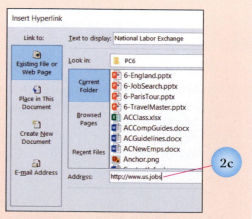

3. Add a hyperlink to the Monster website by completing the following steps:
   a. Select the text *Monster* in Slide 6.
   b. Click the Hyperlink button in the Links group.
   c. At the Insert Hyperlink dialog box, type www.monster.com in the *Address* text box. (PowerPoint automatically inserts *http://* at the beginning of the address.)
   d. Click OK to close the Insert Hyperlink dialog box.
4. Save **6-JobSearch.pptx**.

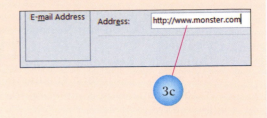

3c

Check Your Work

Hint Hyperlinks are active only when running the slide show, not when creating the presentation.

In addition to linking to a website, a hyperlink can be created that links to another location in the presentation with the Place in This Document button in the *Link to* group at the Insert Hyperlink dialog box. Click the slide to link to in the presentation in the *Select a place in this document* list box. Use the Create New Document button in the Insert Hyperlink dialog box to create a hyperlink to a new presentation. Click this button, type a name for the new presentation, and specify if the new presentation is to be edited now or later.

A graphic such as an image, picture, chart, or text box, can be used as a hyperlink to a file or website. To create a hyperlink with a graphic, select the graphic, click the Insert tab, and then click the Hyperlink button or right-click the graphic and then click *Hyperlink* at the shortcut menu. At the Insert Hyperlink dialog box, specify what to link to and the text to display in the hyperlink.

Insert a hyperlink to an email address using the E-Mail Address button in the *Link to* group in the Insert Hyperlink dialog box. Click the button and the options change in the Insert Hyperlink dialog box. With options that display, type the email address in the *E-mail address* text box, type a subject for the email in the *Subject* text box, and type the text to display in the presentation in the *Text to display* text box. To use this feature, the email address must be set up in Outlook.

Navigate to a hyperlink by clicking the hyperlink in the slide when running the slide show. Hover the mouse over the hyperlink and a ScreenTip displays with the hyperlink. To display specific information in the ScreenTip, click the ScreenTip button in the Insert Hyperlink dialog box, type the text in the Set Hyperlink ScreenTip dialog box, and then click OK.

Project 3d Inserting Hyperlinks to a Website, to Another Presentation, and to a Word Document

Part 4 of 5

1. With **6-JobSearch.pptx** open, make Slide 3 active.
2. Create a link to another presentation by completing the following steps:
   a. Move the insertion point immediately to the right of the word *Picture*, press the Enter key, press Shift + Tab, and then type Resume design.
   b. Select *Resume design*.
   c. Make sure the Insert tab is active and then click the Hyperlink button in the Links group.

d. At the Insert Hyperlink dialog box, make sure the Existing File or Web Page button is selected.
e. If necessary, click the *Look in* option box arrow and then navigate to the PC6 folder on your storage medium.
f. Double-click ***DesignResume.pptx***.

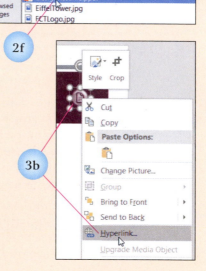

3. Create a hyperlink from a graphic to a Word document by completing the following steps:
   a. Make Slide 4 active.
   b. Right-click the small image in the upper right corner of the slide and then click *Hyperlink* at the shortcut menu.
   c. At the Insert Hyperlink dialog box, make sure the Existing File or Web Page button is selected.
   d. If necessary, click the *Look in* option box arrow and then navigate to the PC6 folder on your storage medium.
   e. Double-click ***ContactInfo.docx***.
4. Make Slide 6 active and then insert a chart by completing the following steps:
   a. Press Ctrl + F12 to display the Open dialog box.
   b. Navigate to the PC6 folder on your storage medium and then double-click ***USBLSChart.pptx***.
   c. Select the chart.
   d. Click the Copy button.
   e. Click the PowerPoint button on the taskbar and then click the thumbnail representing **6-JobSearch.pptx**.
   f. Click the Paste button.
   g. With the chart selected, drag the chart down so it is positioned attractively on the slide.
5. Create a hyperlink from the chart to the United States Bureau of Labor Statistics website by completing the following steps:
   a. With the chart selected, click the Hyperlink button in the Links group on the Insert tab.
   b. At the Insert Hyperlink dialog box, make sure the Existing File or Web Page button is selected and then type www.bls.gov in the *Address* text box.
   c. Click OK to close the Insert Hyperlink dialog box.
6. Hover the mouse pointer on the PowerPoint button on the taskbar, click the thumbnail representing **USBLSChart.pptx**, and then close the presentation.
7. Run the slide show by completing the following steps:
   a. Make sure you are connected to the Internet.
   b. Make Slide 1 active.
   c. Click the Slide Show button in the view area on the Status bar.
   d. Navigate through the slides to Slide 3 and then click the Resume design hyperlink in the slide.
   e. Run the **DesignResume.pptx** slide show that displays. Continue clicking the mouse button until you return to Slide 3 of **6-JobSearch.pptx**.
   f. Click the mouse button to display Slide 4.
   g. Display the Word document by clicking the small image in the upper right corner of the slide.

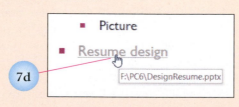

h. Look at the information that displays in the Word document and then click the Close button in the upper right corner of the Word window.

i. Continue running the slide show to Slide 6.

j. At Slide 6, click the <u>National Labor Exchange</u> hyperlink.

k. Scroll through the website and then close the web browser.

l. Click the <u>Monster</u> hyperlink.

m. Scroll through the website and then close the web browser.

n. Click the chart.

o. Scroll through the Bureau of Labor Statistics website and then close the web browser.

p. Continue viewing the remainder of the presentation using the Action buttons. (When Slide 1 displays, press the Esc key to end the slide show.)

8. Save **6-JobSearch.pptx**.

Check Your Work

The hyperlinked text or the hyperlink destination can be edited. To do this, right-click the hyperlink and then click *Edit Hyperlink* at the shortcut menu. At the Edit Hyperlink dialog box, make changes and then close the dialog box. The Edit Hyperlink dialog box contains the same options as the Insert Hyperlink dialog box.

In addition to modifying the hyperlink, the hyperlinked text can be edited. For example, a different font, font size, text color, or text effect can be applied to the hyperlink text. Remove a hyperlink from a slide by right-clicking the hyperlinked text and then clicking *Remove Hyperlink* at the shortcut menu.

Project 3e Modifying, Editing, and Removing a Hyperlink Part 5 of 5

1. With **6-JobSearch.pptx** open, make Slide 4 active and then modify the hyperlink in the image by completing the following steps:

   a. Right-click the small image in the upper right corner of the slide and then click *Edit Hyperlink* at the shortcut menu.

   b. At the Edit Hyperlink dialog box, click the ScreenTip button in the upper right corner of the dialog box.

   c. At the Set Hyperlink ScreenTip dialog box, type Click this image to display information on typing contact information.

   d. Click OK to close the Set Hyperlink ScreenTip dialog box.

   e. Click OK to close the Edit Hyperlink dialog box.

2. Make Slide 3 active and then remove the <u>Resume design</u> hyperlink by right-clicking the hyperlinked text (the text is dimmed and barely visible) and then clicking *Remove Hyperlink* at the shortcut menu.

3. Run the slide show and click the hyperlinks as they appear in the slides.

4. Print the presentation as a handout with six slides displayed horizontally per page.

5. Save and then close **6-JobSearch.pptx**.

Check Your Work

Chapter Summary

- Display a presentation in Slide Master view by clicking the View tab and then clicking the Slide Master button in the Master Views group. In Slide Master view, slide master thumbnails display in the slide thumbnails pane.

- Use buttons in the Background group on the Slide Master tab to change theme colors and fonts, apply a predesigned background style, display the Format Background task pane with options for applying background styles, and hide background graphics.

- Delete a placeholder by clicking in the placeholder, clicking the placeholder border, and then pressing the Delete key.

- Delete a slide master in Slide Master view by clicking the slide master thumbnail in the slide thumbnails pane and then clicking the Delete button in the Edit Master group.

- Create a custom slide layout by clicking the Insert Layout button in the Edit Master group on the Slide Master tab. Rename the custom slide layout with the Rename button in the Edit Master group.

- Insert a placeholder in a slide layout or custom slide layout by clicking the Insert Placeholder button arrow in the Master Layout group on the Slide Master tab and then clicking the desired placeholder at the drop-down list.

- In Slide Master view, create a custom prompt by selecting generic text in a placeholder and then typing the specific text.

- Click the Insert Slide Master button in Slide Master view to insert a new slide master and associated slide layouts. A new slide master can also be inserted by applying a design theme using the Themes button in the Edit Theme group on the Slide Master tab.

- Save a presentation as a template by changing the *Save as type* option at the Save As dialog box to *PowerPoint Template (*.potx)*.

- Open a presentation based on a template by clicking the *PERSONAL* option at the New backstage area and then double-clicking the template thumbnail.

- Customize handouts with options on the Handout Master tab. Display this tab by clicking the Handout Master button on the View tab.

- Customize notes pages with options on the Notes Master tab. Display this tab by clicking the Notes Master button on the View tab.

- In addition to changing views, use buttons on the View tab to show/hide the ruler and/or gridlines; change the zoom display; view slides in color, grayscale, or black and white; and work with multliple windows.

- Action buttons are drawn objects in a slide that have an attached routine, such as displaying the next slide, the first slide, a website, or another PowerPoint presentation.

- Create an action button by clicking the Insert tab, clicking the Shapes button, clicking the specific button at the drop-down list, and then clicking or dragging in the slide to create the button.

- Apply an action to text or an object in a slide by selecting the text or object, clicking the Insert tab, and then clicking the Action button.

- Use options at the Insert Hyperlink dialog box to create a hyperlink to a web page, another presentation, a location within a presentation, a new presentation, or to an email.

- A hyperlink can be created using a graphic and can be modified, edited, or removed.

Commands Review

FEATURE	RIBBON TAB, GROUP/OPTION	BUTTON	KEYBOARD SHORTCUT
action buttons	Insert, Illustrations		
Action Settings dialog box	Insert, Links		
arrange all windows	View, Window		
cascade windows	View, Window		
Handout Master view	View, Master Views		
Insert Hyperlink dialog box	Insert, Links		Ctrl + K
Move split	View, Window		
New backstage area	File, *New*		
Notes Master view	View, Master Views		
Slide Master view	View, Master Views		
Switch Windows	View, Window		
Zoom dialog box	View, Zoom		

Microsoft®
PowerPoint®
Applying Custom Animation and Setting Up Shows

Performance Objectives

Upon successful completion of Chapter 7, you will be able to:

1 Apply, modify, and remove animations
2 Apply a build
3 Animate shapes, images, SmartArt, and chart elements
4 Draw motion paths
5 Set up a slide show
6 Set rehearse timings for slides
7 Hide and unhide slides
8 Use ink tools
9 Create, run, edit, and print a custom slide show
10 Insert and customize audio and video files
11 Create and insert a screen recording

Precheck

Check your current skills to focus your study.

Animation, or movement, can add visual appeal and interest to a slide show when used appropriately. PowerPoint provides a number of animation effects that can be applied to elements in a slide. In this chapter, you will learn how to apply animation effects, use ink tools on slides, insert audio and video files, and make a screen recording to create dynamic presentations.

In some situations, you may want to prepare an automated slide show that runs on a continuous loop. A presentation can be customized to run continuously with a specific amount of time set for each slide to remain on the screen. A custom slide show can be created to present only specific slides in a presentation. In this chapter, you will learn how to prepare automated presentations and how to create and edit custom slide shows.

SNAP

If you are a SNAP user, launch the Precheck and Tutorials from your Assignments page.

Data Files

Before beginning chapter work, copy the PC7 folder to your storage medium and then make PC7 the active folder.

Tutorial

Applying and Removing Animations

Quick Steps

Apply an Animation
1. Click item.
2. Click Animations tab.
3. Click More Animations button.
4. Click animation at drop-down gallery.

 Effects Options

💡 **Hint** You can animate text, objects, graphics, SmartArt diagrams, charts, hyperlinks, and sound.

 Preview

Applying and Removing Animations

Animate items such as text or objects in a slide to add visual interest to a slide show. PowerPoint includes a number of animations that can be applied to items in a slide and the animations can be modified to fit specific needs. For example, an animation can be applied and then customized to display items in a slide one at a time to help the audience focus on each topic or point as it is being presented. An animation can be applied and then customized to specify the direction from which items enter a slide and the rate of speed for the entrance. When considering what animations to apply to a presentation, try not to overwhelm the audience with too much animation. In general, the audience should remember the content of the slide show rather than the visual effects.

To animate an item, click the item, click the Animations tab, click the More Animations button in the Animation group, and then click an animation option at the drop-down gallery. Once an animation is applied, animation effects can be specified using options in the Effect Options button drop-down gallery. Some of the animation effect options may include the direction from which the item appears and whether bulleted text or SmartArt appear as one object, all at once, or by paragraph or object.

Use options in the Timing group on the Animations tab to specify when the animation starts on a slide, the duration of the animation, the delay between animations, and the order in which animations appear on the slide. To view the animation applied to a slide without running the slide show, click the Preview button on the Animations tab and the animation effect displays in the slide in the slide pane. When animation effects are applied to items in a slide, an animation icon displays below the slide number in the slide thumbnails pane.

When inserting or modifying an animation, PowerPoint automatically previews the animation in the slide in the slide pane. This preview feature can be turned off by clicking the Preview button arrow and then clicking *AutoPreview* at the drop-down list to remove the check mark.

1. Open **MarketPres.pptx** and then save it with the name **7-MarketPres**.
2. Make sure Slide 1 is active and then apply animations to the title and subtitle by completing the following steps:
   a. Click in the title *DOUGLAS CONSULTING*.
   b. Click the Animations tab.
   c. Click the *Fade* animation in the Animation group.

   d. Click in the subtitle *Marketing Report*.
   e. Click the *Fade* animation in the Animation group.
   f. Click the Preview button on the Animations tab to see the animation effects in the slide pane.
3. Apply animations to Slides 2 through 4 in Slide Master view by completing the following steps:
   a. Click the View tab and then click the Slide Master button in the Master Views group.
   b. Click the third slide master layout in the slide thumbnails pane (*Title and Content Layout*).
   c. Click in the text *Click to edit Master title style*.
   d. Click the Animations tab and then click the *Fly In* animation that displays in the Animation group.
   e. Click the Effects Options button in the Animation group and then click *From Top* at the drop-down gallery.
   f. Click in the bulleted text *Click to edit Master text styles*.
   g. Click the *Fly In* animation in the Animation group.
   h. Click the Slide Master tab and then click the Close Master View button.

4. Make Slide 1 active and then run the slide show. Click the mouse button to advance items in slides and to move to the next slide. Notice how the bulleted text in Slides 2 through 4 displays one item at a time.
5. Save **7-MarketPres.pptx**.

Quick Steps

Remove an Animation
1. Click item.
2. Click Animations tab.
3. Click *None* option.

To remove an animation effect from an item, click the item in the slide in the slide pane, click the Animations tab, and then click the *None* option in the Animation group. An animation effect also can be removed from an item by clicking the item in the slide pane, clicking the assigned animation number icon, and then pressing the Delete key. To apply a different animation to an item, make sure to delete any existing animations first. If the first animation is not deleted, both animations will be assigned to the item.

Project 1b   Removing Animations

1. With **7-MarketPres.pptx** open, make Slide 1 active and then remove the animation from the title and subtitle by completing the following steps:
   a. Click in the title *DOUGLAS CONSULTING*.
   b. Click the Animations tab.
   c. Click the *None* option in the Animation group.
   d. Click in the subtitle *Marketing Report*.
   e. Click the *None* option in the Animation group.

2. Remove the animation effects for Slides 2 through 4 by completing the following steps:
   a. Click the View tab and then click the Slide Master button in the Master Views group.
   b. Click the third slide master layout in the slide thumbnails pane (*Title and Content Layout*).
   c. Click in the text *Click to edit Master title style*.
   d. Click the Animations tab and then click the *None* option in the Animation group.
   e. Click in the text *Click to edit Master text styles*.
   f. Click the *None* option in the Animation group.
   g. Click the Slide Master tab and then click the Close Master View button.
3. Make Slide 1 active and then run the slide show.
4. Save **7-MarketPres.pptx**.

Quick Steps

Apply an Animation Effect

1. Click item.
2. Click Animations tab.
3. Click Add Animation button.
4. Click animation effect.

 Add Animation

Quick Steps

Apply Effects with Animation Painter

1. Click item.
2. Apply animation effect.
3. Click item with animation effect.
4. Double-click Animation Painter button.
5. Click each item to apply the animation effect.
6. Click Animation Painter button to deactivate it.

Animation
Painter

Applying Animation Effects

The Add Animation button in the Advanced Animation group on the Animations tab provides four types of animation effects that can be applied to an item. An effect can be applied that specifies how an item enters and exits the slide, an emphasis can be applied to an item, and a motion path can be created that will dictate the specific pattern for an item to move on, or even off, the slide.

To apply an entrance effect to an item, click the Add Animation button in the Advanced Animation group and then click the animation effect in the *Entrance* section of the drop-down gallery. Customize the entrance effect by clicking the Effect Options button in the Animation group and then clicking the specific entrance effect. Additional entrance effects are available at the Add Entrance Effect dialog box. Display this dialog box by clicking the Add Animation button and then clicking *More Entrance Effects* at the drop-down gallery. Complete similar steps to apply an exit effect and an emphasis effect. Display additional emphasis effects by clicking the Add Animation button and then clicking *More Emphasis Effects*. Display additional exit effects by clicking the Add Animation button and then clicking *More Exit Effects*.

Applying Animations with Animation Painter

An animation that has been applied to one item in a slide can also be applied to other items in the presentation with the Animation Painter. To use the Animation Painter, apply an animation to an item, position the insertion point anywhere in the animated item, and then double-click the Animation Painter button in the Advanced Animation group on the Animations tab. Using the mouse, select or click each additional item in the presentation that should have the same animation. After applying the animation to the items in the presentation, click the Animation Painter button to deactivate it. To apply animation to only one other item in a presentation, click the Animation Painter button once. The first time an item is selected or clicked, the animation is applied and the Animation Painter is deactivated.

Project 1c Applying Animation Effects   **Part 3 of 6**

1. With **7-MarketPres.pptx** open, apply an animation effect to the title and subtitle in Slide 1 by completing the following steps:
   a. Make Slide 1 active.
   b. Click in the title *DOUGLAS CONSULTING*.
   c. Click the Animations tab.
   d. Click the Add Animation button in the Advanced Animation group and then click the *Wipe* animation in the *Entrance* section of the drop-down gallery.

e. Click the Effect Options button in the Animation group and then click *From Top* at the drop-down gallery.

f. Click in the subtitle *Marketing Report*.

g. Click the Add Animation button and then click the *Zoom* animation in the *Entrance* section.

2. Apply an animation effect to the titles in Slides 2 through 4 by completing the following steps:

a. Click the View tab and then click the Slide Master button in the Master Views group.

b. Click the third slide master layout in the slide thumbnails pane (*Title and Content Layout*).

c. Click in the text *Click to edit Master title style*.

d. Click the Animations tab, click the Add Animation button in the Advanced Animation group, and then click the *More Emphasis Effects* option at the drop-down gallery.

e. At the Add Emphasis Effect dialog box, click the *Grow With Color* option in the *Moderate* section.

f. Click OK to close the dialog box.

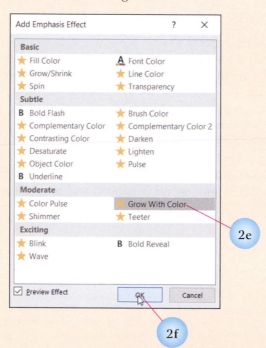

g. Click the Slide Master tab and then click the Close Master View button.

3. Use the Animation Painter to apply an animation effect to the bulleted text in Slides 2 through 4 by completing the following steps:

a. Make Slide 2 active.

b. Click in the bulleted text to make the placeholder active.

c. Click the Animations tab, click the Add Animation button, and then click the *Split* animation in the *Entrance* section.

d. Click in the bulleted text.

e. Double-click the Animation Painter button in the Advanced Animation group.

f. Make Slide 3 active.

g. Click in the bulleted text. (The mouse pointer displays as an arrow with a paintbrush attached. The animations are applied to all four bulleted items.)

h. Make Slide 4 active and then click in the bulleted text.

i. Click the Animation Painter button to deactivate it.

4. Click the Preview button on the Animations tab to view the animation effects.

5. Run the slide show by clicking the Start From Beginning button on the Quick Access Toolbar. Click the mouse button to advance slide elements and to move to the next slide.

6. Save **7-MarketPres.pptx**.

Modifying Animation Effects

Start

An animation effect applied to an item can be modified with options in the Timing group. Use the *Start* option box drop-down list to specify when the item should be inserted in the slide. Generally, items display in a slide when the mouse button is clicked. Click the *Start* option box arrow and then click *With Previous* or *With Next* at the drop-down list to make the item appear in the slide with the previous or next item.

Duration

Use the *Duration* measurement box to specify the length of an animation. Click the *Duration* measurement box up arrow to increase the length of time the animation displays on the slide and click the down arrow to decrease the length of time. The duration time also can be changed by selecting the current time in the *Duration* measurement box and then typing a specific time.

Delay

Use the *Delay* measurement box to specify the number of seconds an animation delays before playing after the previous animation has finished playing. Click the *Delay* measurement box up arrow to increase the delay time and click the down arrow to decrease the time. The delay time can also be changed by selecting the current time in the *Delay* measurement box and then typing a specific time.

Öuick Steps

Reorder an Animation Item
1. Click item in slide.
2. Click Move Earlier button or Move Later button.

Move Earlier

Move Later

Reordering Items

When an animation effect is applied to an item, an animation number displays next to the item in the slide in the slide pane. This number indicates the order in which the item will appear in the slide. When more than one item displays in the slide, the order can be changed with options in the *Reorder Animation* section of the Timing group on the Animations tab. Click the Move Earlier button to move an item before another item or click the Move Later button to move an item after another item.

Project 1d Removing, Modifying, and Reordering Animation Effects   Part 4 of 6

1. With **7-MarketPres.pptx** open, make Slide 1 active.

2. Modify the start setting for the animation effect you applied to the slide title by completing the following steps:

a. Click in the title to activate the placeholder.

b. Click the *Start* option box arrow in the Timing group on the Animations tab.

c. Click <mark>*With Previous* at the drop-down list. (The title animation effect will begin as soon as the slide displays, without you having to click the mouse button.</mark> Notice that the number *1* located to the left of the item in the slide changes to a 0.)

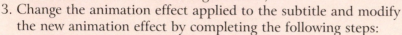

2b

Start: On Click ▾   Reorder Animation
Durati| On Click | ▲ Move Earlier
Delay | With Previous | ▼ Move Later
| After Previous |

2c

3. Change the animation effect applied to the subtitle and modify the new animation effect by completing the following steps:

a. Click in the subtitle *Marketing Report*.

b. Click the More Animations button in the Animation group and then click the *None* option in the drop-down gallery.

3d

Start: With Previous ▾   Reorder Animation
Duration: 01.00 ▲▾   ▲ Move Earlier
Delay: 00.00 ▲▾   ▼ Move Later
Timing

c. Click the Add Animation button in the Advanced Animation group and then click the *Grow/Shrink* animation in the *Emphasis* section.

d. Click the *Start* option box arrow and then click *With Previous* at the drop-down list.

e. Click the *Duration* measurement box down arrow four times. (This displays *01.00* in the measurement box.)

3e

4. Remove animations from slide titles in Slide Master view by completing the following steps:

a. Click the View tab and then click the Slide Master button in the Master Views group.

b. Click the third slide master layout in the slide thumbnails pane (*Title and Content Layout*).

c. Click in the text *Click to edit Master title style*.

d. Click the Animations tab.

e. Click the More Animations button in the Animation group and then click the *None* option.

f. Click the Slide Master tab and then click the Close Master View button.

5. Remove animations from the bulleted text in Slides 2 through 4 by completing the following steps:

a. Make Slide 2 active.

b. Click in the bulleted text.

c. Click the Animations tab and then click the *None* option in the Animation group.

d. Make Slide 3 active, click in the bulleted text, and then click the *None* option in the Animation group.

e. Make Slide 4 active, click in the bulleted text, and then click the *None* option in the Animation group.

6. Make Slide 2 active and then apply and customize animation effects by completing the following steps:

a. Click in the title *Department Reports*.

b. Click the Add Animation button in the Advanced Animation group and then click the *More Entrance Effects* option at the drop-down gallery.

c. At the Add Entrance Effect dialog box, scroll down the list box and then click *Spiral In* in the *Exciting* section.

d. Click OK to close the dialog box.

Add Entrance Effect   ?   ✕

★ Random Bars   ★ Split
★ Strips   ★ Wedge
★ Wheel   ★ Wipe
Subtle
★ Expand   ★ Fade
★ Swivel   ★ Zoom
Moderate
★ Basic Zoom   ★ Center Revolve
★ Compress   ★ Float Down
★ Float Up   ★ Grow & Turn
★ Rise Up   ★ Spinner
★ Stretch
Exciting
★ Basic Swivel   ★ Boomerang
★ Bounce   ★ Credits
★ Curve Up   ★ Drop
★ Flip   ★ Float
★ Pinwheel   ★ Spiral In
★ Whip
☑ Preview Effect   OK   Cancel

6c

6d

e. Click the bulleted text.

f. Click the Add Animation button and then click the *Zoom* animation in the *Entrance* section.

g. Click the image in the slide.

h. Click the Add Animation button and then click the *Zoom* animation in the *Entrance* section.

7. Click the Preview button at the left side of the Animations tab to view the animation effects.

8. After viewing the animation effects, you decide that you want the image to animate before the bulleted text and you want the animation effects to begin with the previous animation (instead of with a mouse click). With Slide 2 active, complete the following steps:

a. Click the image. (The number 5 will display outside the upper left corner of the image placeholder because the image is the fifth item to enter the slide.)

b. Click the Move Earlier button in the *Reorder Animation* section of the Timing group. (The number displayed to the left of the image changes to *2* because you moved the image animation before the three bulleted items.)

c. Click the *Start* option box arrow in the Timing group and then click *With Previous* at the drop-down list.

d. Click in the title *Department Reports*.

e. Click the *Start* option box arrow in the Timing group and then click *With Previous* at the drop-down list.

9. Make Slide 3 active and then apply the same animation effects you applied in Slide 2. (Do this by completing steps similar to those in Steps 6a through 6h and Steps 8a through 8e.)

10. Make Slide 4 active and then apply the same animation effects you applied to Slide 2. (Do this by completing steps similar to those in Steps 6a through 6f and Steps 8d through 8e.)

11. Make Slide 1 active and then run the slide show.

12. Save **7-MarketPres.pptx**.

Customizing Animation Effects at the Animation Pane

Quick Steps

Reorder Animation Items

1. Click item in Animation Pane.
2. Click Move Earlier button or Move Later button.

Remove an Animation Effect

1. Click item in Animation Pane.
2. Click down arrow.
3. Click *Remove.*

 Animation Pane

The Animation Pane provides options for customizing and modifying animation effects. Display the Animation Pane, shown in Figure 7.1, by clicking the Animation Pane button in the Advanced Animation group on the Animations tab. When an animation is applied to an item, the item name or description displays in the Animation Pane. Hover the mouse pointer over an item and a description of the animation effect applied to the item displays in a box below the item. Click the down arrow at the right side of an item in the Animation Pane and a drop-down list displays with options for customizing or removing the animation effect.

When an effect is applied to an item, the item name and/or description displays in the Animation Pane preceded by a number. This number indicates the order in which the item will appear in the slide. When more than one item displays in the Animation Pane, the order of an item can be changed by clicking the item and then clicking the Move Earlier or the Move Later buttons at the top of the Animation Pane.

Figure 7.1 Animation Pane

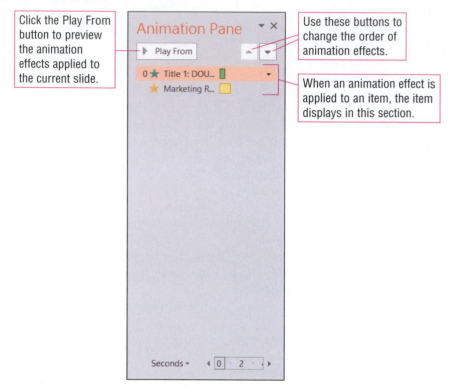

Click the Play From button to preview the animation effects applied to the current slide.

Use these buttons to change the order of animation effects.

When an animation effect is applied to an item, the item displays in this section.

All animation effects applied to a slide can be played by clicking the Play All button at the top of the pane. (The name of the button varies depending on the contents of the Animation Pane and what is selected in the pane.) The animation effects display in the slide in the slide pane and a time indicator displays along the bottom of the Animation Pane with a vertical line indicating the progression of time (in seconds). Play only the selected animation effect in the Animation Pane by clicking the animation effect in the pane and then clicking the Play From button at the top of the pane.

Project 1e **Removing, Customizing, and Reordering Animation Effects in the Animation Pane**

Part 5 of 6

1. With **7-MarketPres.pptx** open, make Slide 1 active.
2. Click in the title *DOUGLAS CONSULTING*, click the Animations tab, and then click the *None* option in the Animation group.
3. With the title placeholder selected, click the Add Animation button in the Advanced Animation group and then click the *Grow & Turn* animation in the *Entrance* section.
4. Click the *Duration* measurement box down arrow two times. (This displays *00.50* in the measurement box.)
5. Click in the subtitle *Marketing Report*, click the More Animations button in the Animation group, and then click the *None* option.
6. With the subtitle placeholder selected, click the Add Animation button in the Advanced Animation group and then click the *Grow & Turn* animation in the *Entrance* section.
7. Click the *Duration* measurement box down arrow two times. (This displays *00.50* in the measurement box.)

8. Modify the start setting for the slide title animation effect in the Animation Pane by completing the following steps:

a. Click the Animation Pane button in the Advanced Animation group on the Animations tab. (This displays the Animation Pane at the right side of the screen.)

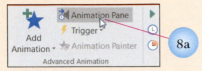

b. Click the Title 1 item in the Animation Pane.

c. Click the down arrow at the right side of the item and then click *Start With Previous* at the drop-down list.

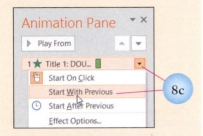

9. Remove animations from slides using the Animation Pane by completing the following steps:

a. Make Slide 2 active.

b. Click the Picture 3 item in the Animation Pane.

c. Click the down arrow at the right side of the item and then click *Remove* at the drop-down list.

d. Click the image in the slide pane, click the Add Animation button in the Advanced Animation group, and then click the *Pulse* animation in the *Emphasis* section.

10. Make Slide 3 active and then complete steps similar to those in Steps 9b through 9d to remove the animation effect from the image and add the *Pulse* emphasis animation effect.

11. With the Picture 3 image selected in the Animation Pane, click the Play From button at the top of the pane to view the animation effect applied to the image.

12. Play all animation effects applied to the slide by clicking anywhere in the blank area below the animation effects in the Animation Pane (this deselects the Picture 3 animation effect) and then click the Play All button (previously the Play From button) at the top of the pane.

13. After viewing the animation effect, you decide that you want the image to animate before the title and bulleted text and you want the animation effect to begin with the previous animation. With Slide 3 active, complete the following steps:

a. Click the Picture 3 item in the Animation Pane.

b. Click the up arrow at the top of the Animation pane two times. (This moves the Picture 3 item above the Title 1 and the Content Placeholder items.)

c. Click the down arrow at the right side of the Picture 3 item and then click *Start With Previous* at the drop-down list.

14. Reorder animation effects in Slide 2 to match the changes made to Slide 3.

15. Make Slide 1 active and then run the slide show.

16. Close the Animation Pane.

17. Save **7-MarketPres.pptx**.

Applying Sound to Animations

Enhance an animation by adding a sound to the animation. To apply a sound, click the Animation Pane button to display the Animation Pane, click the animated item in the Animation Pane, click the down arrow at the right side of the item, and then click *Effect Options* at the drop-down list. At the effect options dialog box (the name of the dialog box varies depending on the animation applied) with the Effect tab selected, click the down arrow at the right side of the *Sound* option box and then click a sound at the drop-down list. Sound can also be added to an animation by clicking the animated item in the slide in the slide pane, clicking the Animation group dialog box launcher, and then choosing the sound effect at the dialog box that displays.

Applying a Build

Hint You can group text (in a bulleted text placeholder) at the effect options dialog box by first, second, third, fourth, or fifth levels.

In Project 1a, a build was applied to bulleted text in a slide. A build displays important points on a slide one point at a time, keeping the audience's attention focused on the current point. A build can be further customized by causing a previous point to dim when the next point displays. To customize a build, click the Animation Pane button to display the Animation Pane, click the bulleted item in the Animation Pane, click the down arrow at the right side of the item, and then click *Effect Options* at the drop-down list. At the effect options dialog box (the name of the dialog box will vary) with the Effect tab selected, choose a color option with the *After animation* option box.

Project 1f Applying Sound and a Build to Animations

Part 6 of 6

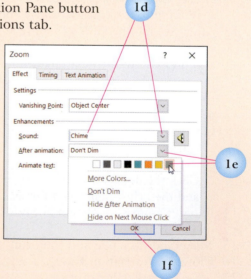

1. With **7-MarketPres.pptx** open, make Slide 2 active and then apply sound and a build to the bulleted text by completing the following steps:
   a. Click in the bulleted text.
   b. Open the Animation Pane by clicking the Animation Pane button in the Advanced Animation group on the Animations tab.
   c. Click the down arrow at the right side of the Content Placeholder item in the Animation Pane and then click *Effect Options* at the drop-down list.
   d. At the Zoom dialog box, make sure the Effect tab is selected, click the *Sound* option box arrow, scroll down the list box, and then click the *Chime* option.
   e. Click the *After animation* option box arrow and then click the light gray color (last option).
   f. Click OK to close the dialog box.
2. Click in the bulleted text in the slide.
3. Double-click the Animation Painter button.
4. Display Slide 3 and then click in the bulleted text.
5. Display Slide 4 and then click in the bulleted text.
6. Click the Animation Painter button to deactivate it.
7. Close the Animation Pane.
8. Make Slide 1 active and then run the slide show.
9. Save and then close **7-MarketPres.pptx**.

You will open an online learning presentation and then apply animation effects to shapes, an image, elements in SmartArt graphics, and elements in a chart. You will also draw a motion path in a slide.

Preview Finished Project

Animating Shapes and Images

Animate individual shapes or objects, such as images, in a slide in the same way a title or text or objects in a content placeholder are animated. More than one shape can be selected and then the same animation effects can be applied to the shapes. To select more than one shape, click the first shape, press and hold down the Shift key, click any additional shapes, and then release the Shift key.

Project 2a Animating Shapes and an Image

Part 1 of 6

1. Open **OLLearn.pptx** and then save it with the name **7-OLLearn**.
2. Make Slide 8 active (this slide contains one large object with three smaller objects hidden behind it) and then animate objects and apply exit effects by completing the following steps:
   a. Click the Animations tab and then click the Animation Pane button in the Advanced Animation group.
   b. Click the large green shape in the slide.
   c. Click the Add Animation button in the Advanced Animation group and then click the *More Exit Effects* option.
   d. At the Add Exit Effect dialog box, click the *Spiral Out* option in the *Exciting* section. (You will need to scroll down the list to display this option.) Watch the animation effect in the slide and then click OK.

   e. Click the large green shape to select it and then drag it up the slide to display a portion of the three shapes behind.
   f. Click the small shape at the left, click the Add Animation button, and then click the *More Entrance Effects* option.
   g. At the Add Entrance Effect dialog box, click *Spinner* in the *Moderate* section, and then click OK.

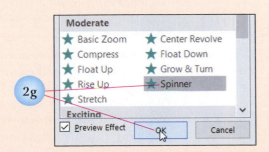

   h. Select the middle shape, press and hold down the Shift key, click the shape at the right, and then release the Shift key. (This selects both shapes.)
   i. Click the Add Animation button and then click the *More Entrance Effects* option.

j. At the Add Entrance Effect dialog box, click *Spinner* in the *Moderate* section and then click OK. (Notice that the two objects are numbered *3* in the Animation Pane and are set to enter the slide at the same time. You will change this in the next step.)

k. Click the small shape at the right, click the down arrow at the right of the *Start* option box in the Timing group, and then click *On Click* at the drop-down list.

l. Apply emphasis to the middle shape by clicking the middle shape, clicking the Add Animation button, and then clicking the *Grow/Shrink* option in the *Emphasis* section of the drop-down gallery.

m. Click the large green shape to select it and then reposition it over the three smaller shapes.

n. Click the Preview button to play the animation effects in the slide.

3. Make Slide 9 active and apply and customize animation effects and change animation order by completing the following steps:

a. Click anywhere in the text *Online learning continues to evolve!* (this selects the text box), click the Add Animation button, and then click *Grow & Turn* in the *Entrance* section.

b. Click anywhere in the text *Stay tuned!* (this selects the text box), click the Add Animation button, and then click the *Swivel* option in the *Entrance* section.

c. Click the image to select it.

d. Click the Add Animation button and then click the *Spin* animation in the *Emphasis* section.

e. Click the Effect Options button in the Animation group and then click *Two Spins* at the drop-down gallery.

f. Click the *Duration* measurement box down arrow until *01.00* displays.

g. Click the Move Earlier button in the Timing group. This moves the image item in the list box above the *Stay tuned!* text box item.

h. Click the Preview button to play the animation effects in the slide.

4. Save **7-OLLearn.pptx**.

Animating a SmartArt Graphic

Animation effects can be applied to a SmartArt graphic and then customized to specify whether the entire SmartArt graphic displays at once or the individual elements in the SmartArt graphic display one at a time. Specify a sequence for displaying elements in a SmartArt graphic with the Effect Options button in the Animation group.

When an animation effect is applied to a SmartArt graphic, animations can be applied to individual elements in the graphic. To do this, click the Effect Options button and then click the *One by One* option at the drop-down list. Display the Animation Pane and then expand the list of SmartArt graphic objects by clicking the small double arrows that display in a gray shaded box below the item in the Animation Pane. Click an individual item in the Animation Pane and then click an animation in the Animation group.

1. With **7-OLLearn.pptx** open, make Slide 4 active and then animate objects in the SmartArt graphic by completing the following steps:
   a. Click the shape in the SmartArt graphic containing the word *Convenient*. (Make sure white sizing handles display around the shape. White sizing handles will also display around the entire SmartArt graphic.)
   b. With the Animations tab active, click the *Float In* animation in the Animation group.
   c. Click the Effect Options button in the Animation group and then click *One by One* at the drop-down gallery. (This will allow you to apply different effects to the objects in the SmartArt graphic.)
   d. Make sure the Animation Pane displays. (If not, click the Animation Pane button in the Advanced Animation group.)
   e. Expand the list of SmartArt graphic objects in the Animation Pane by clicking the small double arrows that display in a gray shaded box below the Content Placeholder item. (This expands the list to display four items.)
   f. Click the item in the Animation Pane that begins with the number *2*.
   g. Click the More Animations button in the Animation group and then click the *Grow & Turn* animation in the *Entrance* section.
   h. Click the item in the Animation Pane that begins with the number *4*.
   i. Click the More Animations button in the Animation group and then click the *Grow & Turn* animation in the *Entrance* section.
2. Click the Preview button on the Animations tab to view the animation effects applied to the SmartArt graphic objects.
3. Make Slide 6 active and then apply animation effects by completing the following steps:
   a. Click the shape in the SmartArt graphic containing the text *Multi-Media*. (Make sure white sizing handles display around the shape. White sizing handles will also display around the entire SmartArt graphic.)
   b. Click the Add Animation button and then click the *More Entrance Effects* option.
   c. At the Add Entrance Effect dialog box, click the *Circle* option in the *Basic* section.
   d. Click OK to close the dialog box.
   e. Click the Effect Options button in the Animation group and then click *Out* in the *Direction* section of the drop-down list.
   f. Click the Effect Options button again and then click *One by One* in the *Sequence* section of the drop-down list.
   g. Click the *Duration* measurement box down arrow until *00.50* displays.
4. Click the Play Selected button at the top of the Animation Pane to view the animation effects applied to the SmartArt graphic objects.
5. Save **7-OLLearn.pptx**.

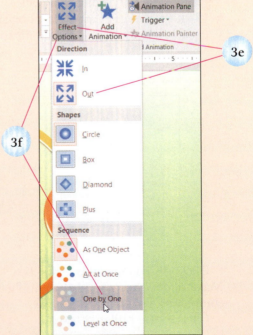

Animating a Chart

Like a SmartArt graphic, a chart or elements in a chart can be animated. Displaying data in a chart may have a more dramatic effect if the chart is animated. Bringing in one element at a time also allows the presenter to discuss each piece of the data as it displays. How the chart is animated in the slide and how the chart elements are grouped can be specified. For example, group chart elements on one object or by series or category. Apply animation to elements in a chart in a manner similar to animating elements in a SmartArt graphic.

Project 2c   Animating Elements in a Chart

Part 3 of 6

1. With **7-OLLearn.pptx** open, make Slide 3 active and then animate chart elements by completing the following steps:
   a. Click in the chart placeholder to select the chart. (Make sure you do not have a chart element selected and that the Animations tab is active.)
   b. Click the Add Animation button and then click the *More Entrance Effects* option.
   c. At the Add Entrance Effect dialog box, click the *Dissolve In* option in the *Basic* section.
   d. Click OK to close the dialog box.
   e. Make sure the Animation Pane displays and then click the down arrow at the right side of the Content Placeholder item in the list box.
   f. At the drop-down list that displays, click *Effect Options*.
   g. At the Dissolve In dialog box, click the *Sound* option box arrow, scroll down the drop-down list, and then click the *Click* option.
   h. Click the Timing tab.
   i. Click the *Duration* option box arrow and then click *1 seconds (Fast)* at the drop-down list.
   j. Click the Chart Animation tab.
   k. Click the *Group chart* option box arrow and then click *By Category* at the drop-down list.

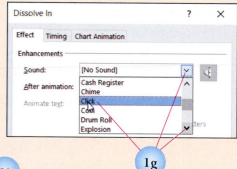

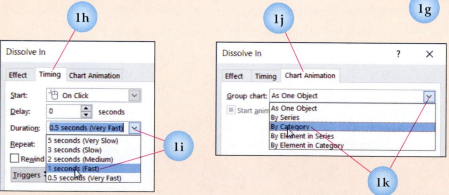

   l. Click OK to close the dialog box.
2. Make Slide 7 active and then apply a build animation effect to the bulleted text by completing the following steps:
   a. Click in the bulleted text.
   b. Click the *Fly In* animation in the Animation group on the Animations tab.

c. Click the Effect Options button and then click *From Right* at the drop-down gallery.

d. Make sure the Animation Pane displays, click the down arrow at the right side of the Content Placeholder item in the pane, and then click *Effect Options* at the drop-down list.

e. At the Fly In dialog box, make sure the Effect tab is selected, click the *After animation* option box arrow, and then click the light green color (second from the right).

f. Click OK to close the dialog box.

3. Save **7-OLLearn.pptx**.

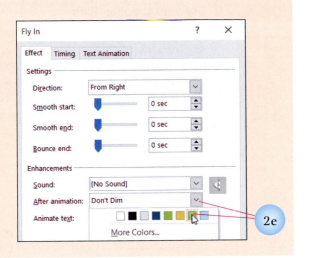

Creating a Motion Path

Quick Steps

Insert a Motion Path
1. Click item in slide.
2. Click Animations tab.
3. Click Add Animation button.
4. Click path in *Motion Paths* section.

Draw a Motion Path
1. Click item in slide.
2. Click Animations tab.
3. Click Add Animation button.
4. Click *Custom Path* in *Motion Paths* section.
5. Drag in slide to create path.
6. Double-click mouse button.

Use options in the *Motion Paths* section of the Add Animation button drop-down gallery to specify a motion path. A motion path is a path created for an object that specifies the movements of the object when running the slide show. Click the Add Animation button in the Advanced Animation group and a gallery of options for drawing a motion path in a specific direction can be found in the *Motion Paths* section. For example, to move an item left in a line when running the slide show, click the Add Animation button in the Advanced Animation group and then click the *Lines* option in the *Motion Paths* section of the drop-down gallery. Click the Effect Options button in the Animation group and then click *Left* at the drop-down gallery. A motion path can also be applied by clicking the Add Animation button, clicking *More Motion Paths* at the drop-down gallery, and then clicking the motion path at the Add Motion Path dialog box.

To draw a motion path freehand, select the object in the slide, click the Add Animation button, and then click the *Custom Path* option in the *Motion Paths* section of the drop-down gallery. Using the mouse, drag in the slide to create the path. When the path is completed, double-click the mouse button.

1. With **7-OLLearn.pptx** open, make Slide 1 active and then apply a motion path to the image by completing the following steps:
   a. Click the image.
   b. Click the Add Animation button and then click the *More Motion Paths* option.
   c. At the Add Motion Path dialog box, scroll down the list box and then click the *Spiral Right* option in the *Lines Curves* section.
   d. Click OK to close the dialog box.
   e. Notice that a spiral line object displays in the slide and a dimmed copy of the image is selected. Hover the mouse pointer over the spiral line until the mouse pointer turns into an arrow with a four-headed arrow attached and then drag the spiral line and dimmed copy of the image so they are positioned over the original image (see the image at the right).

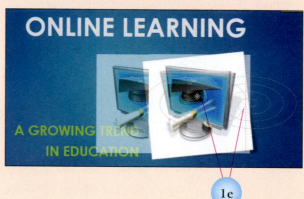

   f. Click the *Start* option box arrow in the Timing group and then click *With Previous* at the drop-down list.
   g. Click the *Duration* measurement box up arrow in the Timing group until *03.00* displays in the measurement box.
   h. Click the *Delay* measurement box up arrow in the Timing group until *01.00* displays in the measurement box.
   i. Click outside the image to deselect it.
2. Make Slide 5 active and then animate the star on the map by completing the following steps:
   a. Click the star object in the slide below the heading *North America*.
   b. Click the Add Animation button, scroll down the drop-down gallery, and then click the *Custom Path* option in the *Motion Paths* section.
   c. Position the mouse pointer (displays as crosshairs) on the star, click and hold down the left mouse button, drag a path through each of the five locations on the map ending back in the original location in the star object, release the mouse button, and then double-click the mouse button.

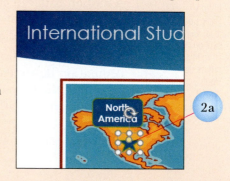

3. Run the slide show and click the mouse to advance slides and elements on slides as needed.
4. Save **7-OLLearn.pptx**.

Applying a Trigger

Use the Trigger button in the Advanced Animation group to make an animation effect occur by clicking an item on the slide during a slide show. A trigger creates a link between two items and provides additional information about that item. For example, a trigger can be applied to a bulleted item to cause another item, such as a picture or chart, to appear. When running the slide show, hover the mouse pointer

Quick Steps

Apply a Trigger
1. Click object in slide.
2. Click Animations tab.
3. Click Trigger button.
4. Point to *On Click of* and then click trigger item.

⚡ Trigger

over the item containing the trigger until the mouse pointer displays as a hand and then click the mouse button to display the trigger item.

The advantage to applying a trigger to an item is that the presenter can control whether or not the item displays when running the slide show. For example, suppose a presentation contains product sales information and the presenter wants to provide additional specific sales data to one group but not another. When presenting to the group that should view the additional sales data, the trigger can be clicked to display the data. When presenting to the other group, the trigger is not clicked, and the sales data remains hidden.

To insert a trigger, apply an animation effect to both items, display the Animation Pane, and then click the item that will become the trigger. Click the Trigger button in the Advanced Animation group, point to *On Click of*, and then click the item to be triggered at the side menu.

Project 2e Inserting Triggers

Part 5 of 6

1. With **7-OLLearn.pptx** open, make Slide 2 active.
2. Apply animation effects to the text and charts by completing the following steps:
   a. Click in the bulleted text.
   b. Click the Animations tab.
   c. Click the *Split* animation in the Animation group.
   d. Select the pie chart at the left. (To do this, click in the chart and then click within the chart border but not on a specific item in the chart. Make sure the chart is selected and not an individual chart element.)
   e. Click the *Split* animation in the Animation group.
   f. Select the middle pie chart and then click the *Split* animation. (Make sure you select the chart and not a chart element.)
   g. Select the pie chart at the right and then click the *Split* animation. (Make sure you select the chart and not a chart element.)
3. Make sure the Animation Pane displays.
4. Apply a trigger to the first bulleted item that, when clicked, will display the chart at the left by completing the following steps:
   a. Click the *Chart 5* item in the Animation Pane.
   b. Click the Trigger button in the Advanced Animation group, point to *On Click of*, and then click *Content Placeholder 2* at the side menu.
   c. Click the *Chart 6* item in the Animation Pane, click the Trigger button, point to *On Click of*, and then click *Content Placeholder 2* at the side menu.
   d. Click the *Chart 7* item in the Animation Pane, click the Trigger button, point to *On Click of*, and then click *Content Placeholder 2* at the side menu.
5. Close the Animation Pane.
6. Run the slide show by completing the following steps:
   a. Run the slide show from the beginning and when you get to Slide 2, click the mouse button until the first bulleted item displays (the item that begins with *Traditional*).

Check Your Work ▶

b. Hover your mouse pointer over the bulleted text until the pointer turns into a hand and then click the left mouse button. (This displays the first chart.)

c. Position the mouse pointer anywhere in the white background of the slide and then click the left mouse button to display the second bulleted item (the item that begins with *Hybrid*).

d. Hover your mouse pointer over the text in the second bulleted item until the pointer turns into a hand and then click the left mouse button. (This displays the middle chart.)

e. Position the mouse pointer anywhere in the white background of the slide and then click the left mouse button to display the third bulleted item (the item that begins with *Internet*).

f. Hover your mouse pointer over the text in the third bulleted item until the pointer turns into a hand and then click the left mouse button. (This displays the third chart.)

g. Continue running the remaining slides in the slide show.

7. Save **7-OLLearn.pptx**.

8. Print the presentation as a handout with all nine slides displayed horizontally on the page.

Setting Up a Slide Show

Set Up Slide Show

Control how the presentation displays with options at the Set Up Show dialog box, shown in Figure 7.2. With options at this dialog box, set slide presentation options, specify how slides advance, and set screen resolution. Display the Set Up Show dialog box by clicking the Slide Show tab and then clicking the Set Up Slide Show button in the Set Up group.

Figure 7.2 Set Up Show Dialog Box

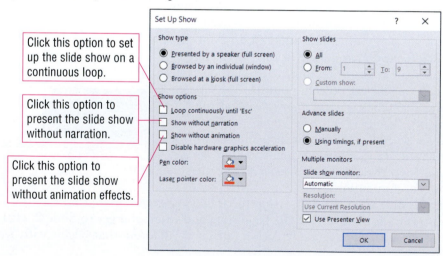

Ǭuick Steps

Run a Slide Show without Animation
1. Click Slide Show tab.
2. Click Set Up Slide Show button.
3. Click *Show without animation*.
4. Click OK.

A slide show can be run without the animations. To do this, display the Set Up Show dialog box, click the *Show without animation* check box to insert a check mark, and then click OK. Changes made to the Set Up Show dialog box are saved with the presentation.

Project 2f **Running a Slide Show without Animation**   Part 6 of 6

1. With **7-OLLearn.pptx** open, specify that you want to run the slide show without animation by completing the following steps:
   a. Click the Slide Show tab.
   b. Click the Set Up Slide Show button in the Set Up group.
   c. At the Set Up Show dialog box, click the *Show without animation* check box to insert a check mark.
   d. Click OK to close the dialog box.
2. Run the slide show to see that the animation effects do not play.
3. Specify that you want the slide show to run with animations by completing the following steps:
   a. Click the Set Up Slide Show button on the Slide Show tab.
   b. At the Set Up Show dialog box, click the *Show without animation* check box to remove the check mark and then click OK.
4. Save and then close **7-OLLearn.pptx**.

Project 3 **Prepare a Self-Running Adventure Slide Show, Use Ink Tools, and Create Custom Slide Shows**   **7 Parts**

You will open a travel tour presentation and then customize it to be an automated slide show set on a continuous loop. You will also hide slides, use ink tools, and create and edit custom slide shows.

Preview Finished Project

Tutorial

Looping a Slide Show Continuously

Setting Up a Slide Show to Loop Continuously

Ǭuick Steps

Loop a Slide Show Continuously
1. Click Slide Show tab.
2. Click Set Up Slide Show button.
3. Click *Loop continuously until 'Esc'*.
4. Click OK.

To advance a slide automatically, insert a check mark in the *After* check box in the Advance Slide section in the Timing group on the Transitions tab and then insert the specific number of seconds in the measurement box. To advance a slide before the specified amount of time has elapsed, leave the check mark in the *On Mouse Click* option. With this option active, the slide will advance after the specified number of seconds or clicking the mouse button will advance the slide sooner. To control the slide show and have slides advanced the specified number of seconds and not allow advancing by clicking the mouse, remove the check mark from the *On Mouse Click* option.

Hint Use an automated slide show to communicate information without a presenter.

In some situations, such as at a trade show or convention, an automated slide show may be needed. An automated slide show is set up on a continuous loop and does not require someone to advance the slides or restart the slide show. To design an automated slide show, display the Set Up Show dialog box and then insert a check mark in the *Loop continuously until 'Esc'* option. With this option active, the slide show will continue running until the Esc key is pressed.

Project 3a **Preparing a Self-Running Slide Show** **Part 1 of 7**

1. Open **AdvTours.pptx** and then save it with the name **7-AdvTours**.
2. Insert slides by completing the following steps:
   a. Click below the last slide thumbnail in the slide thumbnails pane.
   b. Make sure the Home tab is selected, click the New Slide button arrow, and then click *Reuse Slides* at the drop-down list.
   c. At the Reuse Slides task pane, click the Browse button and then click *Browse File*.
   d. At the Browse dialog box, navigate to the PC7 folder on your storage medium and then double-click *PeruTour.pptx*.
   e. Click each slide in the Reuse Slides task pane in the order in which they display, beginning with the top slide.
   f. Close the Reuse Slides task pane.
3. Add transition and transition sound effects and specify a time for automatically advancing slides by completing the following steps:
   a. Click the Transitions tab.
   b. Click the *On Mouse Click* check box in the Timing group to remove the check mark.
   c. Click the *After* check box to insert a check mark.
   d. Click the *After* measurement box up arrow until *00:05.00* displays.
   e. Click the *Fade* slide transition in the Transition to This Slide group.
   f. Click the *Sound* option box arrow in the Timing group and then click *Breeze* at the drop-down list.
   g. Click the Apply To All button.

4. Set up the slide show to run continuously by completing the following steps:
   a. Click the Slide Show tab.
   b. Click the Set Up Slide Show button in the Set Up group.
   c. At the Set Up Show dialog box, click the *Loop continuously until 'Esc'* check box to insert a check mark. (Make sure *All* is selected in the *Show slides* section and *Using timings, if present* is selected in the *Advance slides* section.)
   d. Click OK to close the dialog box.

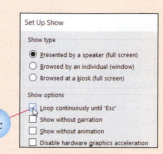

5. Click Slide 1 to select it and then run the slide show. (The slides will advance automatically after five seconds.)
6. After viewing the slide show, press the Esc key on the keyboard.
7. Save **7-AdvTours.pptx**.

Check Your Work

Setting Automatic Times for Slides

Tutorial

Setting Timings
for a Slide Show

Ouick Steps

**Set Automatic Times
for Slides**
1. Click Slide Show tab.
2. Click Rehearse
   Timings button.
3. Using Recording
   toolbar, specify time
   for each slide.
4. Click Yes.

Rehearse
Timings

Hint Enter a
specific recording
time by selecting the
time in the *Slide Time*
measurement box,
typing the time, and
then pressing Enter.

Applying the same time to all slides is not very practical unless the same amount of text appears on every slide. In most cases, some slides should be left on the screen longer than others. Apply specific times to a slide using buttons on the Recording toolbar. Display this toolbar by clicking the Slide Show tab and then clicking the Rehearse Timings button in the Set Up group. This displays the first slide in the presentation in Slide Show view with the Recording toolbar in the upper left corner of the slide. The buttons on the Recording toolbar are identified in Figure 7.3.

When the slide displays on the screen, the timer on the Recording toolbar begins. Click the Next button on the Recording toolbar when the slide has displayed for the appropriate amount of time. To stop the timer, click the Pause button. Click the Resume Recording button to resume the timer. Use the Repeat button on the Recording toolbar to reset the time for the current slide. Continue through the presentation until the slide show is complete. After the last slide, a confirmation message displays showing the total time for the slide show. At this message, click Yes to set the times for each slide recorded during the rehearsal, or click No to delete the times. A slide show can be run without the rehearsed timings. To run the slide show without the timings, click the Slide Show tab and then click the *Use Timings* check box to remove the check mark.

The times applied to slides will display below each slide in the Slide Sorter view. The time that displays below the slide will generally be one second more than the time applied to the slide. So, if 5 seconds were applied to Slide 1, the time *00.06* will display below the slide in Slide Sorter view.

The slide times recorded for individual slides can be edited with the *After* measurement box in the Advance Slide section in the Timing group on the Transitions tab. Make the slide active in the slide pane or click the slide in the Slide Sorter view and then click the up or down arrows to increase or decrease the slide duration.

Figure 7.3 Recording Toolbar

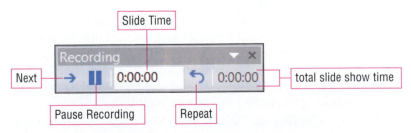

1. With **7-AdvTours.pptx** open, remove the automatic times for slides by completing the following steps:
   a. Click the Slide Show tab.
   b. Click the Set Up Slide Show button.
   c. At the Set Up Show dialog box, click the *Loop continuously until 'Esc'* check box to remove the check mark.
   d. Click OK to close the dialog box.
2. Set times for the slides to display during a slide show by completing the following steps:
   a. Make Slide 1 active.
   b. With the Slide Show tab active, click the Rehearse Timings button in the Set Up group.
   c. The first slide displays in Slide Show view and the Recording toolbar displays. Wait until the time displayed for the current slide reaches :04 (4 seconds) and then click Next. (If you miss the time, click the Repeat button to reset the clock back to 0 for the current slide.)

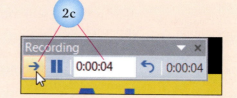

   d. Set the times for the remaining slides as follows:

   Slide 2 = 5 seconds
   Slide 3 = 6 seconds
   Slide 4 = 5 seconds
   Slide 5 = 6 seconds
   Slide 6 = 3 seconds
   Slide 7 = 6 seconds
   Slide 8 = 7 seconds
   Slide 9 = 7 seconds

   e. After the last slide displays, click Yes at the message asking if you want to record the new slide timings. (The slide times may display with one additional second for each.)
   f. If necessary, click the Normal button in the view area on the Status bar.
3. Click the Set Up Slide Show button to display the Set Up Show dialog box, click the *Loop continuously until 'Esc'* check box to insert a check mark, and then click OK to close the dialog box.
4. Run the slide show. (The slide show will start and run continuously.) Watch the slide show until it has started for the second time and then end the show by pressing the Esc key.
5. Save **7-AdvTours.pptx**.

Recording Narration

A narration can be recorded for a presentation that will play when the slide show is running. To record a narration, a microphone must be connected to the computer. To begin the narration, click the Record Slide Show button in the Set Up group on the Slide Show tab. At the Record Slide Show dialog box, click the Start Recording button. The slide show begins and the first slide fills the screen. Begin the narration, clicking the mouse to advance each slide.

Clicking the Record Slide Show button arrow displays a drop-down list with three options. Click the *Start Recording from Beginning* option to begin recording the narration with the first slide in the presentation or click the *Start Recording from Current Slide* option to begin recording the narration with the currently active slide. Position the mouse on the third option, *Clear*, and a side menu displays with options for clearing the timing on the current slide or all slides and clearing the narration from the current slide or all slides.

Record Slide
Show

Click the Record Slide Show button on the Slide Show tab and the Record Slide Show dialog box displays. This dialog box contains two options: *Slide and animation timings* and *Narrations and laser pointer*, so that just the slide timings can be recorded, just the narration, or both at the same time.

With the *Slide and animation timings* option active (containing a check mark), PowerPoint will keep track of the timing for each slide. When the slide show runs, the slides will remain on the screen the number of seconds recorded. To narrate a presentation without slides being timed, remove the check mark from the *Slide and animation timings* check box. With the *Narrations and laser pointer* option active (containing a check mark), the narration and laser pointer gestures made with the mouse can be recorded. To make laser pointer gestures, press and hold down the Ctrl key, click and hold down the left mouse button, drag in the slide, and then release the Ctrl key and the mouse button.

The narration in a presentation plays by default when running the slide show. To run the slide show without narration, display the Set Up Show dialog box and then click the *Show without narration* check box in the *Show options* section to insert a check mark.

Project 3c Recording Narration

Part 3 of 7

This is an optional project. Before beginning the project, check with your instructor to determine if you have a microphone available for recording.

1. With **7-AdvTours.pptx** open, save it with the name **7-AdvTours-NarrateSlide**.
2. Make Slide 9 active and then narrate the slide by completing the following steps:
   a. Click the Slide Show tab.
   b. Click the Record Slide Show button arrow in the Set Up group and then click *Start Recording from Current Slide* at the drop-down list.
   c. At the Record Slide Show dialog box, make sure both options contain a check mark and then click the Start Recording button.
   d. Speak the following text into the microphone: *Call Adventure Tours today to receive an additional ten percent savings when you book a Fiji or Peru tour.*
   e. Press the Esc key to end the narration.

3. Make Slide 1 active and then run the slide show. If your computer has speakers, you will hear your narration when Slide 9 displays. After viewing the slide show at least once, press the Esc key to end it.
4. Save and then close **7-AdvTours-NarrateSlide.pptx**.
5. Open **7-AdvTours.pptx** and then save it with the name **7-AdvTours-Narration**.

6. Remove the timings and the continuous loop option by completing the following steps:
   a. Click the Slide Show tab.
   b. Click the Record Slide Show button arrow, point to *Clear* at the drop-down list, and then click *Clear Timings on All Slides* at the side menu.
   c. Click the Set Up Slide Show button.
   d. At the Set Up Show dialog box, click the *Loop continuously until 'Esc'* check box to remove the check mark.
   e. Click OK to close the dialog box.

7. Make Slide 1 active and then record narration by completing the following steps:
   a. Click the Record Slide Show button in the Set Up group on the Slide Show tab.
   b. At the Record Slide Show dialog box, make sure both options contain a check mark and then click the Start Recording button.
   c. When the first slide displays, either read the information or provide your own narrative of the slide and then click the left mouse button. (You can also click the Next button on the Recording toolbar that displays in the upper left corner of the slide.)
   d. Continue narrating each slide (either using some of the information in the slides or creating your own narration). Try recording laser pointer gestures by pressing and holding down the Ctrl key, clicking and holding down the left mouse button, dragging in the slide, and then releasing the Ctrl key and the mouse button.
   e. After you narrate the last slide (about accommodations for the Peru tour), the presentation may display in Slide Sorter view.
8. Make Slide 1 active and then run the slide show. If your computer has speakers, you will hear your narration as the slide show runs.
9. Run the slide show without narration by completing the following steps:
   a. Click the Set Up Slide Show button in the Set Up group on the Slide Show tab.
   b. At the Set Up Show dialog box, click the *Show without narration* check box to insert a check mark.
   c. Click OK.
   d. Run the slide show beginning with Slide 1. (The slide show will still run automatically with the timing established when you were recording your narration but without the narration.)

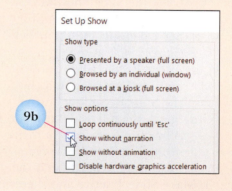

10. Save and then close **7-AdvTours-Narration.pptx**.

Tutorial

Hiding and Unhiding Slides

 Hide Slide

Hiding Slides

A slide show may be presented to a number of different groups or departments. In some situations the presenter may want to hide specific slides in a slide show depending on the audience. To hide a slide in a slide show, make the slide active, click the Slide Show tab, and then click the Hide Slide button in the Set Up group. When a slide is hidden, a slash displays over the slide number in the slide thumbnails pane and the slide in the slide thumbnails pane displays in a dimmed

Quick Steps

Hide/Unhide a Slide
1. Make slide active.
2. Click Slide Show tab.
3. Click Hide Slide button.

manner. The slide is visible in the slide thumbnails pane in Normal view and also in the Slide Sorter view. To remove the hidden icon and redisplay the slide when running a slide show, click the slide in the slide thumbnails pane, click the Slide Show tab, and then click the Hide Slide button.

Managing Monitors

If two monitors are connected to the computer or PowerPoint is running on a laptop with dual-display capabilities, specify which monitor to use when running the slide show with the *Monitor* option in the Monitors group on the Slide Show tab. By default, PowerPoint automatically chooses a monitor to display the slide show. Change the monitor for viewing the slide show by clicking the *Monitor* option box arrow and then clicking the monitor at the drop-down list.

Using Presenter View

Insert a check mark in the *Use Presenter View* check box in the Monitors group on the Slide Show tab if PowerPoint is running on a computer with two monitors or on a laptop with dual-display capabilities. With this option active, the slide show will display in full-screen view on one monitor and in a special speaker view on the other, similar to what is shown in Figure 7.4. The buttons that display below the slide are the same buttons as those that display in Slide Show view. Other options in Presenter View include the display of slide durations, a preview of the next slide in the slide show, a notes pane, and navigation buttons.

Figure 7.4 Presenter View

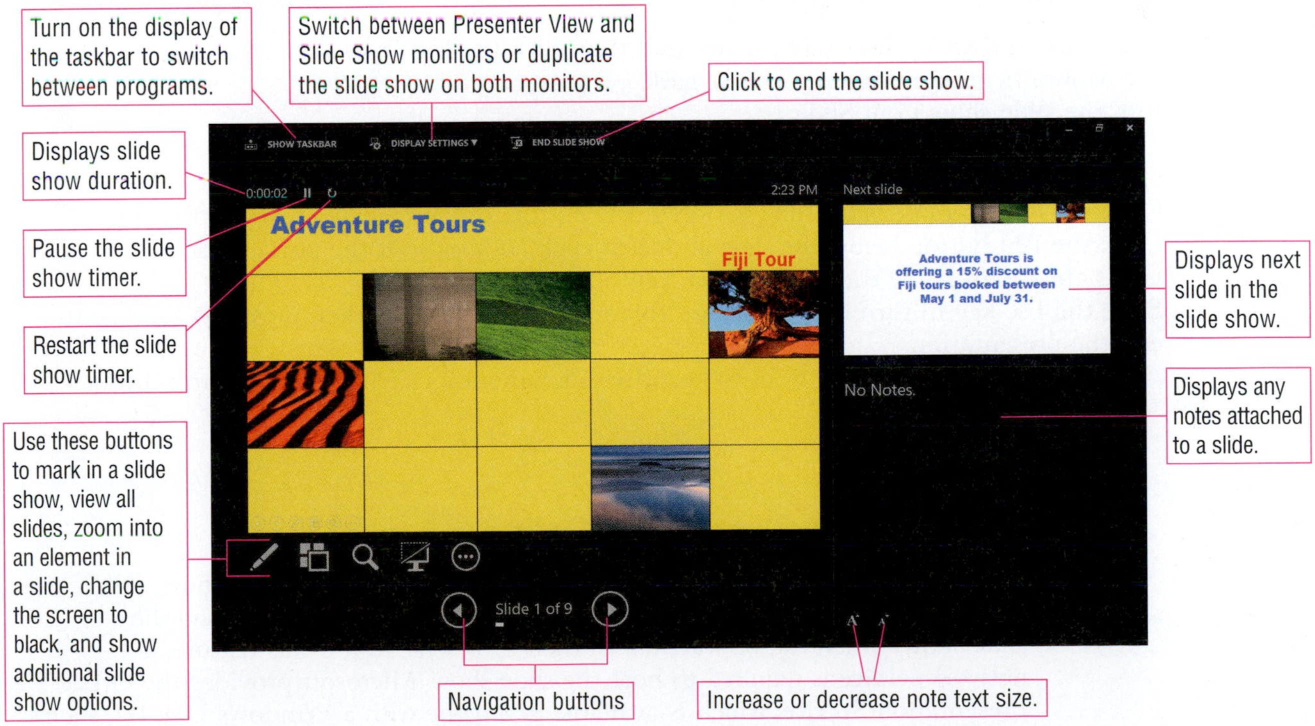

Turn on the display of the taskbar to switch between programs.

Switch between Presenter View and Slide Show monitors or duplicate the slide show on both monitors.

Click to end the slide show.

Displays slide show duration.

Pause the slide show timer.

Restart the slide show timer.

Use these buttons to mark in a slide show, view all slides, zoom into an element in a slide, change the screen to black, and show additional slide show options.

Displays next slide in the slide show.

Displays any notes attached to a slide.

Navigation buttons

Increase or decrease note text size.

1. Open **7-AdvTours.pptx**.
2. Remove the continuous loop option and remove timings by completing the following steps:
   a. Click the Slide Show tab.
   b. Click the Set Up Slide Show button.
   c. At the Set Up Show dialog box, click the *Loop continuously until 'Esc'* check box to remove the check mark.
   d. Click OK to close the dialog box.
   e. Click the Transitions tab.
   f. Click the *After* measurement box down arrow until *00:00* displays in the box.
   g. Click the *After* check box to remove the check mark.
   h. Click the *On Mouse Click* check box to insert a check mark.
   i. Click the Apply To All button.
3. Hide Slide 2 by completing the following steps:
   a. Click Slide 2 in the slide thumbnails pane.
   b. Click the Slide Show tab and then click the Hide Slide button in the Set Up group.
4. Run the slide show to see that Slide 2 does not display (since it is hidden).
5. Unhide Slide 2 by clicking Slide 2 in the slide thumbnails pane and then clicking the Hide Slide button in the Set Up group on the Slide Show tab.

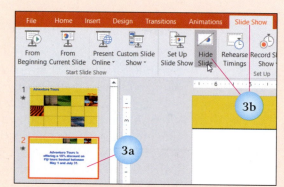

If you have two monitors connected to your computer, you can run the slide show in Presenter View. Complete these optional steps only if you have two monitors connected to your computer.

6. Make sure the Slide Show tab is active and then click the *Use Presenter View* check box in the Monitors group to insert a check mark.
7. Run the slide show from Slide 1.
8. Click the See all slides button below the slide.
9. Click the Slide 3 thumbnail.
10. Click the Return to previous slide button at the bottom of Presenter View to display Slide 2.
11. Click the Pen button below the slide and then click *Highlighter* at the pop-up list.
12. Using the mouse, drag through the text *May 1*.
13. Press the Esc key to turn the highlighter to an arrow pointer, and then press the Esc key to end the presentation.
14. At the message asking if you want to keep the ink annotations, click the Discard button.
15. Save **7-AdvTours.pptx**.

Presenting a Slide Show Online

PowerPoint includes the Present Online feature for sharing a slide show with others over the Internet by sending a link to the people who will view the slide show, which can be watched in their browsers. To use this feature, a network service is required to host the slide show. Microsoft provides the Office Presentation Service, which is available to anyone with a Windows Live ID, such as a OneDrive account, and Microsoft Office 2016.

To present a presentation online, click the Present Online button in the Start Slide Show group on the Slide Show tab. At the Present Online window that displays, click the CONNECT button, and, if necessary, enter a Windows Live ID user name and password. When PowerPoint has connected to an account and prepared the presentation, the Present Online window will display with a unique link PowerPoint created for the presentation. Click the Copy Link hyperlink in the Present Online window to copy the unique link, and then paste the link into an email that will be sent to the people who will be viewing the slide show. If the person presenting the slide show online has an Outlook account, clicking the Send in Email hyperlink opens Outlook and the link can be pasted in the message window.

After everyone has opened the presentation link in a web browser, click the START PRESENTATION button in the Present Online window. People viewing the slide show do not need PowerPoint installed on their computers to view the slide show since the slide show will display through their web browsers. When the slide show has ended, click the End Online Presentation button on the Present Online tab. At the confirmation message that displays, click the End Online Presentation button. The Present Online tab provides options for running the slide show, managing monitors, sharing the slide show through OneNote, and displaying the unique link to send to more people. The Present Online window can also be accessed by clicking the File tab, clicking the *Share* option, clicking *Present Online*, and then clicking the Present Online button.

When presenting a slide show online, the presenter can allow the viewers to download the presentation. To do this, the presenter would click the *Enable remote viewers to download the presentation* check box at the Present Online window before clicking the CONNECT button.

Project 3e Presenting a Slide Show Online   Part 5 of 7

This is an optional project. To complete this project, you will need a Windows Live ID account. Depending on your system configuration and what services are available, these steps will vary.

1. With **7-AdvTours.pptx** open, click the Slide Show tab and then click the Present Online button in the Start Slide Show group.
2. At the Present Online window that displays, click the CONNECT button.
3. If necessary, type your user name and password into the Windows Security dialog box.
4. At the Present Online window with the unique link selected, click the Copy Link hyperlink.
5. Send the link to colleagues by opening your email account, pasting the link into a new message window, and then sending the email to the viewers. Or, if you are using Microsoft Outlook, click the Send in Email hyperlink and Microsoft Outlook opens in a new message window with the link inserted in the message. In Outlook, send the link to people you want to view the presentation.
6. When everyone has received the link, click the START PRESENTATION button at the Present Online window.
7. Run the slide show.
8. When the slide show has ended, press the Esc key and then click the End Online Presentation button on the Present Online tab.
9. At the message that displays telling you that all remote viewers will be disconnected if you continue, click the End Online Presentation button.

Start Inking

Using Ink Tools

Similar to drawing and highlighting in slides during a slide show, as completed in Chapter 1, draw or highlight items in slides in Normal view with options on the Ink Tools Pens tab, as shown in Figure 7.5. Display this tab by clicking the Start Inking button in the Ink group on the Review tab. The Ink Tools Pens tab contains options for drawing and highlighting on slides; erasing markings on slides; selecting multiple options such as ink marks, shapes, and text boxes; selecting a variety of pen and highlighter colors; changing the color and thickness of the pen or highlighter; and converting drawings to shapes. The ink tools feature is useful when using a pen, stylus, or finger when drawing on a tablet or touchscreen computer.

Figure 7.5 Ink Tools Pens Tab

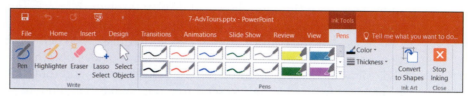

Project 3f Using Ink Tools

Part 6 of 7

1. With **7-AdvTours.pptx** open, make Slide 2 active.
2. Click the Review tab.
3. Click the Start Inking button in the Ink group.
4. With the Ink Tools Pens tab active, draw and highlight on the slide by completing the following steps:
   a. Click the More Pens button in the Pens group.
   b. Click the *Red Pen (1.0 mm)* option at the drop-down list (second column, second row in the *Built-In Pens* section).
   c. Using the mouse, draw a line below the text *15% discount*.

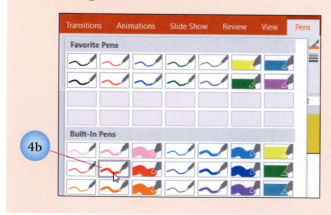

d. Click the More Pens button in the Pens group.

e. Click the *Yellow Highlighter (4.0 mm)* option at the drop-down list (sixth column, first row in the *Favorite Pens* section).

f. Using the mouse, draw through the text *May 1 and July 31.*

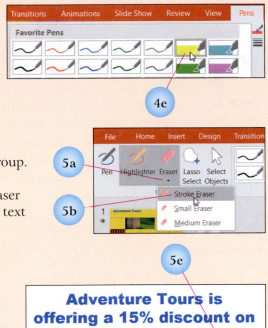

5. Erase drawing and highlighting on the slide by completing the following steps:

a. Click the Eraser button arrow in the Write group.

b. Click *Stroke Eraser* at the drop-down list.

c. Click the mouse pointer (displays with an eraser attached) anywhere in the red line below the text *15% discount.*

d. Click the Eraser button arrow and then click *Medium Eraser* at the drop-down list.

e. Using the mouse, which displays as a white box, drag over the text *and July 31.* to erase the yellow highlighting. (The text *May 1* should remain highlighted.)

f. Press the Esc key to change the mouse pointer to an arrow.

6. Make Slide 5 active.

7. Convert drawings to shapes and select shapes by completing the following steps:

a. Click the Convert to Shapes button in the Ink Art group.

b. Click the More Pens button in the Pens group and then click the *Orange Pen (0.35 mm)* option at the drop-down list (first column, third row in the *Built-In Pens* section).

c. Using the mouse, draw a rectangle around the text *Coral reef* in the second bulleted item. Notice that PowerPoint automatically converted the drawn rectangle into a more precise rectangle. If you are not satisfied with the appearance of the rectangle, click the Undo button on the Quick Access Toolbar two times, select the orange pen again, and then redraw the rectangle.

d. Click the Select Objects button in the Write group.

e. Hover the mouse pointer over the orange rectangle until the mouse pointer displays with a four-headed arrow attached and then click the border to select it.

f. Using the middle sizing handle at the right side of the orange border, drag the border to the right to include the word *cruise.*

g. Click the Thickness button in the Pens group and then click *4½ pt* at the drop-down gallery.

8. Run the slide show to see the highlighting and rectangle applied to the slides.

9. Save **7-AdvTours.pptx**.

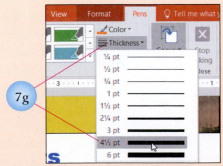

Check Your Work

Tutorial

Creating and
Running a
Custom Slide
Show

 Custom
Slide Show

Quick Steps

**Create a Custom
Slide Show**
1. Click Slide Show tab.
2. Click Custom Slide
   Show button.
3. Click *Custom Shows*.
4. Click New button.
5. Make changes at
   Define Custom Show
   dialog box.
6. Click OK.

**Run a Custom Slide
Show**
1. Click Slide Show tab.
2. Click Custom Slide
   Show button.
3. Click custom show.

**Edit a Custom Slide
Show**
1. Click Slide Show tab.
2. Click Custom Slide
   Show button.
3. Click *Custom Shows*.
4. Click custom show's
   name.
5. Click Edit button.
6. Make changes at
   Define Custom Show
   dialog box.
7. Click OK.

Hint Create
custom slide shows
to customize a
presentation for a
variety of audiences.

Creating a Custom Slide Show

A custom slide show is a slide show within a slide show. Creating a custom slide show might be useful in situations where only a select number of slides will be presented to a particular audience. To create a custom slide show, click the Slide Show tab, click the Custom Slide Show button in the Start Slide Show group, and then click *Custom Shows* at the drop-down list. At the Custom Shows dialog box, click the New button and the Define Custom Show dialog box displays, similar to what is shown in Figure 7.6.

At the Define Custom Show dialog box, type a name for the custom slide show in the *Slide show name* text box. To insert a slide in the custom slide show, click the check box for the specific slide in the *Slides in presentation* list box to insert a check mark and then click the Add button. This inserts the slide in the *Slides in custom show* list box. Continue in this manner until all specific slides have been added to the custom slide show. A check mark can be inserted in all of the specific slide check boxes first and then clicking the Add button will add all the slides in the *Slides in custom show* list box at once.

To change the order of the slides in the *Slides in custom show* list box, click one of the arrow keys to move the selected slide up or down in the list box. When all slides have been inserted in the *Slides in custom show* list box and are arranged in the desired order, click OK. More than one custom slide show can be created in a presentation.

Running a Custom Slide Show

To run a custom slide show within a slide show, click the Custom Slide Show button on the Slide Show tab and then click the custom slide show's name at the drop-down list. A custom slide show can also be run by displaying the Set Up Show dialog box and then clicking the *Custom show* option. If the presentation contains more than one custom slide show, click the *Custom show* option box arrow and then click the custom slide show's name at the drop-down list.

Figure 7.6 Define Custom Show Dialog Box

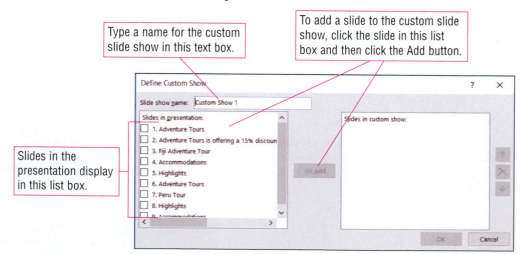

Editing a Custom Slide Show

A custom slide show is saved with the presentation and can be edited. To edit a custom slide show, open the presentation, click the Custom Slide Show button on the Slide Show tab, and then click *Custom Shows* at the drop-down list. At the Custom Shows dialog box, click the custom slide show name to be edited and then click the Edit button. At the Define Custom Show dialog box, make changes to the custom slide show, such as adding or removing slides or changing the order of slides and then click the OK button.

Printing a Custom Slide Show

Print a custom slide show with options in the *Settings* category of the Print backstage area. To do this, click the File tab and then click the *Print* option to display the Print backstage area. Click the first gallery in the *Settings* category and then click the custom slide show in the *Custom Shows* section.

Quick Steps

Print a Custom Slide Show
1. Display Print backstage area.
2. Click first gallery in *Settings* category.
3. Click custom show at drop-down list.
4. Click Print button.

Project 3g   Creating, Editing, and Running Custom Slide Shows   Part 7 of 7

1. With **7-AdvTours.pptx** open, save the presentation with the name **7-AdvTours-Custom**.
2. Create two custom slide shows by completing the following steps:
   a. Click the Slide Show tab, click the Custom Slide Show button, and then click *Custom Shows* at the drop-down list.
   b. At the Custom Shows dialog box, click the New button.
   c. At the Define Custom Show dialog box, select the text in the *Slide show name* text box and then type PeruTourCustom.
   d. Click the Slide 6 check box in the *Slides in presentation* list box to insert a check mark and then click the Add button. (This adds the slide to the *Slides in custom show* list box.)
   e. Click the check boxes for Slides 7, 8, and 9 in the list box to insert check marks and then click the Add button.
   f. Click OK to close the Define Custom Show dialog box.
   g. At the Custom Shows dialog box, click the New button.
   h. At the Define Custom Show dialog box, select the text in the *Slide show name* text box and then type FijiTourCustom.
   i. Add Slides 1 through 5 to the *Slides in custom show* list box.
   j. Click OK to close the dialog box.
   k. Click the Close button to close the Custom Shows dialog box.
3. Run the custom slide shows by completing the following steps:
   a. Click the Custom Slide Show button on the Slide Show tab and then click *PeruTourCustom* at the drop-down list.

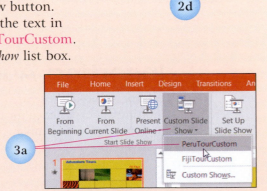

b. Click the left mouse button to advance slides.

c. Click the Custom Slide Show button, click *FijiTourCustom* at the drop-down list, and then view the slide show. (Click the left mouse button to advance the slides.)

4. Edit the FijiTourCustom custom slide show by completing the following steps:

a. Click the Custom Slide Show button on the Slide Show tab and then click *Custom Shows* at the drop-down list.

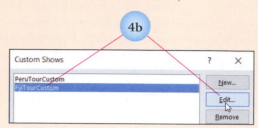

b. At the Custom Shows dialog box, click *FijiTourCustom* in the list box and then click the Edit button.

c. At the Define Custom Show dialog box, click Slide 2 in the *Slides in custom show* list box and then click the Down button at the right side of the list box three times. (This moves the slide to the bottom of the list.)

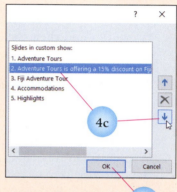

d. Click OK to close the dialog box.

e. Click the Close button to close the Custom Shows dialog box.

5. Run the FijiTourCustom slide show.

6. Print the FijiTourCustom slide show by completing the following steps:

a. Click the File tab and then click the *Print* option.

b. At the Print backstage area, click the first gallery in the *Settings* category and then click *FijiTourCustom* in the *Custom Shows* section.

c. Click the second gallery in the *Settings* category and then click *6 Slides Horizontal* at the drop-down list.

d. Click the Print button.

7. Save and then close **7-AdvTours-Custom.pptx**.

> **Check Your Work**

Project 4 **Insert Audio and Video Files in an Eco-Tours Presentation**   **5 Parts**

You will open a presentation and then insert an audio file, a video file, and an image with motion. You will also customize the audio and video files to play automatically when running the slide show.

> **Preview Finished Project**

Inserting Audio and Video Files

Adding audio and/or video files to a presentation will turn a slide show into a true multimedia experience for the audience. Including a variety of elements in a presentation will stimulate interest in the slide show and keep the audience motivated.

Inserting an Audio File

To add an audio file to a presentation, click the Insert tab, click the Audio button in the Media group, and then click *Audio on My PC* at the drop-down list. At the Insert Audio dialog box, navigate to the folder containing the audio file and then double-click the audio file.

If an audio recording device is attached to the computer, audio can be recorded for the presentation by clicking the Audio button and then clicking *Record Audio* at the drop-down list. At the Record Sound dialog box, name the audio, click the Record button, and then record the audio.

When an audio file is inserted in a presentation, the Audio Tools Format tab and the Audio Tools Playback tab display. Click the Audio Tools Format tab and options display that are similar to options on the Picture Tools Format tab. Click the Audio Tools Playback tab and options display for previewing the audio file, inserting a bookmark at a specific time in the audio file, specifying fade in and fade out times, and specifying how to play the audio file.

Quick Steps

Insert an Audio File
1. Click Insert tab.
2. Click Audio button.
3. Click *Audio on My PC*.
4. Double-click audio file.

Project 4a   Inserting an Audio File   **Part 1 of 5**

1. Open **EcoTours.pptx** and then save it with the name **7-EcoTours**.
2. Insert an audio file that plays music at the end of the presentation by completing the following steps:
   a. Make Slide 8 active and then click the Insert tab.
   b. Click the Audio button in the Media group, and then click *Audio on My PC* at the drop-down list.
   c. At the Insert Audio dialog box, navigate to the PC7 folder on your storage medium and then double-click **AudioFile-01.mid**.
   d. With the Audio Tools Playback tab active, click the *Start* option box arrow in the Audio Options group and then click *Automatically* at the drop-down list.
   e. Click the *Loop until Stopped* check box in the Audio Options group to insert a check mark.
   f. Click the *Hide During Show* check box to insert a check mark.
3. Click the Start from Beginning button on the Quick Access Toolbar to run the slide show starting with Slide 1. When the last slide displays, listen to the audio file and then press the Esc key to return to the Normal view.
4. Save **7-EcoTours.pptx**.

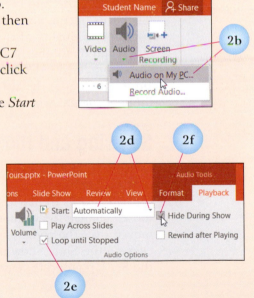

Check Your Work

Inserting a Video File

Inserting a video file in a presentation is a similar process to inserting an audio file. Click the Video button in the Media group on the Insert tab and then click *Video on My PC* at the drop-down list to display the Insert Video dialog box. At this dialog box, navigate to the folder containing the video file and then double-click the file.

Quick Steps

Insert a Video File
1. Click Insert tab.
2. Click Video button.
3. Click *Video on My PC*.
4. Double-click video file.

The Video button drop-down list also includes the *Online Video* option. Click this option to display the Insert Video window. At this window, search for videos online using the *YouTube* search option or paste an embedded code into the *From a Video Embed Code* option to insert a video from a website. To embed code from an online video, locate and copy the embedded code of the video, paste the embedded code in the *From a Video Embed Code* section of the Insert Video window, and then click the Insert button. Another way to insert a video in a presentation is to click the Insert Video button in the content placeholder on a slide. This displays the Insert Video window with the additional option to browse for a file on the computer.

When a video file is inserted in a presentation, the Video Tools Format tab and the Video Tools Playback tab display. Click the Video Tools Format tab and options display for adjusting the video file color and frame, applying video styles, and arranging and sizing the video file. Click the Video Tools Playback tab and options display that are similar to the options on the Audio Tools Playback tab. Formatting also can be applied to a video with options in the Format Video task pane.

Optimizing and Compressing Video Files

If a video with an older file format is inserted in a presentation, the Info backstage area may display an Optimize Compatibility button. Optimize compatibility of a video file to increase the likelihood that the video file will play on multiple devices.

Compress Media

When a video file is inserted in a presentation, consider compressing the file to improve playback performance and save disk space. If a presentation contains a video file, the Info backstage area contains the Compress Media button. Click this button and a drop-down list displays with options for specifying the compressed quality of the video. Click the *Presentation Quality* option to save space and maintain the quality of the video. Click the *Internet Quality* option and the compressed video file will be comparable to a video file streamed over the Internet. Choose the last option, *Low Quality*, to compress the file when space is limited, such as when sending the presentation as an email attachment.

Showing and Hiding Media Controls

When a slide with an audio or video file displays during a slide show, media controls appear along the bottom of the audio icon or video window. Use these media controls to play the audio or video file, move to a specific location in the file, or change the volume. The media controls display when the mouse pointer is moved over the audio icon or video window. Media controls can be turned off by clicking the Slide Show tab and then clicking the *Show Media Controls* check box in the Set Up group to remove the check mark.

Project 4b **Inserting a Video File in a Presentation**   **Part 2 of 5**

1. With **7-EcoTours.pptx** open, make Slide 8 active.
2. You will insert a video file in the slide that contains audio, so delete the audio file you inserted in Project 4a by clicking the audio file icon that displays in the middle of Slide 8 and then pressing the Delete key.
3. Insert a video file by completing the following steps:
   a. Click the Insert tab.

b. Click the Video button in the Media group and then click *Video on My PC* at the drop-down list.

c. At the Insert Video dialog box, navigate to the PC7 folder on your storage medium and then double-click the file named **Wildlife.wmv**.

d. Click the Play button in the Preview group (on the left side of the Video Tools Format tab) to preview the video file. (The video plays for approximately 30 seconds.)

4. Format the video by completing the following steps:

a. Make sure the video image is selected on the slide and the Video Tools Format tab is selected.

b. Click the *Beveled Frame, Gradient* option in the Video Styles group (fourth option).

c. Click the Video Shape button in the Video Styles group and then click *Rounded Rectangle* at the drop-down gallery (second option in the *Rectangles* section).

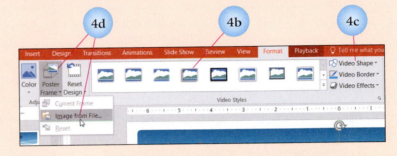

d. Click the Poster Frame button in the Adjust group and then click *Image from File* at the drop-down list.

e. At the Insert Pictures window, click the Browse button to the right of the *From a file* option, navigate to the PC7 folder on your storage medium, and then double-click **Olympics.jpg**.

f. Click the Corrections button in the Adjust group and then click *Brightness: 0% (Normal) Contrast: +20%* at the drop-down gallery (third column, fourth row).

g. Click the Rotate button in the Arrange group and then click *Flip Horizontal* at the drop-down list.

h. Click the Size group dialog box launcher to display the Format Video task pane.

i. With the Size & Properties icon selected, make sure the *Size* options display.

j. Select the current measurement in the *Height* measurement box and then type 4.9.

k. Click *Position* to display the options.

l. Select the current measurement in the *Horizontal position* measurement box and then type 2.3.

m. Select the current measurement in the *Vertical position* measurement box and then type 1.8.

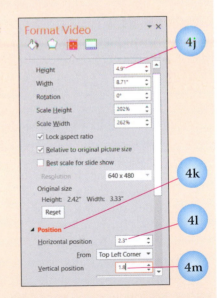

n. Close the Format Video task pane.

o. Click the Video Tools Playback tab.

p. Click the Volume button in the Video Options group and then click *Low* at the drop-down list.

q. Click the *Loop until Stopped* check box in the Video Options group to insert a check mark.

5. Make Slide 1 active and then run the slide show. When the slide containing the video file displays, move the mouse over the video file window and then click the play button at the bottom left side of the window.

6. After viewing the video a couple of times, press the Esc key two times.
7. Specify that you want the video window to fill the slide, the video to automatically start when the slide displays, the video to play only once, and the display of media controls turned off by completing the following steps:

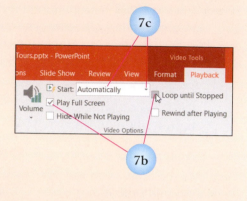

a. Make sure Slide 8 is active, click the video file window, and then click the Video Tools Playback tab.
b. Click the *Play Full Screen* check box in the Video Options group to insert a check mark and click the *Loop until Stopped* check box to remove the check mark.
c. Click the *Start* option box arrow in the Video Options group and then click *Automatically* at the drop-down list.
d. Click the Slide Show tab.
e. Click the *Show Media Controls* check box in the Set Up group to remove the check mark.
8. Make Slide 1 active and then run the slide show. When the slide displays containing the video, the video will automatically begin. When the video is finished playing, press the Esc key to return to Normal view.
9. Print Slide 8.
10. Compress the video file by completing the following steps:

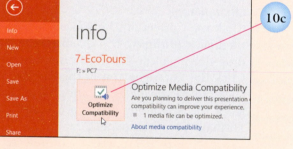

a. Make Slide 8 active and then click the video file window.
b. Click the File tab.
c. At the Info backstage area, click the Optimize Compatibility button.
d. When the optimization is complete, click the Close button in the Optimize Media Compatibility dialog box.
e. Click the Compress Media button and then click *Internet Quality* at the drop-down list.
f. At the Compress Media dialog box, wait until the compression is complete (notice the progress bar along the bottom of the dialog box) and then the initial size of the video file and the number of megabytes saved by the compression.
g. Click the Close button to close the dialog box and then click the Back button to return to the presentation.
11. Save **7-EcoTours.pptx**.

Complete these optional steps to insert a video from the Internet into a slide.

12. With Slide 8 active, insert a new slide with the Blank layout.
13. Click the Insert tab, click the Video button in the Media group, and then click *Online Video* at the drop-down list.
14. Click in the *Search YouTube* box, type Antarctica wildlife, and then press the Enter key.
15. At the search results window, double-click a video that interests you.
16. Size and position the video window in the slide to better fill the slide.
17. Make Slide 1 active and then run the slide show. When the slide with the video file you inserted displays, click the Play button in the video window. When the video is finished playing, press the Esc key to return to Normal view.
18. Save **7-EcoTours.pptx**.

Check Your Work

Trimming a Video File

Quick Steps

Trim a Video File
1. Insert video file.
2. Click Video Tools Playback tab.
3. Click Trim Video button.
4. Specify start time and/or end time.
5. Click OK.

 Trim Video

Use the Trim Video button on the Video Tools Playback tab to trim the beginning and end of a video. This might be helpful in a situation where a portion of the video should be removed that is not pertinent to the message in the presentation. Trimming is limited to a portion of the beginning and end of the video.

To trim a video, insert the video file in the slide, click the Video Tools Playback tab, and then click the Trim Video button in the Editing group. At the Trim Video dialog box, specify the start and/or end time for the video. To trim the start of the video, insert a specific time in the *Start Time* measurement box or drag the green start point marker on the slider bar below the video. Zero in on a very specific starting point by clicking the Next Frame button or the Previous Frame button to move the display of the video a single frame at a time. Complete similar steps to trim the ending of the video except use the red end point marker on the slider bar or insert the specific ending time in the *End Time* measurement box.

Project 4c Trimming a Video   Part 3 of 5

1. With **7-EcoTour.pptx** open, make Slide 8 active.
2. Trim the first part of the video that shows the running horses by completing the following steps:
   a. Click the video to select it and then click the Video Tools Playback tab.
   b. Click the Trim Video button in the Editing group.
   c. At the Trim Video dialog box, position the mouse pointer on the green start point marker on the slider bar until the pointer displays as a double-headed arrow pointing left and right. Click and hold down the left mouse button, drag the start point marker to approximately the *00:04.0* time, and then release the mouse button.
   d. Click the Next Frame button until the first image of the birds displays and the horses have completely disappeared off the screen. (Depending on where you dragged the start point marker, you may need to click the Previous Frame button.)
   e. Click the OK button.

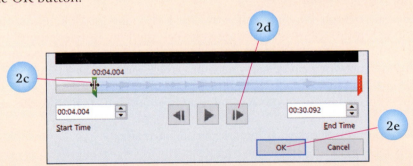

3. Click the *Fade In* measurement box up arrow in the Editing group until *01.00* displays and then click the *Fade Out* measurement box up arrow until *01.00* displays.
4. Run the slide show and then press the Esc key to return to the Normal view.
5. Save **7-EcoTours.pptx**.

Playing an Audio File throughout a Slide Show

An audio file can be inserted in a presentation to play when a specific slide displays when running the slide show. An audio file can also be customized to play continually through all of the slides when running the slide show. Generally, an audio file that plays continually throughout the presentation would be used when setting up an automated presentation.

 Play in Background

To specify that the audio file plays throughout the presentation, click the Play in Background button in the Audio Styles group on the Audio Tools Playback tab. When this button is clicked, the *Start* option box in the Audio Options group changes to *Automatically*, and a check mark is inserted in the *Play Across Slides* check box, the *Loop until Stopped* check box, and the *Hide During Show* check box. To make the presentation automated, display the Set Up Show dialog box and then insert a check mark in the *Loop continuously until 'Esc'* check box.

Project 4d Playing an Audio File throughout a Slide Show

Part 4 of 5

1. With **7-EcoTours.pptx** open, make Slide 8 active and then make the following changes:
   a. Select and then delete the video file.
   b. Apply the Title Only slide layout.
   c. Type the title Let the adventure begin! and then change the font size to 54 points and the font color to standard dark blue.
   d. Distribute the title placeholder vertically on the slide. (Do this by clicking the Align button on the Drawing Tools Format tab and then clicking *Distribute Vertically* at the drop-down list.)
2. Make Slide 1 active and then insert an audio file that plays throughout all slides by completing the following steps:
   a. Click the Insert tab, click the Audio button in the Media group, and then click *Audio on My PC* at the drop-down list.
   b. At the Insert Audio dialog box, navigate to the PC7 folder on your storage medium and then double-click ***AudioFile-02.mid***.
   c. With the Audio Tools Playback tab active, click the Play in Background button in the Audio Styles group. (Notice that when you click the Play in Background button, the *Start* option box in the Audio Options group changes to *Automatically*, and a check mark is inserted in the *Play Across Slides* check box, the *Loop until Stopped* check box, and the *Hide During Show* check box.)
   d. Click the Volume button in the Audio Options group and then click *Medium* at the drop-down list.
3. Specify that you want slides to automatically advance after five seconds by completing the following steps:
   a. Click the Transitions tab.
   b. Click the *After* measurement box up arrow in the Timing group until *00:05.00* displays.
   c. Click the *On Mouse Click* check box to remove the check mark.
   d. Click the Apply To All button.
4. Set up the slide show to run continuously by completing the following steps:
   a. Click the Slide Show tab.
   b. Click the Set Up Slide Show button.
   c. At the Set Up Show dialog box, click the *Loop continuously until 'Esc'* check box to insert a check mark.

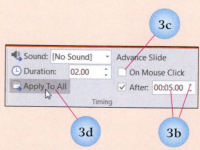

d. Click OK to close the dialog box.
5. If necessary, make Slide 1 active and then run the slide show. When the slide show begins for the second time, press the Esc key to return to Normal view.
6. Save and then close **7-EcoTours.pptx**.

Check Your Work

Creating a Screen Recording

Screen Recording

PowerPoint includes a screen recording feature that will record actions as they are being performed on the screen. A screen recording is automatically inserted into the active slide as a video file, and the Video Tools Format tab and Video Tools Playback tab are available. Format a screen recording in the same manner as formatting a video file.

Create a screen recording by opening any necessary files (other PowerPoint presentations, different applications, or an Internet browser), clicking the Insert tab, and then clicking the Screen Recording button in the Media group. At the Screen Recording toolbar that displays, click the Select Area button. When the mouse pointer displays as crosshairs, click and hold down the left mouse button, drag to select the screen area that will be used in the screen recording, and then release the mouse button. Once the area is selected, click the Record button on the Screen Recording toolbar, as shown in Figure 7.7. A message will display stating how to end the recording and a countdown to begin the recording. When the countdown is complete, the screen recording will record all mouse movements and actions performed on the screen. Press the Windows logo key + Shift + Q to end the recording. The recording is automatically inserted in the active slide.

A screen recording file is saved with the presentation. To make the recording available for other presentations, save it as a separate file by right-clicking the recording and then clicking *Save Media As* at the shortcut menu. At the Save Media As dialog box, navigate to the desired folder, type a name for the recording in the *File name* text box, and then click the Save button. Insert the recording into a different presentation with the Video button in the Media group.

Figure 7.7 Screen Recording Toolbar

Click the Record button to begin recording. This button displays as a Pause button once recording begins.

time duration of recording

Use the Select Area button to determine the section of the screen to be used during the recording.

Click the Record Pointer button to include the arrow pointer in the screen recording.

Click the Audio button to include audio in the recording.

1. Open **Animations.pptx** and save it with the name **7-Animations.pptx**.
2. Make Slide 6 active.
3. Open **MotionPath.pptx**. Make sure no other applications are open except for **7-Animations.pptx** and **MotionPath.pptx**.
4. Click the PowerPoint button on the taskbar and then click **7-Animations.pptx**.
5. Create a screen recording of the steps to insert a custom motion path in a slide by completing the following steps:
   a. Click the Insert tab.
   b. Click the Screen Recording button in the Media group.
   c. When the Screen Recording toolbar displays, click the Select Area button.
   d. Using the mouse, drag to select the entire PowerPoint window for the **MotionPath.pptx** file.
   e. Click the Record button on the Screen Recording toolbar.
   f. In the **MotionPath.pptx** window, click the moon image to select it.
   g. Click the Animations tab.
   h. Click the More Animations button in the Animations group.
   i. Scroll down the drop-down list and then click *Custom Path* in the *Motion Paths* section.
   j. Using the mouse, click and drag the moon around the Earth image, ending in the original location, release the mouse button, and then double-click the mouse button.
   k. Press the Windows logo key + Shift + Q to end the screen recording.
6. Format the screen recording by completing the following steps:
   a. With the Video Tools Format tab active, click in the *Shape Height* measurement box, type 4.5, and then press the Enter key.
   b. Drag the screen recording down so it is positioned below the title and centered vertically on the slide.
7. View the screen recording by clicking the Play button in the Preview group.
8. Save the screen recording to your storage medium by completing the following steps:
   a. Right-click anywhere in the screen recording.
   b. Click the *Save Media as* option at the shortcut menu.
   c. At the Save Media As dialog box, navigate to the PC7 folder on your storage medium.
   d. Type the name 7-Motion in the *File name* text box.
   e. Click the Save button.
9. Make Slide 1 active and then run the slide show. When the slide with the screen recording displays, click the Play button in the video window. When the video is finished playing, press the Esc key to return to Normal view.
10. Print Slide 6.
11. Save and then close **7-Animations.pptx**.
12. Close **MotionPath.pptx** without saving changes.

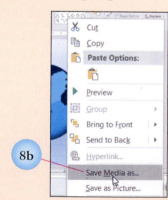

Check Your Work

Chapter Summary

- Apply animation to an item in a slide with options in the Animation group on the Animations tab. Specify animation effects with options from the Effect Options button drop-down gallery.

- Click the Preview button on the Animations tab to view the animation effects without running the slide show.

- Remove an animation effect from an item in a slide by clicking the *None* option in the Animation group on the Animations tab.

- The Add Animation button in the Advanced Animation group on the Animations tab provides four types of animation effects—entrance, exit, emphasis, and motion paths.

- Use the Animation Painter button in the Advanced Animation group on the Animations tab to apply the same animation to items in more than one location in a slide or slides.

- Use options in the Timing group on the Animations tab to determine when an animation starts on a slide, the duration of the animation, the delay between animations, and the order in which animations appear on the slide.

- Use the Animation Pane to customize animation effects. Display the pane by clicking the Animation Pane button in the Advanced Animation group on the Animations tab.

- Apply a sound to an animation with the *Sound* option box at the effect options dialog box with the Effect tab selected. The name of the dialog box varies depending on the animation effect selected.

- A build displays important points on a slide one point at a time. A build can be applied that dims the previous bulleted point with the *After animation* option box at the effect options dialog box with the Effect tab selected.

- Specify a path an item is to follow when it displays on the slide with options in the *Motion Paths* section of the Add Animation button drop-down gallery. To draw a motion path, choose the *Custom path* option at the drop-down gallery.

- Use the Trigger button in the Advanced Animation group to specify that an animation effect occurs during a slide show by clicking an item on the slide.

- Customize a slide show with options in the Set Up Show dialog box. Display the dialog box by clicking the Slide Show tab and then clicking the Set Up Slide Show button.

- To prepare an automated slide show, insert a check mark in the *Loop continuously until 'Esc'* check box at the Set Up Show dialog box.

- To apply specific times to slides, click the Rehearse Timings button in the Set Up group on the Slide Show tab. Use buttons on the Recording toolbar to set, pause, or repeat times.

- To record narration for a presentation, click the Record Slide Show button in the Set Up group on the Slide Show tab and then click the Start Recording button at the Record Slide Show dialog box.

- Hide or unhide a slide in a slide show by clicking the Hide Slide button in the Set Up group on the Slide Show tab.

- Specify on which monitor to run the slide show with the *Monitor* option in the Monitors group on the Slide Show tab.

- If PowerPoint is running on a computer with two monitors or on a laptop with dual-display capabilities, the slide show can be displayed in full-screen view on one monitor and in Presenter view on the other monitor.

- Use the Present Online feature to share a slide show with others over the Internet. Send a link to the people who will view the slide show and then everyone can watch the slide show in their web browsers.

- Draw or highlight text or objects in slides while in Normal view using options on the Ink Tools Pens tab. Display the Ink Tools Pens tab by clicking the Start Inking button in the Ink group on the Review tab.

- Create a custom slide show, which is a slide show within a slide show, with options in the Define Custom Show dialog box.

- To run a custom slide show, click the Custom Slide Show button in the Start Slide Show group on the Slide Show tab and then click the custom show at the drop-down list.

- Print a custom slide show at the Print backstage area by clicking the first gallery in the *Settings* category and then clicking the custom show in the *Custom Shows* section.

- Insert an audio file in a slide by clicking the Audio button in the Media group on the Insert tab and then clicking *Audio on My PC*. Use options on the Audio Tools Format tab and the Audio Tools Playback tab to format and customize the audio file.

- Insert a video file in a slide by clicking the Video button in the Media group on the Insert tab and then clicking *Video on My PC*. Use options on the Video Tools Format tab and the Video Tools Playback tab to format and customize the video file.

- When a slide show runs, media controls display along the bottom of an audio icon or video window in a slide when the mouse is moved over the icon or window. Turn on or off the display of these media controls with the *Show Media Controls* check box in the Set Up group on the Slide Show tab.

- Compress a video file to improve playback performance and save disk space. Compress a video file by clicking the File tab to display the Info backstage area, clicking the Compress Media button, and then clicking the specific compression.

- Use the Trim Video button on the Video Tools Playback tab to trim the beginning and/or end of a video.

- Create and insert a screen recording by clicking the Screen Recording button in the Media group on the Insert tab, selecting the recording area, beginning the recording, and then formating the recording that is inserted in the selected slide.

Commands Review

FEATURE	RIBBON TAB, GROUP/OPTION	BUTTON, OPTION
add animations	Animations, Advanced Animation	
Animation Painter	Animations, Advanced Animation	
Animation Pane	Animations, Advanced Animation	
animations	Animations, Animation	
compress video file	File, *Info*	
Define Custom Show dialog box	Slide Show, Start Slide Show	, *Custom Shows*, New
hide/unhide slide	Slide Show, Set Up	
ink tools	Review, Ink	
insert audio file	Insert, Media	
insert video file	Insert, Media	
optimize video file	File, *Info*	
present online	Slide Show, Start Slide Show	
Recording toolbar	Slide Show, Set Up	
screen recording	Insert, Media	
Set Up Show dialog box	Slide Show, Set Up	
Trim Video dialog box	Video Tools Playback, Editing	

Microsoft®
PowerPoint®

Integrating, Sharing, and Protecting Presentations

Performance Objectives

Upon successful completion of Chapter 8, you will be able to:

1. Import a Word outline into a presentation
2. Copy and paste data between programs and use the Clipboard
3. Share presentations with others
4. Export a presentation to Word
5. Save a presentation in different file formats
6. Embed and link objects
7. Download templates
8. Compare and combine presentations
9. Insert, edit, and delete comments
10. Manage presentation properties
11. Protect a presentation
12. Inspect a presentation and check for accessibility and compatibility issues
13. Manage autosave versions of presentations
14. Customize PowerPoint options

Precheck

Check your current skills to focus your study.

Share data between programs in the Microsoft Office suite by importing and exporting, copying and pasting, copying and embedding, or copying and linking data. The method for sharing data depends on the data and whether it is static or dynamic. Use options in the Share backstage area to share a presentation online or as an email attachment and use options at the Export backstage area to create a video or handout of a presentation and save a presentation in a variety of file formats. If PowerPoint is used in a collaborative environment, comments can be inserted in a presentation and then the presentation can be shared with others. Use options in the Info backstage area to manage presentation properties, password protect a presentation, insert a digital signature, inspect a presentation, and manage versions. In this chapter, you will learn how to complete these tasks as well as how to download design templates from Office.com.

SNAP

If you are a SNAP user, launch the Precheck and Tutorials from your Assignments page.

Data Files

Before beginning chapter work, copy the PC8 folder to your storage medium and then make PC8 the active folder.

Tutorial

Importing a Word Outline

Importing a Word Outline

A Word document containing text formatted as an outline with heading styles can be imported into a PowerPoint presentation. Text formatted with a Heading 1 style becomes the title of a new slide. Text formatted with a Heading 2 style becomes first-level text, paragraphs formatted with a Heading 3 style become second-level text, and so on.

Quick Steps

Import a Word Outline
1. Open blank presentation.
2. Click New Slide button arrow.
3. Click *Slides from Outline*.
4. Double-click document.

To import a Word outline, open a blank presentation, click the New Slide button arrow in the Slides group on the Home tab, and then click *Slides from Outline* at the drop-down list. At the Insert Outline dialog box, navigate to the folder containing the Word document and then double-click the document. If text in the Word document does not have heading styles applied, PowerPoint creates an outline based on each paragraph of text in the document.

Project 1a Importing a Word Outline

Part 1 of 9

1. At a blank presentation, click the New Slide button arrow in the Slides group on the Home tab and then click *Slides from Outline* at the drop-down list.
2. At the Insert Outline dialog box, navigate to the PC8 folder on your storage medium and then double-click *ATTopFive.docx*.
3. Click the Design tab and then apply the Parallax design theme.
4. Change the background by completing these steps:
   a. Click the Format Background button in the Customize group on the Design tab.
   b. At the Format Background task pane, click the *Solid fill* option.
   c. Click the Color button and then click the *White, Background 1* option (first column, first row in the *Theme Colors* section).
   d. Click the Apply to All button.
   e. Close the task pane.
5. Delete Slide 1.

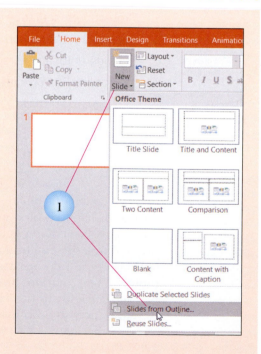

6. Format the new Slide 1 by completing the following steps:
    a. Change the slide layout by clicking the Home tab, clicking the Layout button in the Slides group, and then clicking *Title Only* at the drop-down list.
    b. Drag the placeholder containing the text *Adventure Tours* toward the bottom of the slide and center it horizontally.
    c. Insert the **FCTLogo.jpg**, located in the PC8 folder on your storage medium (do this with the Pictures button on the Insert tab), and then increase the size of the logo so it fills a good portion of the white area of the slide.
7. Make Slide 2 active and then apply the Title Only layout.
8. Make Slide 3 active and then change the bulleted text line spacing to 2.0 lines.
9. Make Slide 4 active and then change the bulleted text line spacing to 1.5 lines.
10. Save the presentation and name it **8-ATTopFive**.

> **Check Your Work**

Tutorial

Copying and Pasting Data

Copying and Pasting between Programs

Use the Copy and Paste buttons in the Clipboard group on the Home tab to copy data such as text or an object from one program and then paste it into another program. For example, in Project 1b, an Excel chart will be copied and then pasted into a PowerPoint slide. A copied object, such as a chart, can be moved and sized like any other object.

Project 1b Copying an Excel Chart to a PowerPoint Slide   Part 2 of 9

1. With **8-ATTopFive.pptx** open, make Slide 2 active.
2. Open Excel and then open **Top5Tours.xlsx**, located in the PC8 folder on your storage medium.
3. Click in the chart to select it. (Make sure you select the chart and not just an element in the chart.)
4. Click the Copy button in the Clipboard group on the Home tab.
5. Close **Top5Tours.xlsx** and then close Excel.
6. In PowerPoint, with Slide 2 active, click the Paste button in the Clipboard group on the Home tab.
7. Move the chart so it is centered below the title *Top Five Destinations*.
8. Display Slide 1 in the slide pane and then run the slide show.
9. Print only Slide 2.
10. Save **8-ATTopFive.pptx**.

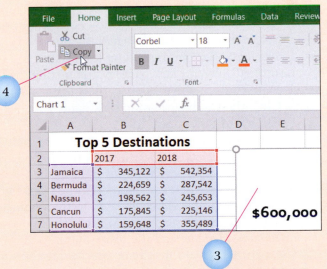

> **Check Your Work**

Hint Click the Options button at the bottom of the Clipboard task pane to customize the display of the task pane.

Use the Clipboard task pane to collect and paste multiple items. Up to 24 different items can be collected and then pasted in various locations. Turn on the display of the Clipboard task pane by clicking the Clipboard group task pane launcher. The Clipboard task pane displays at the left side of the screen.

Select data or an object to be copied and then click the Copy button in the Clipboard group. Continue selecting text or items and clicking the Copy button. To insert an item, position the insertion point in the specific location and then click the item in the Clipboard task pane representing that item. If the copied item is text, the first 50 characters display. When all items are inserted, click the Clear All button to remove any remaining items from the Clipboard task pane. To paste all items from the Clipboard task pane at once, click the Paste All button.

Project 1c Collecting and Pasting Text Between a Document and a Presentation   **Part 3 of 9**

1. With **8-ATTopFive.pptx** open, make Slide 4 active and then insert a new slide with the Title and Content layout.
2. Click in the title placeholder and then type Spring Treks.
3. Copy text from Word by completing the following steps:
   a. Open Word and then open **AdvTrek.docx**.
   b. Click the Clipboard group task pane launcher to display the Clipboard task pane.
   c. If any data displays in the Clipboard task pane, click the Clear All button at the top of the task pane.
   d. Select the text *Yucatan Adventure – 10 days* (including the paragraph mark following the text—consider turning on the display of nonprinting characters) and then click the Copy button in the Clipboard group.
   e. Select the text *Mexico Adventure – 14 days* and then click the Copy button.
   f. Select the text *Caribbean Highlights – 16 days* and then click the Copy button.
   g. Select the text *California Delights – 7 days* and then click the Copy button.
   h. Select the text *Canyon Adventure – 10 days* and then click the Copy button.
   i. Select the text *Canadian Parks – 12 days* and then click the Copy button.
   j. Select the text *Royal Canadian Adventure – 14 days* and then click the Copy button.
4. Click the PowerPoint button on the taskbar and then paste items from the Clipboard task pane by completing the following steps:
   a. With Slide 5 active, click in the *Click to add text* placeholder.
   b. Click the Clipboard group task pane launcher to display the Clipboard task pane.
   c. Click the *California Delights* item in the Clipboard task pane.
   d. Click the *Canadian Parks* item in the Clipboard task pane.
   e. Click the *Caribbean Highlights* item in the Clipboard task pane.
   f. Click the *Mexico Adventure* item in the Clipboard task pane
   g. Click the *Yucatan Adventure* item in the Clipboard task pane. (Press the Backspace key two times to remove the bullet below *Yucatan Adventure* and the blank line.)
5. Clear the Clipboard task pane by clicking the Clear All button in the upper right corner of the task pane.
6. Close the Clipboard task pane by clicking the Close button (contains an *X*) in the upper right corner of the task pane.
7. Make Slide 1 the active slide and then run the slide show.

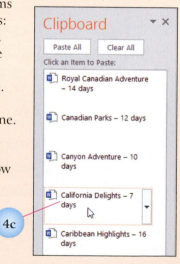

4c

Check Your Work

Sharing Presentations

PowerPoint provides a number of options for sharing presentations between programs, sites on the Internet, other computers, and as attachments. Options for sending and sharing presentations are available at the Share backstage area. Display this backstage area by clicking the File tab and then clicking the *Share* option.

Using the *Share with People* Option

Hint If you have a person's contact information stored, you only have to enter their name in the Invite people text box.

Use the *Share with People* option at the Share backstage area to invite people to view a presentation. To use this feature, the PowerPoint presentation must be saved to a OneDrive account or a shared location such as a website or SharePoint library. (Microsoft SharePoint is a collection of products and software that includes a number of components. If a company or organization uses SharePoint, a presentation can be saved in a library on the organization's SharePoint site so colleagues have a central location for accessing presentations.)

To share a PowerPoint presentation, open the presentation from a OneDrive account (or other shared location) and then click the Share with People button at the Share backstage area. This closes the backstage area and the Share task pane displays at the right side of the screen similar to what is shown in Figure 8.1.

If a presentation is open that is not saved to a OneDrive account, the information at the right side of the Share backstage area will specify that the presentation needs to be saved. To do this, click the Save to Cloud button and, at the Save As backstage area, double-click the OneDrive account. At the Save As dialog box with the OneDrive account folder active and the presentation name in the *File name* text box, click the Save button. With the presentation saved to the OneDrive account, click the File tab, click the *Share* option, and then click the Share with People button. This closes the backstage area and the presentation displays with the Share task pane at the right side of the screen.

In the *Invite people* text box in the Share task pane, type the names or email addresses of people to invite them to view and/or edit the presentation. Type more than one name or email address by separating them with a semicolon. The option box below the *Invite people* text box contains the default setting *Can edit*. At this setting, the people invited will be able to edit the presentation. Change this option to *Can view* if the invited people should only be able to view the presentation.

When all names or email addresses are entered, click the Share button. An email is sent to the email address(es) typed and, in a few moments, the name or names display in the Share task pane. Any time the presentation is opened in the future, displaying the Share backstage area and then clicking the Share with People button will close the backstage area and open the Share task pane in the presentation. To stop sharing the presentation with a person, right-click the person's name in the Share task pane and then click *Remove User* at the shortcut menu.

Figure 8.1 Share Task Pane

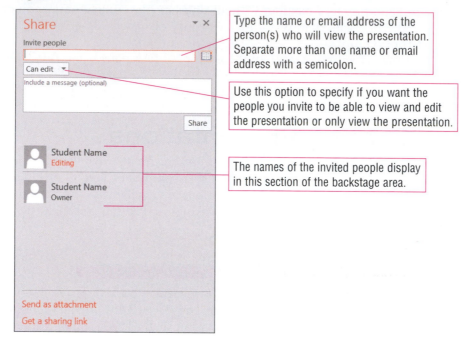

Type the name or email address of the person(s) who will view the presentation. Separate more than one name or email address with a semicolon.

Use this option to specify if you want the people you invite to be able to view and edit the presentation or only view the presentation.

The names of the invited people display in this section of the backstage area.

Project 1d Inviting People to View Your Presentation

Part 4 of 9

Note: To complete this optional project, you need to be connected to the Internet and have a OneDrive account.

1. With **8-ATTopFive.pptx** open, save the presentation to your OneDrive folder and name it **8-ATTopFive-Shared**. (To do this, click the File tab, click the *Save As* option, and then double-click the OneDrive account in the middle panel. At the Save As dialog box with the OneDrive account folder active, type 8-ATTopFive-Shared in the *File name* text box and then click the Save button.

2. With **8-ATTopFive-Shared.pptx** open, click the File tab and then click the *Share* option.

3. At the Share backstage area with the *Share with People* option selected, click the Share with People button.

4. Type the email address for your instructor and/or the email address of a classmate or friend in the *Invite people* text box in the Share task pane.

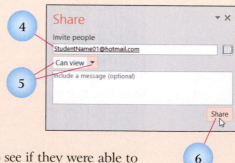

5. Click the option box arrow for the option box containing the text *Can edit* and then click *Can view* at the drop-down list.

6. Click the Share button.

7. After a few moments, notice the name(s) that display in the Share task pane.

8. Check with your instructor, classmate, and/or friend to see if they were able to open the email containing the link to your PowerPoint presentation.

9. Remove the name (or one of the names) that displays in the Share task pane by right-clicking the name and then clicking *Remove User* at the shortcut menu.

10. If you have **8-ATTopFive.pptx** saved on a removable device, close **8-ATTopFive-Shared.pptx** saved to your OneDrive folder and then reopen **8-ATTopFive.pptx** from your removable device.

Use the <u>Send as attachment</u> hyperlink that displays near the bottom of the Share task pane to send a copy of the presentation or a PDF version of the presentation as an attachment to the email. The letters PDF stand for *portable document format*, which is a file format developed by Adobe Systems that captures all of the elements of a presentation as an electronic image. To send the presentation as an attachment, an Outlook account must be established.

The Share task pane also contains the <u>Get a sharing link</u> hyperlink that, when clicked, displays options for creating a link for viewing or for editing. Click the Create an edit link button and a link displays for viewing and editing the presentation. Copy the link and paste it an email, instant message, social media site, and so on. To paste a link for viewing the presentation without the ability to edit, click the View-only link button. Copy the link that displays and then paste it in the specific locations.

Using the *Email* Option

Click the *Email* option at the Share backstage area and options display for sending a copy of the presentation as an attachment to an email, sending a link to the presentation, attaching a PDF or XPS copy of the open presentation to an email address, and sending an email as an Internet fax.

As mentioned earlier, to send the presentation as an attachment, an Outlook email account must be established. To create an email that contains a link to the presentation, the presentation must be saved to a OneDrive account or a shared location such as a website or SharePoint library.

Click the Send as PDF button and the presentation is converted to a PDF file and attached to the email. Click the Send as XPS button and the presentation is converted to an XPS file and attached to the email. The XPS file format is a Microsoft file format for publishing content in an easily viewable format. The letters XPS stand for *XML paper specification*, and the letters XML stand for *extensible markup language*, which is a set of rules for encoding presentations electronically. Information displays to the right of both buttons providing a brief description of the formats. Systems that captures all of the elements of a presentation as an electronic image.

Click the Send as Internet Fax button to fax the current presentation without using a fax machine. To use this button, the sender must be signed up with a fax service provider.

Using the *Present Online* Option

Click the *Present Online* option at the Share backstage area to present a presentation through the Office Presentation Service. This process was covered in Chapter 7.

Using the *Publish Slides* Option

Use the *Publish Slides* option at the Share backstage area to save slides in a shared location such as a slide library or a SharePoint site so that other people have access to the presentation and can review or make changes to it.

Note: Before completing this optional project, check with your instructor to determine if you have Outlook set up as your email provider.

1. With **8-ATTopFive.pptx** open, click the File tab and then click the *Share* option.
2. At the Share backstage area, click the *Email* option and then click the Send as Attachment button.
3. At the Outlook window, type your instructor's email address in the *To* text box.
4. Click the Send button.

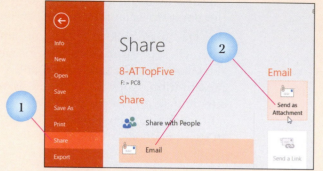

Tutorial

Exporting Presentations

Exporting Presentations

The Export backstage area contains a number of options for saving and exporting a presentation. Options at the Export backstage area include saving a presentation as a PDF or XPS file, creating a video of a presentation, packaging a presentation for a disc, creating handouts, and saving a presentation in a different file format.

Saving a Presentation as a PDF or XPS File

Quick Steps

Save a Presentation as a PDF/XPS File
1. Open presentation.
2. Click File tab.
3. Click *Export* option.
4. Click *Create PDF/XPS Document* option.
5. Click Create PDF/XPS button.
6. Specify PDF or XPS format.
7. Click Publish button.

As explained earlier, the portable document format (PDF) captures all of the elements of a presentation as an electronic image and the XPS format is used for publishing content in an easily viewable format. To save a presentation in PDF or XPS format, click the File tab, click the *Export* option, make sure the *Create PDF/XPS Document* option is selected, and then click the Create PDF/XPS button. This displays the Publish as PDF or XPS dialog box with the *PDF (*.pdf)* option selected in the *Save as type* option box. To save the presentation in XPS format, click the *Save as type* option box and then click *XPS Document (*.xps)* at the drop-down list. At the Save As dialog box, type a name in the *File name* text box and then click the Publish button.

A PDF file can be opened in Adobe Reader, Microsoft Edge, and Microsoft Word. An XPS file can be opened in Adobe Reader, Internet Explorer, and XPS Viewer. One method for opening a PDF or XPS file is to open File Explorer, navigate to the folder containing the file, right-click on the file, and then point to *Open with*. This displays a side menu with the programs that will open the file.

Creating a Video of a Presentation

Quick Steps

Save a Presentation as a Video
1. Open presentation.
2. Click File tab.
3. Click *Export* option.
4. Click *Create a Video* option.
5. Click Create Video button.

Create a video that incorporates all of a presentation's recorded timings and narrations and preserves animations and transitions using the *Create a Video* option. The information at the right side of the Export backstage area describes creating a video and provides a hyperlink to get help on burning a slide show video to a DVD or uploading it to the Web. Click the Get help burning your slide show video to DVD or uploading it to the web hyperlink and information displays on burning a slide show video to disc and publishing a slide show video to YouTube.

Quick Steps

Package a Presentation for CD
1. Open presentation.
2. Click File tab.
3. Click *Export* option.
4. Click *Package Presentation for CD* option.
5. Click Package for CD button.
6. Click Copy to CD button or Copy to Folder button.

Packaging a Presentation

Use the *Package Presentation for CD* option to copy a presentation and include all of the linked files, embedded items, and fonts. Click the *Package Presentation for CD* option and then click the Package for CD button and the Package for CD dialog box displays. At this dialog box, type a name for the CD and specify the files to be copied. The presentation can be copied to a CD or to a specific folder.

Project 1f Saving a Presentation as PDF and XPS Files, as a Video, and Packaged for a CD   Part 6 of 9

1. With **8-ATTopFive.pptx** open, save the presentation in PDF format by completing the following steps:
   a. Click the File tab and then click the *Export* option.
   b. Make sure the *Create PDF/XPS Document* option is selected.
   c. Click the Create PDF/XPS button.
   d. At the Publish as PDF or XPS dialog box, make sure the *Save as type* option is set to *PDF (*.pdf)*, insert a check mark in the *Open file after publishing* check box, and then click the Publish button. (In a few moments the presentation displays in PDF format in Adobe Acrobat Reader.)

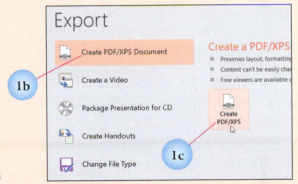

   e. Scroll through the presentation in Adobe Acrobat Reader.
   f. Click the Close button in the upper right corner of the window to close Adobe Acrobat Reader.
2. Save the presentation in XPS format by completing the following steps:
   a. Click the File tab and then click the *Export* option.
   b. With the *Create PDF/XPS Document* option selected, click the Create PDF/XPS button.
   c. At the Publish as PDF or XPS dialog box, click the *Save as type* option box and then click *XPS Document (*.xps)* at the drop-down list.
   d. Make sure the *Open file after publishing* check box contains a check mark and then click the Publish button. (In a few moments the presentation displays in the XPS Viewer.)

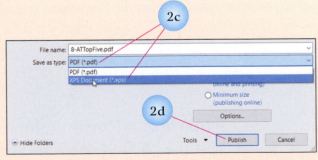

   e. Scroll through the presentation in the XPS Viewer.
   f. Close the XPS viewer by clicking the Close button in the upper right corner of the window.

3. Save **8-ATTopFive.pptx** as a video by completing the following steps:
   a. Click the File tab and then click the *Export* option.
   b. Click the *Create a Video* option.
   c. Click the Create Video button.
   d. At the Save As dialog box, click the Save button. (Saving as a video takes a minute or so. The Status bar displays the saving progress.)
4. When the video has been saved, play the video by completing the following steps:
   a. Click the File Explorer button on the taskbar.
   b. Navigate to the PC8 folder on your storage medium and then double-click **8-ATTopFive.mp4**. (This opens the presentation video in a viewing window.)
   c. Watch the presentation video and, when it is finished, click the Close button in the upper right corner of the window.
   d. Close File Explorer.
5. With **8-ATTopFive.pptx** open, package the presentation by completing the following steps:
   a. Click the File tab and then click the *Export* option.
   b. Click the *Package Presentation for CD* option.
   c. Click the Package for CD button.
   d. At the Package for CD dialog box, select the text in the *Name the CD* text box and type ATTopFiveforCD.
   e. Click the Options button.
   f. At the Options dialog box, make sure the *Embedded TrueType fonts* check box contains a check mark and then click OK.
   g. Click the Copy to Folder button.
   h. At the Copy to Folder dialog box, click the Browse button.
   i. Navigate to the PC8 folder on your storage medium.
   j. Click the Select button.
   k. At the Copy to Folder dialog box, click OK.
   l. At the message asking if you want to include linked files in the presentation, click the Yes button.
   m. When a window displays with the folder name and files, close the window by clicking the Close button in the upper right corner of the window.
   n. Close the Package for CD dialog box by clicking the Close button.

Check Your Work

Exporting a Presentation to a Word Document

Slides can be printed as handouts in PowerPoint; however, exporting a presentation to Word provides greater control over the formatting of the handouts. Use the *Create Handouts* option at the Export backstage area to export a PowerPoint presentation to a Word document. Open the presentation, click the File tab, click the *Export* option, click the *Create Handouts* option, and then click the Create Handouts button. This displays the Send to Microsoft Word dialog box, shown in Figure 8.2. At this dialog box, select the page layout to use in Word and then click OK.

The first four page layout options will export slides as they appear in PowerPoint with lines to the right or below the slides. The last option will export the text only as an outline. Select the *Paste link* option and the Word document will be updated automatically whenever changes are made to the PowerPoint presentation.

Figure 8.2 Send to Microsoft Word Dialog Box

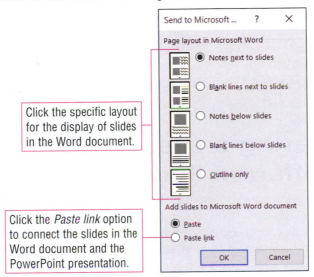

Click the specific layout for the display of slides in the Word document.

Click the *Paste link* option to connect the slides in the Word document and the PowerPoint presentation.

Part 7 of 9

Project 1g Exporting a Presentation to Word

1. Make sure **8-ATTopFive.pptx** is open, click the File tab, and then click the *Export* option.
2. At the Export backstage area, click the *Create Handouts* option.
3. Click the Create Handouts button.
4. At the Send to Microsoft Word dialog box, click the *Blank lines next to slides* option and then click OK.
5. If necessary, click the Word button on the taskbar.
6. In Word, select the first column (the column that contains *Slide 1*, *Slide 2*, and so on) and then turn on bold formatting. (The presentation was inserted in a table in Word.)

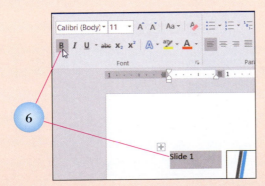

7. Select the third column (contains the lines) and then apply the standard red font color.
8. Save the document and name it **8-ATTopTours**.

9. Print and then close **8-ATTopTours.docx**.
10. Close Word.
11. In PowerPoint, export **8-ATTopFive.pptx** as an outline by completing the following steps:
    a. Click the File tab and then click the *Export* option.
    b. At the Export backstage area, click the *Create Handouts* option.
    c. Click the Create Handouts button.
    d. At the Send to Microsoft Word dialog box, click the *Outline only* option and then click OK.
    e. If necessary, click the Word button on the taskbar.
    f. In Word, scroll through the document and then close Word without saving the document.
12. In PowerPoint, save **8-ATTopFive.pptx**.

Check Your Work

Saving a Presentation in a Different Format

A presentation is saved, by default, as a PowerPoint presentation with the .pptx file extension. If the presentation will be used by someone who is using a different presentation program or a different version of PowerPoint, the presentation may need to be saved in another format. At the Export backstage area, click the *Change File Type* option and the backstage area displays as shown in Figure 8.3.

Figure 8.3 Export Backstage Area with *Change File Type* Option Selected

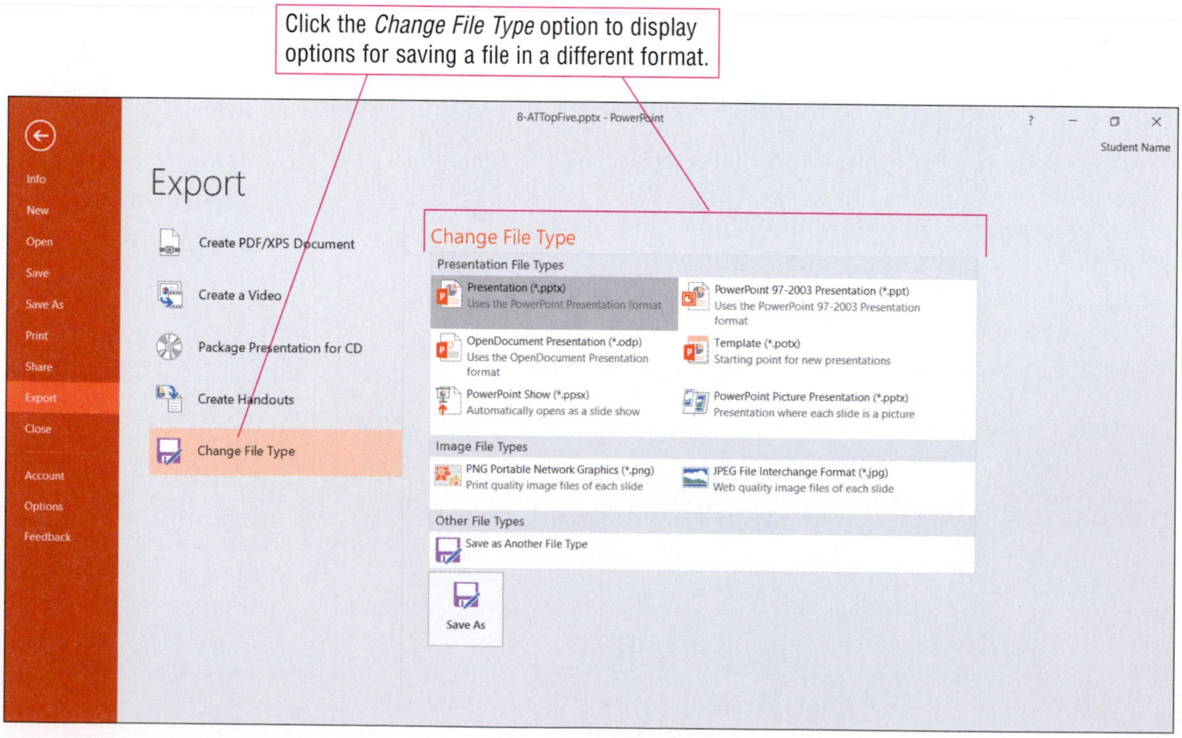

Click the *Change File Type* option to display options for saving a file in a different format.

Save a Presentation in a Different Format
1. Click File tab.
2. Click *Export* option.
3. Click *Change File Type* option.
4. Click format.
5. Click Save As button.

With options in the *Presentation File Types* section, a PowerPoint presentation can be saved with the default file format (.pptx) or in a previous version of PowerPoint. Use the *OpenDocument Presentation (*.odp)* option to save a presentation and make it available to open in other applications. The OpenDocument format enables files to be exchanged, retrieved, and edited with any OpenDocument-compliant software. Save a presentation as a template to use the presentation as a basis for creating other presentations. (Saving a presentation as a template was explained in Chapter 6.) Save a presentation in the PowerPoint Show (*.ppsx) format and the presentation automatically starts when it is opened. When a presentation is saved using the *PowerPoint Picture Presentation (*.pptx)* option, the contents of the presentation are flattened to a single picture per slide. A presentation saved in this format can be opened and viewed but not edited.

Project 1h Saving a Presentation in Different Formats

1. Make sure that **8-ATTopFive.pptx** is open.
2. Save the presentation as a PowerPoint Show by completing the following steps:
   a. Click the File tab and then click the *Export* option.
   b. At the Export backstage area, click the *Change File Type* option.
   c. Click the *PowerPoint Show (*.ppsx)* option in the *Presentation File Types* section and then click the Save As button.

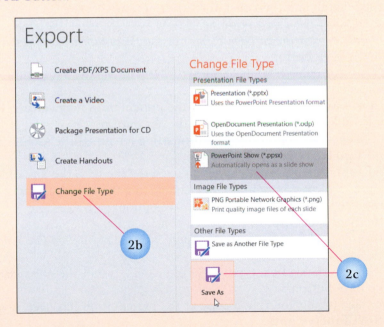

   d. At the Save As dialog box, click the Save button. (This saves the presentation with the file extension *.ppsx*.)
3. Close **8-ATTopFive.ppsx**.
4. Open the **8-ATTopFive.ppsx** file in File Explorer by completing the following steps:
   a. Click the File Explorer button (button containing yellow file folders) on the taskbar.
   b. In File Explorer, double-click the drive representing your storage medium.
   c. Navigate to the PC8 folder on your storage medium and then double-click **8-ATTopFive.ppsx**.

d. If a *How do you want to open this file?* window displays, double-click the *Microsoft Office PowerPoint Viewer* option in the window. (This starts the presentation in Slide Show view.)

e. Run the slide show.

f. When the slide show has ended, click the left mouse button.

g. Close File Explorer by clicking the File Explorer button on the taskbar and then clicking the Close button in the upper right corner of the window.

5. Open **8-ATTopFive.pptx** (make sure you open the file with the .pptx file extension) and then save it as a previous version of PowerPoint by completing the following steps:

a. Click the File tab and then click the *Export* option.

b. Click the *Change File Type* option.

c. Click *PowerPoint 97-2003 Presentation (*.ppt)* in the *Presentation File Types* section and then click the Save As button.

d. At the Save As dialog box, type 8-ATTopFive-2003format in the *File name* text box and then click the Save button.

e. At the Microsoft PowerPoint Compatibility Checker dialog box, click the Continue button.

f. At the presentation, notice that the file name at the top of the screen displays followed by the words *[Compatibility Mode]*.

6. Close **8-ATTopFive-2003format.ppt**.

7. Open **8-ATTopFive.pptx** (make sure you open the file with the .pptx file extension) and then save it in OpenDocument Presentation format by completing the following steps:

a. Click the File tab and then click the *Export* option.

b. Click the *Change File Type* option.

c. Click *OpenDocument Presentation (*.odp)* in the *Presentation File Types* section and then click the Save As button.

d. At the Save As dialog box, make sure *8-ATTopFive.odp* displays in the *File name* text box and then click the Save button.

e. When a message displays stating that the presentation may contain features that are not compatible with the format, click the Yes button.

f. Run the slide show and notice that formatting remained the same.

8. Close **8-ATTopFive.odp**.

9. Open **8-ATTopFive.pptx** (make sure you open the file with the .pptx file extension) and then save it as a picture presentation by completing the following steps:

a. Click the File tab and then click the *Export* option.

b. Click the *Change File Type* option.

c. Click *PowerPoint Picture Presentation (*.pptx)* in the *Presentation File Types* section and then click the Save As button.

d. At the Save As dialog box, type 8-ATTopFive-Picture in the *File name* text box and then click the Save button.

e. At a message telling you that a copy of the presentation has been saved, click OK.

f. Close **8-ATTopFive.pptx**.

g. Open **8-ATTopFive-Picture.pptx**.

h. Click Slide 1 in the slide pane and notice how the entire slide is selected rather than a specific element in the slide. In this format you cannot edit a slide.

10. Close **8-ATTopFive-Picture.pptx**.

Check Your Work

Save slides in a presentation as graphic images in PNG or JPEG format with options in the *Image File Types* section of the Export backstage area. Save slides as PNG images for print quality, and save slides as JPEG images if the slide images will be posted to the Internet. To save a slide or all slides as graphic images, click either the *PNG Portable Network Graphics (*.png)* option or the *JPEG File Interchange Format (*.jpg)* option in the *Image File Types* section and then click the Save As button. At the Save As dialog box, type a name for the slide or presentation and then click the Save button. At the message that displays, click the All Slides button if every slide in the presentation is to be saved as a graphic image or click the Just This One button if only the current slide is to be saved as a graphic image. Click the All Slides button and a message displays indicating that all slides in the presentation were saved as separate files in a folder. The name of the folder is the name typed in the *File name* text box in the Save As dialog box.

Project 1i   Saving Slides as Graphic Images

1. Open **8-ATTopFive.pptx**.
2. Click the File tab and then click the *Export* option.
3. At the Export backstage area, click the *Change File Type* option.
4. Click the *PNG Portable Network Graphics (*.png)* option in the *Image File Types* section and then click the Save As button.
5. At the Save As dialog box, make sure **8-ATTopFive.png** displays in the *File name* text box and then click the Save button.
6. At the message that displays, click the All Slides button.
7. At the message telling you that each slide has been saved as a separate file in the 8-ATTopFive.png folder, click OK.

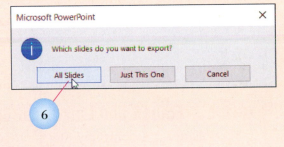

8. Open Word.
9. At a blank document, change the font size to 18 points, turn on bold formatting, change the alignment to center, and then type Adventure Tours.
10. Press the Enter key two times and then insert one of the slides saved in PNG format by completing the following steps:
    a. Click the Insert tab and then click the Pictures button in the Illustrations group.
    b. At the Insert Picture dialog box, navigate to the 8-ATTopFive folder in the PC8 folder on your storage medium and then double-click **Slide3.PNG**.

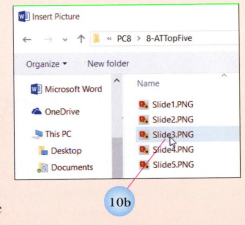

11. Format the image in the document by completing the following steps:
    a. Click in the *Shape Height* measurement box in the Size group on the Picture Tools Format tab, type 2.8, and then press the Enter key.
    b. Click the *Drop Shadow Rectangle* option in the Picture Styles group (fourth option).

12. Press Ctrl + End to move the insertion point to the end of the document, press the Enter key, and then complete steps similar to those in Steps 10 and 11 to insert and format the image Slide4.PNG in the document.
13. Save the document and name it **8-ATTours**.
14. Print and then close **8-ATTours.docx**.
15. Close Word.
16. Capture an image of the Open dialog box and insert the image in a PowerPoint slide by completing the following steps:
    a. Press Ctrl + N to display a new blank presentation.
    b. Click the Layout button in the Slides group on the Home tab and then click *Blank* at the drop-down list.
    c. Press Ctrl + F12 to display the Open dialog box.
    d. At the Open dialog box, navigate to the PC8 folder on your storage medium.
    e. Click the option button at the right side of the *File name* text box (the option button contains the text *All PowerPoint Presentations*) and then click *All Files (*.*)* at the drop-down list.
    f. Make sure all of your project files display. You may need to scroll down the list box to display the files.
    g. Press and hold down the Alt key, press the Print Screen button on your keyboard, and then release the Alt key. (This captures an image of the Open dialog box and not the entire screen.)
    h. Click the Cancel button to close the Open dialog box.
    i. Click the Paste button. (This inserts the image of the Open dialog box into the slide.)
17. Print the slide as a full page slide.
18. Close the presentation without saving it and then close **8-ATTopFive.pptx**.

Check Your Work

Project 2 Embed and Link Excel Charts to a Presentation   3 Parts

You will open a company funds presentation and then copy an Excel pie chart and embed it in a PowerPoint slide. You will also copy and link an Excel column chart to a slide and then update the chart in Excel.

Preview Finished Project

Embedding and Linking Objects

One of the reasons the Microsoft Office suite is used extensively in business is because it allows data from one program to be seamlessly integrated into another program. For example, a chart depicting sales projections created in Excel can easily be added to a slide in a PowerPoint presentation to the company board of directors on the new budget forecast.

Integration is the process of adding content from other sources to another file. Integrating content is different than simply copying and pasting it. While it makes sense to copy and paste objects from one application to another when the content is not likely to change, if the content is dynamic, the copy and paste method becomes problematic and inefficient. To illustrate this point, assume one of the outcomes from the presentation to the board of directors is a revision to the sales projections, which means that the chart originally created in Excel has to be updated to reflect the new projections. If the first version of the chart was copied and pasted into PowerPoint, it would need to be deleted and then the revised chart in Excel would need to be copied and pasted into the slide again. Both Excel and PowerPoint would need to be opened and edited to reflect this change in projection. In this case, copying and pasting the chart would not be efficient.

To eliminate the inefficiency of the copy and paste method, objects can be integrated between programs. An object can be text in a presentation; data in a table, a chart, a picture, a slide; or any combination of data. The program that was used to create the object is called the *source* and the program the object is linked or embedded to is called the *destination*.

Embedding and linking are two methods for integrating data in addition to the copy and paste method. When an object is embedded, the content in the object is stored in both the source and the destination programs. When editing an embedded object in the destination program, the source program in which the program was created opens. If the content in the object is changed in the source program, the change is not reflected in the destination program and vice versa.

Hint Static data remains the same while dynamic data changes periodically or continually.

Linking inserts a code into the destination file connecting the destination to the name and location of the source object. The object itself is not stored within the destination file. When linking, if a change is made to the content in the source program, the destination program reflects the change automatically. The decision to integrate data by embedding or linking will depend on whether the data is dynamic or static. If the data is dynamic, then linking the object is the most efficient method of integration.

Tutorial

Embedding Objects

Embedding Objects

An object that is embedded is stored in both the source *and* the destination programs. The content of the object can be edited in *either* the source or the destination; however, a change made in one will not be reflected in the other. The difference between copying and pasting and copying and embedding is that embedded objects can be edited with the source program's editing tabs and options.

Quick Steps

Embed an Object
1. Open source program.
2. Select object.
3. Click Copy button.
4. Open destination program.
5. Click Paste button arrow.
6. Click *Paste Special*.
7. Click source of object.
8. Click OK.

Since embedded objects are edited within the source program, the source program must reside on the computer when the presentation is opened for editing. If a presentation will be edited on another computer, check before embedding any objects to verify that the other computer has the same programs.

To embed an object, open both programs and both files. In the source program, click the object and then click the Copy button in the Clipboard group on the Home tab. Click the button on the taskbar representing the destination program file and then position the insertion point at the location where the object is to be embedded. Click the Paste button arrow in the Clipboard group and then click *Paste Special* at the drop-down list. At the Paste Special dialog box, click the source of the object in the *As* list box and then click OK.

Edit an embedded object by double-clicking the object. This displays the object with the source program tabs and options. Make changes and then click outside the object to exit the source program tabs and options. Animation effects can be applied to an embedded object with the same techniques learned in Chapter 7.

1. Open **FundsPres.pptx** and then save it with the name **8-FundsPres**.
2. Open Excel and then open **Funds01.xlsx**, located in the PC8 folder on your storage medium.
3. Click in the chart to select it. (Make sure the entire chart is selected and not an element in the chart.)
4. Click the Copy button in the Clipboard group on the Home tab.
5. Click the PowerPoint button on the taskbar.
6. Make Slide 4 active.
7. Click the Paste button arrow and then click *Paste Special* at the drop-down list.

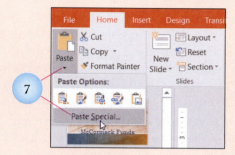

8. At the Paste Special dialog box, click *Microsoft Office Graphic Object* in the *As* list box and then click OK.

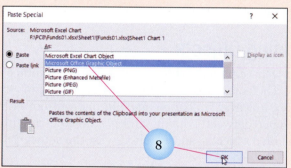

9. Click the Chart Tools Format tab.
10. Change the height of the chart to 5.5 inches and change the width to 9 inches.
11. Center the pie chart in the slide below the title.
12. Save **8-FundsPres.pptx**.
13. Click the Excel button on the taskbar, close the workbook, and then close Excel.

Check Your Work

Tutorial

Linking Objects

Linking Objects

💡 **Hint** Since linking does not increase the size of the file in the destination program, consider linking objects if file size is a consideration.

If the content of the object to be integrated between programs is likely to change, link the object from the source program to the destination program. Linking the object establishes a direct connection between the source and destination programs. The object is stored in the source program only. The destination program will have a code inserted into it that indicates the name and location of the source of the object. Whenever the presentation containing the link is opened, a message displays saying that the presentation contains links and the user is then prompted to update the links.

To link an object, open both programs and open both program files. In the source program file, click the object and then click the Copy button in the Clipboard group on the Home tab. Click the button on the taskbar representing the destination program file and then position the insertion point in the desired location. Click the Paste button arrow in the Clipboard group on the Home tab and then click *Paste Special* at the drop-down list. At the Paste Special dialog box, click the source program for the object in the *As* list box, click the *Paste link* option at the left side of the *As* list box, and then click OK.

Project 2b   Linking an Excel Chart to a Presentation   **Part 2 of 3**

1. With **8-FundsPres.pptx** open, open Excel and then open **Funds02.xlsx**, located in the PC8 folder on your storage medium.
2. Save the workbook with the name **8-MMFunds**.
3. Copy and link the chart to a slide in the presentation by completing the following steps:
   a. Click in the chart to select it. (Make sure you select the chart and not just an element in the chart.)
   b. Click the Copy button in the Clipboard group on the Home tab.
   c. Click the PowerPoint button on the taskbar.
   d. Make Slide 5 active.
   e. Click the Paste button arrow and then click *Paste Special* at the drop-down list.
   f. At the Paste Special dialog box, click the *Paste link* option.
   g. Make sure *Microsoft Excel Chart Object* is selected in the *As* list box and then click OK.
   h. Click the Drawing Tools Format tab, change the height of the chart to 5 inches, and then drag the chart so it is centered on the slide.

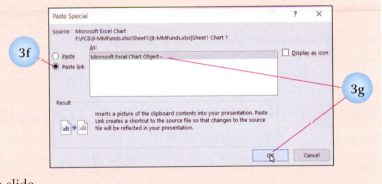

4. Click the Excel button on the taskbar, close **8-MMFunds.xlsx**, and then close Excel.
5. Make Slide 1 active and then run the slide show.
6. Save and then close **8-FundsPres.pptx**.

Check Your Work

Editing Linked Objects

Edit linked objects in the source program in which they were created. Open the document, workbook, or presentation containing the object; make the changes as required; and then save and close the file. If both the source and destination programs are open at the same time, the changed content is reflected immediately in both programs.

1. Open Excel and then open **8-MMFunds.xlsx**.
2. Make the changes as indicated to data in the following cells:
   a. Cell B2: Change *13%* to *17%*.
   b. Cell B3: Change *9%* to *12%*.
   c. Cell B6: Change *10%* to *14%*.
3. Click the Save button on the Quick Access Toolbar to save the edited workbook.
4. Close **8-MMFunds.xlsx** and then close Excel.
5. In PowerPoint, open **8-FundsPres.pptx**.
6. At the message telling you that the presentation contains links, click the Update Links button.
7. Make Slide 5 active and then notice the updated changes in the chart data.
8. Print the presentation as a handout with six slides displayed horizontally per page.
9. Save and then close **8-FundsPres.pptx**.

	A	B
1		Percentage
2	2014	17%
3	2015	12%
4	2016	18%
5	2017	4%
6	2018	14%

2a
2b
2c

Check Your Work

Project 3   **Download and Apply a Design Template to a Presentation and Prepare a Presentation for Sharing**   **10 Parts**

You will download a design template and apply the template to a company presentation. You will insert, edit, and delete comments in the presentation; modify the presentation properties; inspect the presentation; and encrypt the presentation with a password.

Preview Finished Project

Tutorial

Downloading and Applying a Design Template

Quick Steps

Download a Template
1. Click File tab.
2. Click *New*.
3. Click in search text box.
4. Type key word or phrase.
5. Press Enter.
6. Double-click template.

Downloading Templates

A number of PowerPoint templates are available for downloading at the New backstage area. To search for and download a template, click the File tab and then click the *New* option to display the New backstage area. Click in the search text box, type a keyword or phrase, and then press the Enter key or click the Start searching button at the right side of the search text box. PowerPoint searches the Office.com templates gallery and displays templates that match the key word or phrase. To download a template, double-click the template or click once on the template to display a download window. At this window, read information about the template and view additional template images by clicking the right- or left-pointing arrows that display below the template image. To download the template, click the Create button. When a template is downloaded, a presentation based on the template opens and the downloaded template is added to the New backstage area.

Many presentations opened from a downloaded template contain predesigned slides. Use these slides to help create a presentation or delete the predesigned slides and create a presentation using just the template layouts.

To make the downloaded template (not a customized version of the template) available for future presentations, pin the template to the New backstage area. To do this, display the New backstage area, hover the mouse over the template to be pinned, and then click the push pin that displays. Complete the same steps to unpin a template from the New backstage area.

If a customized template is saved to the Custom Office Templates folder, it can be applied to an existing presentation. To do this, open the presentation, click the Design tab, click the More Themes button in the Themes group, and then click the *Browse for Themes* option at the drop-down list. At the Choose Theme or Themed Document dialog box, navigate to the Custom Office Templates folder in the Documents folder on the computer's hard drive and then double-click the template in the dialog box Content pane.

Project 3a Downloading and Applying a Design Template Part 1 of 10

Note: Check with your instructor before downloading a design template. To download a template, you must have access to the Internet and access to the hard drive. If you do not have access to the design template or cannot download it, open ISPres.pptx, save it with the name 8-ISPres, apply a design theme of your choosing, and then continue to Step 13.

1. At a blank PowerPoint screen, click the File tab and then click the *New* option.
2. At the New backstage area, click in the search text box, type marketing plan, and then press the Enter key.
3. Scroll down the backstage list box and view some of the templates.
4. Click in the search text box, type red radial lines, and then press the Enter key.
5. Click the *Red radial lines presentation (widescreen)* template.
6. At the template window, view some of the images for the template by clicking the right-pointing arrow below the template image several times.
7. Click the Create button. (This downloads the template and opens a presentation based on the template.)

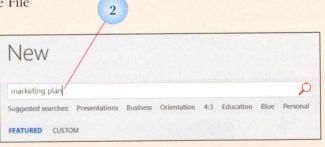

8. Delete the sample slides in the presentation by completing the following steps:
   a. With the first slide selected in the slide thumbnails pane, scroll down the slide thumbnails pane to the last slide, press and hold down the Shift key, click the last slide, and then release the Shift key. (This selects all of the slides in the presentation.)
   b. Press the Delete key. (When you press the Delete key, the slides are deleted and a gray screen displays with the text *Click to add first slide.*)

9. Save the presentation as a template to the Custom Office Templates folder by completing the following steps:
   a. Press the F12 function key to display the Save As dialog box.
   b. Click the *Save as type* option box and then click *PowerPoint Template (*.potx)* at the drop-down list. (Make sure the Custom Office Templates folder in the Documents folder on the computer's hard drive is active.)
   c. Click in the *File name* text box, type XXX-ISTemplate (type your initials in place of the *XXX*) and then click the Save button.

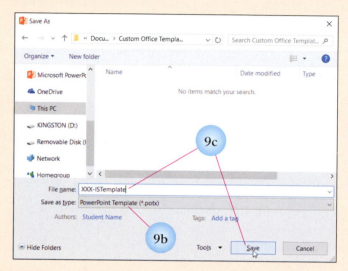

   d. Close the **XXX-ISTemplate.potx** file.
10. Open **ISPres.pptx** from the PC8 folder on your storage medium.
11. Save the presentation with the name **8-ISPres**.
12. Apply **XXX-ISTemplate.potx** to the presentation by completing the following steps:
    a. Click the Design tab.
    b. Click the More Themes button in the Themes group.
    c. Click the *Browse for Themes* option at the drop-down list.
    d. At the Choose Theme or Themed Document dialog box, double-click the *Custom Office Templates* folder in the Content pane.
    e. Double-click **XXX-ISTemplate.potx** (where your initial display in place of the **XXX**).
13. Run the slide show.
14. Print the presentation as a handout with all nine slides displayed horizontally on the page.
15. Save **8-ISPres.pptx**.

Check Your Work

Comparing and Combining Presentations

Use the Compare button in the Compare group on the Review tab to compare two PowerPoint presentations to determine the differences between the presentations. When the presentations are compared, options are available for combining only specific changes, accepting only specific changes, and rejecting some or all of the changes.

To compare and combine presentations, open the first presentation, click the Review tab, and then click the Compare button in the Compare group. This displays the Choose File to Merge with Current Presentation dialog box. At this dialog box, navigate to the folder containing the presentation to be compared with the current presentation, click the presentation name in the Content pane, and then click the Merge button. (The presentation name can also be double-clicked.)

Click the Merge button (or double-click the presentation name) and a Reviewing task pane with the heading *Revisions* displays at the right side of the screen containing changes to slides and the presentation. The *DETAILS* option is selected in the Reviewing task pane and the task pane displays with the *Slide Changes* section and the *Presentation Changes* section. Click a revision that displays in either section of the task pane and the revision mark in the slide or slide thumbnails pane is selected. A revision mark displays in a slide indicating a difference between slides in the two presentations. If a difference occurs to the entire presentation, such as a difference between design themes, a revision mark displays at the left side of the screen near the top of the slide thumbnails pane. Click a revision in the Revisions task pane or click a revision mark in the slide or slide thumbnails pane to expand the revision mark to display a revision check box followed by information about the change.

To accept a change, click the revision check box and then click the Accept button in the Compare group. A change can also be accepted by clicking the Accept button arrow. Clicking the Accept button arrow displays a drop-down list with options to accept the current change, accept all changes to the current slide, or accept all changes to the presentation. To reject a change, click the Reject button in the Compare group. Click the Reject button arrow and options display for rejecting the current change, rejecting all changes to the current slide, or rejecting all changes to the presentation.

Use the Previous and Next buttons in the Compare group to navigate to changes in the presentation. Click the Reviewing Pane button to turn the display of the Reviewing task pane on or off. When finished comparing the presentations, click the End Review button and the review ends and the accept or reject decisions that were made are applied.

Quick Steps

**Compare
and Combine
Presentations**
1. Click Review tab.
2. Click Compare button.
3. Navigate to folder containing presentation to be compared.
4. Click presentation.
5. Click Merge button.
6. Accept or reject changes.
7. Click End Review button.

 Compare

 Accept

 Reject

 Previous

 Next

 Reviewing Pane

 End Review

Project 3b   Comparing and Combining Presentations

Part 2 of 10

1. With **8-ISPres.pptx** open, click the Review tab and then click the Compare button in the Compare group.
2. At the Choose File to Merge with Current Presentation dialog box, navigate to the PC8 folder on your storage medium, click *ISSalesMeeting.pptx* in the Content pane, and then click the Merge button in the lower right corner of the dialog box.

3. Notice the Reviewing task pane (with the heading *Revisions*) at the right side of the screen with the *DETAILS* option selected. This option contains a *Slide Changes* section and a *Presentation Changes* section. A message displays in the *Slide Changes* section indicating that the current slide (Slide 1) contains a change to the slide properties and title. The *Presentation Changes* section displays with *Theme (1 - 9)*.

4. Click the *Title 1: International Security* revision that displays in the *Slide Changes* section of the task pane.

5. Click the revision check box that displays before the text *All changes to Title 1* at the right side of the slide in the slide pane to insert a check mark.

6. You do not want to change the title name, so click the Reject button in the Compare group to reject this change.

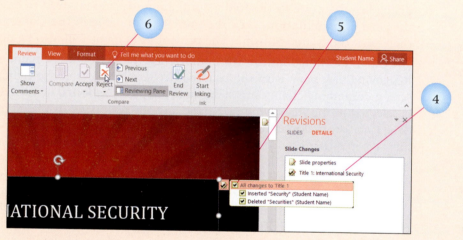

7. Click the Next button.

8. With the chart selected in Slide 3, click the Accept button arrow in the Compare group and then click the *Accept All Changes to This Slide* option.

9. Click the Next button.

10. Accept the remaining changes to the presentation by clicking the Accept button arrow and then click the *Accept All Changes to the Presentation* option.

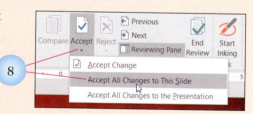

11. Click the Next button until Slide 9 displays in the slide pane.

12. Notice the check mark at the left of the text *Inserted Picture 3* in Slide 9. This picture was inserted in the slide from **ISSalesMeeting.pptx**.

13. Click the Next button.

14. At the message that displays telling you that was the last change and asking if you want to continue reviewing from the beginning, click the Cancel button.

15. Click the End Review button in the Compare group.

16. At the message asking if you are sure you want to end the review, click the Yes button.

17. Save **8-ISPres.pptx**.

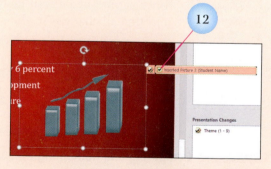

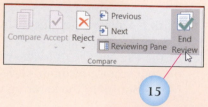

Check Your Work

Managing Comments

If a presentation is to be sent to others for review, specific questions or additional information can be included in the presentation by inserting a comment. To insert a comment, display a specific slide and then position the insertion point where the comment is to appear or select an element in the slide on which to comment. Click the Review tab and then click the New Comment button in the Comments group. This displays an orange active icon at the location of the insertion point or next to the selected element and opens the Comments task pane with a text entry box in the pane. Type the comment in the text entry box and then click outside the text entry box, press the Tab key, or press the Enter key.

To insert another comment in the presentation, position the insertion point or select an element in the slide and then click the New button in the Comments task pane or click the New Comment button in the Comments group and then type the comment in the text entry box. To view a comment in a presentation, click the comment icon and then read the information in the Comments task pane.

To move between comments in a presentation, click the Next or Previous buttons in the upper right corner of the Comments task pane. Or, click the Previous or Next buttons in the Comments group on the Review tab.

Other methods for displaying the Comments task pane include clicking the Comments button on the Status bar or clicking the Show Comments button in the Comments group on the Review tab. When the Comments task pane is open, the Show Comments button is active (displays with a gray background). Turn off the display of the Comments task pane by clicking the Comments button on the Status bar, clicking the Show Comments button, or by clicking the Close button in the upper right corner of the Comments task pane.

To print comments, display the Print backstage area and then click the second gallery in the *Settings* category. (This is the gallery containing the text *Full Page Slides*.) At the drop-down list, make sure the *Print Comments and Ink Markup* option is preceded by a check mark. Comments print on a separate page after the presentation is printed.

Quick Steps

Insert a Comment
1. Click Review tab.
2. Click New Comment button.
3. Type comment text.

 New Comment

 Next

 Previous

 Comments

 Show Comments

Project 3c Inserting Comments

Part 3 of 10

1. With **8-ISPres.pptx** open, make Slide 2 active and then insert a comment by completing the following steps:
   a. Position the insertion point immediately to the right of the word *Australia*.
   b. Click the Review tab.
   c. Click the New Comment button in the Comments group.
   d. Type the following in the text entry box in the Comments task pane: Include information on New Zealand division.
2. Make Slide 3 active and then insert a comment by completing the following steps:
   a. Click in the chart to select it. (Make sure you select the entire chart and not a chart element.)

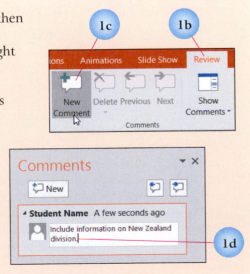

b. Click the New button in the Comments task pane.

c. Type the following in the text entry box: Include a chart showing profit amounts.

3. Make Slide 5 active, position the insertion point immediately to the right of the word *line* at the end of the third bulleted item, and then insert the comment Provide detailed information on how this goal will be accomplished.

4. Make Slide 8 active, position the insertion point immediately to the right of the word *Singapore* in the second bulleted item, and then insert the comment Who will be managing the Singapore office?

5. Click the Previous button in the Comments task pane to display the comment box in Slide 5.

6. Click the Previous button in the Comments group on the Review tab to display the comment box in Slide 3.

7. Click the Next button in the Comments task pane to display the comment in Slide 5.

8. Click the Next button in the Comments group on the Review tab to display the comment in Slide 8.

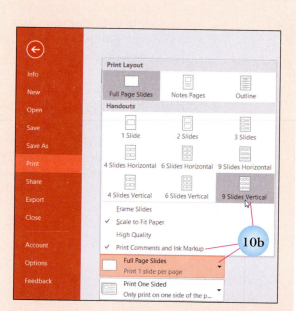

9. Click the Show Comments button in the Comments group on the Review tab to turn off the display of the Comments task pane.

10. Print the presentation and the comments by completing the following steps:

a. Click the File tab and then click the *Print* option.

b. At the Print backstage area, click the second gallery in the *Settings* category, make sure the *Print Comments and Ink Markup* option is preceded by a check mark, and then click the *9 Slides Vertical* option.

c. Click the Print button.

11. Make Slide 1 active and then run the slide show.

12. Save **8-ISPres.pptx**.

Check Your Work

Hint Move a comment in a slide by selecting the comment icon and then dragging it to the new location.

Delete

To edit a comment, click the comment in the Comments task pane, click in the text entry box and then edit the comment. Reply to a comment by clicking the comment in the Comments task pane, clicking in the reply entry box and then typing the response. To delete a comment from a slide, click the comment icon and then click the Delete button in the Comments task pane or the Delete button in the Comments group on the Review tab. A comment can also be deleted by right-clicking the comment icon and then clicking *Delete Comment* at the shortcut menu. Delete all comments in a presentation by clicking the Delete button arrow in the Comments group and then clicking *Delete All Comments and Ink in This Presentation* at the drop-down list.

1. With **8-ISPres.pptx** open, make Slide 8 active and then edit the comment by completing the following steps:
   a. Click the comment icon to the right of *Singapore*. (This displays the Comments task pane.)
   b. Click the comment text in the text entry box in the Comments task pane (this selects the comment text) and then type Check with Sandy Cates to determine who will be appointed branch manager.
2. Delete the comment in Slide 3 by completing the following steps:
   a. Click the Previous button in the upper right corner of the Comments task pane two times to display Slide 3 and the comment in the slide.
   b. Click the Delete button (contains an *X*) in the upper right corner of the comment box.
3. Close the Comments task pane.
4. Print the presentation as a handout with all nine slides displayed horizontally on the page and make sure the comments print.
5. Save **8-ISPres.pptx**.

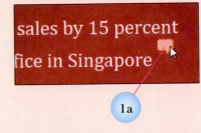

Check Your Work

Tutorial

Managing Presentation Information and Properties

Managing Presentation Information

If a presentation will be distributed or shared with others, check the presentation information and decide if presentation properties should be inserted in the presentation file, if the presentation should be protected with a password, and if the compatibility of the presentation should be checked or versions of the presentation should be accessed. These tasks and others can be completed at the Info backstage area shown in Figure 8.4. Display this backstage area by clicking the File tab and, if necessary, clicking the *Info* option.

Managing Presentation Properties

Each presentation created has certain properties associated with it, such as the type and location of the presentation and when the presentation was created, modified, and accessed. View and modify presentation properties at the Info backstage area and at the Properties dialog box.

Property information about a presentation displays at the right side of the Info backstage area. Add or update a presentation property by hovering the mouse over the information that displays at the right of the property (a rectangular box with a light orange border displays) and then typing the information. In the *Related Dates* section, dates display for when the presentation was created and when it was last modified and printed. The *Related People* section displays the name of the author of the presentation and also contains options for adding additional author names. Click the folder below the *Related Documents* section to display the folder contents where the current presentation is located.

Figure 8.4 Info Backstage Area

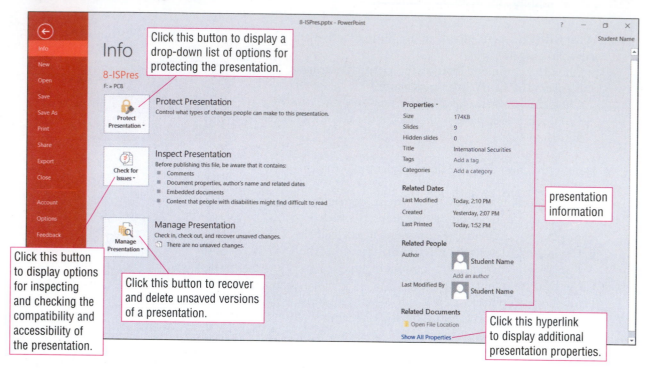

Display additional presentation properties by clicking the Show All Properties hyperlink. Presentation properties also can be managed at the presentations Properties dialog box shown in Figure 8.5. (The name of the dialog box reflects the name of the open presentation.) Display this dialog box by clicking the Properties button at the top of the property information and then clicking *Advanced Properties* at the drop-down list. Inserting text in some of the text boxes can help organize and identify the presentation.

Figure 8.5 Properties Dialog Box

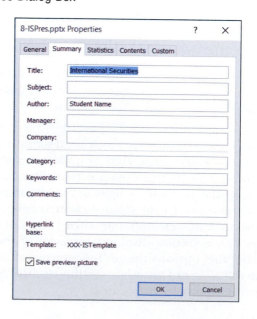

1. With **8-ISPres.pptx** open, click the File tab. (This displays the Info backstage area.)
2. At the Info backstage area, hover your mouse over the text *International Securities* at the right of the *Title* property, click the left mouse button (this selects the text), and then type IS Sales Meeting.
3. Display the 8-ISPres.pptx Properties dialog box by clicking the Properties button at the top of the property information and then clicking *Advanced Properties* at the drop-down list.

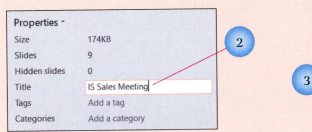

4. At the 8-ISPres.pptx Properties dialog box with the Summary tab selected, press the Tab key (this makes the *Subject* text box active) and then type IS Corporate Sales Meeting.
5. Click in the *Category* text box and then type sales meeting.
6. Press the Tab key to make the *Keywords* text box active and then type International Securities, sales, divisions.
7. Press the Tab key to make the *Comments* text box active and then type This is a presentation prepared for the corporate sales meeting.
8. Click OK to close the dialog box.
9. Save **8-ISPres.pptx**.

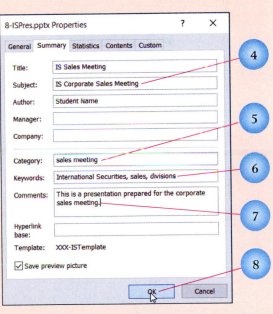

Protecting a Presentation

Protect Presentation

Click the Protect Presentation button in the middle panel at the Info backstage area and a drop-down list displays with the following options: *Mark as Final*, *Encrypt with Password*, and *Add a Digital Signature*. Click the *Mark as Final* option to save the presentation as a read-only presentation. When that option is clicked, a message displays indicating that the presentation will be marked and then saved. At this message, click OK. This displays another message indicating that the presentation has been marked as final and that editing is complete. The message further indicates that when a presentation is marked as final, the status property is set to *Final*; typing, editing commands, and proofing marks are turned off; and that the presentation can be identified by the Mark As Final icon, at the left side of the Status bar. At this message, click OK.

After a presentation is marked as final, a message displays above the ruler indicating that the author has marked the presentation as final and includes an Edit Anyway button. Click this button to edit the presentation. When a presentation is marked as final an additional message displays to the right of the Protect Presentation button in the Info backstage area stating "This presentation has been marked as final to discourage editing."

Encrypting a Presentation

Protect a presentation with a password by clicking the Protect Presentation button at the Info backstage area and then clicking the *Encrypt with Password* option at the drop-down list. At the Encrypt Document dialog box, type a password in the text box (the text will display as round bullets) and then press the Enter key or click OK. At the Confirm Password dialog box, type the password again (the text will display as round bullets) and then press the Enter key or click OK. When a password is applied to a presentation, the message *A password is required to open this document* displays to the right of the Protect Presentation button.

If a presentation is encrypted with a password, keep a copy of the password in a safe place because Microsoft cannot retrieve lost or forgotten passwords. Change a password by removing the original password and then creating a new one. To remove a password, open the password-protected presentation, display the Encrypt Document dialog box, and then remove the password (round bullets) in the *Password* text box.

Project 3f **Marking a Presentation as Final and Encrypting with a Password**   **Part 6 of 10**

1. With **8-ISPres.pptx** open, click the File tab.
2. At the Info backstage area, click the Protect Presentation button and then click *Mark as Final* at the drop-down list.
3. At the message telling you the presentation will be marked as final and saved, click OK.
4. At the next message, click OK.
5. Notice the message bar that displays above the ruler.
6. Close the presentation.
7. Open **8-ISPres.pptx**, click the Edit Anyway button on the yellow message bar, and then save the presentation.

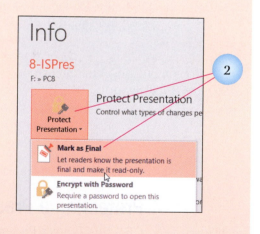

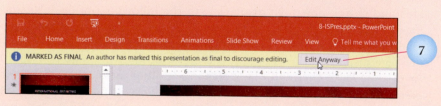

8. Encrypt the presentation with a password by completing the following steps:
   a. Click the File tab, click the Protect Presentation button at the Info backstage area, and then click *Encrypt with Password* at the drop-down list.
   b. At the Encrypt Document dialog box, type your initials in uppercase letters. (Your text will display as round bullets.)
   c. Press the Enter key.
   d. At the Confirm Password dialog box, type your initials again in uppercase letters (your text will display as bullets) and then press the Enter key.
9. Click the Back button to return to the presentation.
10. Save and then close **8-ISPres.pptx**.
11. Open **8-ISPres.pptx**. At the Password dialog box, type your initials in uppercase letters and then press the Enter key.
12. Change the password by completing the following steps:
    a. Click the File tab.
    b. At the Info backstage area, click the Protect Presentation button and then click *Encrypt with Password* at the drop-down list.
    c. At the Encrypt Document dialog box, delete the round bullets in the *Password* text box, type your first name in lowercase letters, and then press the Enter key.
    d. At the Confirm Password dialog box, type your first name again in lowercase letters and then press the Enter key.
    e. Press the Esc key to return to the document.
13. Save and then close **8-ISPres.pptx**.
14. Open **8-ISPres.pptx**. At the Password dialog box, type your first name in lowercase letters and then press the Enter key.
15. Remove the password protection by completing the following steps:
    a. Click the File tab.
    b. At the Info backstage area, click the Protect Presentation button and then click *Encrypt with Password* at the drop-down list.
    c. At the Encrypt Document dialog box, delete the round bullets in the *Password* text box and then press the Enter key.
    d. Press the Esc key to return to the presentation.
16. Save **8-ISPres.pptx**.

8b

Encrypt Document

Encrypt the contents of this file

Password:

••

Caution: If you lose or forget the password, it cannot be recovered. It is advisable to keep a list of passwords and their corresponding document names in a safe place. (Remember that passwords are case-sensitive.)

OK   Cancel

Adding a Digital Signature

Add a digital signature, which is an electronic stamp that vouches for a presentation's authenticity. When a digital signature is added, the presentation is locked so that it cannot be edited or changed unless the digital signature is removed. To add a digital signature, a digital signature must be obtained from a commercial certification authority. With the commercial digital signature obtained, add it to a presentation by clicking the Protect Presentation button at the Info backstage area and then clicking *Add a Digital Signature* at the drop-down list.

Inspecting a Presentation

Check for Issues

Use options from the Check for Issues button drop-down list at the Info backstage area to inspect a presentation for personal and hidden data and to check a presentation for compatibility and accessibility issues. Click the Check for Issues button and a drop-down list displays with the options *Inspect Document*, *Check Accessibility*, and *Check Compatibility*.

PowerPoint includes a document inspector feature that inspects a presentation for personal data, hidden data, and metadata. Metadata is data that describes other data, such as presentation properties. If a presentation is shared with others, some personal or hidden data may need to be removed before sharing the presentation. To check a presentation for personal or hidden data, click the File tab, click the Check for Issues button at the Info backstage area, and then click the *Inspect Document* option at the drop-down list. This displays the Document Inspector dialog box.

Quick Steps

Inspect a Presentation
1. Click File tab.
2. Click Check for Issues button.
3. Click *Inspect Document.*
4. Remove check marks from items that should not be inspected.
5. Click Inspect button.
6. Click Close button.

By default, the document inspector checks all of the items listed in the dialog box. To exclude items for inspection, remove the check mark preceding the item. For example, if a presentation contains comments and/or ink annotations, click the *Comments and Annotations* check box to remove the check mark. Click the Inspect button toward the bottom of the dialog box, and the document inspector scans the presentation to identify information.

When the inspection is complete, the results display in the dialog box. A check mark before an option indicates that the inspector did not find the specific item. If an exclamation point is inserted before an option, the inspector found and displays a list of the items. To remove the found items, click the Remove All button at the right of the option. Click the Reinspect button to ensure that the specific items were removed and then click the Close button.

Project 3g Inspecting a Presentation

1. With **8-ISPres.pptx** open, click the File tab.
2. At the Info backstage area, click the Check for Issues button and then click *Inspect Document* at the drop-down list.

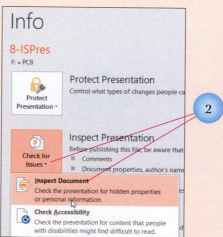

---

3. At the Document Inspector dialog box, you decide that you do not want to check the presentation for XML data, so click the *Custom XML Data* check box to remove the check mark.

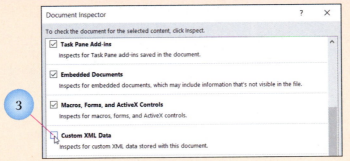

4. Click the Inspect button.
5. Read through the inspection results and then remove all comments by clicking the Remove All button at the right side of the *Comments and Annotations* section.

6. Click the Close button to close the Document Inspector dialog box.
7. Click the Back button to return to the presentation. (If necessary, close the Comments task pane.)
8. Save **8-ISPres.pptx**.

Checking the Accessibility of a Presentation

Quick Steps
Check Accessibility
1. Click File tab.
2. Click Check for Issues button.
3. Click *Check Accessibility*.

PowerPoint includes the accessibility checker feature, which checks a presentation for content that a person with disabilities, such as a visual impairment, might find difficult to read. Check the accessibility of a presentation by clicking the Check for Issues button at the Info backstage area and then clicking *Check Accessibility*. The accessibility checker examines the presentation for the most common accessibility problems in PowerPoint presentations and groups them into three categories: errors—content that is unreadable to a person who is blind; warnings—content that is difficult to read; and tips—content that may or may not be difficult to read. The accessibility checker examines the presentation, closes the Info backstage area, and displays the Accessibility Checker task pane.

At the Accessibility Checker task pane, unreadable errors are grouped in the *Errors* section, content that is difficult to read is grouped in the *Warnings* section, and content that may or may not be difficult to read is grouped in the *Tips* section. Select an issue in one of the sections and an explanation of how to fix the issue and why displays at the bottom of the task pane.

1. With **8-ISPres.pptx** open, click the File tab.
2. At the Info backstage area, click the Check for Issues button and then click *Check Accessibility* at the drop-down list.
3. Notice the Accessibility Checker task pane that displays at the right side of the screen. The task pane displays an *Errors* section. Click *Content Placeholder 7 (Slide 3)* in the *Errors* section and then read the information in the task pane describing why and how to fix the error.
4. Add alternative text (which is a text-based representation of the chart) to the chart by completing the following steps:
   a. Make Slide 3 active, click in the pie chart, right-click the chart border (mouse pointer displays with a four-headed arrow attached), and then click *Format Chart Area* at the shortcut menu.
   b. At the Format Chart Area task pane, click the Size & Properties icon.
   c. Click *Alt Text* to display the options.
   d. Click in the *Title* text box and then type Division Profit Chart.
   e. Click in the *Description* text box and then type Profits: North America, 35%; Europe, 22%; Asia, 17%; Australia, 14%; and Africa, 12%.
   f. Close the Format Chart Area task pane.
5. Click the remaining item in the Accessibility Checker task pane in the *Tips* section and then read the information in the task pane.
6. Close the Accessibility Checker task pane by clicking the Close button in the upper right corner of the task pane.
7. Save **8-ISPres.pptx**.

Checking the Compatibility of a Presentation

Quick Steps
Check Compatibility
1. Click File tab.
2. Click Check for Issues button.
3. Click *Check Compatibility*.
4. Click OK.

Use the Check for Issues button drop-down option, *Check Compatibility*, to check a presentation and identify elements that are either not supported or will act differently in previous versions of PowerPoint from PowerPoint 97 through PowerPoint 2003.

To run the compatibility checker, open a presentation, display the Info backstage area, click the Check for Issues button, and then click *Check Compatibility* at the drop-down list. This displays the Microsoft PowerPoint Compatibility Checker dialog box that provides a summary of the elements in the presentation that are not compatible with previous versions of PowerPoint and indicates what will happen when the presentation is saved and then opened in a previous version. Click OK to close the dialog box.

Opening an Autosave Presentation

Quick Steps

Open an Autosave Backup Presentation
1. Click File tab.
2. Click presentation name at right of Manage Presentation button.

When working in a presentation, PowerPoint automatically saves the presentation every 10 minutes. This automatic backup feature can be very helpful if the presentation is closed without saving it, or if the power to the computer is disrupted. The automatically saved versions of a presentation are listed to the right of the Manage Presentation button in the Info backstage area. Each autosave presentation displays with *Today*, followed by the time and *(autosave)*. When a presentation is saved and then closed, the autosave backup presentations are deleted.

To open an autosave backup presentation, click the File tab to display the Info backstage area and then click the autosave backup presentation at the right of the Manage Presentation button. The presentation opens as a read-only presentation and a message bar displays above the horizontal ruler that includes a Restore button. Click the Restore button and a message displays indicating that the selected version will overwrite the last saved version. At this message, click OK.

Manage Presentations

When a presentation is saved, the autosave backup presentations are deleted. However, if a presentation is closed after 10 minutes without saving it or if the power is disrupted, PowerPoint keeps the backup file in the *UnsavedFiles* folder on the hard drive. Access this folder by clicking the Manage Presentation button in the Info backstage area and then clicking *Recover Unsaved Presentations*. At the Open dialog box, double-click the specific backup file to be opened. The *UnsavedFiles* folder can also be displayed by clicking the File tab, clicking the *Open* option, and then clicking the Recover Unsaved Presentations button below the *Recent* option list.

Delete an autosave backup file by displaying the Info backstage area, right-clicking the autosave file (to the right of the Manage Presentation button), and then clicking *Delete This Version* at the shortcut menu. At the confirmation message that displays, click the Yes button. To delete all unsaved files from the UnsavedFiles folder, display a blank presentation, click the File tab, click the Manage Presentation button, and then click the *Delete All Unsaved Presentations* option at the drop-down list. At the confirmation message that displays, click the Yes button.

Project 3i Checking the Compatibility of Elements in a Presentation and Managing the Presentation

Part 9 of 10

1. With **8-ISPres.pptx** open, click the File tab.
2. Click the Check for Issues button and then click *Check Compatibility* at the drop-down list.
3. At the Microsoft PowerPoint Compatibility Checker dialog box, read the information in the *Summary* list box.
4. Click OK to close the dialog box.
5. Click the File tab and then check to see if any versions of your presentation display to the right of the Manage Presentation button. If so, click the version (or the first version, if more than one displays). This opens the autosave presentation as read-only.
6. Close the read-only presentation.
7. Click the File tab, click the Manage Presentation button, and then click *Recover Unsaved Presentations* at the drop-down list.

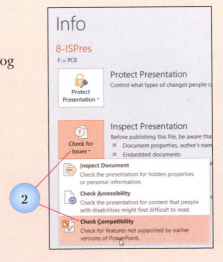

8. At the Open dialog box, check to see if recovered presentation file names display along with the date and time, and then click the Cancel button to close the Open dialog box.
9. Save the presentation.

Customizing PowerPoint Options

Customize PowerPoint with options at the PowerPoint Options dialog box, shown in Figure 8.6. Display this dialog box by clicking the File tab and then clicking *Options*. Click an option at the left side of the dialog box to display specific options for customizing PowerPoint. For example, click the *General* option in the left panel and options display for turning the display of the Mini toolbar on or off when text is selected, enabling or disabling live preview, and changing the user name and password.

Click the *Proofing* option at the PowerPoint Options dialog box and the dialog box displays with options for customizing the spell checker, such as specifying what should or should not be checked during a spelling check and creating a custom spell check dictionary. Click the AutoCorrect Options button and the AutoCorrect dialog box displays with options for changing how PowerPoint corrects and formats text as it is typed.

Click the *Save* option at the PowerPoint Options dialog box and the dialog box displays with options for customizing how presentations are saved. The format

Figure 8.6 PowerPoint Options Dialog Box

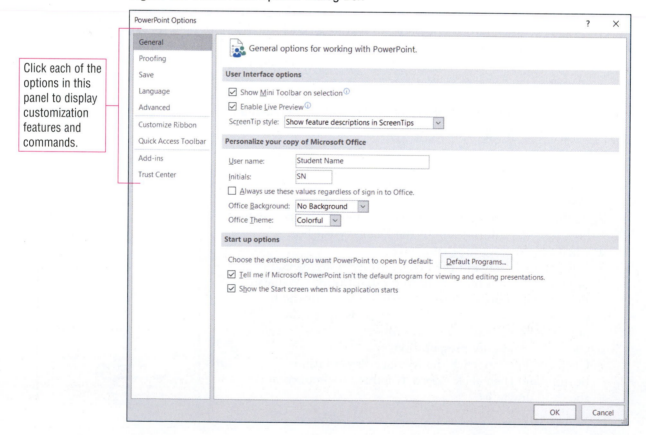

Click each of the options in this panel to display customization features and commands.

in which files are saved can be changed from the default of *PowerPoint Presentation* (**.pptx*) to a macro-enabled PowerPoint presentation, a 97-2003 presentation, a strict open XML presentation, or an OpenDocument presentation. Use other options to specify, by minutes, how often PowerPoint automatically saves a presentation, whether or not to save an autosave version of a presentation if a presentation is closed without first saving it, and a default location for saving presentations.

Project 3j Customizing PowerPoint Options

1. With **8-ISPres.pptx** open, insert new slides in the presentation by completing the following steps:
   a. Click below the bottom slide in the slide thumbnails pane.
   b. Click the New Slide button arrow and then click *Reuse Slides* at the drop-down list.
   c. At the Reuse Slides task pane, click the Browse button and then click *Browse File* at the drop-down list.
   d. At the Browse dialog box, navigate to the PC8 folder on your storage medium and then double-click ***ISPresAfrica.pptx***.
   e. Click each of the three slides in the Reuse Slides task pane to insert the slides into the current presentation.
   f. Close the Reuse Slides task pane.
2. Make Slide 1 active.
3. Change PowerPoint options by completing the following steps:
   a. Click the File tab and then click *Options*.
   b. At the PowerPoint Options dialog box, click the *Save* option in the left panel.
   c. Click the down arrow for the *Save AutoRecover information every* measurement box containing *10* until *1* displays.
   d. Specify that you want presentations saved in the 97-2003 format by clicking the *Save files in this format* option box arrow and then clicking *PowerPoint Presentation 97-2003* at the drop-down list.

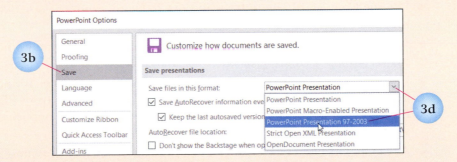

   e. Click the *Proofing* option in the left panel of the PowerPoint Options dialog box.
   f. Click the *Ignore words in UPPERCASE* check box to remove the check mark.
   g. Click the *Ignore words that contain numbers* check box to remove the check mark.
   h. Click OK to close the PowerPoint Options dialog box.
4. Complete a spelling check of the presentation and make changes as needed.

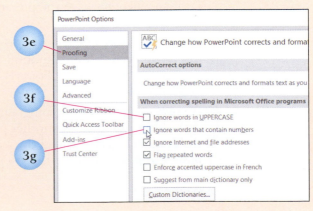

5. Save the presentation, print six slides displayed horizontally per page, and then close the presentation.
6. Press Ctrl + N to open a new blank presentation.
7. Press F12 to display the Save As dialog box.
8. At the Save As dialog box, notice that the *Save as type* option is set to *PowerPoint 97-2003 Presentation (*.ppt)* because you changed the default format at the PowerPoint Options dialog box.
9. Click Cancel to close the dialog box.
10. Display the PowerPoint Options dialog box and then make the following changes:
    a. Click the *Save* option in the left panel.
    b. Change the number in the *Save AutoRecover information every* measurement box to *10*.
    c. Click the *Save files in this format* option box arrow and then click *PowerPoint Presentation* at the drop-down list.
    d. Click the *Proofing* option in the left panel of the PowerPoint Options dialog box.
    e. Click the *Ignore words in UPPERCASE* check box to insert a check mark.
    f. Click the *Ignore words that contain numbers* check box to insert a check mark.
    g. Click OK to close the PowerPoint Options dialog box.
    h. At the message that displays telling you that you are changing the default file format to Office Open XML and asking if you want to change this setting for all Microsoft Office applications, click the No button.
11. Close the blank presentation.

Check Your Work

Chapter Summary

- Create a PowerPoint presentation by importing a Word document containing text with heading styles applied using the *Slides from Outline* option at the New Slides drop-down list.

- Use the Copy and Paste buttons in the Clipboard group to copy data from one program to another.

- Use the Clipboard task pane to collect and paste up to 24 items and paste the items into a presentation or other program files.

- Use options at the Share backstage area to invite people to view and/or edit a presentation, send a presentation as an email attachment or in PDF or XPS file format and as a fax, present a presentation online, and publish slides to a shared location.

- At the Export backstage area, create a PDF or XPS file with a presentation, create a video, package the presentation in a folder or on a CD, and create handouts.

- Click the *Change File Type* option at the Export backstage area and options display for saving a presentation in a different file format such as a previous version of PowerPoint, a PowerPoint show, an OpenDocument presentation, and as graphic images.

- An object created in one program in the Microsoft Office suite can be copied, embedded, or linked in another program in the suite. The program containing the original object is called the *source program* and the program the object is pasted to is called the *destination program*.

- An embedded object is stored in both the source and the destination programs. A linked object is stored in the source program only. Link an object if the contents in the destination program should reflect any changes made to the object stored in the source program.
- Download templates from the Office.com templates gallery at the New backstage area.
- Use the Compare button in the Compare group on the Review tab to compare two presentations to determine the differences between the presentations. Use options in the Compare group to accept or reject differences and display the next or previous change.
- Insert, edit, and delete comments with buttons in the Comments group on the Review tab or with options at the Comments task pane. Display the task pane by clicking the New Comment button or the Show Comments button in the Comments group on the Review tab.
- View and modify presentation properties at the Info backstage area and at the presentation properties dialog box. Display the presentation properties dialog box by clicking the Properties button at the Info backstage area and then clicking *Advanced Properties* at the drop-down list.
- Use options from the Protect Presentation button drop-down list at the Info backstage area to mark a presentation as final, encrypt the presentation with a password, and add a digital signature.
- Use options from the Check for Issues button drop-down list at the Info backstage area to inspect a document for personal and hidden data, check a presentation for content that a person with disabilities, such as a visual impairment, might find difficult to read, and check the compatibility of the presentation with previous versions of PowerPoint.
- PowerPoint automatically saves a presentation every 10 minutes. When a presentation is saved, the autosave backup presentation(s) are deleted.
- Use the Manage Presentation button at the Info backstage area to recover or delete unsaved presentations.
- Customize PowerPoint with options at the PowerPoint Options dialog box. Display this dialog box by clicking the File tab and then clicking *Options*.

Commands Review

FEATURE	RIBBON TAB, GROUP/OPTION	BUTTON, OPTION
Accessibility Checker task pane	File, *Info*	, *Check Accessibility*
Clipboard task pane	Home, Clipboard	
compare presentations	Review, Compare	
Document Inspector dialog box	File, *Info*	, *Inspect Document*
Encrypt Document dialog box	File, *Info*	, *Encrypt with Password*
Export backstage area	File, *Export*	
Insert Outline dialog box	Home, Slides	, *Slides from Outline*

FEATURE	RIBBON TAB, GROUP/OPTION	BUTTON, OPTION
Microsoft PowerPoint Compatibility Checker dialog box	File, *Info*	, Check Compatibility
Package for CD dialog box	File, *Export, Package Presentation for CD*	
Paste Special dialog box	Home, Clipboard	, Paste Special
Publish as PDF or XPS dialog box	File, *Export, Create PDF/XPS Document*	
Send to Microsoft Word dialog box	File, *Export, Create Handouts*	
Share backstage area	File, *Share*	

Workbook

Chapter study tools and assessment activities are available in the *Workbook* ebook. These resources are designed to help you further develop and demonstrate mastery of the skills learned in this chapter.

Unit assessment activities are also available in the *Workbook*. These activities are designed to help you demonstrate mastery of the skills learned in this unit.

Index

Sound option box, 224
source, 275
spelling, checking, 40–42
Spelling task pane, 40–41
Start From Beginning button, 7, 22, 59
Start Inking button, 242
Start option box, 219
Status bar, 5
stock chart, 162
sunburst chart, 162
surface chart, 162
Switch Row/Column button, 166
Switch Windows button, 199
symbol
    inserting, 135
    inserting as bullet, 82
Symbol button, 135
Symbol dialog box, 82, 83

T

table, 144–153
    AutoExpansion feature, 161
    changing design of, 146–147
    changing layout of, 148–150
    creating, 144–146
    drawing, 152–153
    entering text in cells, 144
    inserting Excel spreadsheet, 150–152
    selecting cells, 144–145
Table button, 144
Table Tools Design tab, 146–147, 152
Table Tools Layout tab, 148–149, 152
tabs, 5
    setting, in text box, 112–114
Tabs dialog box, 112–113
Tell Me feature, 5, 63–64
template
    downloading, 278–280
    saving presentation as, 194–195
text
    checking spelling, 40–42
    converting SmartArt graphic to, 160
    converting to SmartArt, 158–160
    cutting, copying and pasting in slides, 45–47
    deleting, in slides, 11–12
    entering in cells, 144
    finding and replacing, in slides, 43–44
    fitting text in placeholder, 74
    formatting

with Format Painter, 72–73
    with Mini toolbar, 70
    inserting
        in placeholder, 10
        in slides, 11–12
    pasting text between document and presentation, 262–263
    rearranging in outline pane, 47–48
    rotating, 80–81
    selecting, in slides, 11–12
    thesaurus, 41
    WordArt text, 133–134
text box
    aligning, 107
    change size of, 106–107
    formatting, 106–110
    inserting, 106–110
    moving, 106
    selecting multiple objects, 107
    set default, 111–112
    setting tabs in, 112–114
Text Box button, 106
Text Direction button, 80
Text Effects button, 133
Text Fill button, 133
Text Options tab, 86
Text Outline button, 133
Text pane, inserting text in, 158
Text Pane button, 158
themes
    applying to Slide Master, 183–184
    custom
        deleting, 101–102
        editing, 101
        saving, 100–101
        theme colors, 97–98
        theme fonts, 99
    design theme templates, 9–10, 13–15, 27
Themes button, 183
Thesaurus, 41
time, inserting, into Slide Master, 187–188
Title bar, 5
Title Slide layout, 11
transitions
    adding, 32–33
    defined, 31
    removing, 32
Transitions tab, 31, 233
trigger, applying for animation, 230–232

U

Undo button, 59
ungrouping objects, 120–121
unpin presentation, 7

V

vertical ruler, turning on/off, 115
vertical scroll bar, 5
video, saving presentation as, 266–268
Video button, 247
video file
    creating screen recording, 253–254
    inserting, 247–250
    optimizing and compressing, 248
    showing and hiding media controls, 248
    trimming, 251
view area, 5
views, changing, 16
View tab, 16, 29
    changing zoom, 199
    managing windows, 199
    viewing color and grayscale, 200
    viewing presentation, 200–201

W

waterfall chart, 162
website
    inserting hyperlinks, 207–209
    linking, to another presentation, 204–205
WordArt
    converting to SmartArt, 158–160
    creating and formatting, 133–134
WordArt button, 133
Word document
    exporting presentation to, 268–270
    inserting hyperlinks, 207–209
Word outline, importing, 260–261
word-wheeling, 63

X

XPS format, 266–268
xy (scatter) chart, 162

Z

zoom, changing, 199
Zoom button, 23, 199